From Castle Rackrent
to Castle Dracula

For Anthony & Mary
with best wishes, love & thanks
Paul
4/3/20.

From Castle Rackrent to Castle Dracula
Anglo-Irish Agrarian Fiction in the Nineteenth-Century

By
Paul E H Davis

The University of Buckingham Press

First published in Great Britain in 2011 by

The University of Buckingham Press
Yeomanry House
Hunter Street
Buckingham MK18 1EG

© Paul E H Davis

The moral right of the author has been asserted.

A CIP catalogue record for this book is available at the British Library

ISBN 9780956071675

For

Derek, Sylvia, and Victoria-Louise

With love and thanks

Acknowledgements

I would like to thank Professor Valerie Sanders of the University of Hull, Dr Barry Sloan of the University of Southampton New College, Andrew Hadfield of the University of Wales and Professor Robert Welch of the University of Ulster for initially pointing me in the right direction and, Professor John Sutherland of University College London. Also for their continued support and encouragement: Dr Stefan Hawlin, Professor Jane Ridley, Professor Dennis O'Keeffe and Dr Michael Conolly.

I am also grateful to all those who replied to my persistent questioning at various meetings connected with the Bath Spa University Irish Lecture Programme, the British Association of Irish Studies, the Society for the Study of Nineteenth-Century Ireland, the Canadian Association of Irish Studies, *Fin de Siècle* Seminar Series, Oxford, and the International Association for the Study of Irish Literature.

Since my area of study has been so wide, I have been especially dependent on the help and advice of the staff of various libraries. I would particularly like to the thank Dr C J Wright of The British Library, Michael Webb of The Bodleian Library, Oxford, Jacqueline Cox of King's College Library, Cambridge, Dr David C Sutton of The University of Reading Library, Una O'Sullivan of The Royal Commission on Historical Manuscripts, Catherine Fahy of The National Library of Ireland, Stuart Ó Seanóir of Trinity College Dublin Library, Siobhan O'Rafferty of the Royal Irish Academy, Dublin, and Hoang-My Dunkle of The Huntington Library, California.

In addition, I am deeply grateful to the staff of The London Library, The University of Sussex Library, The University of Brighton Library, and The University of Southampton New College Library. But particular thanks must go to Jackie Harris, Margaret Surzyn, and all the staff of the University of Buckingham Hunter Street Library, for their unwavering support, understanding, help and friendliness throughout my research.

Since this is my first book, I am particularly grateful to Christopher Woodhead of The University of Buckingham Press Ltd for taking a chance on me in the first place, and for his continuing friendly help and advice.

Although many people have helped in the preparation of this book, it simply would not have been possible without two key individuals. First, Dr John Drew who, at a critical stage in its development, stepped in and kept the project alive; since then, he has been both friend and guide which I sincerely appreciate. Secondly, Prof John Clarke who, since we first met in the 1980s, has been mentor, friend and editor of this book. His unwavering support, advice and apparently inexhaustible knowledge, have not only made this book possible, but also made the doctorate that inspired it a reality; to him, I remain ever grateful.

Finally, I would like to thank my family for all their support and, above all, for their understanding and patience.

The illustrations used in this book are from the author's own collection.

CONTENTS

IRELAND.

Drawn & Engraved by Sid.l Hall.

English Miles.
5 10 20 30 40 50

London, Published by Longman, Hurst, Rees, Orme & Brown, Paternoster Row, 1823.

R G Collingwood was surely right when he insisted that 'All History is Contemporary History.' What Collingwood meant was that every age reinterprets the past – and I would add to that the literature of the past – in the light of its own values, preoccupations and prejudices. It follows that historians and literary critics can never achieve complete objectivity – at least not in this life. Post-modernism is based on an acknowledgement of this huge intellectual limitation, yet I believe that the Post-modernists take things too far. If total objectivity is impossible, that does not necessarily exclude a search for relative objectivity. In other words, we are still entitled to say that some interpretations are more convincing than others. My position is that of St Paul, who said, 'For now we see through a glass darkly, but we shall see face to face.' It is important to stress that Paul did *not* say 'For now we see nothing at all …'

I hope that readers will bear these simple reflections in mind when they turn to *From Castle Rackrent to Castle Dracula*. On the face of it, this is a work of Literary Criticism – though I hope to show that is really much more – in that it explores the significance of a specific literary genre: The Irish Agrarian Novel. Much of what earlier critics – most of them Irish – have said about these novels strikes me as confusing. Dangerous though it is to speculate about national characteristics, it may not be too far off the mark to say that the Irish are wonderful writers but not so good at Literary Criticism – at least not on the basis of what they have said about Irish Agrarian Novels. In this book, Paul Davis says much about fantasy, but it is hard to escape the feeling that even the fantasy of *Dracula* is closer to reality than the fantastic web of distortion and debate that has been woven around these novels. Extreme fantasy invites parody and satire. Perhaps only a Swift, or a Lewis Carroll, could have done full justice to the absurdity of much that has been said. The key to it all is that nothing is what it seems.

On the face of it, whatever their political, religious, or economic point of view, these novelists have much in common. They write in the same language (English), follow many of the same literary conventions and clearly borrow extensively from each other.

The critics, however, insist that the Irish agrarian novelists as a whole have little in common. They are portrayed as belonging to hostile tribes, with entirely different identities and value systems, engaged in a life or death battle for Ireland itself. While it has to be admitted – grudgingly – that they use the same language, it is proposed that each tribe has a distinctive 'accent'. Indeed it seems that in some mysterious way 'accent' creates a chasm of mutual incomprehension deeper than any normal language barrier.

1. In view of the obvious similarities between the writers, one might have thought that the logical thing to do would be to ask whether the 'accents' thesis was really credible. Rather than doing this, however, the critics assume that it is true and then devote their energy and ingenuity to debating just how many 'accents' there really are – two, three or more? But if the thesis itself is wrong, does it matter how many 'accents' are identified? We are entering 'Angels on Pinheads' territory.

2. On the face of it, between about 1800 and 1900, a number of writers, some born in Ireland and some born in England – though both groups spent some years in Ireland – wrote novels set against a background of the problems of Irish agriculture. One might have thought that the sensible thing would be to call all these books 'Irish agrarian novels' and their authors 'Irish agrarian novelists'.

3. Yet, once more, the critics will not accept the obvious. Rather, they debate whether some of the novels and novelists, especially those seen as having close links with England, should be included in the category of 'Irish agrarian novelists' at all - on the grounds that they might not be sufficiently Irish. Of course, as the criteria for inclusion become 'tighter', so the range of books counting as 'real' Irish agrarian novels must become narrower. The ultimate *reductio ad absurdum* – to which some critics come dangerously close – would be that none of the 'candidate' Irish agrarian novels satisfy the conditions of admission to the category. In other words, we could be writing about a club with no members, a singularly fruitless undertaking.

4. If none of the applicants satisfy the conditions of entry to a club, the logical thing to do is to relax the conditions – or invent another club with completely different rules. But the critics do neither. They keep the same club, with its entry requirements unchanged, yet they contrive to 'elect' members! Again we are confronted with something that looks puzzling. Indeed, the only possible explanation is that – consciously or unconsciously – an element of deception or distortion has been introduced. In other words, if most of the 'Irish agrarian novels' and their authors seem in danger of being denied the title because they are not Irish enough, the only way to admit them is *to make them seem more 'Irish' than they really are.*

As Davis shows, this is exactly what has happened. Novelists are portrayed as more humble in their origins, more unambiguously committed to the cause of the tenants, more strongly Catholic in their identities and more committed to political – rather than just cultural nationalism – than the evidence will bear. There is the astonishing treatment of Carleton who somehow emerges as a Catholic even though conversion to Protestantism was clearly the most important event in his life.

This summary of the 'received wisdom' on the Irish agrarian novel may border on the caricature but, even if it approximates to what has been said, we are bound to wonder why the critics have tied themselves into such extraordinary knots and devoted so much ingenuity to answering seemingly absurd questions. We must return to Collingwood's idea of all ages interpreting and reinterpreting the past in the light of their own values and preoccupations. The crucial question to ask here is what do we mean by 'contemporary'? The answer must surely be that the critics' 'take' on Irish Agrarian Novels is not only 'Irish' but largely 'twentieth-century Irish' too.

When this point is appreciated many of the seemingly peculiar aspects of the critics' treatment become easier to understand. Twentieth-century Ireland was a very political and very violent place, probably more violent and more political than it was in the nineteenth century – a point not sufficiently appreciated. Politics and violence leads to polarisation, where everything is based on the postulate, 'He who is not with me must be against me '. It is a world of the Easter Rising, of the Black and Tans, of

Civil War in the South in the 1920s and Civil War in the North in the 1970s and 80s. In the last resort the crucial question for twentieth-century Ireland was 'Are you a Republican?'

To that question most of the literary critics could reply – correctly – in the affirmative. The problem is that they seek to legitimatise their Republicanism by giving it a long ancestral pedigree. It is probably true that the hidden agendas behind most literary criticism are political. But some agendas are more political than others and commentary on the Irish Agrarian Novel has been intensely political. In effect the critics want to present those writers they accept as true 'Irish Agrarian Novelists' not just as nationalists – which in the broad sense many of them undoubtedly were – but as political nationalists too. In fact, with the exception of Kickham – actually not a very good novelist – none came close to an explicit avowal of Republicanism, but this is brushed aside. The argument is that these writers would have been Republicans had it not been for fear of prosecution or – perhaps less nobly – for fear of loss of sales. Even if they said they were not Republicans, they were Republicans inside themselves, even if they did not realise it. It is the same story as Carleton's 'Catholicism' all over again – moulding the past in the image of the present with a vengeance.

While Davis appreciates that a search for hidden meanings – even for unconscious meanings – has its place in literary criticism, he is also well aware of the dangers of this approach. He is refreshingly old-fashioned in his willingness to accept that, when considering any sort of literature, it is sometimes worth developing one's analysis on the assumption that writers actually mean what they say. For example, writers such as Griffin, the Banims and Carleton said they were trying to extol certain human qualities to solve or mitigate the social and economic problems of Ireland.

Davis suggests they may have been telling the truth – after all was not this precisely the approach taken by Dickens to the social and economic problems of Victorian England? Of course, Davis accepts that there was an important political dimension to these novels but it was often a back-drop to a more human drama. Hence, rather than treating the novelists as politicians, he restores them to their proper role – as novelists. He also reminds us that they did not know what the future held; indeed even if they had known, it would still be dangerous to assume that they would have applauded everything later critics applaud or deplored everything they deplore

While Davis certainly performs a valuable service exposing the strange contortions of much of earlier writing about the Irish Agrarian Novel, he still faces the challenge of whether he can construct an alternative interpretation. In the light of the Relativism proclaimed at the beginning of this Introduction, it must be acknowledged that Davis's own treatment reflects his own times and circumstances every bit as much as the analysis he rejects. For our purposes, the two most important things to say about Paul Davis are that is he is not Irish and that he is writing quite a long time after most of the literary critics he takes issue with – and even longer after the Irish Agrarian Novels themselves. On the whole, I think these essential facts constitute advantages rather than disadvantages.

Although Davis may disagree with the Irish Nationalist critics, he never suggests that the task facing them – or him – is easy. The Irish Agrarian Novels are difficult to interpret, not least because some of them cannot be described as outstandingly successful in literary terms and, in many instances, their social, economic and political analysis appears contradictory and feeble. On several occasions, Davis remarks that there are times when the Agrarian Novel seems to be dying of exhaustion. Endless permutations have been played on a few basic themes and readers are left wondering what has been achieved in literary, social or political terms.

Davis has no truck with pointless debates about what constitutes a 'proper' Irish agrarian novel. His definition is broad – and rightly so. Yet he does follow the Nationalist commentators by trying to make sense of the novelists by grouping them into categories or tribes. But the tribes and their respective 'accents' now have very different characteristics. The old tribes are defined by the national identity, religious affiliation and by social or economic status. In other words, the proposed categorisation is only literary in the secondary sense. It seems that writers are bound – even condemned – to speak (write novels) in particular 'accents' because of the nature of their backgrounds. This is Determinism, representing a kind of diluted Marxism that is really rather depressing. It may have a limited appeal to some historians, but it must surely repel anyone whose first and real love is literature. Of course, all writers are influenced by their backgrounds, but that does not mean that they are enslaved by them. No great writers – and many not so great ones – can be regarded as mere symbols of their social, political or religious affiliations. The very fact that they are writers makes them different. To some extent, all literature is an exercise in escapism, in that writers try to transcend their own backgrounds and personalities by 'creating' other people, often very different from themselves. Thus the 'accents' approach is not only flawed but it is also essentially 'anti-literary', because it implicitly denies the uniqueness of the creative process itself.

In contrast, it seems to me that one of the most attractive features of Davis's approach is that his scheme of categorisation, which cuts across the various 'accents' or 'voices' however defined, is at least unquestionably and truly literary. This is because Davis's categories are based, not on what the authors were, but on what they wrote, what they tried to do and how they set about it. Davis proposes three categories:

1. Those novelists (Edgeworth, Griffin, the Banims and Carleton) who sought to point a way to the solution of Ireland's agrarian problems through reconciliation, compromise and the renunciation of violence, whether 'institutional' or 'agrarian'. They did so by using their heroes to show how landlords and tenants alike could mend their ways, so producing a more harmonious and prosperous Ireland. The solutions were 'Irish', in that all the elements to the 'solution' were already present in Ireland; they simply had to be more generous and sensible. The literary form of these novelists was essentially realist.

2. Those novelists (Trollope and Kickham) who felt that there could be no 'internal' solution. Hence, they introduced 'foreign' elements, English in the case of Trollope and American in the case of Kickham, to achieve the desired result. They also differed from members of the first category, by their implicit acceptance that a degree of violence – though within limits – was necessary to solve the underlying problems. Trollope was therefore prepared to endorse – or rather deplore the absence of – an appropriate amount of institutional violence, whereas Kickham was ready to condone agrarian violence to an extent greater than those Davis locates as ultimately belonging to the 'Edgeworth' tradition. The literary form of these novelists is best described as quasi-realist.

3. Those writers (Moore and Stoker) who did not seek a solution, because they regarded the conflict between landowners and tenants as eternal. They therefore investigated the violence in all its psychological nuances. In the process they not only accepted violence but even revelled in it. Their assumptions may have been well-founded but they were not rational in the conventional sense and hence their literary form was one of fantasy rather than of realism.

Whether we agree with Davis or not, it cannot be denied that this is a new and distinctive way of approaching the Irish Agrarian Novel, one that avoids the glaring pitfalls and distortions of earlier approaches.

Modern literary critics may cultivate a veneer of reticence in their judgements, but the fundamental question about any piece of literature can never be far from the surface: 'Does it work?' While acknowledging the achievements and contributions of all the writers under investigation, Davis concludes that, in most instances – especially for the authors in the first and second of his categories – that it does not. He shows that the search for a solution based on compromise and renunciation of violence, even one involving a fair degree of violence and the intervention of foreign elements, proved maddeningly elusive. Many of the authors themselves came to the same conclusion, either giving up writing altogether or turning to more satisfactory, or perhaps more profitable literary forms. Curiously, therefore, those who accepted that there was no solution of any kind, the fantasy novelists who accepted the inevitability of an eternal cycle of violence emerge as the most 'realistic'. It is fitting, therefore that the last Agrarian Novel to be considered, Stoker's *Dracula*, the bleakest, the most disturbing, and the most truly violent, is also seen as the most successful.

Davis argues that, with Stoker, the tradition of the Agrarian Novel, stretching back to Edgeworth, came to an end, as Irish Literature turned to other themes, to the urban, to the psychological and to a level of fantasy where even conventional notions of language were discarded. The most obvious explanation for the end of the Agrarian Novel is that the Land Question had been 'solved' – essentially by land purchase. But this may too simplistic. Despite a degree of urbanisation, the tensions and conflicts inherent in the Land Question had not really disappeared. The issues of identity were still present – often in the Irish themselves – and the result was more violence and polarisation lasting for most of the twentieth century.

But if the Land Question did not truly disappear, what of the Agrarian Novel? It is sometimes said that Stoker had no real successors, that, unlike Edgeworth, he had 'no children'. With Stoker, Irish literature could be said to have been firmly set on a course of fantasy. Perhaps his real heir was Joyce, but there is another possibility. As we have seen, the nationalist critics' treatment of the agrarian novelists involved a large degree of fantasy. Could it be that they were Stoker's true heirs? The parallels are striking. The Land Question was not truly dead, but continued in other, more frightening and violent forms. In other words it was 'un-dead' – just like Dracula! We must not be too harsh on the critics Davis so rightly takes issues with. Nor can we be totally dismissive of Determinism. It may not be entirely true but it is not entirely false either – especially if its victims lack the freedom that goes with being an imaginative writer. In other words, much of what has been said about the Irish agrarian novelists can be seen as a violent and polarised twentieth-century fantasy imposed on the nineteenth century. Perhaps the critics simply could not help it.

Of course, this poses the difficult challenge of trying to attempt the 'reality' of nineteenth-century Ireland. It may well be an impossible task; as Davis stresses 'reality' is in the eye of the beholder. Nineteenth-century Ireland was certainly deeply troubled, experiencing both agrarian and institutional violence so graphically described by its novelists. But it was not really unique; other parts of Europe experienced similar problems that were as bad if not worse. The lot of the Irish tenant farmer may have been bad but was that of the peasant in Czarist Russia any better? Probably not. Those novelists who sought a solution may not have found one, perhaps there was none. But, if they are to be believed, they spent much of their lives thinking that there was a chance, if only an outside one – an elusive goal certainly, but one still worth striving for.

It is now more than a hundred years since the publication of the last Irish Agrarian Novel and that is the context in which Davis is writing. Recent developments in both the South and the North of Ireland bring some hope that the Land Question – and its painful 'un-dead' half life in the twentieth century – has finally been laid to rest. Now seems the right time to reassess the Agrarian Novels, not through the lens of Ireland's many twentieth-century 'Troubles', but through the lens of the Peace Process.

Most of the 'solution' Agrarian Novels have happy endings. We may be sceptical about whether these endings are credible and suspect that they were provided because that was what readers wanted. But still they are part of the novels – and important parts too. There is actually a striking similarity between these happy endings and the principles that underlie the Peace Process. Both involve a renunciation of violence, a recognition of the legitimacy of other traditions and a readiness to compromise a little to achieve a more secure and prosperous future. In the long run the novelists' 'solutions' may seem less implausible today than they did even fifty years ago. Despite all the frustrations they encountered, the Agrarian Novelists may have been true prophets: wrong in their lifetimes but right in the future.

History and geography dictate that the British and Irish must live alongside each other and, inevitably, some will live in the other's land. The institutions that shaped the relationship may not be ideal. The Union was probably always too unequal to work properly – what a tragedy that Home Rule did not pass in 1886! In some circumstances, however, the two peoples get on pretty well together, in good times and in bad. Before completing this Introduction, I walked into the centre of Buckingham to buy my Remembrance Poppy and, with Paul's book in my mind, recalled the proud names of the Irish Regiments in the British Army and how British and Irish had fought alongside against so many common foes. The combination works well in other scenarios too. When a hugely wealthy Canadian tycoon was asked for his advice on how to succeed in life, he replied, 'Dress British, look Irish and think Yiddish!' Even if he is not Irish, Paul Davis himself fulfils all these requirements, and brings them to bear to show that the Irish Agrarian Novels have more relevance now than ever before.

John Clarke, University of Buckingham

I notice very distinctly in all Irish literature two different accents.[1]

A new map is being made of the whole country.[2]

'The Noble Savage'

The birth of the agrarian novel must be seen against the background of economic and political conditions in eighteenth-century Ireland – even though it has to be admitted that, in reality, contemporary writers had little to say about social or economic matters. The exception is Jonathan Swift – most famously in Gulliver's Travels (1726) and A Modest Proposal (1729). At first sight this relative silence seems surprising, not least because there was a good deal of agrarian and institutional violence in Ireland, especially from the 1760s onwards.

Ireland may exemplify aspects of the thesis proposed by historians such as Palmer and Godechot, who have argued that there was an 'Atlantic Revolution' in the second half of the eighteenth century. According to Godechot, population levels stagnated throughout Europe between 1650 and 1750. Coupled with the introduction of new crops from America or Asia, this resulted in a modest improvement in living standards. Around 1750, however, numbers began to rise again and soon the temporary improvement in living standards disappeared; as things deteriorated, social and political protest became virtually inevitable.

Although relatively stable, England experienced some unrest in the second half of the eighteenth century. The Established Church was challenged by the rise of Methodism among the poor, and by the growth

---

[1] Representative Irish Tales (1891), ed by W B Yeats (Gerrards Cross: Colin Smythe Ltd, 1979), p. 25.
[2] Brian Friel, *Translations* (1981) (London: Faber and Fabern Ltd, 2000), p. 33.

of a dissenting middle class. The Government's decision to grant Catholics additional civil rights resulted in the 'Gordon' or 'No-Popery' riots (1780) – arguably the most spectacular breakdown of law and order in an English city since the Middle Ages. There was an unpopular war in America, martial law in London during the French Revolutionary Wars, opposition to Enclosures in rural areas and protest, associated with John Wilkes, in towns. These troubles seem to have reflected a universal pattern; almost invariably, when numbers grew, living standards and real wages declined. This had happened in England in the early fourteenth and in the late sixteenth centuries, and may have been occurring now in Ireland and much of the rest of Europe. Between the 1780s and 1820s, however, something unprecedented began in England. The rate of economic growth kept pace with, or even exceeded, the growth in numbers; ultimately, that meant rising living standards. But this did not happen in Ireland, where population surpassed what the economic system could sustain – although there are doubts as to precisely when this happened.

The Irish economy was not stagnant in the eighteenth century; both exports and imports increased substantially. Like other Europeans, the Irish had cause to be grateful to the potato – at least initially. The relative prosperity of England may have increased some of Ireland's problems. Rising English demand for grain encouraged Anglo-Irish landowners to grow more corn, and to reduce the acreage under pasture. This seems to have been the immediate cause of the agrarian outrages of the 1760s. In the 1770s, Ireland was regarded as poor, but not perhaps noticeably poorer than other parts of Europe. When Arthur Young visited Ireland to collect material for *A Tour of Ireland* (1780), he noted that tenants 'live upon potatoes and milk [...] with some oatmeal', they 'are in a better situation in most respects than twenty years ago [and] are much better clad than they were'. Cormac Ó Gráda believes that the Irish economy was performing quite well at this time:

> Agricultural output and rents undoubtedly rose, traditional industries such as provisioning, brewing, and distilling prospered, and the new techniques of the Industrial Revolution also made inroads. All sectors benefited from buoyant conditions in foreign, especially British, markets.[3]

---

[3] Cormac Ó Gráda, *Ireland* (Oxford: Clarendon Press, 1995), p. 5.

Reliable statistical evidence for the Irish population and economy in the eighteenth century is scanty. The Palmer-Godechot analysis may not fit the situation in Ireland in the 1750s or 60s, because the widespread introduction of the potato could have been later than generally supposed. If so, the years between 1760 and 1800 would have seen the upswing of the potato-cycle, with serious problems only occurring around the turn of the century.

Why then did the first agrarian novel appear in 1800? While there is a case for thinking that the Irish economy had been performing tolerably well in the 1770s, this was certainly no longer true by 1800. The negative effects of rapid population growth – together with monoculture (crop failure and famine) and the trend to economically non-viable and smaller holdings – began to bite. The famine of 1766 was followed by some thirty-four years of relative plenty but famine returned in 1800-01. There was now virtually universal agreement that the Irish tenantry was one of the worst off in Europe. The first half of the nineteenth century was marked by recurrent famine and economic crisis: economic panic in 1810, followed by a decline in agricultural prices, famine in 1817-19, again in 1822, 1831 and, most devastatingly, between 1845 and 1849.

Political Economy first emerged as a frame of reference and a moral discipline for Government policy in the last quarter of the eighteenth century. The message of Adam Smith's *Enquiry into the Causes of the Wealth of Nations* (1776) was optimistic. Smith sought to discredit earlier notions, which he associated with assumptions behind 'The System of Commerce', that the amount of wealth in the world was finite and that one nation could only become rich if others became poorer. Smith argued that economic growth, if not infinite, was possible for the foreseeable future. He claimed that the presence of a wealthy neighbouring state was an advantage, rather than a disadvantage, and would assist economic growth. The implications for Ireland of Britain's economic success were mainly positive but, to derive maximum advantage, other conditions were required. These included the application of the principle of the 'Division of Labour' and clear property rights. Since Smith's preconditions were met more closely in Britain than in Ireland, it seemed that the way forward for Ireland was to become like Britain – and that would involve extensive changes, especially in agriculture. Significantly, Smith, a Scot, supported the Act of Union between England and Scotland (1707); perhaps Ireland could also benefit from a Union with England and Scotland. But that would involve drastic changes and might induce previously resident landowners to become absentees.

While the implications of Smith's ideas for Ireland were mixed, those of T R Malthus were overwhelmingly negative. In his *First Essay on Population* (1798), Malthus argued that population had an inherent tendency to expand more rapidly than resources. Population might increase in a 'geometrical ratio' of 1:2:4:8:16:32, whereas resources could never increase in more than an 'arithmetical ratio' of 1:2:3:4:5:6:7. After a while, the gap between population and resources would become so wide that many would starve, succumb to disease or die in the inevitable social convulsion and violence that ensued. Malthus feared that England might experience such a fate, but it must have been obvious that Ireland, about to experience another famine, corresponded more closely to the Malthusian prophecy. But did Malthus mean that famine might actually be necessary and that, far from seeking to avert it, the authorities and the landowners should welcome famine as a means of restoring the natural balance between people and resources? On occasion, Anthony Trollope was to imply that they should.

Ireland's links with England were by no means universally popular, even among the relatively privileged landowners and Protestants. The Irish as a whole had economic grievances similar to the Americans before 1776, in that existing arrangements favoured England's industries and discriminated against those of the colonies. Some of the issues raised at the time of the American Revolution re-emerged with greater force in 1789, as the French Revolution had a distinct agrarian dimension. It began as a peasant revolt against landowners and resulted in many French tenants obtaining their own land. Perhaps Irish tenants should have followed the revolutionaries' advice to tenants everywhere: '*Coupez le cou aux Seigneurs, comme on avait fait en France.*' The French Revolution, however, was directed as much against the Catholic Church as against the Crown or the nobility; Bishops were some of the most notable victims of 'The Terror'. In the past, the Papacy might have regarded Protestant England as perhaps its principle enemy but, when faced with revolution in France and the spread of revolutionary ideas in Italy, it concluded that atheistic Republicanism was worse than Protestantism or British rule. The Catholic Church and Great Britain allied against a common foe – a process much facilitated when the British took over Malta and established a remarkably harmonious relationship with the Church. Whatever the attitude of individual priests, the Catholic hierarchy in Ireland, let alone

4

the Papacy itself, would certainly never endorse movements directed against landowners or against the British Government.

For a time, it seemed just possible that the dissenting Protestant community in Ireland, especially the Presbyterians, might take the revolutionary lead. While privileged in relation to the Catholics, Presbyterians were discriminated against in relation to members of the Established Church. Some had been exposed to Enlightenment ideas and were close in spirit to the American rebels. To achieve anything against the British, however, they would have to make common cause with the Catholic majority. Some were prepared for this – the real meaning of the United Irishmen Rebellion of 1798 – but the rising failed because of mutual distrust between Catholics and Protestants. Most Presbyterians, though eager to escape discrimination at the hands of the Established Church, wished to retain the privileges they enjoyed in relation to Catholics.

There was a more fundamental difference between Ireland and America. From the sixteenth century onwards, comparisons had been made between American natives and those of Ireland. Yet Native Americans had been treated even more harshly than Irish natives; their numbers had been decimated by what amounted to genocide. There might still be 'Indian Wars' as the frontier moved westwards but, by the time of the American Revolution, there was no danger that the native population would ever take over – hence British protection was unnecessary. In Ireland, the danger was very real. Thousands of native Irish may have been killed, but they had in no sense been wiped out. They still represented the overwhelming majority of the total population, and their numbers were increasing. If the Irish Protestants cut their links with Britain, would they have sufficient strength to maintain their privileges? If not, continuing British protection was essential.

For a while, everything seemed possible in Ireland: rapprochement between Catholics and Protestants – or at least Catholics and Presbyterians – against the British, or Civil War between different classes and religions. For the British Government, the solution appeared to be an Act of Union, similar to the apparently successful Union between England and Scotland. In its original form, as devised by William Pitt the Younger, the Union project had promising features. There would no longer be any obstacles facing Irish exports into the rest of Britain and that would encourage agricultural improvements in Ireland. The Catholics demanded political equality (Emancipation) but, if they were admitted to the Dublin Parliament, they would probably gain a majority of the seats – an alarming prospect for the Protestants. If the Dublin Parliament was abolished, however, and an Irish Catholic contingent came to Westminster, it would still be a small minority among the overwhelmingly Protestant members from England, Scotland and Wales. Unfortunately, George III vetoed Catholic Emancipation, and so the Union went ahead without Emancipation; as a result Pitt resigned in 1801.

The political convulsions of the late 1700s and now the fact of the Union meant that Irish agriculture had reached a turning point and was confronted by a number of opportunities and threats. Politically, this may help to explain the appearance of novels seeking to explore the various possible outcomes. But there was also a strong cultural dimension. The implications of the cultural shift to what would shortly be defined as Romanticism were significant in that there were important links between Romanticism and nationalism. Nationalists everywhere believed that each of the peoples of Europe had distinctive 'characters' and an inherent right to an allotted area in which to live, a land forming and reflecting their special spirit. For some Romantics at least, the logical conclusion to be derived from this belief was that all peoples had the right to form a state of their own, and that this state should be dominated by the majority population within its borders. Romantics, however, tended to have a special interest in peasants – partly because of sympathy for their plight and partly because they were often seen as the true repository of the national character – untainted by superficial and artificial influences often found in towns. Significantly, there was a good deal of sympathy in England for oppressed peoples and oppressed tenants and peasants. In contrast to earlier views that tenants were of little interest, there was now a tendency to idealise rustic simplicity and the supposed moral value of primitivism, to believe, with Jean-Jacques Rousseau, that tenants possessed virtues that had been corrupted by the advance of civilization elsewhere in society. The tenants' cause might perhaps be assisted if they could be presented as the Irish version of 'the noble savage'.

Inclusivity or Exclusivity?

Tension between landowners and tenants has been a recurrent feature in many European and Asian societies. Such tensions have often resulted in protest and violence: examples include events in England in 1381 (the so-called Peasants' Revolt), the Pugachev Rising in Russia in the

1770s, Revolution in France in 1789, and the Troubles in southern Italy in the 1860s, Spain in the 1930s, and China in the 1940s. In this book, violence perpetrated by tenants against landowners/agents is termed 'agrarian violence', whereas repression and exploitation of tenants by landowners/agents is termed 'institutional violence'. Institutional violence, implicitly supported by the State and imposed within the parameters of the Rule of Law, can lead to a cycle of agrarian and institutional violence. The literary portrayal of the resultant tensions and conflicts is at the core of the 'agrarian novel' to be investigated in subsequent chapters.

Tensions between landowners and tenants were particularly acute in Eastern Europe, where divergence of economic interest was frequently sharpened by differences of race, culture, language and religion – often present simultaneously. For centuries, Eastern Europe was a frontier zone disputed between Protestants, Catholics and Orthodox Christians, and indeed sometimes with Muslims: between Germans, Hungarians and Slavs – and between sub-groups within these larger categories. In the nineteenth century, each was to produce distinctive literatures and histories based on its fears and aspirations, and embodying its own unique and troubled *volksgeist*.

The permutations of divergence were complex. In parts of 'Greater Hungary', Orthodox Romanian tenantry rose against Catholic Magyar landowners, but religion was not always a factor; there was tension between German Catholic landowners and Czech Catholic tenants in Bohemia and Moravia. Some of the peoples of Eastern Europe owned no land of their own, while others were tenants in one area and landowners in another. So, for instance, Catholic Polish tenants and labourers in Posen complained of Protestant and German [Prussian] oppression, while Orthodox Ruthene tenants in Galicia complained of oppression by Polish Catholic landowners. Each landlord/tenant flashpoint had its unique features, but the overall situation in Eastern Europe had striking similarities with the one in Ireland; indeed, whereas the Eastern problem was largely the result of the German expansion to the East, the *Drang nach Ostern*, the problems of Ireland were ultimately caused by a westward expansion of the Germans' near cousins, the Anglo-Saxons.

This book aims to investigate the literary representation of Ireland's agrarian problems in the nineteenth century. Of course, there had been tension and violence for centuries, but they had found no place in literature. The first Irish agrarian novel, Maria Edgeworth's *Castle Rackrent*, appeared in 1800, the same year as the Act of Union. From then until the

1890s, agrarian issues played a central role both in Irish fiction and in fiction about Ireland. For our purposes, the agrarian novel ends with Bram Stoker's *Dracula* (1897) – apparently set in Eastern Europe.

Agrarian novelists of the nineteenth century explored the Land Question in terms of the violence it produced, the accompanying religious antagonisms, and the socio-political ramifications for England and Ireland. Key writers to be considered are Maria Edgeworth, John and Michael Banim, Gerald Griffin, William Carleton, Charles Kickham, Anthony Trollope, Thomas Moore and Bram Stoker. These authors have at least one thing in common: with the exception of Stoker – and to a lesser extent Moore – they are not fantasy novelists. Whatever their differences of definition, explanation or solution, all make similar assumptions about how to represent reality in prose fiction, and follow accepted, if artificial, conventions of social realism.

There can be few less promising candidates for an agreed reality than nineteenth-century Ireland. Aspects of high civilization exist alongside the misery of the tenant hovels, which so shocked even hardened European travellers that paralipsis becomes the rhetorical strategy of choice in their accounts. The problem of reality is acute because the issues of nineteenth-century Ireland still bear upon our prejudices and emotions, upon our own identities. Real objectivity is impossible – as the divergent interpretations of present-day historians demonstrate. In other words, facts are not neutral; inevitably, they are interpreted differently and deployed selectively.

The authors considered here came from diverse backgrounds and subscribed to differing views about society. Their differences will be examined later, but we must first consider what they had in common. Without some parameters, it is impossible to speak of a canon of Irish agrarian literature at all; meaningful comparison depends on an element of common ground. Taking the term in the broadest sense, most of the writers under investigation are social realists, but exactly what kind are they?

While some English social novels are set in wholly rural locations, many are partly rural and partly urban or, in other terms, partly romantic and partly industrial. Writers such as Benjamin Disraeli in *Coningsby* (1844) and Elizabeth Gaskell in *Mary Barton* (1848) deplore the emerging industrial society and contrast an idyllic rural life with the misery of the new towns. Significantly, major episodes of social violence (such as the murder in *Mary Barton*) occur in towns. Even a writer such as Thomas

Hardy, who exposes some unpleasant features of rural life in novels like *Tess of the D'Urbervilles* (1891), still idealizes aspects of the countryside. Traditional rural values are contrasted with new urban ones and pronounced superior. This contrast is largely absent in novels set in Ireland – with the possible exception of the Banims' *The Nowlans* (1826). Until James Joyce, Irish fiction has little to say about the lives of ordinary people in towns. Apart from Belfast, a city largely ignored by novelists, there were no industrial towns in Ireland; social novels about nineteenth-century Ireland are agrarian novels, and deal with country matters.

One further difference between English and Irish fiction is that even if English novelists exaggerate the delights of rural life, compared to Ireland, the English countryside was a model of harmony. No social novelist aspiring to realism could idealize contemporary Irish rural life in the way that was still possible in England. An element of contrast, arguably essential to the patterning of the social novel as an art form, is present in novels about Irish life. However, whereas the dominant element of contrast in the English social novel is spatial (good countryside, bad industrial towns), the dominant contrast in social novels about Ireland is temporal. Regardless of ideological stance, Irish novels portray the present or near present as terrible. The element of idealization comes in the yearning for better times – set either in a mythic past or in the future.

While the novelists considered in this book view Irish tenants with varying degrees of sympathy, none could be truly described as a tenant themselves. None were engaged in manual labour at the time of writing. They had private means, received a pension from the State, or supported themselves by their writing. They possessed or aspired to possess middle class status, or even higher. None wholly rejected the principle of private property or challenged conventional notions of morality. Remarkably, with the possible exception of Kickham, not one openly subscribed to republicanism or advocated complete independence for Ireland.

There is a further point of common ground: these authors shared an identity as writers. Writers may be vain, competitive and individualistic, but they see still themselves as part of a group of creative artists whose work is often undervalued by society. They read each other's books and engage in what, in *Hidden Rivalries in Victorian Fiction* (1987), Jerome Meckier terms 'hidden rivalries' that manifest themselves, consciously or otherwise, in ways that combine to form a vibrant tradition. Sometimes writers derive inspiration (either positive or negative) from the works of others, which give them ideas for their own novels. This was especially true of the Irish agrarian novelists; since they moved in a relatively small, even closed community of readers and of treatises on Irish affairs, it would be astonishing if there had been no cultural interaction between them.

Here it may be appropriate to reveal the political and literary perspectives that inform this book. At the outset of my research, I felt strongly that, overall, Irish agrarian fiction was curiously neglected and undervalued, and that it deserved more attention and recognition. I also believed that literary criticism should strive to be objective and to seek political impartiality. My views have since changed; though no Marxist, I now agree with those who doubt whether either goal is attainable. If they are right, I have an obligation to declare my own perspective as one of 'enlightened Conservatism'. This perspective has led me to explore the reasons for the relative neglect of the Irish agrarian novel. It has not, of course, been entirely neglected; it has been discussed, but in ways that seem to me to involve an unacceptable level of distortion and manipulation. I acknowledge that some of this may not have been deliberate – although I fear that in some instances it might have been. I also agree that things may look quite different to those who subscribe to other perspectives.

The emergence of 'Irish Studies' in the latter half of the twentieth century resulted in frequent and understandable attempts to define Irish literature. There has been acute controversy as to how the agrarian novelists should be treated in this respect. Logically, there are no fewer than nine distinct positions – though some critics seem to slide between more than one – which, at risk of over-simplification, may be stated as follows:

All novels written about the Irish Land Question, even indirectly, and by authors of any nationality should be regarded as part of Irish literature. This is my own position and permits the inclusion of the Englishman, Anthony Trollope – who is discussed in this book.

Only agrarian novels written directly about the Irish Land Question should be considered as part of Irish literature. This excludes Stoker, who seems to be writing about Transylvania.

Only agrarian novels written by Irish authors should be included. This excludes Trollope.

Only those writers whose national identity was unquestionably Irish should be included. This excludes Edgeworth.

Only Catholics should be included, thus excluding Protestants such as Edgeworth, Carleton and Stoker. Those wishing to include Carleton for other reasons have to explain away his Protestantism.

Only those who were in some sense Irish nationalists should be included. This almost certainly excludes Edgeworth, but the biggest problem is with those who followed her – Griffin, the Banims and Carleton. They could be included if they could be portrayed as nationalists who had moved a long way from Edgeworth's agenda. Yet, as with Carleton's Protestantism, such portrayals require considerable ingenuity and sleight of hand.

Griffin, the Banims and Carleton have to be excluded if they cannot be described as nationalists, and are really too close to Edgeworth in outlook.

If, however, Edgeworth, Griffin, the Banims and Carleton are excluded, together with Trollope (English and anti-Irish nationalism) and Stoker (Transylvania) – we are left with Moore, who spent most of his adult life in England, and with Kickham, arguably the weakest of the agrarian writers on literary grounds.

The entire sub-genre should be excluded from the canon of Irish Literature because it follows English literary conventions too closely and is written in English rather than in Irish.

A Story Repeated?

Initially, commentary and discussion on the Irish agrarian novel came largely in the form of biographies of individual writers. These biographies, produced in the closing decades of the nineteenth century, tended to stress – and probably to exaggerate – the subject's identification with the tenants, with the Catholic Church, and with political Nationalism. This tendency, particularly marked in the treatments accorded to the Banim brothers and to William Carleton, may reflect developments in Ireland in the 1870s and 1880s, not least the emergence of the Land League and the increasing power of the Home Rule movement.

Around the turn of the nineteenth and twentieth centuries, however, attempts were made to investigate the agrarian novels and their authors as a whole – an approach effectively precluded by the earlier emphasis on biography. Now critics sought to 'organise' the agrarian novelists into

11

categories, largely based on perceptions of 'degrees of Irishness'. Later, some went further and attempted to evaluate the relationship of the agrarian novel as a sub-genre with the totality of Irish literature, culture and identity.

Perhaps the most intriguing feature of the story of the literary criticism devoted to the Irish agrarian novel, largely a phenomenon of the twentieth century, is its close resemblance to the story of the agrarian novels themselves. Both the novels and the literary criticism are dominated – perhaps too dominated – by a single figure: Edgeworth dominates the novels and W B Yeats dominates the literary criticism. Subsequent developments follow a similar pattern. Edgeworth's successors try to distance themselves from her – but ultimately they cannot escape. Their analysis may be different but they still deal with the same issues and ask pretty much the same questions. Precisely the same is true of Yeats and his successors. In both cases, the 'founder's' dominance leads to lack of real originality, to intellectual exhaustion and, on occasion, comes dangerously close to absurdity – though more frequently in the case of the critics than of the novelists.

But it is not just a matter of 'permutations on Edgeworth' and 'permutations on Yeats'. The literary critics of the twentieth century cannot deny the importance of Edgeworth or Yeats, but these writers are actually huge obstacles to what most of the critics would really like to do. Ideally, they would like to portray the agrarian novels, their authors – and indeed the tradition of criticism that has subsequently developed around them – as the embodiments of a narrowly defined vision of Irish identity, whose chief manifestations are the Irish language, poetry, advocacy of the expropriation of landed estates, Catholicism, and radical Nationalism. As we shall see, Daniel Corkery was to advance some very peculiar ideas, but before we attempt to expose the extent of his confusion, we should at least his acknowledge his honesty in appreciating the difficulties of any description on these lines. The root of the problem lies in Edgeworth and Yeats themselves. Both Edgeworth and Yeats were Protestants, both came from landowning families, Edgeworth supported the Union and Yeats's attitude to independence was – to say the least of it – decidedly ambiguous. With 'founders' like that, the task was impossible. Of course, the final irony is that Maria Edgeworth and William Butler Yeats were actually related. They were both members of the great Butler clan, whose own founders had been Anglo-Norman adventurers who had arrived in Ireland in the Middle Ages. In the last resort, the question of whether the

Butlers should be considered Irish is the same as whether the agrarian novel is Irish.

Thus any discussion about the treatment of the agrarian novel as a genre by literary critics must begin with Yeats. We find the first attempt at 'categorisation' in Yeats's Introduction to *Representative Irish Tales* (1891) – which seeks to do something similar to what F R Leavis's *The Great Tradition* (1948) was later propose for English literature. Yeats insists.

> I notice very distinctly in all Irish literature two different accents – the accent of the gentry, and the less polished accent of the peasantry and those near them; a division roughly into the voice of those who lived gayly, and those who took man and his fortunes with much seriousness and even at times mournfully.[4]

This scheme of categorisation is far from exclusive. While Yeats may distinguish between the accents the gentry (who live gayly) and those of the peasantry (who are more serious and even mournful), he has no hesitation in placing both accents under a common heading of 'Irish Literature'. Like all schemes of categorisation, Yeats's model may be too simplistic. Even if we accept his idea of accents, it does not necessarily follow that the gentry accent is always 'gay' (and by implication rather superficial) or that the peasant accent is always serious and sometimes mournful. So, while Yeats's inclusion of Lover and Lever in the gentry accent and Carleton and Kickham in the peasant accent category may seem reasonable, Lever's *Lord Kilgobbin (1872)* contains a serious analysis of the Land Question and, although Carleton examines issues facing his countrymen 'with much seriousness', he also deploys humour even in seriously-minded novels like *Valentine M'Clutchy* (1845). Indeed, Yeats seems to have forgotten that the most 'genteel' of the agrarian novelists, Edgeworth herself, was in many ways also the most 'serious' of all.

Perhaps appreciating that his initial categorization had been too simplistic, Yeats later modified his scheme by postulating the existence of a third accent:

> In Gerald Griffin, the most finished storyteller among Irish novelists, and later on in Charles Kickham, I think I notice a new accent – not quite clear enough to be wholly distinct; the accent of people who have not the recklessness of the landowning class, nor

[4] Yeats, *Representative*, p. 25.

the violent passions of the peasantry, nor the good frankness of either.[5]

Yeats's third accent, which in social terms seems to be that of the middle classes, is rather elusive, not least when he suggests implausibly that Kickham belongs both to the second accent of the peasantry and to the third accent, the 'middle way'. It is not even clear whether Yeats approves of the third accent. The fact that it avoids both 'the recklessness of the landowning classes' and 'the violent passions of the peasantry' tempts us to expect a ringing endorsement of the moral and other qualities of people like Griffin and Kickham. Yeats goes so far as to say that the new accent 'may sometime give Ireland a new literature'.[6] Indeed, it is said that he sought to build the Irish canon on the 'few perfect tales'[7] of Griffin and Kickham. Yet there are hints that such a literature would not have been to Yeats's taste – not least because the new accent from which it might spring does not possess 'the good frankness' of either the gentry or the peasant accents. Yeats does praise, *Knocknagow* (1879) and describes Kickham as one of the 'the leading national writers'. Yet he goes on to castigate Kickham for seeing 'everything with the rose-spectacles of the returned exile' and, while his portrayals of his own class are good, his 'Orangemen, landlords and agents [...] are seldom in any way human, nor are they artistically true'.[8]

The problem is recurrent in Yeats. A few words of praise are followed by brutal dismissal. Thus, Samuel Lover's stories are 'seldom more than the allowable exaggerations of the humorist', while Thomas Crofton Croker suffers from a 'narrow conception of Irish life'. Charles Lever writes 'mainly for his own [Protestant Ascendancy] class' while the Banims' works are 'of little account'. The only exception is Maria Edgeworth, Yeats's own kinswoman: the 'most serious novelist coming from the upper classes' and 'the most finished and famous produced by any class'.[9] Some years later, (14 September 1910), when writing about J M Synge, Yeats again praises Edgeworth:

---

[5] Yeats, *Representative*, p. 31.
[6] Yeats, *Representative*, p. 31.
[7] Roy F Foster, *W B Yeats* (Oxford: Oxford University Press, 1997), Vol I, p. 98.
[8] Yeats, *Representative*, p. 31.
[9] Yeats, *Representative*, pp. 26-30.

In no modern writer that has written of Irish life before him [Synge], except, it may be, Maria Edgeworth in *Castle Rackrent*, was there anything to change a man's thought about the world or stir his moral nature.[10]

Yeats considers *Castle Rackrent* 'one of the most inspired chronicles written in English'. While admiring Edgeworth's depiction of the peasant narrator Thady Quirk, Yeats is even more impressed by her portrayal of the Ascendancy:

When writing of people of her own class she saw everything about them as it really was. She constantly satirised their recklessness, their love for all things English, their oppression of and contempt for their own country.

For a while, we are teased with the possibility that other writers, perhaps speaking in the 'peasant accent', could equal Edgeworth in ability and importance. William Carleton seems a promising candidate:

Beside Miss Edgeworth's well-finished four-square house of the intelligence, Carleton raised his rough clay 'rath' of humour and passion. Miss Edgeworth has outdone writers like Lover and Lever because of her fine judgement, her serene culture, her well-balanced mind. Carleton [...] has, I believe, outdone not only them but her also by the sheer force of his powerful nature.

But Yeats proceeds to express so many reservations about Carleton that it becomes increasingly hard to believe that he really rates him as high, let alone higher, than Edgeworth. Thus Yeats insists that Carleton's work suffered because there was 'no national cultivated public' to receive or respond to it and he also argues that, after *Fardorougha the Miser* (1839) 'and the two or three other novels that followed [...] came decadence – ruinous, complete'.[11] In fact, some of Carleton's best novels, including *Valentine M'Clutchy* (1845), *The Black Prophet* (1847) and *The Tithe Proctor* (1849) were published long after 1839. Indeed, *The Squanders of Castle Squander*, published as late as 1852, contains a powerful analysis of the

---

[10] W B Yeats, *Essays and Introductions* (London: Macmillan Publishers Limited, 1989), p. 322.
[11] Yeats, *Representative*, pp. 27-29.

Land Question. Yeats's distaste for aspects of Carleton's work stems from his belief that, 'landlords, agents, and their class are described as falsely as peasants are in the books of Lover and Croker'. Yeats identifies *Valentine M'Clutchy* as 'the first novel of his [Carleton's] decadence', yet the novel obviously involves a reworking of Edgeworth's *The Absentee* (1812) and this book will argue that Carleton's depiction of the appalling Valentine M'Clutchy is an effective satire on Edgeworth's novel – and not an example of 'misdirected power'.[12] Yeats certainly knew Carleton's work well and was reading *The Black Prophet* (1847) when he wrote *The Countess Kathleen* (1892), indeed, Roy Foster suggests that Carleton's novel 'supplied the background of a Famine-ravaged land'. While Yeats criticised Carleton, he was ready to defend him against those who followed *The Nation* in attacking Carleton's 'apostasy' – and entirely proper response from a Protestant like Yeats.

It has been said of Yeats that:

[His] view of authentic Irishness still stressed a peasant and Catholic identity; and his immersion in early nineteenth-century Catholic Irish fiction, together with his contemporary denunciation of the 'braggadocio' peddled for English audiences by the supposedly Anglo-Irish Charles Lever and Samuel Lover, helped dictate this view.

Of course, the problem is that Edgeworth, according to Yeats the best of all the agrarian novelists, was also the least 'Irish' and Carleton – probably the best of the 'Irish' writers – not only succumbed to ruinous and complete decadence but also embraced 'un-Irish' Protestantism. In other words, while Yeats's idea of 'accents' may have been valuable as a starting-off point for a tradition of literary criticism, it is also extremely elusive – in fact, just as elusive as Edgeworth's 'legacy' of the search for a solution to the Land Question, mutually advantageous to landowners and tenants alike.

Yeats's approach to the agrarian novels must be seen in the context of his own preoccupations in the closing years of the nineteenth century. When writing his introduction to 'March 1891',[13] he was involved in the Irish Literary Revival and developing his dream of 'a new Irish Literary movement – like that of '48 – that will show itself at the first lull in this

---

[12] Yeats, *Representative*, pp. 28-30.
[13] Foster, *Yeats*, I, pp. 97-98.

storm of politics'.[14] According to Foster, Yeats's plan was not universally welcomed:

> [Yeats's] original ambition was to produce 'a kind of social history', with stories 'illustrative of some phase of Irish life', defending the 'square built power' of unfashionable Irish novelists like Gerald Griffin and the Banim brothers [...]. In July 1891 the *Irish Monthly* would attack him for including tasteless and anti-Catholic material, and overly emphasizing 'the rollicking, savage and droll elements' of Irish life.[15]

Perhaps the *Irish Monthly* did not see – as Yeats clearly did – that the 'gentry accent' had to be included if a significant canon of literature was to be established. This was the obvious conclusion to be drawn from Yeats's reservations about the Banims, Griffin, Carleton and Kickham. But, if the 'gentry' accent (especially Edgeworth) was included – and accepted as Irish – then it did not matter so much if the 'peasant' or 'third' accents contributed little of real literary value. The problem became far more acute for critics, perhaps taking their cue from the *Irish Monthly,* who were unwilling to accept the gentry accent as Irish in any meaningful sense. Unless they disagreed with Yeats's less than enthusiastic evaluation of the products the peasant and third accents, they would have to concede that, shorn of the gentry accent, the genre would look pretty thin.

Logically, there are two courses open to those who wish to challenge a particular interpretation of literature, or indeed of almost anything else. Either they can say that the writer concerned is wrong – and show why he is wrong – or they can say that is broadly right yet fails to take his ideas far enough. The first approach shows real independence of mind; the second implies a continuing degree of intellectual dependence. This was precisely the dilemma facing critics who examined the agrarian novels after Yeats. They might have argued that the Banims, Griffin, Kickham and Carleton were much greater writers than Yeats had allowed. In Carleton's case, at least, such a task should have been relatively easy. Inevitably, that would have meant a truly radical break with Yeats – though it might have 'saved' the agrarian novel as an authentic expression of peasant as well as of gentry accents, and ultimately of 'Irishness' itself. But the new critics did not do that. In effect, they said that Yeats had been right to be critical of

---

[14] Yeats, *Representative*, p. 32.
[15] Foster, *Yeats*, I, p. 98.

the 'peasant' or 'third' accent agrarian novels; unfortunately, he had not been critical enough. In other words, the new critics were as much in Yeats's shadow as the later agrarian novelists had been in Edgeworth's. Nowhere is the better demonstrated than in the writings of Daniel Corkery.

At first sight it seems unsurprising that Corkery and others found it as hard to escape from Yeats's shadow as many agrarian writers had done from Edgeworth's. After all, Yeats was a commanding literary figure, a poet rather than a novelist, but with an international standing at least comparable to Edgeworth's. Yet it should have been easier for the critics to escape. Although they might disagree with Edgeworth, the agrarian novelists held her in enormous respect. There can be little doubt that Carleton was genuinely delighted when he learned that Edgeworth had praised his writing. In contrast, most of the later critics despised Yeats. When Daniel Corkery heard Yeats lecture, he quickly wrote him off as 'a *poseur*'.[16] Furthermore, whatever its faults, Edgeworth had produced a substantial and detailed agenda for the agrarian novel. However important in other areas, Yeats's main contributions to the literary evaluation of the agrarian novel – his theory of accents and his low regard for the 'peasant' and 'third' accent versions of it – are altogether less impressive than Edgeworth's contributions to the novels themselves.

Here we must examine the terminologies employed by Yeats and Corkery. As we have seen, the key element in Yeats's scheme of categorisation is the idea of 'accents'. He uses this word in the normal way. Common usage does not equate 'different accents' with 'different languages'; neither does Yeats. The normal meaning of 'different accents' is that they describe variations, based on social or regional differences, within a common language. This is Yeats's meaning too – although he is more concerned with social than with regional differences. Of course, in the case of the agrarian novels, the common language is English.

The word 'accent' has fairly flexible connotations. As they change their stations in society or move their place of residence, people often change their accent. Sometimes this is done deliberately; more often the process is largely unconscious. It is true that differences of accents can lead to misunderstandings, but this is comparatively rare. For the most part, people speaking in different accents can communicate with each other quite easily.

---

[16] Patrick Maume, *'Life that is Exile': Daniel Corkery and the Search for the Irish Ireland* (Belfast: The Institute of Irish Studies, 1993), p. 20.

When proposing his own scheme of categorisation, Corkery, in *Synge and Anglo-Irish Literature* (1931), makes two major departures from Yeats's terminology; Yeats's 'accents' become 'moulds' and his 'gentry accent' becomes the 'Colonial mould'.

> Its earliest moulds cannot be distinguished from those of contemporary English literature. Later it certainly did develop somewhat different moulds, which can be distinguished. These second-period moulds we may speak of as Colonial moulds. The earliest writers never thought of themselves as cut off from English life and letters; the Colonial writers did.[17]

At first sight, these changes seem insignificant but further reflection suggests that they are profound. 'Mould' is more obviously metaphorical than 'accent' and carries with it an association of rigidity that 'accent' lacks. Moulds must stay exactly as they are or risk being totally smashed to pieces. You cannot 'modify' a mould as you can an accent; 'moulds' do not communicate with each other like accents do. But there is more. Yeats's distinction between 'gentry' and 'peasant' accents implies no essential division of race or language; Corkery's introduction of the 'colonial' concept raises the possibility of both. Above all, whereas Yeats includes 'gentry accent' works as part of Irish literature, Corkery's 'Colonial mould' becomes identified with 'Anglo-Irish literature'. Whatever their superficial similarities, Corkery's 'moulds' are much further apart than Yeats's accents had been.

The difference becomes sharper still when we learn that Corkery believes that 'literature written in English by Irishmen is […] Anglo-Irish literature, while by Irish literature we mean the literature written in the Irish language and that alone'.[18] Corkery is not only 'transferring' Yeats's 'gentry accent' writers from 'Irish Literature' to 'Anglo-Irish Literature' but is also moving Yeats's 'peasant' and 'third' accent writers – the Banims, Griffin, Carleton, and Kickham – into 'Anglo-Irish Literature' too. In short, because Corkery equates Irish Literature with the Irish language, none of the agrarian novelists – who all wrote in English – can remain part of Irish literature.

It is not that Corkery is entirely ungenerous. He describes *Castle Rackrent* as 'the best specimen of the ['Colonial'] style of literature, noting

---

[17] Daniel Corkery, *Synge and Anglo-Irish Literature* (Cork: The Mercier Press, 1966), p. 7.
[18] Corkery, *Synge*, p. 1.

– with impressive accuracy – that [n]o other book did as much in the creation of what was to become the most favoured of the moulds which subsequent writers were to use'. There are times when Corkery seems to retreat from his insistence that to qualify as Irish literature, books must be written in the Irish language. There are hints that Griffin, a 'native-born Catholic Irishman whose forebears had not come out of England' is held in some regard, but ultimately that fact that Griffin was both Catholic and Irish is not enough to keep him out of the 'Colonial mould': 'he may be taken as the type of the non-Ascendancy writer who under the stress of the literary moulds of his time wrote Colonial Literature'.[19]

There are suggestions too that some works written in English might be considered for inclusion in a canon of Irish literature if it could be shown that they were targeted at Irish rather than English readers. Writers such as Carleton and Kickham were possible candidates for such inclusion. Another possible way was to admit works not tainted by 'movements and fashions in literature which do not take their rise in this country [Ireland]'[20] or were truly relevant to the concerns and interests of the Irish people. Such flexibility promises a more liberal interpretation. No doubt there is much to criticize in the agrarian novels of Thomas Moore, Edgeworth, Griffin and Carleton. Yet these writers' obsession with the Land Question was an essentially Irish phenomenon; indeed, it was the repeated analysis of this issue that simultaneously reveal both the sub-genre's artistic limitations and its greatest strengths. The agrarian novels considered here, especially *Castle Rackrent*, *Memoirs of Captain Rock* (1824) and *Dracula*, owe little to foreign literary fashions – though they do echo wider European conflicts over land-ownership. Corkery blames expatriation for excessive 'foreign' influence on Anglo-Irish literature: '[e]xpatriation is the badge of all the tribe of Anglo-Irish literary men'.[21] But Edgeworth, Michael Banim, Griffin, Carleton and Kickham were not expatriates.

Yet the doors are firmly closed again when Corkery faces the ultimate question: in what does 'Irishness' consist? He suggests that Ireland's 'national consciousness may be described [...] as a quaking sod. [...] It is not English, nor Irish, nor Anglo-Irish'.[22] Metaphors can be helpful on occasion, but not in this case. We are never told of what 'the quaking sod'

---

[19] Corkery, *Synge*, pp. 7-9.
[20] Corkery, *Synge*, p. 4.
[21] Corkery, *Synge*, p. 4.
[22] Corkery, *Synge*, p. 14.

and its associated 'national literature' is really made. Corkery implies that the only literature that really counts is some distant Gaelic poetry that, by custom, was part of an oral tradition, or arises from the 'quaking sod'. In the search for national identity and consciousness, poetry may be more important than novels. After all, the novel is only the product of the last three hundred years, whereas poetry takes us much further into the past. Furthermore, in many cultures, the novel as an art form was 'imported' from elsewhere – however much 'national colouring' it may have acquired subsequently – while poetry is more likely to be spontaneous and 'home grown'. In principle, therefore, Corkery's claim – that the poetry and land of Ireland are inextricably linked – does seem credible:

> The future conquest of the soil was part of Irish consciousness [...] those of us who have read Irish poetry know that it has for many centuries been one of the deepest things in Irish consciousness; our 'national' writers however either were not aware of it, or, aware of it, could not or would not give it utterance.[23]

But the juxtaposition of readers of Irish poetry and 'national writers' is more problematic. The claim – that 'national' writers (the quotation marks are obviously ironic and the reference can only be to the novelists) were either ignorant of the relationship between the soil and poetry or unwilling or unable to reflect that relationship in their own literary works – raises huge questions, especially if their failure arose from inability. If so, was that failure due to the fact that they were writing in English or even that they were novelists rather than poets?

Clearly, Corkery is suspicious of the notion – accepted by Yeats – that novelists who wrote in English could do anything to foster Irish consciousness. There might have been more to say for his position if the novelists had been 'crowding out' a more purely Irish alternative, one that would have provided a large readership of literate, moderately affluent, and poetry-loving Gaelic speakers with exactly what it needed. In nineteenth-century Ireland, such a project would have been completely unviable – and twentieth-century attempts, backed by the Irish state, have enjoyed not much better success. Certainly, if Irish consciousness was to be articulated in a cultural form in the nineteenth century, novelists – and

---

[23] Corkery, *Synge*, p. 17.

novelists writing in English too – were best placed to do it. The consciousness they articulated may not have been 'Irish' enough for Corkery – or indeed for other critics more anxious to accommodate them into some sort of 'Irish category' – but what they wrote did in some ways reflect the complex reality of the national consciousness of nineteenth century Ireland.

In theory, the Irish were as British as the Scots, the Welsh and the English – as Jonathan Clark states, in *Our Shadowed Present* (2003): 'If the United Kingdom was a composite state, it was appropriate that "[e]very Briton in 1800 possessed a composite identity".[24] It may be debated as to how far the Irish actually 'participated' in such a composite identity and, if so, what form it took. The agrarian novels, however, suggest that there was a kind of British dimension and hence that, for a while at least, Irish consciousness included elements of 'Britishness', even if that did not entail commitment to the political arrangements of the Union. Yet if to be Irish was also to be even slightly British, it follows that it is impossible to exclude the agrarian novels from the canon of 'Irish' literature. In other words, Corkery's argument depends on a very selective analysis of the writers and their works. In a way similar to Yeats's 'third accent,' Corkery refines his argument:

All Anglo-Irish literature […] may be divided into two kinds – the literature of the Ascendancy writer and that of the writer for the Irish people. Roughly, the first kind includes all the literature that lives by foreign suffrage; the second, all that lives by native suffrage.[25]

Corkery's analysis seems to put most of the agrarian novelists in the category of Ascendancy writers. He is claiming that these novelists wrote for a 'foreign' – that is English readership – and that the Irish themselves did not read them because their subject matter was irrelevant to Ireland. Although it is hard to determine patterns of readership, most of the novels were published in Ireland and not in England. Above all, it is surely very odd to suggest that novels written about the Land Question – after all, the dominant problem in Irish society for the best part of a century – were not relevant to the Irish. It is true that Corkery does accept Kickham, who like the other agrarian novelists wrote in English, as a

[24] Jonathan C D Clark, *Our Shadowed Present* (London: Atlantic Books, 2003), p. 105.
[25] Corkery, *Synge*, p. 23.

writer who lived 'by native suffrage' – that is as someone who wrote for the Irish and was read by them. Corkery's enthusiasm for Kickham, however, is as qualified as Yeats's is for Carleton. He says of *Knocknagow*:

> It is a book unknown except to the Irish; and again one is not sorry, for, when all is said, it is only good in parts, and not great anywhere. The emotional content here is also right; the mental equipment, however, that shaped it out was not hardened by culture and discipline.[26]

Knocknagow has remained in print and is one of the most popular nationalist novels. Yet if Corkery is right – and *Knocknagow* is neither great nor hardened by culture or discipline – that must mean that the only genuinely 'Irish' agrarian novelist has little literary significance.

In the last resort, therefore, of all the agrarian novelists, only Kickham, seen by Corkery as by no means outstanding as a writer, is left with a chance of inclusion as a 'national writer'. Even then it is only an outside chance – because Kickham was a novelist and wrote in English, both characteristics which, elsewhere in Corkery's analysis, would seem to disqualify him. For 'nationalist' purposes, therefore, the agrarian novel has been effectively written off.

We have noted earlier that there are similarities between the story of literary criticism devoted to the agrarian novel and that of the agrarian novels themselves. In particular, we have suggested that, in the field of criticism, Yeats is the 'equivalent' of Edgeworth in the novels. But does the pattern continue and, if so, to whom is Corkery the equivalent? The answer may seem surprising, but the closest equivalence is with Kickham and Trollope. It is ironic that Corkery, the fairly extreme nationalist and xenophobe, should be included in this category. In their different ways, Kickham and Trollope looked to other countries to 'escape' the impasse into which Edgeworth's agenda had descended by seeking essentially 'foreign' answers to the underlying problems facing Ireland. Trollope looked to England and Kickham looked to America. In seeking to complete the 'demolition' of Yeats's scheme of categorisation and to further undermine the stature of the agrarian novelists, Corkery too looked abroad in search of literary, social and political inspiration.

---

[26] Corkery, *Synge*, p. 25.

Corkery's most obvious 'foreign source' was England and derived from the ideas and values of the Bloomsbury group – with its contempt for most 'Victorian' writers, public figures and values. In England, the Bloomsbury group ridiculed what its members saw as typically 'Victorian' narrow-mindedness and hypocrisy and sought to replace it with a more morally and sexually-liberated aesthetic and lifestyle. Duncan Grant, Vanessa Bell, Roger Fry (through the Omega Workshops), and Clive Bell sought to create a new wave in art – in painting, decorating, furniture design, and art criticism. Lytton Strachey's *Eminent Victorians* (1918) re-interpreted key Victorian figures 'from a slightly cynical standpoint'.[27] Perhaps most strikingly, it was Virginia Woolf who, after a brief visit to Ireland, insisted that there had been no worthwhile Irish writer since Dean Swift – 'I'm trying to get the Irish back to the great men of the eighteenth century. Swift!'[28] Whereas Woolf despised the oppressive culture of the nineteenth century while embracing that of the eighteenth century, Corkery rejected about eight hundred years of Irish history. But while Corkery might be regarded as a sort of 'detached' member of the Bloomsbury set – who happened to live in Ireland – Bloomsbury values were highly untypical of Ireland in the 1930s. The Puritan Catholic theocracy that underpinned De Valera's Ireland, though admittedly more nationalist, was surely much closer in spirit to the moral earnestness of most of the agrarian novelists Corkery so readily dismissed as un-Irish.

The ultimate origin of Corkery's other 'foreign borrowing' – though probably acquired indirectly through contact with Bloomsbury ideas – is even more remarkable. Its true homeland was Soviet Russia in the days of Josef Stalin. In 1928, Stalin had turned his back on the former NEP agenda, to embark on a massive programme in which peasants were deprived of their lands and herded – most unwillingly – into collective farms. At the same time Stalin also embarked on a similarly massive programme of 'break-neck' industrialization. Now, peasants were demonised and the industrial proletariat lauded as the true embodiment of socialist virtue. The death and suffering involved was horrendous. Corkery's writings neatly reflect the latest twist in Soviet ideology. Patrick Maume notes:

---

[27] Lytton Strachey, *Eminent Victorians* (1918) (New York: Continuum, 2002), p. xi.
[28] Virginia Woolf, *The Diary of Virginia Woolf*, ed by Anne Olivier Bell and Andrew McNeil lie (New York: Harcourt Brace Jovanovich, 1982), IV, p. 255.

[Corkery] complained that the farmers were only interested in the land; he accepted the necessity of the Land War, but believed it hindered the development of an Irish national culture by stifling discussion and ignoring the interests of other elements of Irish society such as the urban working man. He wrote in his diary that while the mind of the farmer was dominated by land, the townsman valued 'personal freedom'.[29]

Corkery's position reflects a twentieth-century intellectual's preoccupation with urban issues – but he hints that his real objection to the agrarian novels springs from distaste for the values of the tenants themselves, perhaps even the values of rural societies. It is true that Karl Marx was extremely rude about 'peasants' but Corkery seems to be verging on another 'might have been', equally as counter-factual as the idea of Gaelic poetry as the only authentic voice of Irish consciousness. This time the 'alternative' is the voice of an industrial proletariat – who either did not exist or, if they did, were staunchly Protestant and Unionist. Perhaps Corkery 'corresponds' to more than one of the agrarian novel categories proposed in this book; not only does he resemble Kickham and Trollope in his 'foreign borrowings' but he also reminds us of the 'fantasy writers' – Moore and Stoker – in his strange 'counterfactuals'; indeed he goes further. If Stoker was really writing about Ireland when he set *Dracula* in Transylvania, perhaps Corkery was really writing about the Ukraine when he appeared to be talking about Ireland.

Corkery is, however, nowhere near as good as either Moore or Stoker. The more we investigate him, the more confused he appears. Echoing Yeats's habit of a few words of praise followed by the stab in the back, he first says that Carleton should be regarded as Edgworth's equal (almost quoting Yeats verbatim) but then attacks him with even greater ferocity than Yeats had ever done. Maume explains:

Reading *Tess of the D'Urbervilles*, he [Corkery] noted 'the peasants in their coarseness are very different from our Irish peasants but then our peasants have not got into print – I know nothing of them'.

In other words, Corkery had learned nothing about the Irish peasants from Carleton! But if Corkery knows nothing of Irish peasants, how is he

---

[29] Maume, *Life*, pp. 12-13.

qualified to judge novels largely devoted to them? The confusion is so great – much greater than in Yeats – that in the end Corkery, having rejected both the agrarian novelists and Yeats's analysis of Irish literature, just blames everything on the English.

There would have been little point in subjecting Corkery to this extended analysis if he had been merely a lone voice, untypical of other writers of this time. This is not the case and views quite similar to Corkery's can be found in the writings of many of his contemporaries or near contemporise. In virtually all cases, a low evaluation or complete exclusion of the agrarian novelists stems from a narrow definition of Irish national identity. Douglas Hyde's *A Literary History of Ireland* (1899) insists:

> The present volume has been styled [...] a 'Literary History of Ireland,' but a 'Literary History of Irish Ireland' would be a more correct title, for I have abstained altogether from an analysis or even mention of the works of Anglicised Irishmen of the last two centuries. Their books, as those of Farquhar, of Swift, of Goldsmith, of Burke, find, and have always found their true and natural place in every history of *English* literature that has been written by Englishmen themselves or by foreigners.[30]

For Hyde, writers like Swift and Goldsmith are English rather than Irish and, despite the title's inclusive inference, they would taint a true literary history of Ireland. De Blacam's *A First Book of Irish Literature* (1934) appears slightly more generous:

> While I regard the Gaelic tradition as the very core of our heritage, I hold that the old nation justly may take pride in the merits of Anglo-Irish writings – the limpid style, in which they are the best of English models, and the strength and passion which the writers draw from Gaelic blood or association. The value to us of Anglo-Irish writings, however, is in exact proportion to the affiliation of the writers to historic Ireland.[31]

[30] Douglas Hyde, *A Literary History of Ireland* (1899) (London: T. Fisher Unwin, 1906), p. ix.
[31] Aodh de Blacam, *A First Book of Irish Literature* (1934) (Dublin & Cork: The Educational Company of Ireland Limited, nd), p. viii.

The question then arises as to which 'Anglo-Irish writers' have a significant affiliation to historic Ireland. Despite a few polite words about earlier authors, De Blacam's essential conclusion is that no Anglo-Irish writer before Yeats had sufficient affiliation to be worthy of serious notice.

There were a few critics who spoke up for the cultural achievements of the Anglo-Irish. For instance, in 1935, John Eglinton wrote in *Irish Literary Portraits*:

> I find myself wondering whether that event ['the "Treaty" of 1921'] has not already begun to eliminate the elect breed of those to whom England and Ireland were equally dear. To the Unionist, Ireland was, exactly like England and Scotland, a mother-country, whose sons are over all the world.

Eglinton challenges claims of the primacy of the Gaelic language stating that 'the ancient Irish language is no more a bond of union among the Irish than Hebrew has been among the modern Jews'.[32] His interpretation was accurate as the Treaty ultimately condemned the Ascendancy to oblivion and the Irish language was never to be universally spoken across Ireland.

Historians in disguise

Literary criticism flourished in Ireland after 1945, displaying considerably greater sophistication than is to be found in the criticism produced by Yeats or Corkery. In respect of the agrarian novelists, however, the underlying question remains the same: did they – or even some of them – belong to 'Irish Literature' or not? Continuing disagreement is obvious from the titles of two important works. Thomas Flanagan's *The Irish Novelists 1800-1850* (1958), includes many authors who wrote in English, while Barry Sloan's study of the same authors is significantly entitled *The Pioneers of Anglo-Irish Fiction 1800-1850*. (1986). Yet Flanagan and Sloan were both unusual in choosing to write about the agrarian novelists at all. For the most part, the greater sophistication of literary criticism was directed towards other genres. In short, the most striking thing about the agrarian novel was that so little was said about it.

---

[32] John Eglinton, *Irish Literary Portraits* (London: Macmillan & Co Ltd, 1935), p. 4.

In 1966, Horatio Sheafe Krans wrote in *Irish Life in Irish Fiction*:

No attempt has, I believe, been made before to bring into a single
survey the Irish novelists of the first half of the nineteenth century
and their work. [...] In the novels may be seen [...] the racial
antipathies, the religious antagonisms, the sleepless consciousness
of past wrongs.[33]

Krans may have been exaggerating a little but he had a point. Krans
identifies Edgeworth, Carleton and Lever as a part of Irish literature, yet P
J Drudy in his book, *Anglo-Irish Studies* (1976), argues that, despite its title,
it investigates 'Irish and Anglo-Irish culture and learning' as if they were
separate cultures.[34] In other words, Corkery's 'moulds' have barely
cracked.

In the 1980s, more works appeared investigating nineteenth-century
Irish literature including *Anglo-Irish Literature* (1982), *History and Violence in
Anglo-Irish Literature* (1986), *The Crows Behind the Plough* (1988), *Anglo-Irish
and Irish Literature* (1988) and *Critical Approaches to Anglo-Irish Literature*
(1989). These titles suggest that, though there might be some debate
about precise boundaries, a clear distinction had been established between
'Irish' and 'Anglo-Irish' writers. There was also implicit rejection of De
Blacam's notion that 'Anglo-Irish' works were only of interest if they
revealed an affiliation with the writers of 'historic' Ireland. While the
critics of the 1980s were less 'restrictive' in their definitions than Corkery
had been, they remained more restrictive than Yeats, who had included
'gentry accent' novels in his overall category of Irish literature.

The 1990s saw a significant change in the academic consideration of
nineteenth-century Ireland, one that might have been expected to 'serve
the cause' of the agrarian novelists. In particular, 'Anglo-Irish Studies'
were increasingly replaced by the more inclusive 'Irish Studies'. Laurence
Geary and Margaret Kelleher note:

[I]nterest in nineteenth-century studies has never been greater, and
contrasts sharply with previous neglect of many aspects of that
century's history and culture. However, many of the changes that

---

[33] Horatio Sheafe Krans, *Irish Life in Irish Fiction* (New York: AMS Press Inc, 1966), p. v.
[34] *Anglo-Irish Studies*, ed by P J Drudy (Chalfont St Giles: Alpha Academic, 1976), no page
numbers.

have taken place in studies of nineteenth-century Ireland have yet
to be fully recognised or sufficiently examined.[35]

Although the change may appear to be little more than semantics, it
reveals a substantial shift in focus. Contemporary critics consistently
suggest that there is a single canon of Irish literature and, in doing so,
hope to be able to choose selectively from among Anglo-Irish writers.
This enables them to avoid the problems encountered by Yeats – and
even more by Corkery – with his essentially 'Ascendancy-versus-
Nationalism' binary. The message is that rather less attention should be
devoted to the politics and/or religion of the agrarian novelists: Moore,
Edgeworth, Carleton and Kickham should be studied primarily as writers
rather than as Catholics or Protestants, Nationalists or Unionists, pro or
anti-British.

As so often, however, any expectation that an apparent change in the
critics' stance will bring the agrarian novelists to the centre of literary
debate has proved premature. Although not always obviously, much of
the critical writing has focussed on the temporal relationship between the
agrarian novelists and works of other periods, and indeed with Irish
history as a whole. The critics have been historians in disguise – sadly for
the most part, not very good historians. It has been claimed, for example,
that Edgeworth's work, especially *Castle Rackrent* – supposedly set in 1782
– is really 'an epitaph for eighteenth century Ireland' and should not be
bracketed with 'genuine' nineteenth century agrarian novelists. Yet it is
clear that *Castle Rackrent* was written in anticipation of the Union and of
the problems and opportunities likely to result from it. If Edgeworth is
removed from the list of the agrarian novelists and many of the later ones
not even mentioned, the relevance of the subgenre becomes highly
marginal.

The suggestion that agrarian novelists should be read as novelists
rather than as symbols of belief systems of politics or religion may seem
to go against the trend towards historical evaluation. It appears that some
writers may now be excluded from the canon of Irish Literature not
because they are not Irish enough but because they are not good enough
writers. Though for different reasons, some late twentieth-century critics
can be as dismissive and almost as exclusive as Corkery about the agrarian
novelists. Even those who remain in the canon are thought rather

---

[35] *Nineteenth-Century Ireland*, ed by Laurence M Geary and Margaret Kelleher (Dublin:
University College Dublin Press, 2005), p. vii.

uninteresting. Sean Ryder notes that 'critical discussions of nineteenth-century Irish writing tended to focus on a relatively narrow range of writers' and viewed 'the period as far less interesting than the early twentieth century'. But this was largely because the criteria of merit and interest were essentially historical. Ryder notes that critics focused on the Revivalists and hence 'mid-century predecessors' (presumably the agrarian novelists) were worth studying only 'insofar as they could be read as the Revivalists' artistic antecedents'. In large measure that meant 'mid-century predecessors of Yeats'. But it has been said of Yeats that he had 'an aesthetic and psychological need to distinguish himself from his precursors'.[36] While he may have written about the agrarian novelists, Yeats would have been loath to acknowledge any direct obligation to them – except perhaps to Edgeworth, who critics like Joep Leerssen think should not be treated as a nineteenth-century agrarian novelist in any case. It is true that some critics have portrayed the best of the agrarian novelists as precursors of Yeats.

In his Preface to *The New Oxford Book of Irish Verse* (1986), Thomas Kinsella reveals his allegiance by commenting that the Irish language created poetry 'for a thousand years before the curse of Cromwell fell upon them [the people], and it, and which for some hundreds of years afterwards flourished in decline'.[37] Yet he is dismissive, not only of Moore – '[n]one of [whose] popular poetry bears close scrutiny' – but also of the whole of the nineteenth century. In *Davis, Mangan, Ferguson?* (1970), Kinsella states 'I believe that silence, on the whole, is the real condition of Irish literature in the nineteenth century'. He argues that 'continuity and shared history' is 'missing from Irish literature, in English and Irish, in the nineteenth century'.[38] Kinsella sees 'the familiar "Anglo-Irish" elements dominate, in a long preparation […] for the career of Yeats'.[39] Yet there is an overwhelming sense that the silence of the Irish elements and the dominance of the Anglo-Irish is a matter for regret – even if those Anglo-Irish elements do prepare the way for Yeats. So, the 'cause' of the agrarian novels is not far advanced – if at all – since the days of Corkery. At best,

[36] Sean Ryder, 'Literature in English', in *Nineteenth-Century Ireland*, ed by Laurence M Geary and Margaret Kelleher (Dublin: University College Dublin Press, 2005), pp. 118-119.
[37] *The New Oxford Book of Irish Verse*, ed by Thomas Kinsella (Oxford: Oxford University Press, 1986), p. vii.
[38] Thomas Kinsella, *Davis, Mangan, Ferguson?* (Dublin: The Dolmen Press, 1970), pp. 58-59.
[39] Kinsella, *New Oxford*, p. xxvi

the agrarian novelists are seen as having limited ability and even individual writers like Edgeworth – who did have some ability – are merely preparing the way for genuine Irish writers. Thus Ryder states: 'the bulk of nineteenth-century Irish writing remained unexamined by critics, or was judged merely as historical background to the twentieth-century'.[40]

It cannot be said, therefore, that the agrarian novelists have been fortunate in the treatment they have received from later writers. It is essentially a story of distortion, dismissal and neglect. Distortion characterised the early biographies by making them seem more 'Nationalist' than they really were. Dismissal characterised their treatment by Yeats and Corkery – either because they were not good enough (Yeats) or not good enough or Irish enough (Corkery). The majority of critics since 1945 ignored them, because they were either not good enough or relevant enough. In order to understand this treatment, it is important to gain a deeper understanding of the standards against which the agrarian novelists were being judged. In part, they were the victims of a literary version of the Whig interpretation of history: those who wrote about them applied the standards of the present to the past. Thus, in the late nineteenth century, their novels were 'squeezed' to fit the criteria of relatively moderate 'Home Rule' nationalism. But it was impossible to 'squeeze' them further to fit the criteria of a more extreme Republican Nationalism and its associated notions of culture and Irish identity.

In some ways it has become easier to see why the agrarian novelists received harsh treatment from most twentieth-century critics now that the works of those critics are being investigated thoroughly. This is especially true of Corkery. In *Strange Country* (1998), Seamus Deane interprets Corkery's theory of moulds as 'a founding act of literary and political criticism for the newly emergent Free State':

> [F]or Yeats and Corkery, to be backward, archaic, is to possess that fullness that a secular temporality has abandoned. Yet the paradox is that such a sacral time must be provided with a history that is organized [...] The telling feature of such writing is its capacity to negotiate between the sacred and the secular, to carry from the former the energies lacking in the latter – in local Irish terms, to translate from the Irish into English all those intensities that modern English lacks and to restore all those energies in Irish that

---

[40] Ryder, *Nineteenth*, p. 121.

have been suppressed [...] it is a matter of some importance to determine the degree of the writer's access to the Irish language.[41]

While his argument is hard to follow, the implications of Deane's analysis are interesting. He seems to dilute Corkery's apparent insistence that to be considered 'Irish' a work must be written in the Irish language. Now it appears that 'access to the Irish language' might be sufficient. The ideal writer seems to be a kind of mediator between English and Irish. He needs to have access to Irish so that his English works can convey a genuinely Irish intensity. It is also hinted, however, that Irish literature needs an input from Anglo-Irish or even English literature to restore its lost energy – though, unsurprisingly, this argument is not fully developed. Yet Deane is surely right to link Corkery's analysis with the needs of the new Irish state. Once more we return to history. New states need identities, and 'agreed' or 'organised' histories are essential to the development and nurture of such identities. These histories are most successful when they go back far into the past, to times that possess a spiritual character lost in the modern world – hence the importance of 'the archaic'. In short, therefore, there is good reason to believe that, despite its literary externals, the debate on the role of the agrarian novels is ultimately a debate about history.

It has been widely acknowledged that contemporary societies need to be aware of their descent from a fairly remote and spiritual past. The Irish literary critics may not have approved of English literature, but at least they seem to have read it. They appear ignorant, however, of a great controversy among historians in Victorian England – in some ways also a new state, one that needed a new understanding of the past. In English history, the nearest equivalent to 'the curse of Cromwell' is surely the Norman Conquest of 1066, which was followed by three centuries during which the English language became submerged and was abandoned by the upper classes – much like the experience of the Irish some five hundred years later. An 'exclusive' interpretation of English history was proposed by E A Freeman who, in *History of the Norman Conquest* (1867-1876), portrayed the Norman Conquest and the subjugation of the Anglo-Saxons as an unmitigated disaster. An equally 'exclusive' version was proposed by J H Round who, in *Feudal England* (1895), saw Anglo-Saxon England as a land of savages, in desperate need of Norman efficiency and ruthlessness.

---

[41] Seamus Deane, *Strange Country* (Oxford: Clarendon Press, 1998), pp. 150-153.

If we had to rely on Freeman and Round alone, it would be tempting to propose a theory of moulds for English historiography, even more rigid than the literary moulds proposed by Corkery. But one historian, William Stubbs, in *Constitutional History of England* (1874-78), broke the mould. He suggested a dialectic: a thesis of Anglo-Saxon and somewhat chaotic liberty; an antithesis of Norman efficiency and despotism; and finally a synthesis, the glory of Medieval England, that produced an ideal balance between liberty and order. If the Corkery model – similar to Freeman's model for Anglo-Saxon England – became the more or less official historical orthodoxy of the Irish Free State, the agrarian novelists would seem virtual collaborators with the occupiers. If an Irish version of Stubbs had been proposed – it was not, but there are hints of it in some of the agrarian novels themselves – then the novelists would have emerged as essential players in the process of synthesis.

The historical dimension is most apparent in the work of Declan Kiberd who, in *Inventing Ireland* (1996), offers a convoluted interpretation of Irish history and culture from 'the first wave of invaders' to the Literary Revival. Kiberd attacks 'the sheer ferocity of Spenser's writings on the Irish resistance' – in his *View of the Present State of Ireland* (1596) – and blames Shakespeare for creating 'the stage-Irishman':

In Shakespeare's rudimentary portrait [of Captain Macmorris in *Henry V*] are to be found those traits of garrulity, pugnacity and a rather unfocused ethnic pride which would later signalize the stage Irishman.

Kiberd proposes an alternative Irish canon beginning with the Gaelic writer Seathrun Ceitinn who 'sought to save the lore of ancient Ireland'. He finds some merit in the work of George Farquhar and Richard Brinsley Sheridan, whose plays 'reminded the London smart-set of the cultural price being paid for empire by its sponsors on the periphery'. Likewise, Goldsmith brought 'the consequences of rural clearances to the attention of his more sensitive metropolitan readers' while Swift offered 'a sharp reminder of the way in which English policy was viewed in Ireland'. But it is Edmund Burke who finds most favour with Kiberd, who argues that Burke's attacks on British excesses in India could readily be applied to Ireland as well. Kiberd endorses Conor Cruise O'Brien's description of Burke as an 'outer Whig and inner Jacobite'. He goes on to lament the early death of Thomas Davis, leader of Young Ireland and founder of the

Nation, but then jumps to Yeats. The agrarian novelists are scarcely mentioned; they are certainly not portrayed as precursors of Yeats. According to Kiberd, the real link to Yeats is not literary but political, and it runs through C S Parnell:

> The poet Yeats met the ship which bore Parnell's remains back to Dublin; [...] The way was open for a literary movement to fill the political vacuum. Its writers would take Standish O'Grady's versions of the Cuchulain legend, and interpret the hero not as an exemplar for the Anglo-Irish overlords but as a model for those who were about to displace them.[42]

The implication must be that the agrarian novelists have not been included because they do not prepare the way for Yeats and have failed to appreciate the significance of the native Irish cultural tradition that was so crucial to the Revival. But Kiberd's enthusiasm for Burke and Davis is curious, because Burke influenced Edgeworth, and Davis influenced Carleton and Stoker. Yet the comments on O'Grady, the son of Viscount Guillamore and a clergyman of the Church of Ireland, are especially revealing. Influenced by Thomas Carlyle's concept of the hero as a man-of-letters, O'Grady was fascinated by Irish myths and legends – especially Cu Chulainn. He developed the idea that the Ascendancy landlords should have led the native Irish, just as Cu Chulainn had done in myth. In works like *History of Ireland: Cuculain and his Contemporaries* (1880) and *Cuculain: An Epic* (1882), O'Grady covers what is essentially an *apologia* for the Ascendancy with a veneer of Celtic legend. It is rather reminiscent of the romance of Old Scotland as presented by Prince Albert and Queen Victoria. It is strange that a man like O'Grady should have been seen as contributing more to the Irish cause than Carleton or even Kickham.

No survey of modern literary criticism can ignore the Marxist dimension which, by its very nature, is essentially 'historical'. Ryder praises the Marxist critic Terry Eagleton for widening the Irish canon by 'recovering nineteenth-century figures like Fr Prout, W E H Lecky, Isaac Butt, George Sigerson, John E Cairnes, William Wilde and John Mitchel'.[43] These are certainly interesting figures and, as a Marxist, Eagleton does not slip too readily into acceptance of essentially Nationalist categories. It is worth noting, however, that Prout [Francis

---

[42] Declan Kiberd, *Inventing Ireland*, (London: Vintage, 1996), pp. 9-25.
[43] Ryder, *Nineteenth*, p. 126.

Sylvester Mahony] and Mitchel were primarily journalists, Lecky an historian, Butt a politician, Sigerson a translator, Cairnes an economist, Wilde a surgeon. In all cases, however, these men could be regarded as 'politically conscious' and hence, from Eagleton's perspective more worthy of study than the apparently a-political agrarian novelists. Although he refers to others, Eagleton does have the merit of engaging directly with some of the 'neglected' agrarian novelists to be discussed in this book. At first sight, there seems to be a good deal to be said in favour of Eagleton's assertion that Irish 'artistic culture' followed 'the trajectory of class power with an exactness enough to embarrass even the most vulgar of Marxists'. On further investigation, however, the chronology and the details do not fit very well and the stress is perhaps excessively political. Eagleton describes Moore as 'the first "national" poet' in the aftermath of 1798 and says of *Memoirs of Captain Rock* that it was one of the 'most powerful political interventions of the period'. It is not clear what period Eagleton is referring to, since *Memoirs of Captain Rock* was not published until 1824, more than a quarter of a century after 1798. Similarly Eagleton claims that the Banims' success reflects the drive towards Catholic Emancipation in the 1820s – but John Banim chose to live in London writing plays for the English Opera House and Griffin also lived and worked in England during this period. Though both the Banims and Griffin supported Emancipation, they were clearly driven by many other considerations. The Banims, for instance, sought financial stability, and continued writing long after Emancipation had been achieved, even setting their stories in English locations such as Eastbourne – as in *The Smuggler* (1831). Eagleton insists, however, that the Banims' fiction is self-consciously an attempt to sketch for a sceptical British reading public the true lineaments of Irish society'. Perhaps on occasion it was but there were many times when it was not. And then what are we to make of Griffin's decision to give up writing, burn his manuscripts and join the Christian Brothers?

Perhaps the greatest challenge to the literary critic is presented by the greatest author: Maria Edgeworth. Eagleton accepts Edgeworth must be regarded as one of 'the true intellectuals of the United Irish epoch', but he seems to accept too readily Joep Leerssen's theory, in *Remembrance and Imagination* (1996), that she should be regarded as an essentially eighteenth-century figure, so ignoring her later novels and her huge influence on later agrarian novelists.

Many of Eagleton's judgements on individual writers remind us strongly of Yeats or Corkery. Thus he claims that Lever 'never seemed to have had an idea in his head' while J S Le Fanu merely articulated 'the interests of the Protestant elite', yet the revolutionaries of Young Ireland wrote 'political propaganda which ranks among some of the finest imaginative writing of the century'.[44] Perhaps Eagleton's greatest service is that he rescues some of the agrarian novelists from neglect, even if he does not rate most of them very highly. Despite the work of Eagleton and others, however, evaluation and analysis still seems dominated by issues raised by Yeats and Corkery. In the past fifty or sixty years, critics have made significant contributions, but historians or philosophers of history might have done a better job. The Yeats/Corkery agenda now seems tired. The prospect of a 'revival' of the agrarian novel appears once more. Roy Foster, in *The Irish Story* (2002), states:

> The idea of narrative is back in the air. [...] the old-style ideological certitudes have worn threadbare, the presentation of history itself in narrative form has come back into a certain vogue. But so has the study of the assumptions and exclusions represented by the narrative form itself.[45]

This book seeks to take up Foster's implicit challenge.

The Traditions of Edgeworth and Moore

If we reject the schemes of categorisation proposed for the agrarian novel by Yeats and Corkery, we must offer an alternative model. It may appear unsatisfactory, but categorisation is essential to any understanding of most literary genres. The task is therefore to produce a different form of categorisation. The proposal here is that the most significant division among agrarian novelists is that between the 'literary children' of Edgeworth and those of Moore. It should be stressed that this division cuts across accents – if not moulds – and across religious affiliation, economic status and political affiliation. It is proposed that there is a tradition that begins with Edgeworth and goes on through the Banims, Griffin, Carleton and Kickham. In their very different ways, all these

---

[44] Terry Eagleton, *Scholars and Rebels in Nineteenth-Century Ireland* (Oxford: Blackwell Publishers Limited, 1999), pp. 29-33.

[45] Roy F Foster, *The Irish Story* (London: Penguin Group, 2002), pp. 1-2.

writers searched for a rational and more or less peaceful solution to the Land Question. Another tradition links Moore, Trollope and Stoker. Despite their apparent differences, all three seem to advocate violence of one kind or another, and either border on or pass into the fantastic and surreal. Significantly, Stoker's Count Dracula, like Moore's Captain Rock, exists outside of time and needs continuous violence and conflict in order to survive.

This book aims to consider agrarian novels and their creators in a new, and perhaps more objective light than has been possible, at least until very recently, in Ireland itself. It will endeavour to show that a hundred years of Irish agrarian writing deserves to be considered both in its own right and for what it reveals about nineteenth-century Ireland. In short, the approach is unashamedly both literary and historical. Of course, in a book that investigates some sixteen novels by eight different writers, it has not been possible to explore many interesting lines of research. There is, consequently, almost nothing on the publishing history, mode of publication and excerpts in periodical reviews. Chapters do not follow a strict chronological order in terms of the novelists, but, reflecting one of the quotations at beginning of this chapter, 'map' the progression of the agrarian novel from its inception to its amalgamation with other forms of literature. In order to give some structure to a book that covers a long period, it has been divided into three main sections, linked by short introductions and conclusions.

The first section considers the search for a solution to the Irish Land Question. The key writer in the development of the agrarian novel is Edgeworth and the next chapter concentrates on identifying her agenda through detailed analysis of her Irish novels. The following chapter, on the Banims and Griffin, examines how they interpreted Edgeworth's agenda from a Catholic perspective. The final chapter in this section considers William Carleton's attempt both to satirize Edgeworth's agenda and to move it forward. The second section considers the situation in post-Famine Ireland and investigates parallel attempts by Charles Kickham and Anthony Trollope to find a solution outside Ireland, through America and England respectively. The third section concentrates on the fantasy and surreal interpretations and presentations of the Land Question in the works of Thomas Moore and Bram Stoker. The final chapter, which also serves as the conclusion, explores what has been gleaned from a detailed analysis of Edgeworth and Moore, and proposes a new critique of the Irish agrarian novel.

Part One:
The Edgeworth Tradition

Although the agrarian novel dominated Irish fiction for most of the nineteenth century, it was at its peak between 1800 and 1850. It was Maria Edgeworth who identified the key elements of the fictional representation of the Irish Land Question - perhaps the most contentious of all Anglo-Irish issues and only resolved in the early twentieth century, when land redistribution finally brought the effective end of the old Anglo-Irish Ascendancy. Edgeworth was also the first to offer a blueprint for a solution, though very different to the one eventually adopted. When Edgeworth was writing her Irish novels (1800-17), there was already widespread agrarian violence, but she believed it was still possible to find a solution without destroying the Ascendancy. Politicians and landowners largely ignored Edgeworth's warnings and advice, though her ideas were taken up and modified – arguably not modified sufficiently – by subsequent agrarian novelists.

The main change was one of focus. While Edgeworth's novels centre on the lives of Ascendancy landowners, those of Gerald Griffin and the Banim brothers introduce two new dimensions: a Catholic perspective, and a tenant perspective. These Catholic writers strove to develop a different stance to Edgeworth's liberal Protestantism, but they remained in her shadow. So, while trying to emulate Edgeworth, Griffin, notably in *Tracy's Ambition* (1829), seeks a solution that includes both landowners and the tenants. Yet his solution, reflecting his upper middle class background, is further removed in spirit from the tenants than Edgeworth is from the landowners. While his novels display an empathy with the tenants, the empathy is Catholic with Catholic – rather than upper middle class landowner with tenant. Ultimately, Griffin's fear of the tenants prevented him from offering a remotely realistic solution and also drove him to abandon literature for the cloister.

John and Michael Banim were Griffin's social inferiors, the sons of a small trader/farmer – the next level down. Since it is hard to attribute many of their works to one brother or the other, they are usually studied

41

together. The Banims' works range widely: plays for Covent Garden, tales of Irish myth, stories set in France, and even a novel about Eastbourne and smugglers. Writing provided the Banims with their main source of income and commercial considerations probably determined their choice of topics. Yet their most interesting and successful works are set in Ireland – especially *Tales of the O'Hara Family* (1826) and *The Anglo-Irish of the Nineteenth Century* (1828), a work heavily influenced by Edgeworth. Like Griffin, the Banims also failed to find a solution, though they did succeed in finding what might be called 'a distinctive voice'.

The Banims were followed by William Carleton, the 'Peasant novelist' and – after Edgeworth – the most significant agrarian novelist of this period. Carleton was also strongly influenced by Edgeworth. He satirizes *The Absentee* (1812) in *Valentine M'Clutchy* (1847) but, as his implausible ending shows, his own solution is less credible than Edgeworth's. Yet Carleton is an important writer. His early tales of Ireland are characterised by an immediacy and authenticity that effectively evokes a lost world, but his longer works, particularly those dealing with the Land Question, do not achieve the same level of understanding. Although he continued to write for twenty years after the Famine, the quality of his later work declined – though with the significant exception of *The Squanders of Castle Squander* (1852).

The first half of the nineteenth century – essentially up to the beginning of The Great Hunger in 1845 – was a turbulent period in Irish history. Substantial concessions to the Catholic community, notably Emancipation in 1829, did little to ameliorate the condition of the tenantry and levels of both institutional and agrarian violence continued to rise through the early 1830s. Whatever their other shortcomings, the agrarian novels of the time do reflect and respond to these developments; indeed, with the notable exception of *Dracula* (1897), their dynamism and creativity compares favourably with agrarian novels of the second half of the century.

*'It is impossible to draw Ireland as she now
is in a book of fiction',*

Maria Edgeworth, 19th February 1834[1]

Edgeworth and Violence

Maria Edgeworth established an agenda for Ireland and for Irish agrarian literature, one dominated by discussions about the rights and wrongs of landed property. Whether or not they agreed with Edgeworth, later agrarian novelists followed in her footsteps. If she had never written, who can say whether the entire genre of agrarian fiction would even have emerged? Edgeworth's importance as the author of acclaimed fiction and educational works is almost universally acknowledged. This unmarried lady, whose works impressed both George III and Robert Peel, produced a very diverse 'family'. Gerald Griffin attempted to expand the world of *Castle Rackrent* in *Tracy's Ambition* (1829), and William Carleton's *Valentine M'Clutchy* (1845) is a parody of *The Absentee* (1812). Edgeworth wrote the first 'regional' novel, a tradition developed, with spectacular success by Scott. John and Michael Banim, who satirized *The Absentee* in *The Anglo-Irish of the Nineteenth Century* (1828), wanted to emulate Scott too; this was also J Sheridan Le Fanu's objective in *The Cock and Anchor* (1845). All of these writers, Scott included, owed much to Edgeworth.

Edgeworth was the first and most complete of the agrarian novelists. Some of her successors may have had greater literary skills and more direct and painful personal experience of the problems facing Ireland. Many, like Carleton, could expose the weaknesses of her analysis, but none could equal Edgeworth's intellectual capacity or produce anything so

---

[1] Maria Edgeworth *The Life and Letters of Maria Edgeworth* (1894), ed by A J C Hare, (New York: Books for Libraries Press, 1971), II, p. 550.

comprehensive as her analysis of what should be done. Edgeworth's solution may have been flawed and unrealistic – it certainly seemed so when she died in 1849 – but at least it was recognizable as a solution. Other writers may have had schemes and policies lurking at the back of their minds, but they lacked either the courage or the ability to articulate them properly. Hence, in terms of a clear programme, Edgeworth both 'represents a distinct step in the history of English fiction' and a decisive step in the history of Irish politics.

This chapter begins with a discussion of Edgeworth's experience of and her approach to violence and goes on to examine three stages in her Irish novels: *Castle Rackrent* (1800) and its analysis of the problems of landownership; *Ennui* (1809) and *The Absentee* containing proposals to solve the problems identified in *Castle Rackrent*; and *Ormond* (1817) reflecting fading belief in the solutions suggested earlier. It concludes with an evaluation of the agenda Edgeworth left to her successors.

Novelists often use their own experiences as bases for their works of fiction – though they do so selectively and in different ways. Although Maria Edgeworth had direct personal experience of institutional and agrarian violence, her novels appear to focus on episodes of institutional violence while agrarian violence – figuring prominently in her letters – is largely absent. During the 1790s, Edgeworth and her father experienced agrarian violence at close quarters. Their rational, Enlightenment view on the world was shaken by the irrationality of the forces unleashed:

> [S]he took the real lesson of 1798 to be the evil of mob feeling. She had seen with her own eyes how a rational well-intentioned individual could be brow-beaten by a tyrannical majority. The individualism she had been taught as a creed was reinforced by the experience of seeing a hysterical reaction at work.[2]

Perhaps Edgeworth never referred to mob violence because she had been so traumatised by it; by its very nature, such violence is 'hysterical' and hence irrational. Unlike other landowners, however, Edgeworth understood that the existing hierarchy was in danger and thus sought to educate her own class, if only for their own good.

---

[2] Marilyn Butler, *Jane Austen and the War of Ideas* (Oxford: Oxford University Press, 1997), p. 126.

Edgeworth's fear of violence was confirmed by her experiences during the 1798 Rebellion. Her letters describe her feelings as violence in County Longford draws closer to Edgeworthstown (now Mostrim); in one she writes, 'we never thought the danger *near* till to-day'. The Edgeworths and their neighbours feared secret society activity more than a French Invasion. The raising of a militia in County Longford in 1795 led to increased agrarian atrocities:

> Last night a poor old woman was considerably roasted: the man, who called himself Captain Roast, is committed to jail, he was positively sworn to here this morning. Do you know what they mean by the White Tooths? Men who stick two pieces of broken tobacco pipes at each corner of the mouth, to disguise the face and voice.[3]

'Captain Roast' echoes 'Captain Rock' and 'Captain Moonlight' – even 'Captain Swing' in England. Such names, along with similar pseudonyms, had been used since the 1760s. 'Rock' implies steadfastness and immovability while 'Moonlight' reflects the timing of most agrarian outrages. It is unclear what 'Captain Roast' did to the old woman but it was undoubtedly violent and cruel. Richard Lovell Edgeworth told his daughter about the rise in violence in some detail. She noted:

> All that I crave for my own part is, that if I am to have my throat cut, it may not be by a man with his face blackened with charcoal.

The fact that Edgeworth thought she might be murdered – and even visualised how – indicates the centrality of violence to her thinking. Shortly before the French invasion, she witnessed, first-hand, the results of this violence – yet these images never appear in any of her Irish novels:

> 'Look to the other side – don't look at it!' cried Mr. Edgeworth; and when we had passed he said it was a car turned up, between the shafts of which a man was hung – murdered by the rebels.

---

[3] Maria Edgeworth, *The Life and Letters of Maria Edgeworth*, ed by Augustus J C Hare, (London: Edward Arnold, 1894), I, pp. 36-39.

The Edgeworths experienced further violence after the French invaded, but this time, at the hands of Protestants. Richard Lovell Edgeworth, known for his impartial treatment of Catholics and Protestants, angered other landowners by insisting that his yeomanry be open to both religions. Significantly, 'Captain Roast' and his followers had spared the Edgeworths' house the destruction suffered by other Ascendancy landowners. With the approach of the French, the Edgeworths fled to Longford where Richard Lovell Edgeworth offered to defend the gaol while his son, Henry, went upstairs to act as lookout. Yet some thought that the Edgeworths were traitors and 'Mr. Edgeworth was accused of having made signals to the French from the gaol'. Richard Lovell Edgeworth, venturing out later in the evening, was attacked and hit 'with a brickbat in the neck'.[4] People actually believed that the Edgeworths, criticized for not being sufficiently religious in their books, were willing to help the enemy because they felt so strongly about religion – albeit, in Protestant eyes, the wrong one.

Some landowners even tried, unsuccessfully, to have Richard Lovell Edgeworth's yeomanry impeached. Yet what truly alarmed Edgeworth was the sheer irrationality and unpredictability of mob violence. She feared all mob activity (violent or otherwise) and, true to her Enlightenment beliefs, rated individualism above collectivism – as Marilyn Butler suggests:

> [Edgeworth's] individualism is anything but rebellious, since she equates moral independence with financial independence within a free-enterprise system. It is a view she might have justified by quotation from her father's favourite Adam Smith. When she urges rich and poor to do an honest day's work, she imagines them as a result both happier and freer.[5]

Edgeworth sympathised with tenants' frustration with absentee landowners and their corrupt agents to the extent that, despite her vivid imagination and personal experience of agrarian violence, she never represented it in her fiction. Instead, she felt that more enlightened landowners offered a better solution than revolution.

---

[4] Edgeworth, *Life and Letters* (1894), I, pp. 41-58.

[5] Butler, 1997, p. 156.

The Problem Stated: *Castle Rackrent*

In *Castle Rackrent*, Edgeworth outlines two of the main strands of the Land Question: the problems caused by landlords and those caused by Agents and middlemen. As Barry Sloan points out, in *The Pioneers of Anglo Irish Fiction 1800-1850* (1986), Edgeworth's position is essentially conservative:

> *Castle Rackrent* is not a subversive novel advocating peasant landownership. Maria Edgeworth may make a plea for the rights of the Irish poor, but those rights are conditional on them serving good and responsible landlords who will fulfill their obligations to the tenantry [...] [She] did not want fundamental change in the structure of Irish society.[6]

Ostensibly, the story is set before 1782, but it is best regarded as a prophecy of what may happen after the Union – that is if the landowners do not mend their ways. *Castle Rackrent* reveals the depth of Edgeworth's disapproval of landowners who do not care how their money is obtained and use the Law to extract every penny from their tenants. As Sloan stresses, Edgeworth insists that landlords are not just responsible for their own property – but also for their tenants' moral and religious welfare. In telling the story of the Rackrents, Edgeworth uses a good deal of humour, but the laughter becomes strained as the family descends to self-destruction.

Thady M'Quirk provides a first-person – though somewhat inconsistent – narrative of the rise and fall of the Rackrent family, in which neither phase is exactly edifying. The rise and inheritance of the estate is achieved through religious and cultural apostasy. The Rackrents change their religion from Catholic to Protestant and their name from O'Shaughlin to Rackrent. But Edgeworth is more concerned with their decline, traced through four masters of Castle Rackrent: Sir Patrick, Sir Murtagh, Sit Kit and Sir Connolly/ Condy. In their different ways they are all wastrels. They are actually very bad at looking after their own interests – let alone the interests of their tenants, who supply them with the rents they squander. Sir Patrick wastes rents on drink, Sir Murtagh on lawsuits

---

[6] Barry Sloan, *The Pioneers of Anglo-Irish Fiction 1800-1850* (Gerrards Cross: Colin Smythe Limited, 1986), pp. 6-7.

and Sir Kit, an absentee, wastes them on gambling. Sir Condy combines all the vices of his predecessors; he is an absentee, a gambler, a spendthrift and an alcoholic. Although Edgeworth clearly deplores the effect of these vices on the Rackrents themselves, her main concern is what they mean for the tenants.

The sequence of vice is interesting. We are told relatively little about the drunken Sir Patrick. It is hardly likely that such a man would make prudent investments in his estate but he probably allowed his tenants some leeway – he certainly appears to have been the most popular of the Rackrents. We learn much more about Sir Murtagh and his repellent wife, a scion of aptly named Skinflint family. Perhaps even more than her husband, Lady Rackrent seems obsessed with money. The Edgeworths were much influenced by Adam Smith and hence one might have expected a more sympathetic treatment. After all, one of Smith's core doctrines is that of the unseen hand – where pursuit of individual and selfish gain actually brings benefit to the entire community. But things do not seem to work like that at Castle Rackrent. They seem to be engaging in a game to extract as much revenue as possible from obsolete feudal rights, using legal chicanery to maximize their advantage. The Rackrent tenants find that in addition to their rents, they must also supply 'duty fowls, and duty turkies and duty geese'.[7] Sir Murtagh cunningly refuses to mend his fences so that he can confiscate his tenants' livestock when they stray onto his land. He takes full advantage of 'his heriots' (*Rackrent*, p. 14) – a payment […] to landowners on the death of a tenant (*Rackrent,* p 121) – and his right to 'duty work' (*Rackrent*, pp 14-15) that required tenants to work his land several days a year without payment. For those who displeased Sir Murtagh, duty work was demanded precisely at the time when absence from his own holding was likely to cause the tenant most inconvenience and loss:

> [When] a man vexed him, why the finest day he could pitch on, when the cratur was getting in his own harvest, or thatching his cabin, Sir Murtagh made it a principle to call upon him and his horse – so that he taught 'em all, as he said, to the know the law of landlord and tenant. (*Rackrent*, p. 15)

---

[7] Maria Edgeworth, *Castle Rackrent* (1800), ed by George Watson, (Oxford: University Press, 1991), p. 14. Further references to this edition are given after quotations in the text, and the title shortened to *Rackrent.*

The same point is made, even more powerfully in Richard Lovell Edgeworth's 'Glossary':

> Whenever a poor man disobliged his landlord, the agent sent to him for his duty work, [...] tenants were often called from their own work to do that of the landlord. Thus the very means of earning their rent were taken from them; whilst they were getting in their landlord's harvest, their own was often ruined, and yet their rents were expected to be paid as punctually as if their time had been at their own disposal. (*Rackrent*, p. 104)

The Rackrents' demands exemplify institutional violence that forces tenants into compliance by a combination of the Law (heavily weighted in the landowners' favour) and fear:

> [Tenants] were kept in such good order, they never thought of coming near Castle Stopgap without a present of something or other – nothing too much for my lady – eggs – honey – meal, growse [sic], and herrings, fresh or salt – all went for something. (*Rackrent*, p. 14)

The Rackrents care nothing for their tenants' welfare and want only to accumulate more wealth. They do not invest in the estate and hence there is no prospect of greater prosperity. As the years go by, Lady Rackrent devises ever more ingenious means of relieving the tenants of what little they have: her rights to 'weed-ashes, and her sealing money upon the signing of all their leases', and money for speaking 'to Sir Murtagh about abatements and renewals.' (*Rackrent*, p. 17)

Despite such appalling treatment, there is no hint of refusal to pay – let alone of agrarian violence. Indeed, throughout *Castle Rackrent*, the tenants emerge as long suffering, though totally loyal. But we are bound to wonder. The Edgeworths' years in France must have made them appreciate that the financial exploitation of feudal devices – long after the reality of mutually supportive 'true' feudalism had disappeared – had been a major cause of discontent and a contributory factor to the French Revolution. Even when they appear to be doing good for their tenants – as when they set up a school – the Rackrents are merely finding additional ways to exploit them. Thus their school, open to Protestants and Catholics alike, is really no more than a factory for child-workers, a device to obtain unpaid labour. If there is any 'charity', the true recipient is Lady Rackrent herself:

> [Lady Murtagh] had a charity school for poor children, where they were taught to read and write gratis, and where they were kept well to spinning for my lady in return; for she had always heaps of duty yarn from the tenants, and got all her household linen out of the estate from first to last; for after the spinning, the weavers on the estate took it in hand for nothing, because of the looms my lady's interest could get from the Linen Board to distribute gratis. (*Rackrent*, p. 13)

It is tempting to imagine that nothing could be worse that the avarice, malice and shabby tricks of the Sir Murtagh and his wife. Sadly, the last of the Rackrents, Sir Kit and Sir Condy, introduce a new and even more sinister dimension: both are absentees. The consequences of absenteeism – developed further in Edgeworth's later novels – represent a crucial facet of the Land Question and provide one of the most powerful and enduring themes in the canon of the agrarian novel. Absenteeism puts power in the hands of Agents, men who, with a very few honorable exceptions, provide the agrarian novelists, from Edgeworth onwards, with their central 'villain' character. Despite their shortcomings, landowners seem to get off relatively lightly compared to the opprobrium that is heaped on the Agent. However unpleasant the Rackrents may be, there can be no doubt that the real villain of *Castle Rackrent* is Jason Quirk, an avaricious and cunning attorney, and the son of the narrator, Thady M'Quirk. It is Jason Quirk, the educated son of a tenant, who ultimately ends the story of the Rackrents by becoming master of Castle Rackrent himself.

It would, of course, have been impossible for Quirk to rise so high if he had not received a reasonably good education. While Edgeworth and her successors certainly had good reason to deplore the behaviour of Agents, it is hard not to detect an element of snobbery – itself an enduring characteristic of the agrarian novels and indeed of the literary criticism devoted to them. There is certainly a decided ambiguity in Edgeworth's attitude to education. In principle she approved, but she was also adamant that such education had to be appropriate to the pupil's station in life:

> The question, whether society could exist without the distinction of ranks, is a question involving a variety of complicated

discussions, which we will leave to the politician and the legislator', as she wrote early in life, in her preface to her collection of children's stories, *The Parent's Assistant* (1796). 'At present it is necessary that the education of different ranks should, in some respects, be different'. (*Rackrent*, Introduction, p. xxii)

In particular, it was highly undesirable that the sons of tenants should be educated in a way that would enable them to become lawyers, middle men and agents. Men like Jason Quirk threatened everything that was good about the past – the harmonious relationship between landowners and tenants. Of course Edgeworth appreciated that it would be wrong to idealize this relationship and wanted to improve it. But a wholesale takeover by Quirk and his kind would destroy landowners and tenants alike.

Of course, landowners have only themselves to blame if their hedonistic lifestyle in London impoverishes their estates, destroys tenants' livelihoods and ultimately allows the agent to usurp their place. Terry Eagleton comments:

[W]ith the destruction of the pathetic Sir Condy Rackrent at the hands of Thady's scheming son Jason, we have been seduced into finding ourselves witness to the triumph of a new, ruthlessly utilitarian order over what might now seem in retrospect a colourful if corrupt traditionalism.[8]

When Quirk takes over the Castle the tenants realize that a sympathetic, if inept, landowner has been replaced by an efficient, ruthless parvenu and 'the people one and all gathered in great anger against my son Jason, and terror at the notion of his coming to be a landlord over them' (*Rackrent*, p.79). But the tenants' support for Sir Condy is as much to do with self-interest as feudal loyalty. Quirk may be resident but, for Edgeworth, he is neither the right class nor her idea of an enlightened landowner.

In the past, whenever the Rackrents wanted more money, the agent increased the rents. The tenants were forced to pay, to avoid eviction, as the Law said they must. Yet the landowners kept increasing their demands and their tenants' lives became intolerable. But Edgeworth's sternest warning lies in the inexorable rise of Jason Quirk. She implies that, in the

---

[8] Terry Eagleton, *Heathcliff and the Great Hunger* (London: Verso, 1995), p. 163.

past, the primal relationship had been between resident landowners and their tenants. There had obviously been some absentees before the Union but now, with the prospect of the centre of the socio-political world moving from Dublin to London, the problem threatens to become worse. Above all, it may create a vacuum, only too likely to be filled by able, though unscrupulous men, like Quirk, who will exploit the opportunity to enrich themselves at the expense of incompetent absentees and tenants alike.

In the text itself, there are strong hints that agents are even worse than landowners. Thus Thady declares:

> The agent was one of your middle men, who grind the face of the poor, and can never bear a man with a hat upon his head – he ferretted the tenants out of their lives – not a week went without a call for money – drafts upon drafts from Sir Kit – but I laid it all to the fault of the agent. (*Rackrent*, p. 21)

Agents and middle men certainly do not enjoy the traditional respect accorded to landowners and often appear as the immediate instigators of institutional violence. Once more, Richard Lovell Edgeworth drives home the point:

> There was a class of men termed middle men in Ireland, who took large farms on long leases from gentlemen of landed property, and set the land again in small portions to the poor, as under tenants, at exorbitant rents. The *head-landlord*, as he was called, seldom saw his *under-tenants*, but if he could not get the *middle man* to pay his rent punctually, he *went to the land, and drove the land for his rent*, that is to say, he sent his steward or bailiff, or driver, to the land, to seize the cattle, hay, corn, flax, oats, or potatoes, belonging to the under-tenants, and proceeded to sell these for his rent; it sometimes happened that these unfortunate tenants paid their rent twice over, once to the *middle man*, and once to the *head landlord*. (*Rackrent*, p. 20n)

Again and again, Maria Edgeworth stresses the burden of rents and insecurity of tenure:

Rents must be all paid up to the day, and afore – no allowance for improving tenants – no consideration for those who had built up their farms – No sooner was a lease out, but the land was advertised to the highest bidder – all the old tenants turned out, when they had spent their substance in the hope and trust of a renewal from the landlord. – All was now set at the highest penny to a parcel of poor wretches who meant to run away, and did so, after taking two crops out of the ground. (*Rackrent*, p. 21)

Tenants are given neither incentives to improve their farms nor any hope for the future: old age brings eviction, homelessness and poverty. The landowner, legally, uses different forms of institutional violence to grab every penny. Corruption is widespread and loyal tenants have to pay their landowner – as well as paying bullying and grasping agents, middle men, drivers and tithe proctors – simply in order to exist. But it is the agent who adds another layer of exploitation that is too much to bear and – though such a thing cannot be stated explicitly – threatens Ireland with Revolution.

The Philosophic Mirage: *Ennui* and *The Absentee*

If *Castle Rackrent* represents the problem as Edgeworth perceived it, then *Ennui* and *The Absentee* explore the solution. These novels will be examined together since they deal with the same problem and identify the solution as a combination of Richard Lovell Edgeworth's landowning skills and the economic principles of Adam Smith. In *Castle Rackrent*, Edgeworth's insistence that the fundamental problem is the shortcomings of the landowners seems to place her firmly in what was later to become the nationalist camp. If she had written no more, the question of whether she should be included in the canon of Irish literature would not have arisen. The issue that separates Edgeworth from her allegedly more Irish successors is not the problem but the solution that she proposed.

In *The Absentee*, Lord Clonbrony's 'personal assistant', Sir Terence O'Fay, expresses the view of many real life landowners:

Well! some people talk of morality, and some of religion, but give me a little snug PROPERTY [sic].[9]

O'Fay identifies the three most important elements in the Land Question – issues that were to dominate Irish agrarian fiction from Edgeworth to Stoker; implicitly, he also raises the question of which was the most important. Different authors and different characters in the fictions they created were to advance a wide variety of views and permutations on the central question raised by O'Fay – indeed, perhaps they did little else.

Sir Terence O'Fay is not actually a landowner himself and some landowners might have disagreed with him. Things would have certainly looked different to other sections of society – to Orange agents and Catholic tenants for example. Some might have accepted that morality and religion and property were indeed opposites, but would have considered morality and religion more important than property. It was, however, more complicated than that; this book will argue that attitudes to the relationship between morality, religion and property cut across the boundaries of class and religious affiliation. Edgeworth herself, the daughter of a Protestant landowner, rejects the view she ascribes to O'Fay. She does not see morality and religion and property as opposites or alternatives – rather her whole thrust is that morality, religion and property complement each other if they are properly understood.

This is an apposite point to consider the exclusion of religion from Edgeworth's Irish novels. Religion was central to the psyche of Irish tenants and pervaded every aspect of their lives – especially their relations with their Protestant masters and their Church of Ireland allies. The Edgeworths were certainly Protestant but, until the second decade of the nineteenth century, they would hardly have described themselves as such. They were certainly not extreme Protestants and had a significant Catholic ancestor, Jane Edgeworth, who 'founded a religious house [...] [and] was considered as a saint'.[10] The Edgeworths' problem was that religion was emotional and abstract rather than rational and concrete:

---

[9] Maria Edgeworth, *The Absentee* (1812), ed by W J McCormack and Kim Walker, (Oxford: Oxford University Press, repr. 1988), p. 25. Further references to this edition are given after quotations in the text, and the title shortened to *Absentee*.

[10] Richard Lovell Edgeworth, *Memoirs of Richard Lovell Edgeworth* (London: Richard Bentley, 1856), p. 4.

The aim of the Enlightenment writers was accordingly to instruct mankind that its destiny on earth could be investigated and understood, not merely accepted in the dumb suffering of 'religious' passivity. Education, clarification, demystification – these were the watchwords of the intellectual leaders of the age, and they were aimed, first and foremost, at the heavy hand of an intellectually oppressive church.[11]

The Edgeworths' cared little whether their tenants were Catholics or Protestants so long as they behaved appropriately. Yet they were still criticized for the absence of religion from their books:

> The omission of religious education brought down on his daughter's novels, as well as on his own works, the hostility of the growing forces of Evangelicalism.[12]

Edgeworth, at heart a rationalist, regarded religion, like violence, as irrational. She knew how central religion was in Ireland but believed its potential for creating conflict could be minimized if landowners were tolerant and treated Catholics and Protestants alike. If Edgeworth had entered the religious debate, she would have undermined her message that landowners must change. Richard Lovell Edgeworth did not respond to the criticism but his daughter found it provoking:

> Maria Edgeworth, who was a more conventional Christian than Richard Lovell Edgeworth (although she does not seem pious by nineteenth-century standards) was understandably nettled by the repeated imputation that her heroines are not Christians. After slurs by Croker in the *Quarterly* and John Foster in the *Eclectic Review* (viii, 1812), she composed a note for private circulation on behalf of the heroine of *The Absentee*: 'Lady Colambre refers the [*Quarterly*] Reviewer to page 148 of the 2nd vol. of *The Absentee* [...] she trusted, that in this Christian land none could have so little

---

[11] Adam Smith, *The Essential Adam Smith*, ed by R L Heilbroner, (Oxford: Oxford University Press, 1986), p. 2.

[12] Marilyn Butler, *Maria Edgeworth*, (Oxford: Oxford University Press, 1972), p. 172.

Christian charity as to suspect her of being an infidel. Clonbrony Castle, 26 August, 1812'.[13]

Where religion is referred to in Edgeworth's Irish novels, it is portrayed as either not a problem or part of the solution. If economic reform is the solution to violence, neutralising religious antagonisms by treating Catholics and Protestants equally – especially educating them together – becomes a means to a greater end. Edgeworth's novels were aimed primarily at her fellow landowners – if they would change their ways, the benefits would eventually filter down to the tenants. As Butler records, Edgeworth's ideas were formed several years before she wrote her Irish novels. In *Letters for Literary Ladies* (1795), she attempts:

[T]o make through fiction certain moral discriminations of a more personal and inward kind. The gentry as she sees them face a choice of role. They may be content to be social parasites, the mindless slaves of pleasure and fashion. Alternatively they can chose to live as active, rational beings, bent on ordering and leading their own small sphere. Rightly or wrongly, she believes the parent can determine the character of the child. Like other progressives of the period, she wants to see the assertion of the conscious will, and a planned programme of education is a method of mastering the all-important element of the environment. But, as well as leading their family and household, her men and women are also landlords and heads of the local community.[14]

While, in self-imposed exile in London, Lord Clonbrony sinks under the weight of his wife's demands and is forever trying to get money from his Irish estate, O'Fay seeks to maximise revenue and cares nothing about the morality of his methods so long as more rent is raised. O'Fay represents an extreme, cynical Ascendancy view that has little time for morality or religion. He does not care about Burke's efforts to provide schooling for Protestant and Catholic children or his attempts to placate both vicar and priest. O'Fay rates property above all; religion and morality are luxuries that he and Clonbrony cannot afford. O'Fay represents the inhumane extreme of rational economic thinking. Property is a real concept not an

---

[13] Butler, 1972, p. 342n.

[14] Butler, 1997, p. 128.

abstract one, like religion or morality, and is backed by the Law; it has rules and usually has one clear owner. It produces money and hence tangible benefits.

It could be suggested that O'Fay's stance represents a satire of Adam Smith's position, but this is inaccurate. While Smith believed that individuals should be driven largely by consideration of self-interest, he was anxious to prove that proper self-interest also worked to the advantage of others. O'Fay's version of self-interest lacks this vital ingredient. He has no interest in agricultural improvement because, in the short term, the costs involved would reduce the landowner's income. Smith took a broader view. He believed that landowners should improve their estates – essentially for their own interests – but he contended that such improvements would benefit the tenants as well. Smith's metaphorical hand may have been hidden but he believed it was very powerful. It is possible that Richard Lovell Edgeworth, an ardent follower of Smith, might have endorsed this approach, but there were other influences present in his outlook – not least that of Rousseau.

Although father and daughter agreed on many practical matters, their outlooks were not identical. While there are certainly traces of Smith in Maria Edgeworth's views – as can clearly be seen in *Ennui* – she is less of a Smithian overall than her father. Whereas in Smith benefit to others is an unintended, though welcome, consequence of essentially selfish actions, in Edgeworth a conscious desire to help others is called for. An enlightened landowner should therefore be concerned with morality and religion. Merely running an estate for personal profit is not enough. With property comes responsibility and, certainly in Ireland, that means responsibility for the moral and religious welfare of one's tenants.

For Edgeworth, her father represented the ideal landowner: a resident, enlightened and benevolent despot. Also, like him, she wanted to make Ireland more like England, as Michael Hurst outlines in *Maria Edgeworth and the Public Scene* (1969):

[B]oth regarded the United Kingdom idea as the great opportunity for taking Ireland ahead. […] Behind the shelter of British power they [landowners] could live up to the Edgeworth ideal of benevolence and yet impose salutary reforms upon a mass peasantry vastly more feckless than they themselves had ever been.

London would provide that very breathing-space so clearly lacking under the state of semi-independence set up in 1782.[15]

In *Emile* (1762), Rousseau stresses the power of example and the Edgeworths took this lesson to heart. Richard Lovell Edgeworth was also influenced by his fellow-countryman, Edmund Burke, whose involvement in Irish affairs is echoed in the thematics of Edgeworth's novels:

> [Burke] was active in connection with the proposals of the Irish parliament to tax absentees in 1773; he took part in supporting Irish demands for free trade in 1778; and he became involved in the affairs of Ireland which culminated in the Revolution of 1782. We find him taking part again in the trade laws controversy of 1785; [...] Burke played an important part in trying to preserve, while purifying, the Irish constitution, and also in pressing the case of the Catholics.[16]

Richard Lovell Edgeworth returned to Ireland from England, in 1782, 'with a firm determination to dedicate the remainder of his life to the improvement of his estate and to the education of his children'. He had to convince his Catholic tenants of his good intentions while facing prolonged antagonism from fellow Ascendancy landowners. Edgeworthstown was no 'snug little property', rather it was 'filled with loungers, followers and petitioners' who 'all had grievances and secret information, accusations reciprocating and quarrels'.[17] The implication is that the Irish are lazy, talk too much and lack solidarity – precisely the impression formed by Virginia Woolf when she visited Ireland in 1934.

In *Memoirs of Richard L. Edgeworth*, Edgeworth portrays her father presiding, energetically and in good humour, over proceedings. His forward thinking treatment of tenants paid dividends on his estate:

> Big House economy depended largely on the wealth and organisation of the owner; [...] The army of servants and tenants

---

[15] Michael Hurst, *Maria Edgeworth and the Public Scene* (London: Macmillan and Co. Ltd., 1969), p. 16.

[16] Cecil Parker Courtney, *Montesquieu and Burke* (Westport, Connecticut: Greenwood Press, 1975), p. 167.

[17] *The Black Book of Edgeworthstown*, ed by Harriet Jessie Butler and Harold Edgeworth Butler, (London: Faber & Gwyer, 1927), p. 156.

in such a household played an inevitable role in its destiny, in which the capacity of the head for good human relationships was tested to the limit. [...] Richard Lovell Edgeworth's manor was progressive and morally responsible.[18]

However, '[e]xamples of firmness were necessary' and 'were chosen from cases where the sympathies of the by-standers were clearly against the culprit'.[19] Landowners needed to be astute politicians with good local intelligence. Edgeworth knew the potential for violence – including the mob violence she so feared – posed by tenants who felt allegiance to one ideology (religion/nationalism/tenantry) or another. Extreme Protestants, especially Orangemen, could stir things up in order to justify further repression. Equally, extreme Catholics, like Ribbonmen, sought to foment agrarian unrest in order to support the Catholic cause against Ascendancy landowners. Whereas, Richard Lovell Edgeworth admitted his underlying fear of his own tenants – '[a]n insurrection of such people, who have been much oppressed, must be infinitely more horrid than anything that has happened in France [...]'[20] – his daughter retained a firm faith in the natural goodness of tenants, as Seamus Deane indicates:

> Edgeworth [...] is like de Stael, confident that the starting point of her great project should be the idea of national character, something which she regards as an indisputable sociological fact.[21]

Edgeworth's ideas for reform relied on both sides seeing the error of their ways and changing accordingly. If landowners improved, the inherent 'goodness' in the Irish *volksgeist* would respond positively. Here, Edgeworth parts company with Smith's ideas on national character. Smith may have had a strong sense that he was a Scot, but he believed that the Act of Union had improved the Scottish national character. To some extent at least, the Scots had become more like the English. His sense of Scottish identity is entirely compatible with political union. This essentially Enlightenment view was challenged by Romantic notions of National

---

[18] A C Partridge, *Language and Society in Anglo-Irish Literature* (Dublin: Gill & Macmillan Ltd, 1984), p. 239.

[19] Partridge, p. 158.

[20] Edgeworth, 1856, p. 337.

[21] Seamus Deane, 'Irish National Character 1790-1900', in *The Writer as Witness*, ed by Tom Dunne, (Cork: Cork University Press, 1987), p. 98.

identity that were underpinned by a belief in an ultimately immutable *volksgeist*. Taken to its logical extreme, this view would lead to advocacy of a separate Irish state – to independence. Edgeworth seems to represent a rather uneasy compromise between Enlightenment and Romantic views. The element of the immutable is stronger in Edgeworth than in Smith; she seems to accept that there is such a thing as a distinct Irish *volksgeist* and that must mean that, despite her avowed intention to make Ireland like England, the Irish will never be like the English.

Perhaps what Edgeworth is really trying to say is that the English and Irish *volksgeists* are not so divergent as they appear; much of the difference is due to bad government and bad landowners in Ireland. If these were remedied, the underlying similarities could be revealed. But that begs a crucial question: if the Irish and English *volksgeists* are different but close, what was the appropriate political arrangement between them? Edgeworth's Unionism seems incompatible with her ideas of national identity. If the Union increased absenteeism, Edgeworth's *bête-noir*, then so much the worse for the Union. Logically, her position would be one of federalism rather than of a unitary state; it is interesting to speculate about how Edgeworth would have reacted to W E Gladstone's proposals in 1886.

In *Ennui*, Glenthorn is another absentee landowner unaware of the condition of his Irish estate and caring little about his tenants. The role of M'Leod, the agent, is primarily to act as an advocate of Smith's ideas. Glenthorn's first experience of his tenants echoes that of Richard Lovell Edgeworth when he encounters them in 'various lounging attitudes, leaning against the walls, or pacing backwards or forwards'.[22] The indolence of the tenants is evident and all want to try to get something for nothing:

> Another had three lives dropped in the *lase* for ever; another wanted a renewal; another a farm; another a house; and one *expected* my lard would make his son an exciseman; and another that I would make him a policeman; and another was *racked*, if I did not settle the *mearing* between him and Corny Corkran. (*Ennui*, p. 182)

---

[22] Maria Edgeworth, *Castle Rackrent and Ennui*, ed by Marilyn Butler, (London: Penguin Books, repr. 1992), p. 182. Further references to this edition are given after quotations in the text.

Glenthorn, however, cannot cope with the voracity of his tenants' demands. His good nature is abused by his lazy tenants who are quick to see an easy opportunity, as M'Leod had foretold:

> I was soon made to comprehend it, by crowds of eloquent beggars, who soon surrounded me: many who had been resolutely struggling with their difficulties, slackened their exertions, and left their labour for the easier trade of imposing upon my credulity. The money I had bestowed was wasted at the dram-shop, or it became the subject of family quarrels. (*Ennui*, p. 190).

In this didactic passage, Edgeworth issues several warnings to landowners, particularly those who are not natural masters like her father. While some tenants are industrious, others will take advantage of a weak landowner. Worse, merely throwing money at the problem only exacerbates matters by encouraging drunkenness and violence. There is no easy solution; landowners must combine encouragement with firmness and not be taken in, however persuasive the Irish 'blarney'.

Glenthorn, who initially sees himself as being in competition with M'Leod, seeks to gain the initiative by granting leases that create middle men. However, M'Leod warns that 'these middle-men, will underset the land, and live in idleness, whilst they *rack* a parcel of wretched under-tenants'. M'Leod supports his argument by explaining that on the neighbouring Ormsby estate 'land [is] let at ten shillings an acre' and the 'tenantry are beggars: and the land now, at the end of the leases, is worn out' (*Ennui*, p. 190). The Smithian M'Leod has a rational solution and launches into an explanation of Political Economy – with distant echoes of Jonathan Swift's *A Modest Proposal* (1729):

> [T]he complaint of each family was, that they had not land for the sons. *It might be doubted* whether, if a farm could support but ten people, it were wise to encourage the birth of twenty. *It might be doubted* whether it were not better for ten to live, and be well fed, than for twenty to be born, and to be half-starved. (*Ennui*, p. 191)

After explaining the problems caused by sub-division, M'Leod describes the ineffectiveness of protectionism and the need for division of labour:

I [Glenthorn] thought my tenants would grow rich and *independent*, if they made every thing *at home* that they wanted: yet Mr. M'Leod perplexed me by his 'doubt whether it would not be better for a man to buy shoes, if he could buy them cheaper than he could make them.' He added something about the division of labour, and Smith's Wealth of Nations. (*Ennui*, p. 191)

Glenthorn, unenlightened, initially believes that Hardcastle, the Ormsby agent, is better than M'Leod. The agents disagree about everything and especially about educating tenants, as Hardcastle explains:

[W]hy, my dear sir, can any man alive, who knows this country, doubt that the common people have already too much education, as it is called – a vast deal too much? Too many of them know how to read, and write, and cipher, which I presume is all you mean by education. (*Ennui*, p. 192)

Hardcastle thinks the Irish can only be controlled if they are kept ignorant. If they are educated, they become 'the most troublesome seditious rascals in the community'. Landowners and agents must control tenants. Hardcastle sees a direct correlation between educated tenants and agrarian unrest – the opposite of Edgeworth's own position:

[K]eep the Irish common people ignorant, and you keep 'em quiet; [...] Teach them any thing, and directly you *set them up*: now it's our business to *keep them down*, unless, sir, you'd wish to have your throat cut. (*Ennui*, p. 193)

Fear lies beneath Hardcastle's analysis. The Irish are dangerous and only a repressive policy will keep them subdued. However, not content with linking education with violence, he goes on to link it with religious antagonism and recounts how he punished a thief by forcing him to learn a Protestant catechism:

[T]he next week I found him stealing my turf again! and when I caught him by the wrist in the fact, he said, it was because the priest would not let him learn the catechism I gave him, because it was a Protestant one. Now you see, sir, there's a bar for ever to all education. (*Ennui*, p. 194)

Edgeworth ensures Hardcastle undermines his own argument by his bigotry. He is shown to be guilty of institutional violence by persecuting an elderly tenant who he 'forced to give up his farm, and retire, with his daughter, to this hovel; and soon afterwards he lost the use of his side by a paralytic stroke' (*Ennui*, p. 197). The eviction clearly caused the old man's stroke. Yet the tenants accept their fate and never talk of revenge. Hardcastle, cynical and cruel, is also an astute businessman. He makes money for himself while following his employer's instructions by taking 'upon him [...] the regulation of the markets in the town of Ormsby' so he could 'keep down the price of oats and potatoes'. If the tenants try to get round the agent's restrictions or complain, then the Law is invoked. The tenant is helpless, however, as the magistrate hearing the case is controlled directly by the agent:

> Then there was a race between *my* [Glenthorn's] justice of the peace and *his* [Hardcastle's] justice of the peace. [...] To English ears the possessive pronouns *my* and *his* may sound extraordinary, prefixed to a justice of the peace; but, in many parts of Ireland, this language is perfectly correct. (*Ennui*, p.198)

Tenants stand little chance of a fair hearing under this corrupt system. Yet Edgeworth does not suggest they need to have more say in legal matters, rather, a fairer system would emerge if tenants were sufficiently educated to understand their cases, and if unbiased magistrates were appointed.

In *Ennui*, Edgeworth comments directly on the level of violence rife in contemporary Ireland:

> [Glenthorn's] tenantry had not yet been contaminated by the epidemic infection, which broke out soon after with such violence as to threaten the total destruction of all civil order.

Yet Edgeworth holds her own class, Ascendancy landowners, more responsible for the violence than Irish tenants and stresses its institutional nature:

> [Glenthorn's] foster-brother's forge was searched for pikes, his house ransacked, his bed and *bellows*, as possible hiding places,

were cut open; by accident, or from private malice, he received a shot in his arm. (*Ennui*, p. 245)

Again, despite provocation, tenants do not seek revenge – they are too terrified to act:

> 'Let it drop, and *plase* your honour; my lord, let it drop, and don't be making yourself *inimies* for the likes of me. Sure, what signifies my arm? and, before the next assizes, sh'n't I be as well as ever, arm and all?' continued he, trying to appear to move the arm without pain.

Christy, Glenthorn's foster-brother, fears what might happen to Glenthorn – if not himself – should the landowner take action. The corruption must be deep and widespread if an Ascendancy landowner could put his own life at risk merely by confronting others of his own class. Even Christy's mother, despite her son's injuries, warns Glenthorn 'you don't know the *natur* of them people, dear – you are *too innocent* for them entirely, and myself does know the mischief they might do *yees*' (*Ennui*, p. 246).

Edgeworth's argument is flawed however. It might have helped if landowners became resident and improved their estates, but the Ireland portrayed by Edgeworth is one inhabited by loyal and non-violent tenants. Despite the outrages she witnessed in the mid-1790s and during the 1798 Rebellion, she insists that the landowners are at fault and that tenants deserve better masters – a point stressed in *The Absentee*, written only three years after *Ennui*.

In *The Absentee*, Edgeworth introduces and judges repressantative examples of the landed gentry. Sir James Brooke represents the pre-Union class in Dublin that has since been replaced by people like Mrs Anastasia Rafferty, the grocer's wife and Nicholas Garraghty's sister. Beyond the Pale, the Killpatricks are resident landowners but do nothing to improve their tenants' situation. In yet another form of institutional violence, they play with their tenants' lives and, with echoes of Marie Antoinette's model farm at Versailles, treat them as objects to be dressed up and housed in order to improve the view from the Big House:

> They had built ornamented, picturesque cottages, within view of their park; and favourite followers of the family, people with half a

century's habit of indolence and dirt, were *promoted* to these fine dwellings. (*Absentee*, p. 108)

Count O'Halloran's Irish name and European title indicate that he is an old-style, Catholic landowner. The implication is that Catholics were more in tune with the land of Ireland and the needs of her people than Protestant landowners. O'Halloran decries the actions of modern landowners:

[W]ho, according to the clause of distress in their leases, lead, drive, and carry away, but never *enter* their lands; one of those enemies to Ireland – those cruel absentees! (*Absentee*, p. 122)

Although O'Halloran influences Colambre, Edgeworth's portrayal of him shows that his time has passed. Modern landowners should certainly possess the Count's love of Ireland, sense of history and moral responsibility, but they should also be willing to share their prosperity.

Colambre discovers that his father's tenants have scant regard for their landowner who, they believe, regards them as 'negroes'. Their opinion, however, of his good agent, Burke, could hardly be higher. The implication is that where Clonbrony's absenteeism risks provoking tenants, an enlightened agent can placate them:

I don't know why God was so kind to give so good an agent to an absentee like Lord Clonbrony, except it was for the sake of us, who is under him, and knows the blessing, and is thankful for the same. (*Absentee*, p.130)

Burke and his wife, who live on the estate, essentially fulfil the role of the paternalistic landowner advocated by Edgeworth:

[N]o duty work called for, no presents, nor *glove money*, nor *sealing money* even, taken or offered; no underhand hints about proposals, when land would be out of lease; but a considerable preference, if desarved [sic], to the old tenant, and if not a fair advertisement, and the best offer and tenant accepted: no screwing of the land to the highest penny, just to please the head landlord for the minute, and ruin him at the end, by the tenant's racking the land, and running off with the year's rent. (*Absentee*, p.132)

Garraghty, who replaces Burke, makes the tenants produce ever more rents that tenants appear merely to regard as an example of escalating institutional violence, as Julian Moynahan emphasises in *Anglo-Irish* (1994):

> Garraghty [...] oppresses the wretched tenants of Clonbrony town and its agricultural estate, partly to line his pockets and rise as his sister did, but also in response to frequent urgent demands from the Clonbronys for money to underwrite their London social campaigning. In this Anglo-Irish and native Irish social pyramid, where nearly everyone is misplaced except the rural tenants at the bottom, it is the bottom class that pays, and dearly, for the folly and vice of the rest.[23]

Unlike Burke's, Garraghty's management of the estate is exploitative. He appoints his brother as under-agent and, together, they pursue schemes to make money for themselves. The under-agent 'gets his own turn out of the roads' (*Absentee*, p.139) which he does by forcing tenants to break stones to pay him the rent and cheat the county. The agent lets animals over-graze fields so that the land loses value and can be bought up cheaply by Garraghty himself. The Garraghty brothers use various forms of institutional violence ranging from the under-agent evicting an innocent family because the daughter rejects his advances, through to erasing Clonbrony's pencilled guarantee of tenure on a tenant's lease, to a sophisticated money-laundering operation (*Absentee*, p.161). The result of this corruption is that the landowner is cheated. Since Clonbrony needs more money, the tenants have to make up the financial shortfall and end up living in 'miserable huts, sunk beneath the side of the road, the mud walls crooked in every direction [and] dunghills before the doors, and green standing puddles' (*Absentee*, p.146). The tenants have no future, they just hope to survive. If the situation worsens then they must choose between begging or emigration.

Neither of these options would be necessary if, as Edgeworth advocates, 'the lord was in it [the house] to give 'em *employ*' (*Absentee*, p.147). If the landowner is resident, the local economy benefits. Yet, amazingly, 'the ill-will of the tenantry' does not develop into any thoughts of violent action. Despite everything, they are so loyal that they are happy

---

[23] Julian Moynahan, *Anglo-Irish* (Princeton, New Jersey: Princeton University Press, 1994), pp. 35-36.

simply because the Clonbronys, nearly broke, return home. However, in truth, the Ascendancy 'had every reason to believe that beneath a surface obsequiousness, the peasantry was sullen, savage, and vindictive'.[24]

Edgeworth's notion of education is closer to Smith's than to Rousseau's. For Smith, '[t]he peace and order of society […] is of more importance than even the relief of the miserable'.[25] For rationalists, order is rational while disorder is not. A combination of schooling and positive examples would result in tenants becoming as enlightened as their landowners, as Smith had argued:

> The more they [the people] are instructed, the less liable they are to the delusions of enthusiasm and superstition, which, among ignorant nations, frequently occasion the most dreadful disorders. An instructed and intelligent people besides are always more decent and orderly than an ignorant and stupid one. They are more disposed to examine, and more capable of seeing through, the interested complaints of faction and sedition, and they are […] less apt to be misled into any wanton or unnecessary opposition to the measures of government.[26]

In his *Lectures on Jurisprudence* (1762-63), Smith predicts the debauched and violent future he foresaw if boys are not educated:

> [W]e may observe the benefit of country schools, and, however much neglected, must acknowledge them to be an excellent institution. But besides this want of education, there is another great loss which attends the putting boys too soon to work. The boy begins to find that his father is obliged to him, and therefore throws off his authority. When he is grown up he has no ideas with which he can amuse himself.[27]

[24] Thomas Flanagan, *The Irish Novelists* (New York: Columbia University Press, 1959), p. 58.
[25] Adam Smith, *The Theory of Moral Sentiments*, ed by A L MacFie and D D Raphael, (Oxford: Clarendon Press, 1976), p. 226.
[26] Smith, *Theory*, p. 307.
[27] Adam Smith, *Lectures on Jurisprudence*, ed by R L Meek, D D Raphael and P G Stein, (Oxford: Oxford University Press, repr 1978), p. 540.

Though Smith is talking about Scotland and England, his point is equally applicable to Ireland. His belief that uneducated men would work only half the week and riot the rest of the time is apt. Ireland's mono-culture, the potato crop, ensured that half the year was spent working and the other half drinking and fighting. The problem is that Smith believed there were only two classes of people: rich landowners and poor tenants. As Edgeworth realised, however, some tenants, having been educated, could well threaten the existing social hierarchy.

Although Edgeworth agreed with Smith on the importance of order and the ability of education to prevent violence, she did not see it as more important than the moral welfare of tenants. In *Ennui*, M'Leod is proud of what he and his wife have achieved. Glenthorn is so impressed by the 'air of neatness and comfort, order and activity [...] that [he] almost thought [himself] in England' (*Ennui*, p. 215). M'Leod has succeeded in making a little corner of Ireland like England. He has created 'a race of our own training [...] and they go on in the way they were taught, and prosper to our hearts' content, and, what is better still, to their hearts' content' (*Ennui*, p. 216). M'Leod's efforts prove that change is possible if only on a small scale and with little money. Change takes time and it is the next generation that is important. While the M'Leods' efforts were doubtless well-intentioned, there is the uncomfortable sense that the children taught in their school have been conditioned almost into a new, super-intelligent race separate from other children. It is not clear if the dominant thinking in their upbringing is Scottish, Irish, English, Protestant or Catholic.

With *The Absentee*, education has become even more crucial, a key element dividing the good from the bad. In Edgeworth's survey of the different types of landowner encountered by Colambre, only the Oranmores have established 'well-attended schools' that show what 'the influence of great proprietors residing on their own estates' (*Absentee*, p. 129) may achieve. On their idealized estate, poor Catholic and Protestant children are educated along rational lines. Absentee landowners, like the Clonbronys, and bad resident landowners, like the Killpatricks, do not appreciate the benefits of educating the poor. It is implied that their estates will become unproductive and violent. Garraghty allows no school on the Clonbrony estate. When Colambre encounters Burke, however, he discovers that the local school, run by the agent's wife, is the perfect blend of Smith's theories and Edgeworth's nurturing landownership. There is 'neither too much interference nor too little attention' and 'protestants and catholics [sic]' learn 'from the same books, and [speak] to one another with the same cordial familiarity' (*Absentee*, p. 133). For Edgeworth, education of the poor is far more important than prolonging religious antagonisms

The Mirage Vanishes: *Ormond*

In *Ormond*, Edgeworth's light but controlling hand, so evident in her previous Irish novels, arguably becomes less sure: 'it does not consistently embody a serious moral purpose' and '[t]ime and again, the progress [...] is halted by an announcement to the effect that some experience [...] has had a salutary effect on the hero's character'.[28] Edgeworth herself realized that her Ireland had disappeared: 'the Tithe War and the general upheaval caused by land agitation convinced her that the union of classes and creeds [...] was no longer a realistic hope'. By the late 1820s, the focus of Irish affairs had switched to Daniel O'Connell – a man 'she hated and feared'[29] – and the fight for Catholic Emancipation. By 1817, even Richard Lovell Edgeworth 'seems to have been uncharacteristically pessimistic concerning the country's future' and began to fear the worst:

> I think we cannot be relieved from our abject distress but by the sword of the avenging angel. The physical and moral cure of our national misery must I fear be famine and pestilence on the one hand and partial bankruptcy on the other.[30]

The world of the Rackrents (where there was still a chance for landowners to change) and the idealized world where paternal landownership would be combined with Smithian principles had faded. By the time she wrote *Ormond*, nearly twenty years after the 1798 Rebellion, Edgeworth's fears of mob violence appear to have distinctly receded.

True to the form of a *bildungsroman*, the novel follows the education of Harry Ormond, but matters begin badly when he loses his temper and, in an overt act of institutional violence, attacks a servant:

---

[28] Murray, pp. 48-53.

[29] Murray, p. 33.

[30] Quoted in Hollingworth, p. 183, (original source: the Butler collection of Edgeworth Correspondence, National Library of Ireland, No. 1291, undated).

[Ormond] lifted his whip to give the fellow [Moriarty] a horse-whipping. Moriarty seized hold of the whip [...] Ormond then snatched a pistol from his holster, telling Moriarty he would shoot him [...] Moriarty, who was in a passion himself, struggled [...] the pistol accidentally went off, the ball entered Moriarty's chest [...] The poor fellow bled profusely.[31]

Ormond's 'neglected and deficient education' (Ormond, p. 9) is blamed. His decision, after reading Henry Fielding, 'to be what he admired – and if possible to shine forth as an Irish Tom Jones' (Ormond, p. 51) – reveals Edgeworth's belief in the improving nature of literature and results in him being 'suddenly seized with a voracious appetite for books' (Ormond, p. 57). He also embraces the concept of education for tenants. As in her earlier novels, Edgeworth confronts the problems caused to education by prolonged religious antagonism:

[H]appily there was in this parish both a good clergyman and a good priest, and still more happily they both agreed, and worked together for the good of their parishoners. Dr. Cambray and Mr. M'Cormuck made it their business continually to follow after Mrs. M'Crule, healing the wounds which she inflicted, and pouring into the festering heart the balm of christian [sic] charity. (*Ormond*, p. 173)

In the same way that M'Leod and Burke create schools to educate Catholic and Protestant children, Dr. Cambray advocates the same idea, and:

. . . had taken pains to secure the co-operation of the catholic [sic] clergyman in all his attempts to improve the lower classes of the people. His village school was open to Catholics as well as Protestants; and father M'Cormuck, having been assured that their religion would not be tampered with, allowed and encouraged his flock, to send their children to the same seminary. (*Ormond*, p. 173)

---

[31] Maria Edgeworth, *Ormond* (1817), ed by John Banville, (Belfast: Appletree Press Ltd, repr 1992), p. 14. Further references to this edition are given after the quotations in the text.

A part of the problem with *Ormond* is that Edgeworth, though still championing education, has nothing new to add to what she has already said. It is simply presented as a standard part of her agenda and consequently feels tired.

One entirely new aspect in *Ormond* however is Edgeworth's depiction of a peculiar, probably unique, form of agrarian violence – 'wrecking'. The indolence of Sir Ulick O'Shane's tenants is evident in the way they lure ships on to the rocks for plunder, completely unconcerned about resultant loss of life:

> [T]he tenants whom he [Annaly] found living near the coast were an idle, profligate, desperate set of people; who, during the time of the late middle landlord, had been in the habit of *making their rents* by nefarious practices. [...] illicit distillers – smugglers – and miscreants who lived by *waifs* and *strays*; in short, by the pillage of vessels on the coast. The coast was dangerous, – there happened frequent shipwrecks; owing partly, as was supposed, to the false lights hung out by these people, whose interest it was that vessels should be wrecked. (*Ormond*, p.168)

The implication is that tenants are naturally drawn to crime unless they are set a good example and can see the rewards for honest work. Sir Herbert Annaly, a caring and reforming landowner, is determined to improve his estate and those who live on it. He is terminally ill but still wants to eliminate agrarian outrages. Annaly's actions produce positive results with the subservient and loyal tenants of earlier novels now replaced by pragmatic and realistic ones:

> Cambray had visited them [Annaly's estates]. The account he gave Ormond of all that had been done there to improve the people and to make them happy; of the prosperous state of the peasantry; their industry and independence; their grateful, not servile attachment to Sir Herbert Annaly and his mother [...] delighted the enthusiastic Ormond. (*Ormond*, p. 168)

Perhaps Annaly's most significant action is his desire to build a lighthouse. Where O'Shane's tenants destroy, Annaly's tenants create:

[Ormond] was struck by all that had been done here in the course of a few months, and especially with the alteration in the appearance of the people. Their countenances had changed from the look of desponding idleness and cunning, to the air of busy, hopeful independence. (*Ormond*, p. 184)

The lighthouse is also a symbolic. It represents the Enlightenment, a beacon of hope, something that will provide positive benefits for tenants and shed its light – knowledge – for all to see.

The problem for Annaly is that his neighbouring Protestant landowner is O'Shane, a jobbing politician and one of Ormond's guardians. It raises the question as to what makes a good landowner. For Edgeworth, a good landowner is somebody, like Annaly, who resides on his estate and adopts a paternalistic approach to improving the tenants' situation. However, tenants with lower morality may equally regard a weak and corrupt landowner, like O'Shane, as a good landowner:

[T]here was Sir Ulick O'Shane, sure! Oh! he was a man to live under – he was the man that knew when to wink and when to blink; and if he shut his eyes *properly*, sure his tenants filled his fist. – Oh! Sir Ulick was the great man for *favour and purtection*, none like him at all! – He is the good landlord, that will fight the way clear for his own tenants through thick and thin – none dare touch them. (*Ormond*, pp. 168-169)

For Edgeworth, landowners like O'Shane were the worst – selfish, ambitious, greedy and immoral. The problem is that a whole generation of tenants had now been raised under repressive Penal Laws and on stories of how their lands were stolen by English invaders. A landowner who encouraged crime and protected his tenants from prosecution may have been more attractive than one offering improvement through hard work.

Ormond's decision to marry into the Annaly family and to live on the Black Islands after the death of his other guardian, the eccentric 'King Corny' (Cornelius O'Shane), is curiously retrograde. Edgeworth appears to be admitting a kind of failure. Her dream of an Ireland full of enlightened landowners, adherents to Smith's ideas, and grateful, basically educated tenants, is not to be. Yet one chance remains. Ormond has learnt, from Annaly, what it means to be a good landowner and even has Annaly's sister as his wife to keep him on track. Ormond's purchase of the Black Islands gives him the chance to put his ideas into action in a microcosm. The Black Islands will become Ireland and what failed on the mainland may work in Ormond's tiny 'kingdom'.

King Corny is eccentric and backward looking – a man 'who has remained loyal to the Catholic religion and Irish ways'[32] and whose home is 'Celtic, primitive and feudal',[33] Like O'Halloran, he belongs to another, more Romantic Ireland – as P H Newby indicates in *Maria Edgeworth* (1950):

> The change from Castle Hermitage to the Black Islands is the change from eighteenth-century Ireland to the world of the Odyssey. King Corny is a Homeric king. Within his dominions his word is law and his subjects worship him yet he lives among them simply.

It is into this old, unreal world that Ormond, along with his Edgeworthian values and Smithian economics, enters at the end of the novel: a world where the existing landowner, like the Rackrents, spends his 'days [...] in the administration of rough justice [...] hard drinking and hunting with hounds and horn'.[34] It is as though everything has come full circle – a version of Thomas Moore's 'wheel of torture'. The writing and publication of *Ormond* was rushed in order to be completed before Richard Lovell Edgeworth's death. However, it was also Edgeworth's last Irish novel. Perhaps her desire to write about Irish issues died with her father, who saw the novel 'as a final contribution to his life-long involvement with the "condition of Ireland" debate'. Another interpretation, however, is that:

> [T]he Edgeworthian ideal of enlightenment, harmony and utilitarian prosperity expounded in the earlier Irish tales was certainly no nearer realization in 1817 than in 1800, despite all suggested remedies.[35]

---

[32] Patrick Murray, *Maria Edgeworth,* (Cork: the Mercier Press, 1971), p. 48.

[33] Brian Hollingworth, *Maria Edgeworth's Irish Writing* (Basingstoke: Macmillan Press Ltd, 1997), p. 186.

[34] P H Newby, *Maria Edgeworth* (London: Arthur Baker Ltd, 1950), p. 81.

[35] Hollingworth, p. 183.

Hollingworth claims that Ormond 'creates a "happy ending" which has not only a personal but also a social and political significance',[36] but this must be disputed. Certainly, *Ormond* has a 'well-made story' ending, but the plot suffers from Edgeworth's rush to finish the novel. *Ormond* is the best of Edgeworth's Irish works if all that is required is a readable novel. Yet, compared to its three predecessors, it offers nothing new on the Land Question, and suggests a future that is frighteningly closer to a retrogression to a bygone era than to a modern progressive Ireland of individual and collective freedom.

Concluding Observations

At the end of *Castle Rackrent*, Edgeworth predicts that, after the Act of Union, '[t]he few gentlemen of education who now reside in this country will resort to England' (*Rackrent*, p. 97). Unlike others, she foresaw that absenteeism would exacerbate the situation in Ireland. She knew intimately about agrarian and mob violence but chose not to portray them. She hoped that, while laughing at the Rackrents, absentee landowners might see the error of their ways. In *Ennui*, she resorted to a didacticism reminiscent of her educational works and supplied a blueprint – a combination of caring paternalism and Smith's political economics – for the improvement of Ireland. In *The Absentee*, she showed in greater detail how destructive the combination of uncaring, absentee landowners and cruel, grasping agents can be. In *Ormond*, although she repeats the central tenets of her argument, we find she has nothing new to say. In 1834, Edgeworth admitted, in a letter to M Pakenham Edgeworth, that the vision of Ireland she had advocated in her novels was no longer feasible as the country had become too divided and violent:

> It is impossible to draw Ireland as she now is in a book of fiction – realities are too strong, party passions too violent to bear to see, or care to look at their faces in the looking-glass. The people would only break the glass, and curse the fool who held the mirror up to nature – distorted nature, in a fever. We are in too perilous a case to laugh, humor [sic] would be out of season, worse than bad taste.[37]

---

[36] Hollingworth, p. 187.
[37] Hare, 1971, February 1834, II, p. 550.

Edgeworth was the first to identify the dangers of institutional violence and portray them in a novel, yet underplays the value of the portraiture she had achieved. Her ideas were not adopted yet they dominated agrarian literature and the cultural debate for most of the ensuing century. Perhaps it is appropriate that she died in the year that the Famine ended (1849), an event in Irish history so catastrophic that it changed forever the destiny of the island. Although Irish, a large part of Edgeworth was English and perhaps that sense of her being an 'outsider' in some way led to her having a more detached, less emotive view of the country. Unlike other agrarian writers, she was not interested in myth and tradition and while this may have undermined her own position, it challenged writers who followed her:

> For the Anglo-Irish to rule, it is not enough to have legal right or British protection. It is necessary to connect in some way with Irish tradition, to recognize and respect that tradition and the attitudes it embodies, to become part of it. 'History', exclaims a character in William Trevor's story 'Beyond the Pale'(1981), 'is unfinished in this island'. That uneasy awareness was to become the subject of most of the Anglo-Irish writers as they examined their role and their rule as a privileged but endangered minority.[38]

While subsequent agrarian writers variously interpreted Edgeworth's agenda, and nationalists have disparaged her solution, subsequent events created a situation of which she might have approved. The change in landownership encouraged by the Government meant that it was now the Catholics and not the Protestants in the ascendancy. It is ironic that the formerly hated Protestants, now '[p]olitically and economically disarmed', may be 'allowed social prestige – a prestige the snobbery endemic among the Catholic masses finds welcome'.[39]

---

[38] Elizabeth Grubgeld, *Anglo-Irish Autobiography* (New York: Syracuse University Press, 2004), p. 40.
[39] Hurst, p. 181.

Thy stone, oh Sisyphus! Stands still,
Ixion rests upon his wheel,
And' – the wild Irish 'dance[1]

They might have forgotten in such
a solitude, the national predilection
for combat.[2]

Many of the issues, themes and stereotypes encountered in Maria Edgeworth's agrarian novels recur in the works of John and Michael Banim and Gerald Griffin. Although the Banims and Griffin are often linked, Griffin is usually regarded as a better writer. Moreover, Griffin is the only Anglo-Irish writer to meet Daniel Corkery's exacting criteria for an acceptably Irish writer. But does the fact that the Banims and Griffin were Catholics necessarily mean that they were nationalist writers and, if so, how might this manifest itself in their agrarian novels?

Thomas Moore was John Banim's literary hero and references to Moore also occur occasionally in the Banims' works. Thus John Banim follows Moore both in using Ixion's 'wheel of torture' as the symbol of the endless violence that is the curse of Ireland (see chapter 7) and in his references to Sisyphus's eternal punishment. Taken in isolation, the quotation from *The Anglo-Irish of the Nineteenth Century* could imply that Ireland's suffering might be stopped, but the context reveals that any such

---

[1] John Banim, *The Anglo-Irish of the Nineteenth Century* (1828), ed by John Kelly (Poole: Woodstock Books, 1997), I, p. 196. Further references to this edition are given after quotations in the text and the title shortened to *Anglo-Irish*.

[2] Gerald Griffin, *The Rivals and Tracy's Ambition* (1829) (New York: D. & J. Sadlier & Co., n.d.), p. 191. Further references to this edition are given after quotations in the text and the titles shortened to *Rivals* and *Tracy's*.

hope is completely unrealistic. The second quotation, from Griffin, also hints at an end to violence but is qualified by an acknowledgement that it is, in some way, part of the national character.

Although the Banims' original aim to be the 'Scott[s] of Ireland' failed – largely because Edgeworth had a much bigger influence upon them – the brothers did produce two historical novels in the manner of Scott – *The Boyne Water* (1826), written principally by John, and *The Croppy* (1828), written principally by Michael. However, these are not true agrarian novels and hence fall outside the scope of this book. John Cronin considers *The Nowlans* (1826) 'explosive material'[3] for the graphic way it examines sex, religion, guilt and identity but, despite echoes of the dissolute Rackrents in Aby Nowlan, much of the novel is set in and around Dublin, and its concerns are not those of an agrarian novel and hence it will not be considered in this chapter.

The first part of this chapter examines claims that the novels of the Banims and Griffin indicate that they were nationalist novelists; it will concentrate on an analysis of *Crohoore of the Bill-Hook* (1826), *The Peep O'Day/John Doe* (1826) and *The Collegians* (1829). The following section will consider Edgeworth's legacy, especially in the context of *The Anglo-Irish of the Nineteenth Century* and *Tracy's Ambition* (1829). The final part examines possible solutions – or lack of them – proposed by the Banims and Griffin.

Nationalist Novelists

The Banims' first major success was the anthology *Tales of the O'Hara Family* (1826) – which includes *Crohoore of the Bill-Hook* – and it was this work that encouraged Griffin to write. The Banims wrote principally about the agrarian violence they observed around them, violence that had escalated to new heights in the early 1820s:

> There was much agrarian unrest in Kilkenny. By 1823 White Boy [sic] activities, shortly to be diverted to the Emancipation agitation, had reached the proportions of guerilla warfare.[4]

---

[3] John Cronin, *The Anglo-Irish Novel* (Belfast: Appletree Press, 1980), p. 54.
[4] Thomas Flanagan, *The Irish Novelists* (New York: Columbia University Press, 1959), p. 169.

The literary portrayal of the Irish to this point had usually centred on the comic 'stage Irishman' or a similarly grotesque, boorish stereotype – both loathed by nationalists. The Banims set out to present the Irish in a truer light and 'to show that causes existed […] creating the lawlessness'[5]:

> In the year 1822 John and Michael Banim conceived the idea of writing a series of novels which should do for the Irish what Scott had done for the Scotch in his 'Waverley Novels'.[6]

The Banims' background is reflected in their work and in their decision to champion the tenants' cause:

> The Banims' social status, as sons of a small tradesman and farmer in Kilkenny, gave them a greater insight into the life of the poor and at the same time made them more eager than Maria Edgeworth had been to assert Irish rights. They condemn terrorism, but remind their readers that Whiteboys and similar groups exist because the Penal Laws left the Irish leaderless and ignorant, and the unjust tithes have made them poor. Tithes ought not to be protested with violence, but they ought to be abolished.[7]

Critics usually regard Patrick Joseph Murray's *The Life of John Banim* (1857) as the seminal early biography on the Banims. Murray argues that it is John Banim, and not Edgeworth who is the key Irish novelist. According to Murray, Edgeworth's works lack 'vigour and individuality' and are 'entirely deficient in the dramatic power, without which any – most of all an Irish – novel must be weak.' Nor do they possess 'attributes peculiar to that phase of genius that can obtain, and keep secure, the title of *the* Irish novelist'.[8] Without supporting evidence, Murray summarises what purports to be John Banim's view of Edgeworth:

> Banim knew well that his countrywoman possessed ability of a very high and polished order; he felt that in entering upon the

---

[5] *Dictionary of National Biography*, ed. by Leslie Stephen, (Oxford: Oxford University Press, 1917; repr. 1973), I, p. 1037.

[6] *DNB*, I, p. 1035.

[7] Robert Tracy, *The Unappeasable Host* (Dublin: University College Dublin Press, 1998), p. 44.

[8] Patrick Joseph Murray, *The Life of John Banim* (London; William Lay, 1857), p. 91.

world of literature as a writer of Irish fiction, he should be prepared to take his place beside, if not above, one who enjoyed all that strength which is derived [...] from a pre-occupation in the public mind. He was fully impressed with all the might and force of these facts, but Sir Walter was his ideal of a National Novelist; from this ideal nothing can be more dissimilar than that discoverable in the style and tone of the works of Miss Edgeworth.[9]

It is true that the Banims' novels do differ from those of Edgeworth, not least because they contain graphic accounts of agrarian violence. The restraint observed by Edgeworth has disappeared and the loyal tenants who longed for the landowner to return now glory in hacking off the ears of the tithe proctor. Similarly, on occasion, the Banims do seem close to a nationalist stance, with Michael stating their aim:

> To insinuate, through fiction, the causes of Irish discontent and to insinuate also that if crime were consequent on discontent, it was no great wonder; the conclusion to be arrived at by the reader, not by insisting on it on the part of the Author, but from sympathy with the criminals.[10]

Terry Eagleton cites the development of the 'national' hero of *The Absentee* into 'a more full blown version' in *The Anglo-Irish of the Nineteenth Century*,[11] while Patrick Rafroidi praises the Banims for being more 'real' while damning Ascendancy writers:

> [T]he works of the Banim brothers, Gerald Griffin and William Carleton, leave the impression of a more depressing side of human nature because it is more true to life than the studies – if one may call them that – made by Maria Edgeworth.[12]

---

[9] Murray, p. 92.

[10] *Ireland in Fiction*, ed. by Stephen J Brown (Dublin: Maunsel and Company Ltd., 1916), p. 18.

[11] Terry Eagleton, *Crazy John and the Bishop* (Cork: Cork University Press, 1998), p. 219.

[12] Patrick Rafroidi, *Irish Literature in English* (1972) (Gerrards Cross: Colin Smythe, 1st English edn., 1980), I, p. 127.

Similarly, Julian Moynahan agrees with Robert Lee Woolf that *The Anglo-Irish* is 'a powerful satiric attack mounted against the very existence of Anglo-Irish identity'[13] and claims that, through the Union, 'the Anglo-Irish surrendered their Irishness [and] ceased to be contenders for a significant role in the Irish future'.[14]

Gerald Griffin is frequently seen as more of a nationalist than the Banims. His novel, *The Collegians* (1829), is 'judged by some as the best nineteenth-century Irish novel'.[15] Flanagan notes that it is 'an Irish novel' rather than a regional novel and, '[i]f the phrase "Catholic novelist" is at all meaningful, it may properly be applied to him'.[16] Seamus Deane makes a similar point believing '*The Collegians* is, self-consciously, a national novel in the form of Romantic melodrama'.[17]

Griffin does not share Edgeworth's paternalistic approach to tenants nor does he regard them as likeable and passive rustics, warning 'the vengeance of an Irish peasant is not to be despised' (*Tracy's*, p. 393). He recognises their potential for violence and concluded that they must be controlled. Griffin identifies three key problems: the tenants' abject poverty, the fact they are unable to own the land they work, and dangerous 'education'. For Griffin, education is not just about book learning but about how children are brought up. He observes that the morals, politics, and attitudes of tenants are passed on from one generation to the next so perpetuating yet more violence. However, he also believes institutional violence is unjust and understands the resulting agrarian violence.

In *Crohoore of the Bill-Hook*, the Banims imply that violence is an inherent part of Irish life, as Barry Sloan notes:

> Violence runs close to the surface of even the most orderly lives and frequently erupts into bloodthirsty actions.[18]

The unlikely hero of the tale, Crohoore, is a sinister and grotesque dwarf. While others celebrate Christmas Eve, he sharpens a Bill-Hook. After a

---

[13] Julian Moynahan, *Anglo-Irish* (Princeton: Princeton University Press, 1995), p. 106.
[14] Moynahan, p. 108.
[15] *The Macmillan Dictionary of Irish Literature*, ed. by Robert Hogan, (Basingstoke: Macmillan Press, 1980), p. 277.
[16] Flanagan, p. 230.
[17] Seamus Deane, *Strange Country* (Oxford: Clarendon Press, 1998), p.58.
[18] Barry Sloan, *The Pioneers of Anglo-Irish Fiction* (Gerrards Cross: Colin Smythe, 1986), p. 52.

murder, he is immediately a suspect, paralleling the way the English often suspected Irish immigrants of crimes merely because they looked and sounded alien and violent. The depiction of the murder scene is graphic:

> [Pierce Shea] found himself slipping on the gory boards. He held the candle over the bed, and there appeared a female form, also lifeless, and presenting marks of the assassin's hand, again too horrible for description. We glance at the object for a moment, only to say that, with the life-stream overflowing the bed, and running down its side, it lay so mangled and deformed as, during a first view, to leave the wretched lover doubtful of its identity.[19]

The self-conscious narrative technique enhances the depravity of the crime by alluding to it as 'too horrible for description'. However, the murderer is not in fact Crohoore but Jack/Rhia Doran, the illegitimate 'son of an opulent gentleman farmer' (*Crohoore*, p. 41) – a landowner – and yet Captain of the local Whiteboys.

The Banims blame the Penal Laws and the tenants' lack of education for Ireland's problems, sympathising with the tenants and representing their violence as the inevitable response to persecution:

> Labouring under the excessive penal code, [...] and excluded by one of its enactments from even an opportunity to become educated, and so gain an enlightened, or, at least, temperate view of their own situation, the Irish peasantry, neglected, galled, and hard-driven, in poverty, bitterness and ignorance, without competent advisers, without leaders a step above themselves, and scarcely with an object, wildly endeavoured to wreak vengeance upon, rather than obtain redress from, the local agents, of some of the most immediate hardships that maddened them. (*Crohoore*, p. 47)

The Banims were strong supporters of Catholic Emancipation and of Daniel O'Connell though, by the mid-1820s, they were having doubts about O'Connell. They feared tenants had been forgotten and left

---

[19] The O'Hara Family, *Crohoore of the Bill-Hook and The Fetches* (1826) (London: Simms and M'Intyre, repr. 1848), p. 17. Further references to this edition are given after quotations in the text and the title shortened to *Crohoore*.

impoverished and bitter. In the last resort, however, the Banims blame the tenants' uneducated state on the Government and Ascendancy.

The Banims, as Catholics, portray the Protestant Church of Ireland as the enemy of both the Catholic Church and the tenants:

> They [tenants] saw their creed denounced; their form of worship, under heavy penalties, interdicted; and they knew that some years before, their priests had been hunted like foxes, and forced to hide in caves and other places of concealment, from the keen scent and vengeance of the most insignificant professors of the rival religion, who, with impunity, took arms in their hands to enforce the rigid letter of an almost exterminating law, still to their knowledge unrepealed. (*Crohoore*, p. 47)

Religious persecution and institutional violence are here inherently linked and indeed the Penal Laws clearly had both religious and political dimensions. The resentment engendered by putting prices on priests' heads and hunting them like animals enrages their congregations. The fact that the most zealous enforcers of the law are some of the worst examples of the Protestant faith, able to act unrestrained, makes matters worse. The key point, however, is that tenants, uneducated, do not realise that the Penal Laws have been repealed. If they were fully informed, they would not resort to violence. To reinforce the picture of a suffering people, the Banims relate an 'anecdote [...] put forward as one laying claim to strict belief':

> [A] rustic congregation had once assembled, with their priest, in the open air, to perform their devotions, then three or four mean mechanics of the other profession appeared, with guns in their hands, fired among the crowd, killed some, and wounded the clergyman. (*Crohoore*, p. 47)

This is not vigorous enforcement of the law, but pre-meditated murder. It implies that the Catholic Church and its adherents are innocents merely seeking peacefully to practise their religion.

The Banims identify a direct correlation between the demand for tithes and agrarian violence:

[The tenant] found himself, while already ground down by unnatural rack-rents, compelled to contribute to the support, in splendour and superiority, of that very rival church – in fact, to pay its ministers the hard-earned pittance he could not afford to his own; and this view of his situation first helped to make the Irish peasant a Whiteboy. (*Crohoore*, p. 47)

It is bad enough that Catholic tenants are persecuted but the fact that tithes have to be paid for the upkeep of the oppressor's alien church drives them into secret societies. In *Crohoore*, the epitome of oppression and corruption is Peery Clancy, the wealthy tithe proctor:

[T]he wretched being who, from the rising of the sun till many hours after his setting, was bent beneath the first malediction of heaven, yet gained thereby but a scanty supply of the meanest food, rags for his covering, and despair for an inmate [...] of the hovel [...] this was the prey Peery contrived to gripe; and the gripe never relaxed till he had crushed his victim. (*Crohoore*, p. 49)

He is corrupt and abuses his power:

[Clancy] got the two douceurs from Dermid; he filled the process; he got it served at a profit of eight hundred per cent; he gained two pounds, at least, on the cow or horse; and, at last, bamboozled and robbed his reverend employer; and sat down in the evening, over the bumper of whiskey punch. To drink (his poor mother calling him a Roman Catholic) long life to the minister's tithes, and may they never fail him! (*Crohoore*, p. 50)

Clancy is loathed by the tenants as he is a Catholic who persecutes them for the benefit of Protestants. But he also cheats his Protestant employer and, by implication, the Church of Ireland.

The Banims opposed tithes and are cautious to affirm that their descriptions are 'carefully copied from the life and the facts' (*Crohoore*, p. 50) – tithe collection is equated with the Spanish Inquisition:

[F]or society may have improved, the arts and sciences may have advanced, the Bastille may have been torn down in one country and the Inquisition abolished in another; but the Irish tithe-proctor of this day, and the Irish tithe-proctor of fifty years ago, are individuals of one and the same species. (*Crohoore*, p. 50)

They address the question as to why tenants do not use the law to help themselves. Dermid, an Irish 'Everyman', returns home having been unjustly treated at the sessions-court feeling that 'for the poor man and the Papist, there was no law or mercy in the land' (*Crohoore*, p. 50) – tenants are forced to take action:

> [B]etween them they agreed to take the tithe-proctors and the law of tithes into their own hands; proposed silly oaths to each other; and the result was 'the boys' of whom Jack Doran made mention, called, apart from the abbreviation, Whiteboys. (*Crohoore*, p. 51)

Yet still the Banims regard secret societies as misguided. They perceive that violence in Ireland is cyclical: the English will not educate tenants but, without understanding, tenants cannot defend their interests other than through violence.

Clancy's ritual punishment is a classic depiction of agrarian violence: the white shirts of the men, the muster in the dead of night answering the sound of a horn and the stealing of horses. Significantly, the local people encourage Whiteboyism:

> [D]oor after door was stealthily opened, half-dressed figures, male and female, appeared at each, and the oft-repeated salutation of '*Dhea liuve – voucheleen*' [God speed you lads], uttered in that bitter and gurgling tone in which they would have set their mastiffs on a detested enemy, told that the mission was understood and appreciated. (*Crohoore*, p. 93)

Whiteboyism is local with perpetrators and victims knowing each other; it is the local community that metes out the punishment.

Clancy's cries for mercy go unheeded and, encouraged by Doran's whip, he is forced to take part in a macabre mockery of an official procession to an execution. The Whiteboys, headed by a musician, are so confident that they will not be stopped or arrested that they set off a cacophony that includes the local community:

[T]he loud shouting of the men rose [...] the inmates of the hovels, at the doors, or lying on their straw, joined in the uproar; and even the shrill scream of women, and the tiny pipes of children, could be distinguished – there was no pity for Peery Clancy. (*Crohoore*, pp. 95-6)

The carnival atmosphere surrounding the torture and mutilation of Clancy is frightening. This is not arbitrary agrarian violence like setting fire to hayricks, but a carefully executed action designed to punish the perpetrator and warn others.

Clancy is buried up to his neck and then a pruning-knife is used to cut off his ears. The passage is reminiscent of a celebrated scene in Quentin Tarantino's *Reservoir Dogs* (1991) – a film also noted for its nonchalant approach to extreme violence. The pseudo-friendliness of the man responsible for the deed, Yemen O'Nase, is disconcerting:

I'd whip the ears aff a bishop, not to talk of a cratur like you, a darker night nor this; divil a taste I'd lave him: an' wouldn't bring any o' the head wid me, neither – musha, what ails you at all?" after he had half accomplished his task; you'd have a better right to give God praise for gittin' into the hands iv a clever boy, like me, that – stop a bit, now – that 'ud only do his captain's orders, an' not be lettin' the steel – slip from your ears across your wind-pipe, Lord save the hearers! – stop, I say – there, now: wasn't that done purty? (*Crohoore*, p. 96)

O'Nase sees himself as an artist rather than a torturer. The pseudo-military aspect changes into a pseudo-religious one when Clancy, with his bleeding orifices, is made to kiss a prayer book and endure mournful singing. The fact that a song has been written for 'all such occasions' (*Crohoore*, p. 97) implies that this violent activity is the norm.

In *The Peep O'Day* (1826), the Banims emphasise that violence is part of Irish life:

The old devotion to private skirmishing of the Irish peasantry is well known. Skirmishing would indeed be too mild a word to express the ferocious encounters that often took place among them [...] when parties, or, as they are locally termed, factions, of fifty or a hundred, met, by appointment, to wage determined war; when blood profusely flowed, and, sometimes, lives were lost.[20]

Faction fighting indicates an inherent willingness to partake in violence and the Banims depict a vicious fight that involves '[e]very male creature in the tent' (*Peep*, p. 36). One side comprises Purcell's men – Purcell being the cruel local landowner and magistrate. The Banims show what will happen if absentee landowners do not change their ways and allow allegedly lesser men to take control:

> What he [Purcell] exactly sprang from, no one can tell [...] he first appeared here the follower of a nobleman we never saw; [...] he became a tithe-proctor; then a fire-brand; and, at last, a bloody traitor and informer. Then [...] a land-jobber, gentleman at large, and county magistrate. (*Peep*, p. 94)

Purcell's various jobs are those most open to abuse and held in contempt by the tenants. As a magistrate, he breaks the Law instead of upholding it. As with Clancy, the Banims are anxious to persuade their English readers that Purcell deserves his violent death:

> Privately [Purcell] stirred up the wretched and ignorant people around him to resist rack-rents, that he throve by as privately exacting. When he got them involved by his agents, he informed against them, running their blood into money. Those who held lands on reasonable terms, he thus contrived to turn adrift on this world, or launch into the next, bidding for the vacant land himself, and then letting it, at tenfold its value, to starving creatures, who, though they sweated like beasts in the field – which they do – could not meet their rent-day. (*Peep*, p. 94)

Purcell plots the downfall of tenants who get in his way and does not stop at eviction but pushes them towards death. He also uses institutional violence for more personal needs:

---

[20] John and Michael Banim, *The Peep O'Day* and *Captain Doe &c.* (1826) (New York: Hurst & Company, n.d.), p. 10. Further references to this edition are given after quotations in the text and the title shortened to *Peep*.

A mother and a son, a daughter and old grandfather – the father was long dead. Purcell, by his underhand practices, ensnared the son, a lad of eighteen or nineteen, in nightly combinations. Then he arraigned him before the landlord; and then – for their lease was expired – son and all were turned out of their home – the old man and all. All, except the daughter. (*Peep*, pp.94-95)

Purcell, although acting legally, is responsible for the mother's death, the grandfather's madness, the daughter Cauthleen's ruin and the son's conviction. When he tires of Cauthleen and wants to replace her with Mary Grace, Howard's lover, he simply beats her up and throws her and their child onto the streets. He compounds this crime by paying his men to abduct Mary and murder Howard. The Banims, however, need Purcell to be seen as unredeemable so that Captain Doe can appear as the heroic champion of the poor. Doe is Henry Kavanagh, Cauthleen's brother and one of those evicted by Purcell. It is significant that, after the eviction, Kavanagh flees to America only to return strengthened and revitalised. Thus, for the first time in an agrarian novel, America is depicted as a haven for the oppressed Irish.

While the Banims claim to oppose secret societies, Doe is depicted as being a local hero and not a random killer:

My poor mother – wretch! my gentle, kind and good mother! My blooming, happy, and till you damned her, my sweet and innocent Cauthleen! my only sister and my only shame! Wronged me! Injured me! Oh, deep and cool villain! See these scalding tears and hear this shivering voice, made childish by a recollection of all your wrongs.[21]

The principle reason behind Doe's actions is personal rather than political – as James Cahalan explains:

[T]he Banims were ardent believers in the nonviolent political approach of Daniel O'Connell, they discredited the anonymous

---

[21] John and Michael Banim, *The Peep O'Day* and *Captain Doe &c.* (1826) (New York: Hurst & Company, n.d.), p. 81. Further references to this edition are given after quotations in the text and the title shortened to *Doe*.

rebel 'John Doe,' whose involvement in political violence is revealed at the end to be an excuse for personal revenge.[22]

The Banims emphasize the link between institutional violence and agrarian violence. Purcell's actions (institutional violence) lead directly to the formation of a secret society (agrarian violence) – Doe explains:

> Look at these unhappy men, and learn, over and over, how you have cursed me! I found them, indeed, ripe for my purpose – and some of them stained with crimes that under me they should never have committed, my revenge alone could have sought their fellowship. I leagued with them – professedly for their views, but really for my own. (*Doe*, p. 81)

The Banims sought to enlist English sympathy for an Irish cause:

> [B]y exposing to English eyes the injustices under which the Catholics laboured they were helping to do their part in the cause of Catholic Emancipation which was then at stake.[23]

Doe condemns some agrarian outrages as readily as the authorities, but he is also a violent man who advocates an alternative law – his law – rather than the Crown's:

> They state it [Doe's aim] to be the lowering of rack-rents and tithes. This Captain Doe professes not to allow any person to set or take land, or pay tithes, but on his own terms. Upon any that transgresses his orders, he wreaks, when he can, summary and often horrible vengeance. (*Peep*, p. 68)

The ambiguity surrounding Doe's position increases with his attitude to the Catholic Church. Howard stresses that Doe is not against the monarch but is against both the Protestant Church and the Catholic Church:

---

[22] James M Cahalan, *The Irish Novel* (Dublin: Gill and Macmillan, 1988), p. 36.
[23] David Gilligan, 'Natural Indignation in the Native Voice: The Fiction of the Banim Brothers' in *Anglo-Irish and Irish Literature*, ed by Birgit Brabsback and Martin Croghan (Stockholm: Almqvist & Wiksell International, 1988), II, p. 84.

I have assured myself that their [secret society] views do not involve the most distant aim at the throne. On the contrary, I believe they indulge a kind of wayward love and reverence for their present good sovereign. As to the Church, they take in the way of resistance to tithes or rates, or dues, almost as much liberty with their own as with ours. (*Peep*, p. 68)

Doe opposes all rents but cannot be a true Catholic hero if he is against both Protestant tithes and Catholic rates; his followers attack Catholic priests:

[E]ven Father O'Clery's spiritual calling was no certain shield against the displeasure of the deluded people, whom the exhortation of the day might have provoked into hostility towards the preacher. [...] It had, before now, happened, that a Roman Catholic pastor was visited with the vengeance which a sense of his efficacious interference had aroused. (*Doe*, p. 22)

The main source of contention is money and not religion or political oppression. O'Clery acts as an unofficial messenger between Doe and Howard and his moderate stance is stressed:

I have to add of my good friend, Father O'Clery, that *he* is the friend of Flood, Grattan, Curran, Lord Avonmore and other Irish stars, who have unanimously elected him a member of the festive body, quaintly denominated 'The Monks of St. Patrick.' Also, that he has officially received notice of the gratitude of government for his most useful as well as talented exertions. (*Peep*, p. 60)

O'Clery reflects the Banims' own political position. They are good Catholics who support Emancipation and oppose violence. Yet they also empathize with the tenants and understand how continual institutional violence drives them into secret societies. Perhaps the key to an understanding of the Banims' attitude lies in O'Clery's spirited diatribe against violence:

And are ye, miserable men, blessed or cursed while your church proclaims you beyond the pale of her obedient children, while in bitterness only she names your names, and while her voice hath gone forth among the desert places, calling you back, as an angry shepherd, to the flock and fold you have abandoned! Woe to the ear that hath not heard the voice! To the rebel that arms himself for the battle that voice hath not ordained! (*Doe*, pp. 74-5)

The Church is against violence but O'Clery's comment about secret society activity not being 'ordained' implies that violence sanctioned by the Church is acceptable.

The Banims identify education as being part of the necessary solution – as Lieutenant Graham's laboured discussion with O'Clery reveals:

Obstinacy was his [Graham's] next word – Irish indolence and obstinacy. They would neither do, nor learn how to do anything, he said; they would not even submit to be educated out of the very ignorance and bad spirit that produced all this Whiteboyism. There was a national establishment, he was well assured, in Dublin, with ample means, that proposed the blessings of education on the most liberal plan; yet the very ministers of the religion of the country would not suffer their ragged and benighted flock to take advantage of so desirable an opportunity. The bigoted rustic pastors actually forbade all parents to send their children to the schools of this institution. (*Peep*, pp. 55-6)

A direct link between ignorance and violence is made. The erroneous myth that violence is the only solution is passed down from one generation to the next. Graham represents English opinion and cites 'bigoted rustic pastors' as the main problem. O'Clery's response, however, that Catholic antagonism to the schools originates with the belief in prescribed reading is a more reasonable excuse than bigotry.

In Griffin's *The Collegians*, Protestant landowners are portrayed as corrupt bullies. The hero, Kyrle Daly, is, like Griffin, a respectable member of the middle class who invariably retains his self-control:

Kyrle Daly, Griffin's middle-class, Catholic image of perfection […] Rather than explicitly announced, Griffin's social values are implicit in his plot and characterizations: he condemns an

Ascendancy that betrays the peasantry and champions a middle class that is seen as living in happy harmony with the peasantry.[24]

Griffin portrays Charles Daly (Kyrle's father) as a middle-class middleman who is colourless but sensible:

> The middle class, as Griffin portrays it, differs from the nobility and gentry in the lack of the dash and go, the frankness and high spirit, the sporting and convivial tastes, the recklessness, and wild wit and gayety [sic]. It wants also the primitive force, the depth, the fervor [sic], the homely but subtle and searching humor [sic] of peasant life. It is more sober and subdued in tone and temper, more decorous. It is prudent, takes thought for the morrow, is domestic, moral, conscientious, and pious, with conventionality, tameness, timidity, and insipidity for its unpleasant features.[25]

The tale is set before Emancipation – as Eagleton indicates:

> [*The Collegians* is] replete with bogus pastoral and discreetly backdated from the tumultuous present to the palmy Grattanite past, is a triumph of arch literary self-consciousness, with its self-preening presentation of the Catholic middle-class Dalys and demonizing of the fast-living squireens or half-sirs.[26]

Griffin emphasises that the landowners portrayed are not those of the 1820s, so Hardress Cregan's behaviour is considered normal for that period:

> [H]e lived at a time when Irish gentlemen fostered a more substantial pride than at present; when appearances were comparatively but little consulted, and the master of a mansion cared not how rude was the interior, or how ruinous the exterior of his dwelling, provided he could always maintain a loaded larder and a noisy board. (*Collegians*, p.203)

---

[24] Cahalan, p. 42.
[25] Horatio Sheafe Krans, *Irish Life in Irish Fiction* (New York: AMS Press, Inc., 1966), p. 165.
[26] Terry Eagleton, *Heathcliff and the Great Hunger* (London: Verso, 1995), p. 204.

Violence is not just an accepted part of a landowner's life but an expected part:

> Hunting, duelling, drinking and defying the bailiffs, these are the primary concerns of men like Cregan senior and his cronies, Connolly and Creagh. Their way of life, which is degenerate, selfish and pleasure-seeking, revolves around a private code of honour with pride as its basis and the duel as its accepted mode of settling disputes.[27]

In *The Collegians*, Griffin's *apologia* for the Irish middle class, Daly, a Catholic, sends his son to Trinity College and decorates his home with aggressively Protestant pictures 'such as Hogarth's Roast Beef, Prince Eugene [and] Schomberg at the Boyne'.[28] The Dalys are respected but fear attack:

> A gun-rack, on which were suspended a long shore gun, a brass-barrelled blunderbuss, a cutlass, and a case of horse pistols, manifested Mr. Daly's determination to maintain, if necessary, by force of arms, his claim to the fair possessions which his honest industry had acquired. (*Collegians*, p. 20)

It is stressed they have legitimately earned their possessions and care for the tenants. Daly intervenes to help Lowry Looby avoid 'the necessity of adopting one of the three ultimata of Irish misery – begging, enlisting, or emigrating.' (*Collegians*, p. 33). Looby has been abandoned by his absentee, English landowner but is saved by a member of the Irish middle class. Griffin recognizes that Irish tenants view what they perceive to be English Law as unjust:

> The peasantry of Ireland have, for centuries, been at war with the laws by which they are governed, and watch their operation in every instance with a jealous eye. Even guilt itself, however naturally atrocious, obtains a commiseration in their regard, from

---

[27] Sloan, pp. 121-2.
[28] Gerald Griffin, *The Collegians* (1829) (New York: D. & J. Sadlier & Co., n.d.), p. 20. Further references to this edition are given after quotations in the text and the title shortened to *Collegians*.

the mere spirit of opposition to a system of government which they consider as unfriendly. (*Collegians*, p. 398)

In *The Collegians*, one incident of institutional violence is remarkable for its viciousness. Danny Mann, deformed because his master, Cregan, threw him down the stairs as a boy, is literally hunted by a group of drunken squireens and half-sirs who think he is a bailiff. Mann receives 'a blow on the head from the loaded handle of a whip, which stunned, staggered, and finally laid him prostrate on the earth' (*Collegians*, p. 263). The landowners then set about 'pinking' their victim:

[H]is cries were drowned in the savage shouts of his beleaguerers. Their swords gathered round him in a fearful circle, and Creagh commenced operations by a thrust in the arm, which left a gash of nearly half an inch in depth. His companions, who did not possess the same dexterity in the exercise of the weapon, and were nevertheless equally free of its use, thrust so frequently, and with so much awkwardness, that the unfortunate deformed ran a considerable risk of losing his life. (*Collegians*, pp. 263-4)

Mann is saved by Cregan who intervenes solely because Mann is his servant – otherwise, he would have joined in.

Both the Banims and Griffin empathize with tenants to a far greater extent than Edgeworth. They also see absentee landowners as perpetrators of institutional violence but hold the Government, the Ascendancy and the Law equally responsible. While they just refrain from advocating or condoning agrarian violence, the Banims and Griffin show that they understand why tenants resort to violence and why they join secret societies.

Edgeworth's Legacy

The Anglo-Irish of the Nineteenth Century, written predominantly by John Banim, exemplifies the way Edgeworth's agenda dominates the brothers' fictional representation of the Land Question, and is also the last of their significant novels. It also shows the Banims are not the nationalists that they are often described as being. The novel is not only a re-working of *The Absentee* but also reflects the pessimism of *Ormond*.

Barry Sloan and David Gilligan correctly identify *The Anglo-Irish* as being a neglected work. As Gilligan states, 'it was seen as uncharacteristic of Banim' and although it has 'many of the characteristics of a novel like *The Absentee* [...] no member of the Ascendancy could have written a book which takes such a critical and embittered look at the political attitudes of the dominant ruling class'.[29] But this is not accurate. While Banim's criticism of the 'ruling class' is more severe than Edgeworth, his analysis and solution are similar to hers.

The Anglo-Irish is often erroneously regarded as an historical novel. While it contains real figures like Lord Castlereagh and General Flood – along with references to Scott and Thomas Moore – it is a novel that looks at social issues linked to the Land Question rather than historical events. One curious aspect is the book's title, which refers to a specific social class but, in the tale, the enemy is the 'English-Irish' and there is no reference to the Anglo-Irish.

The novel, like *The Absentee*, is didactic with a socio-political agenda. The late Lord Clangore was an absentee but his friend and now guardian of his daughter, the aptly named Mr. Knightly, is a good, resident, Irish landowner who is despised as unsophisticated by Clangore's heirs. The new Viscount Clangore and his younger brother Gerald Blount, the hero of the tale, are virulently anti-Irish. The family's Cromwellian roots and subsequent history reveal a willingness to be politically flexible:

> Viscount Clangore [was] willing to rest his ancestral pride chiefly upon the successful bravery, in Ireland, of a soldier of the Commonwealth, who, after the Restoration, had confirmed to him the confiscated Irish property won by his courage and talents from the crimes and turbulence of the natives, and from the admiration and gratitude of the Protector. Similar good services rendered by the immediate successor of this distinguished individual to William III during that monarch's campaigns against the mere Irish abettors of his infatuated father-in-law, ennobled the family. (*Anglo-Irish*, I, pp. 5-6)

Blount initially loathes his connection to Ireland. At his English school, he witnesses the violent behaviour of Irish boys and is informed, by Flood's son, that they are inherently violent:

---

[29] David W Gilligan, 'The Banim Brothers: 1796-1874', unpublished PhD thesis (Ulster University Coleraine, 1990), p. 557.

[The Irish] must have fighting, Blount; 'tis meat, drink, and clothes to them – (indeed, sometimes they want it as a substitute for these matters) – if they can have it with an enemy, and with an Englishman above the world, all the better; but rather than go without it, they must have it from each other. (*Anglo-Irish*, I, p. 41)

At Cambridge, he discovers that Irish students despise their home country:

They called the peasantry of Ireland besotted in superstition, indolent, savage, and treacherous; their priests, illiterate, clownish, bigoted, officious, and an incubus on the mind of the country; the middle ranks of the Catholics, who were starting into professional, or mercantile, or agricultural importance, they described as pert, or rude, or vain, or ill-mannered: they admitted that there was no living quietly or even safely in their beloved country. (*Anglo-Irish*, I, p. 84)

Irish students embark on a drunken rampage destroying college property thereby reinforcing an Irish stereotype.

Much of the institutional violence in *The Anglo-Irish* comes from politicians and Banim exposes their bigotry and naïveté. One English MP's speech outlines the common belief that institutional violence is reactive rather than proactive:

He denied that the firm measures adopted by this country [England] to keep her footing in Ireland ever came under the name of coercion. They naturally sprang up in self-defence, from the continued turbulence, breach of faith, and atrocities committed, century after century, upon the English settlers of the Pale, and afterwards upon the English settlers every where spread through Ireland. In this view, no policy but a strong and severe one could have emanated from British councils, unless Englishmen would consent to show themselves pusillanimous in the face of savage violence. (*Anglo-Irish*, I, p. 90)

The most detested figure in the novel is Mr. Bignell, the Scottish land steward of the Clangore estates. He is the complete antithesis of Edgeworth's Scottish agent, M'Leod, in *Ennui*. Bignell, like Garraghty in

The Absentee, is a corrupt man who evicts women and children, gives land to his own cronies and, because of pressure for more rents from Clangore, squeezes every penny from the impoverished tenants. His actions force one tenant, Michael Farrell, to approach Blount:

> Mr. Bignell, that knew I wrote the last time, is more hard than ever against us, God soften his heart! for he's nothing but a cruel man to us, and everyone around him, as I said before; and he threatens to let the place to a crony of his, and a stranger to us, your honour; and if I'm served in this way, banished from the old house entirely, and the young wife and child on my back, and the wide world before me, what can I do but come to no good in the long run? (*Anglo-Irish*, II, p. 32)

Blount is reassured that 'his Lordship was well advised by Mr. Bignell, his land-steward, or else by his agent, [these letters were] nothing more than shameless efforts to create continued opportunity for living indolently upon spots of ground they would scarcely culture' (*Anglo-Irish*, II, p. 34). Blount recalls that Clangore had identified Farrell as an example of 'how adroitly an Irish knave could represent himself as the injured party, at the very moment he was cajoling and injuring others' (*Anglo-Irish*, II, pp. 34-5). Farrell later emerges as Captain Rock. Banim's main aim is to show that absentee landowners are unsympathetic to their tenants, invariably support their land-stewards and bring about agrarian violence.

The depiction of Bignell ensures the reader will understand why he deserves death. The main source of controversy is the ownership of the land but, beneath the surface, lies the more intractable problem of whether the Union, which has caused absenteeism, itself should continue. Echoing an incident from *The Absentee*, one of Blount's tenants recounts his father's attempt to get a new lease:

> [T]he day came to make the trial any how, and he went up to the lord's house, to talk to the agent, – for, you see, Sir, the lord himself wasn't to the fore, but spending his days in you honor's country, England, ever since ye took our own parliament from us, and sent it across the water, – and no one lived in the fine ould place only him, a bit of a counsellor, from London, that put a Scotch steward over us, one that was mighty fond o' bidding, under the rose, a trifle more than the ould tenant, and by that

manes, many's the comfortable man he made poor. (*Anglo-Irish*, II, p. 101-2)

Bignel not only fixes leases but is also involved in sub-letting and rack-renting:

[T]he Scotch steward bid the money, because, you see, Sir, it was his plan to split the farum into little takes, and re-let it, to twenty or thirty poor divvles, at another rack-rent. (*Anglo-Irish*, V. II, p. 101)

His final act is to 'turn out' a tenant and, despite pleas for time because of the 'ould mother', to do so regardless of consequences. The mere sight of Bignell's face was enough for the old woman and 'killed her' (*The Anglo-Irish*, II, p. 104). To add to his crimes, a woman and her baby are found, by the Rockites, lying at his gate. Bignell has her driven from the premises and the baby dies (*Anglo-Irish*, III, pp. 266-7).

Sir John Lumley, an old-fashioned landowner, laments the changes that have enabled tenants to take legal action if they are beaten by a landowner:

[T]he son of a fellow whom, thirty or forty years ago, you might have paid with a horse-whipping, or with setting your dogs at his heels, if he presumed to teaze you with a complaint of high rent, or a complaint against your land-steward, or for breaking his fence, or for treading down a few of his potatoe-stalks [sic], or a few blades of corn, or what not, out hunting – the son of that same fellow will now threaten to indict you for common assault at the quarter-sessions, when you only lay your whip across his shoulders, upon any such annoying occasion. (*Anglo-Irish*, II, p. 267)

Lumley's outburst may be taken as a humorous outburst by an elderly fool but it shows how far things have progressed in Ireland that tenants are able to make use of the Law to settle grievances.

Much of the agrarian violence in the novel centres around the Rockites:

It was but a few nights before I began my journey to England, that, only three miles from my own house, an industrious

Scotchman, who had recently taken a large farm, fell a victim, along with two of his servants, to the savage vengeance of Captain Rock's desperadoes. (*Anglo-Irish*, I, pp. 21-2)

The current state of Ireland, however, has arisen not just because of Rock but also because of famine and disease:

Famine and he [Rock] now co-operate among the hills, and bogs, and deserts of Ireland; while disease, plague, in fact, under the name of typhus fever, may be said to bring up the rear. (*Anglo-Irish*, I, p. 99).

Since the mid-1700s, 'Captain Rock' had acquired myth-like status in Ireland with the name used by numerous individuals. Rock is portrayed as being the leader of a substantial, disciplined army within which men hold specific ranks. Rumours of Rockite strength lead the English-Irish, in Dublin, to believe they are to be attacked:

[Y]ou behold a man [Flood] expectant of an invasion of this good city of Dublin by a fleet of turf-boats, bearing as many armed Rockites and Ribbonmen, as 'sods of turf,' from various bog-holes in the heart of wild Ireland, who, it is ascertained, propose to themselves the amiable achievement of cutting the throat of each man, woman, and child, that sprinkleth not the forehead with holy water. (*Anglo-Irish*, II, pp. 185-6)

The Ascendancy is portrayed as weak and foolish, reacting hysterically when some boys kick a can in the street.

The key scene in the novel, where Blount is talking to a stranger in a coach about agrarian violence, pays homage to Banim's literary hero Thomas Moore:

The story rapidly moves to a conclusion after this as Gerald travels by coach into the country to meet his sister who is staying with the Knightlys. He is joined on his journey by a stranger (in fact Mr. Knightly incognito) and this part of the novel clearly shows the extent of the influence of Thomas Moore's contemporary pseudo-history of Ireland, *The Memoirs of Captain Rock* (1824) on Banim's novel, down to the green glasses of the incognito traveller who educates Gerald out of his anti-Irish prejudices and political opinions.[30]

This conversation occurs just prior to Bignell's home being attacked, and his capture by the Rockites. It serves again to underscore the Banims' warning that if landowners fail to act like the enlightened Knightly, then agrarian violence will escalate.

Knightly's response to Blount's comment on the Irish propensity for violence is that it is inevitable:

> Tis very wrong, to be sure, but as incidental to the neglected state of society in which they first acquired it, as prancing is to a half-broke colt. In an improved position of Ireland, it will wear down. (*Anglo-Irish*, III, p. 110)

The problems of Ireland truly originate in 'the atrocious act of Legislative Union' (*Anglo-Irish*, III, p. 112), and Knightly believes 'a literal union is not at all necessary' (*Anglo-Irish*, III, p. 123).

Banim presents the Rockites as reasonable people who have been driven into agrarian violence by absentee landowners and corrupt middlemen. Blount is even saved by the intervention of Rockite-supporting tenants who 'crowded round him, to assure Gerald and his "crony" of protection, until the arrival of their chief leader' (*Anglo-Irish*, III, p. 220). However, reflecting Banim's contradictory views, the Rockite murder of a Catholic priest is also revealed:

> Is it Father Dick, that found himself lying in the glin o' Boyle, the other night, with more holes than breath in his body, just for meddling too much with what no ways concerned him? (*Anglo-Irish*, III, p. 215)

The murder of a priest presents a side of the Rockites that is closer to contemporary English perception of them. The justification for killing Bignell comes as tenants deliver a catalogue of his crimes (*Anglo-Irish*, III, p. 271). He is saved only by the intervention of his victim, Rock's wife, who asserts 'ye have no right to harm a hair of his head on our account'

---

[30] Gilligan, 1990, p. 571.

(*Anglo-Irish*, III, pp. 273-4). Rock himself is enlisted to speak against agrarian violence and hints at a solution:

> 'Kneel up, Bignel [sic]', he resumed, 'and take *this* hand to help you. Such as you treat us badly enough, but this is not the way to make ourselves better treated. And, after all, ye are not as much to blame as them that lets ye do it'. (*Anglo-Irish*, III, p. 278)

Banim, echoing Edgeworth, ultimately blames absentee landowners. It is the tenants who must stop the endless cycle of violence.

Tracy's Ambition is considered to be Griffin's 'second-best novel'[31] but, as with Banim in *The Anglo-Irish*, it shows that he was not the nationalist he is often portrayed as being. There are two representatives of institutional violence in the novel: Abel Tracy (a middleman) and Dalton (a magistrate). Dalton is a fundamentally bad man but Tracy, who is good, goes bad but partially redeems himself. Yet neither is likely to become enlightened. Indeed, Tracy's final claim that his 'ambition is entirely set at rest' and that he 'should be a contented man for the remainder of his days' (*Tracy's*, p. 399) if he could become a magistrate indicates he has learned nothing.

Tracy acts as first person narrator (like M'Quirk in *Castle Rackrent*). Encouraged by Dalton, he allows greed to consume him and hence he abuses his tenants. Unlike Garraghty in *The Absentee*, however, there is no reference to Tracy's employer; apparently Tracy himself chooses to persecute his tenants. John Cronin perceives a further link between *Castle Rackrent* and *Tracy's Ambition*:

> In his effectiveness as a narrator, Abel Tracy recalls Maria Edgeworth's Thady Quirke [sic] in *Castle Rackrent*. Dangerously balanced between two classes, two religions, he inhabits a moral no-man's-land which Griffin charts with instinctive skill. This short and powerful work is altogether lacking in the longueurs which affect the much better-known novel, *The Collegians*.[32]

Tracy is also a development of Jason Quirk, Garraghty and M'Leod – as James Cahalan suggests:

---

[31] Cahalan, p.43.
[32] John Cronin, *Gerald Griffin (1803-1840)* (Cambridge: Cambridge University Press, 1978), p. 77.

In the nineteenth-century rural Irish social context, Abel Tracy is the hated 'middle-man,' yet he is an interesting, sympathetic character. It is as if a later version of Edgeworth's Jason Quirk were allowed to tell *his* story.[33]

Like Lady Murtagh, Mrs. Tracy intercedes with her husband on behalf of the tenants but does not require payment and is popular with the tenants:

> A poor man, who owed me some arrears of rent, applied to Mary to procure him some farther time, as the whole support of his family, during the ensuing spring, depended on the stock of potatoes which I had seized for the money due. I wanted the sum, and refused, for the first time in my life, to admit her intercession. (*Tracy's*, p. 235)

Tracy's Ambition, like *The Collegians*, was written at a time of increased agrarian violence; John Cronin writes:

> For Ireland this was to be a period marked by intense agrarian discontent and by several hideous dress rehearsals (e.g. in 1817 and 1822) for the terrible potato famine which was to strike five years after Griffin's early death. This is the period which saw the rise of terrorist bodies such as the 'Whiteboys', the 'Shanavests' and the 'Caravats' and other similar violent organisations formed by a desperate peasantry to hit back against tithes, rents and other oppressions.[34]

Agrarian outrages occur because of absentee landowners but Tracy is a middleman whose social status – an important factor for Griffin – is ambiguous. He is a Protestant married to a Catholic:

> I was one of a race who may be considered the only tenants of land in my native Island. Our castle owners, above us, and our cabin holders, below, are both men of estate; while we occupy the generous position of honorary agents to the farmer, serving to collect their rents in a troublesome country; and of scape goats on

---

[33] Cahalan, p. 44.
[34] Cronin, 1978, p. x.

whom the latter are enabled to repose the burthen of rent, tythes, and county charges. (*Tracy's*, p. 167)

He indicates the potential for violence within tenants made desperate by poverty:

I was not prosperous enough to become intoxicated, nor poor enough to grow moody and dark-hearted, nor sufficiently at ease in my circumstances to sit idle and invent sin. (*Tracy's*, p. 173)

Tracy follows the middle way while tenants below him resort to violence and those above him cause mischief because of *ennui*.

Tracy acts legally but his new, aggressive stance leads to a decline in landowner/tenant relations:

My train of hereditary dependants disappeared at the sight of the police, as fairies used to do at sight of a priest, and began to look on their old master as an altered man. My tenants became more reserved and more respectful; and when I walked into the fields to superintend my workmen, I perceived that the conversation was hushed [...]. They heard me now in silence, with dark and solemn countenances, and without any symptom either of dissent or acquiescence. (*Tracy's*, pp. 234-5)

This breakdown inevitably leads to more agrarian violence. Although sympathetic to the tenants, Griffin opposes secret societies and depicts their actions as vicious and violent. After he is wounded (*Tracy's*, pp. 182-3), Tracy is taken to the house of one of his tenant's. He is accompanied by Dalton – and the Peelers – who deliberately provokes the tenant's wife by accusing her husband of being a 'croppy' (*Tracy's*, p. 184) before planting incriminating evidence in the house. In a rare footnote, Griffin intervenes directly in the tale, insisting that the framing of innocent tenants is not a fictional fantasy and happens in reality – the Anglo-Irish novelist has become the historian:

Notwithstanding my respect for Mr. Tracy's veracity, I felt it my duty, ere I suffered this transaction to appear before the public, to ascertain whether it were without precedent, but my inquiries determined me not to alter the manuscript. I have been assured that expedients as frightfully devoid of principle as that above mentioned were put in operation in some instances in the South of Ireland. (*Tracy's*, p.124n)

The arrival of the corpse of Shanahan's (the tenant's) brother, murdered by Dalton, results in open threats:

Mr. Tracy [...] You see that corpse that is lying there, warm with the life. I give no blame to that tiger for his death [pointing to Dalton] for what could be expected from an open enemy but blows and blood? But you, that were our neighbour, and that had nothing to gain but our blood, nor to lose by our comfort; you that we never injured, you that we often served, you had no reason to turn upon us this way. – There's my brother's blood upon my floor, an' you shed it without reason. Now listen hether", and he crossed the fore-fingers of each hand, while he knitted his brows in fury and stared at me. "You dhrew his blood without in any way being provoked, take care how soon and suddenly you may yourself be called before the same Coort!' (*Tracy's*, pp. 187-8)

Tracy, not Dalton, is blamed for the death because he is seen as a traitor to his fellow Irish Catholics.

Tracy and Dalton offer opposing views on how best to handle tenants. Despite what has occurred, Tracy still wants to retain a good relationship with his tenants (*Tracy's*, pp. 202-3). But Dalton takes an uncompromising, Orange view:

I think them [the Irish people] a base, fawning, servile, treacherous, smooth-tongued, and black-hearted race of men; bloody in their inclinations, debauched and sensual in their pleasures, beasts in their cunning, and beasts in their appetites. They are a disgusting horde, from first to last. (*Tracy's*, p. 203)

Yet Dalton does not regard tenants as utterly beyond redemption and even he blames landowners for encouraging them to turn to drink and violence:

Our landlords give no rural fete, to reward and encourage the industry of their tenants and promote a virtuous spirit of emulation, as some good men do in England. [...] They are taxed for work and money, and then turned off to find their own amusements, if they wish for them. And this they do in good earnest, witness their jig houses, their shebeens, their benefits and balls, their drunkenness, their factious spirit, their night-walking, and all the turbulent and improvident vices of their character. (*Tracy's*, p. 207)

Tracy's regret at condemning tenants to emigration and tearing families apart reveals Griffin's empathy with tenants. Such injustice suffered by tenants is inherent in the system and explains why they turn to secret societies:

[T]here is no law for the poor in Ireland, but what they make themselves, and by that law my child will have blood for blood before the year is out. (*Tracy's*, pp. 211-2)

Those in power use the Law to advance themselves leaving the tenants to be abused as landowners and magistrates deem appropriate:

The makers and not the executors of the law must decide how far its rigid dicta may be violated, and they have yet given no discretionary power to our juries to condemn for a suspected and unalleged offence, while they acquit on that which is declared. The law may decimate, but not the petit juror. I have furnished victims to a self-constituted inquisition! (*Tracy's*, p. 244)

Just as guilt overtakes Tracy, his wife, a good Catholic and defender of the tenants, is viciously murdered. Violence becomes endemic. Even the job to which Tracy's ambition has led him is only vacant because the previous holder 'was murdered a fortnight since' (*Tracy's*, p. 259). However, in order to rehabilitate Tracy with the reader, Griffin needs to underscore the widespread nature of institutional violence:

I had full knowledge of all the woe that I inflicted. The groans of the oppressed were in my ears, the sight of their misery was before my eyes, the wronged, the houseless, the naked, the starving, the unprotected and defenceless were passing continually before and around me [...] the oppression of all, from the legislature which

105

frames a law, to the vilest constable who puts its provisions in effect against the people, all have shocked my observation, and yet have stirred no availing sympathy within my heart. (*Tracy's*, p. 261)

Tracy's claim that his wife was murdered by Irishmen is refuted by the falsely accused Moran who pointedly claims that it could not be an 'Irishmen that murdered Mary Tracy!' (*Tracy's*, p. 267) as '[t]hey had no stake in the country' (*Tracy's*, p. 268).

Once Shanahan realises that Tracy regrets what he has done, they travel together to see the dire condition of the tenants. Shanahan asks why the Government will do nothing to help the Irish poor. He believes that politicians are to blame and not the King who 'has nature in him, an' would do something for us if he could' (*Tracy's*, p. 339) — somewhat undermining Griffin's alleged nationalism. For Griffin, the real problem is that Catholic tenants do not feel they have a vested interest in the land they work and inevitably turn to violence and drink:

I don't know my landlord, nor my landlord doesn't know me. I have no more howld o' my little cabin an' my bit o' ground, than I have o' that smoke that's goen out o' my pipe. I don't know the moment when I an' my little craiturs'll be wheeled out upon the high road, an' the more pains I lay out upon my ground, the sooner, may be, 'twill be taken from me. [...] Let the masther, an' the rent, an' the cabin go, and whistle together, if they like, *I'll* go an' warm my sowl in my body with a glass o' spirits, an' have one happy hour at any rate, if I never have another!' [...] That's the way the drinkin' comes, Mr. Thracy, an' the fightin' comes o' the drinkin'. (*Tracy's*, p. 343)

The Banims and Griffin, respectively, develop the themes found in *The Absentee* and *Castle Rackrent*. The overwhelming influence of Edgeworth's agenda is clear. Despite the claims of nationalist critics, they do not criticize her agenda but develop it. All four novelists share a dislike of absentees, injustice, violence and religious intolerance. The Banims go further than Edgeworth in their criticism of the Ascendancy but *The Anglo-Irish* falls far short of the 'powerful satiric attack' claimed by Moynahan. Griffin goes further than the Banims but his attack, in *Tracy's Ambition*, concentrates on the middle class. Though giving voice to 'the people Thady saw', Griffin reveals the need to share ownership of the land in order to end division and the accompanying violence; nearly a century elapsed before this did indeed occur.

Solutions?

Neither the Banims nor Griffin are truly nationalist novelists – despite attempts by critics like Murray to label them as such. They are, however, national novelists – authors who wrote sympathetically about the Irish and Ireland and sought positive change without violence and within a loose Union. Joep Leerssen seeks to identify a unified canon that is itself sub-divided into two strands:

> [T]he literature of George Moore's *A drama in muslin* [sic], of Somerville and Ross, of Yeats, Jennifer Johnston or Helen Wykham's *Ribstone pippins* [sic] [...] takes its cue [...] from Maria Edgeworth. This is not, however, the romantic tradition of Anglo-Irish literature, the tradition of Mangan, Davis, Pearse; the tradition also of Griffin and Kickham, of Boucicault.[35]

Yet this actually separates Griffin – and implicitly the Banims – from Edgeworth and drifts close to Daniel Corkery's position. Declan Kiberd adopts a more difficult route:

> [N]ineteenth century Irish novelists in English simply repeated the prevailing English methods, in a tradition which stretched from Edgeworth to Griffin, from Carleton to Moore.[36]

Anglo-Irish novelists have become 'Irish novelists' so circumventing socio-religious differences. Yet they are not credited with any achievement as they 'simply repeated the prevailing English methods'. Edgeworth's creation of the regional novel and agrarian novel – and her subsequent dominant agenda are conveniently ignored. Using Kiberd's criteria, they are all national/nationalist writers. W J Mc Cormack also places the writers conveniently together by stating that the same authors 'had

---

[35] Joep Leerssen, *Remembrance and Imagination* (Cork: Cork University Press, 1996), p. 65.
[36] Declan Kiberd, *Inventing Ireland* (London: Vintage, 1996), p. 342.

consolidated a sub-tradition of Anglo-Irish fiction in the wake of Maria Edgeworth's *Castle Rackrent*[37] while Moynahan is more forthright:

> [T]he Anglo-Irish were not to be so easily dismissed into the dustbins of history. For that matter, young Blount, in spite of becoming an enthusiastic nationalist, remains indismissibly a hybrid – half-English, half-Irish in lineage and upbringing.[38]

This simply is not accurate however. Blount is not a nationalist nor ever describes himself as such. His growing affection for the Irish and his understanding of their condition is already encountered in Edgeworth's Irish novels like *The Absentee* that *The Anglo-Irish* re-works: if Blount is a nationalist then so is Lord Colambre.

In the novel, Blount's first encounter with the English responsible for sorting out Ireland reveals his initial belief that the only solution is to make Ireland like England, as Flood outlines:

> Ireland will never be quiet, or prosperous, or worth living in, until English views, interests, industry – English character, in fact, – take place of the views, interests, and indolence, instead of industry – which confer *its* present character. (*Anglo-Irish*, I, p. 23)

On first entering Parliament, Blount advocates Emancipation but only in order to destroy the very people it was meant to liberate:

> [N]o sooner had he uttered the words 'Catholic Emancipation', than he was greeted with a chorus of groans. In vain did he explain that this part of his system went to tear by up the roots Irish Catholicism itself; that hitherto restrictions had provoked that religion into its present predominance in Ireland. (*Anglo-Irish*, I, pp. 93-4)

Banim, like Edgeworth, finally accepts that Ireland will never be like England. Blount's initial belief is rejected by Knightly who agrees that making everybody in Ireland English-Irish:

---

[37] W J Mc Cormack, *Sheridan Le Fanu and Victorian Ireland* (Dublin: The Lilliput Press, 1991), p. 73.
[38] Moynahan, p. 108.

if it had not failed already; failed a hundred times, during the last seven hundred years, and upwards; failed with all possible appliances to speed it on, such as it cannot now muster; failed with attempts at extermination by fire and sword, by chicanery and intrigue, by famine and pestilence; failed with attempts at colonization, even by Scotch experimentalists; failed with attempts at proselytism by 'drum ecclesiastic,' by kidnapping, demoralizing, odious system of charter-schools, by burning mass-houses, by priest-hunting, and by laws passed amid assenting cheers, that might have found an echo in Pandemonium. (*Anglo-Irish*, III, pp. 119-120)

Education is the best prospect for a solution but English prejudice must first be overcome:

[The Irish] have not had mental objects to engage them, and thereby keep them quiet; for a man whose mind is employed on pursuits that tend to improve it, knows and cares little about politics, after coming to one simple conclusion – namely, honour and respect for King, Laws, and Government. (*Anglo-Irish*, I, pp. 150-1)

Like Edgeworth, the Banims champion education but link it with the need for landowners and the middle class to become enlightened. They must appreciate the importance of 'moral power, derived from education amongst the higher and middle classes, and by their communings with, and their example to, the lower classes' (*Anglo-Irish*, III, p. 122).

The end of the novel is, as Terry Eagleton indicates, like Banim's solution, incomplete:

Banim is contradiction incarnate, labouring to present a sanatized image of Catholic nationalism to a sceptical British public while castigating their compatriots in Ireland. Writing for him is intervention as well as representation; yet he is sceptical enough of the transformative powers of art in such dire conditions, as is Gerald Griffin.[39]

---

[39] Eagleton, 1995, p. 203.

Blount, like Lord Colambre at the end of *The Absentee*, becomes an enlightened, resident landowner, marries 'a mere Irishwoman' and believes 'Ireland needs better, but not fewer, landlords'[40] – a point originally made by Edgeworth. The novel ends, however, 'without absolutely concluding' (*Anglo-Irish*, III, p. 303).

Perhaps Banim's insight into Ireland's problems is evident early in the novel. When Blount asks Gunning, a sensible Scotchman, what needs to be done for Ireland, his reply implicitly refers to Moore's 'wheel of torture' in *Memoirs of Captain Rock* (1824):

> Hark you, our Statesman; – first get a majority of one hundred, instead of four or fifteen, in the Commons, and I'll praise you; next get the bishops to give you a majority of one, and I'll praise you more – and – (whisper) – then get a Royal assent, drawn from the coronation-oath and the conscience-keeper, and then –
>
> > *'Thy stone, oh Sisyphus! Stands still,*
> > *Ixion rests upon his wheel,*
> > *And'* – the wild Irish 'dance' –
> > (Anglo-Irish, I, p. 196)

This is a pessimistic view. What is being suggested in 1826 will come to pass but not for nearly a century and, as the Irish Civil War shows, violence did not stop.

For Griffin, however, the solution was more immediate and personal than the Banims'. After his best works, he despaired of literature being able to change anything. His decision to burn his manuscripts appears to have been cathartic but his brother, Daniel, thought it catastrophic:

> The reader will remember his scruples as to the moral tendency of his writings. Besides his published works there were several manuscripts, consisting of novels, tales, and poems, some in a complete, others in an incomplete form, which had been written and laid by from time to time, during the progress of his other labours. Most of these were now devoted to the flames without mercy.[41]

---

[40] Tracy, p. 46
[41] Daniel Griffin, *The Life of Gerald Griffin* (1829) (New York: D & J Sadlier & Co., n.d.), X, pp. 370-1.

When Griffin joined the Christian Brothers and embraced teaching, it was not just a religious calling. He certainly believed tenants deserved better landowners but, throughout *Tracy's Ambition*, when he refers to 'bad education' he is talking of Catholic children being taught to believe in violent revenge. Although he wants to change this misconception, he recognises the need for discipline. The Christian Brothers (founded in Waterford in 1802) were noted for the primacy given to teaching and belief in discipline. Griffin found contentment in abandoning writing:

> [F]rom the moment he [Griffin] got a decidedly serious turn, he never could bring himself to the temperament necessary for works of fiction; that he never produced anything which satisfied himself; and that, whilst occupied in the composition, he often threw the pen out of his hand, from the perfect consciousness that what he was then doing would not be successful.[42]

He was torn between upper middle class values and empathy with the tenants. His initial belief that, like John Banim, he could present Irish life to English readers – who would then demand change – clearly fades. Unlike Edgeworth, however, Griffin does not just blame landowners (aristocratic and middle class). He recognises that tenants also cause problems. Both sides are guilty of perpetuating violence; middle class middlemen have to change but so too do the tenants. He realised that novels were not generally read by tenants and so chose a more direct route. Joining the Order offered the possibility of changing tenants' attitudes. Echoing Edgeworth, Griffin believed that, even if they did not want it, tenants had to be educated and disciplined.

Perhaps the best refutation of the claim that the Banims and Griffin were nationalists may be seen in their personal histories. Griffin, abandoned by his upper middle class parents, the brother and son of a doctor, was ultimately more concerned with religion than politics. His sense of justice came from religious belief rather than a social conscience; indeed, he knew little of what rural tenants truly experienced. As a devout Catholic, he resented Protestant oppression. The stance he adopts in his novels – anti-violence, anti-secret societies, anti-social equality, anti-middlemen, pro-Catholic, pro-Emancipation, pro-tenant – is one widely shared by contemporary Catholics. He does not advocate replacing the

---

[42] A N Jeffares, *Anglo-Irish Literature* (New York: Schocken Books, 1982), p.382.

monarch or indulging in revolution and his close friendship with John Banim indicates a shared set of values. Banim was often visited, at his home, by the Lord Lieutenant of Ireland. He also received a pension from the Government – later given to his wife and daughter – and corresponded with Sir Robert Peel. He would not have been so well connected or have been given a Government pension had he been a true nationalist.

*The only three names which Ireland can point to with pride
are Griffin's, Banim's and [...] my own.*[1]

*What we have to fear for the country [is] the introduction
by the Catholic priesthood of Church principles into every
element of civil, political, and social life.*[2]

Catholicism, Apostasy and Nationalism

The first quotation suggests that, at least on his own valuation, Carleton
should rank as one of the greatest of the Irish agrarian novelists. Many
critics have endorsed this self-assessment. The most important writer on
Carleton is David J O'Donoghue, author of *The Life of William Carleton*
(1896). The first volume of this work consists of Carleton's own
Autobiography, while the second contains O'Donoghue's biography of
Carleton. Carleton's closeness to the tenantry led O'Donoghue and many
of his successors to portray him as a classic Irish nationalist. There is,
however, a major problem as indicated by the second quotation, from *The
Squanders of Castle Squander* (1852), which reveals Carleton's hostility to the
Catholic priesthood and to Church principles. Given that Catholicism
must be central to any definition of Irish identity, O'Donoghue's attempt
to present Carleton as more Irish and more nationalist than other Irish
agrarian novelists faces formidable difficulty.

---

[1] David J O'Donoghue, *The Life of William Carleton*, (London: Covent Garden, 1896), II,
p. 293.
[2] William Carleton, *The Squanders of Castle Squander* (London: Office of the Illustrated
London Library, 1852), II, p. 293. Further references to this edition are given after
quotations in the text and the title shortened to *Squanders*.

Many later commentators, however, have followed O'Donoghue, whose pro-nationalist and even pro-Catholic interpretation of Carleton's life and works has dominated most subsequent discussion. O'Donoghue has the advantage of being Carleton's first biographer and had full access to his papers and letters. He presents Carleton as a crypto-Catholic and nationalist, supporting his argument by seeking to explain the many apparent inconsistencies in Carleton's works. O'Donoghue chose Frances Hoey (wife of John Cashel Hoey, the assistant editor of the *Nation*[3]) to write the introduction to his biography. While acknowledging that Carleton's 'own people held him an "apostate"' and Protestants as a "convert"', Mrs. Hoey re-unites him with 'his own people' by emphasising his hostility to Ribbonism and Orangeism.[4] She contends that this even-handedness 'rates high among his literary achievements, and may fairly cover many of his offences',[5] including his 'liberal conservative'[6] political beliefs and his formal rejection of Catholicism. She asks readers to embrace Carleton just like 'The Young Irelanders' who 'forgave him even his apostasy!'[7]

Yet in *Retrospect of a Long Life*, another contemporary, Samuel Carter Hall, dismisses Carleton as an opportunist who 'was a Catholic to-day and a Protestant to-morrow, turning from one religion to the other as occasion served'. According to O'Donoghue, however, Hall's judgement is clouded by social prejudice. He castigates Hall's description of Carleton as 'peasant-born and peasant-bred, and most at home in a mud cabin or shebeen shop'[8] as 'Pecksniffian'. He argues that the inference that a frequenter of shebeens was unlikely to have been driven by anything other than base motives merely reveals Hall's own snobbery. Dr Patrick A. Murray, 'the professor of Catholic theology at Maynooth', certainly endorsed O'Donoghue's belief that Carleton remained a Catholic at heart; his conversion was merely a result of youthful gullibility:

---

[3] O'Donoghue, II, p. 278.

[4] O'Donoghue, I, p. xxiv.

[5] O'Donoghue, I, p. xxxiv, fn.

[6] O'Donoghue, II, p. 324.

[7] O'Donoghue, I, p. lii.

[8] O'Donoghue, II, p. 134.

Dr. Murray [...] explains the bitterness of some of Carleton's gibes at the priests by the fact that he was patronized at the outset of his career by the worst enemies of Catholic Emancipation.[9]

The fact that Carleton wrote for a wide variety of publications in which he espoused contradictory political and religious positions indubitably makes it hard to determine where he really stood. For example, in 1828, Carleton wrote for Rev. Caesar Otway's *The Christian Examiner*. Some of his tales were later published in *Tales of Ireland* (1834), as O'Donoghue comments:

The charges of intolerance and rank bigotry brought against the work are amply justified. It is deeply to be regretted that Carleton allowed these feeble and illiberal stories [...] to be collected from the pages of the *Christian Examiner*, but it is quite possible that he had no power in the matter. He certainly never knew how to make a business arrangement with his publishers, and the republication may have been as much due to his carelessness as to his publisher's greed.[10]

O'Donoghue dismisses these early stories as inferior juvenilia whose author was probably not responsible for their re-publication. He cites a letter of 1841, in which John Carleton asks his cousin whether he had been truly sincere in much of his early writing. Although Carleton's *Traits and Stories of the Irish Peasantry* (1830, 1833, 1843-44) sold well, O'Donoghue observes 'there are some offensive and regrettable passages in the work, and his countrymen have not forgiven Carleton for them'.[11] Yet O'Donoghue still defends Carleton, who is portrayed as naïve rather than anti-Catholic. This chapter will ask whether O'Donoghue's portrayal of Carleton is credible.

Famine

In *The Black Prophet* (1845) – often seen in nationalist readings as the key Famine novel – Carleton portrays, in fiction and contemporaneous with the event, the catastrophe of the Famine in all its horror:

---

[9] O'Donoghue, II, pp. 180-181
[10] O'Donoghue, II, p. 30.
[11] O'Donoghue, II, p. 13.

Typhus fever had now set in, and was filling the land with fearful and unexampled desolation. Famine, in all cases the source and origin of contagion, had done, and was still doing its work.[12]

Although ostensibly writing about an earlier famine of 1804, Carleton is really referring to the 1840s. He explains how a famine develops, leads to disease, desperation and 'Famine Outrages' (*Prophet*, p. 203). Carleton describes Father Hanratty's discovery of a woman, a metaphor for Ireland, near death and surrounded by her dead and dying children; the cause is clear:

He repeated the question […] he could catch, expressed very feebly and indistinctly, the word – *hunger*. She then made an effort, and bent down her mouth to the infant which now lay still at her breast. She felt for its little heart, she felt its little lips, but they were now chill and motionless. (*Prophet*, p. 388)

The absentee landowner, Lord Mollyborough, allows Henderson or Dick o' the Grange, a middleman, to behave abominably. Henderson's eviction of the Daltons 'was looked upon as much in the character of a matter of right on his part, as one of oppression to them. Long usage had reconciled the peasantry to it' (*Prophet*, 166). Henderson is a magistrate who relies on the subjective judgements of his virtually illiterate clerk Jemmy Branigan. The legal system is unfair and corrupt. If Branigan's judgement is questioned by the tenant, he would '*set his mark*' [sic] on him. Injustice is inherent in the land system: if Dalton does not improve his holding, it will not produce enough. Yet when he improves it by hard work, using his own money, he receives a demand with menaces. Henderson, knowing that Dalton cannot pay 'this rack-rent' and that Skinadre will pay more, legally ejects the Daltons to be 'beggars upon the world, to endure misery and destitution' (*Prophet*, p. 294). Until the law is fair, tenants stand no chance of prosperity and inevitably resort to acts of agrarian violence. When tenants finally act, they do so in the most peaceable manner by submitting a petition to Travers (the landowners' agent).

Travers provides the landowner with a true picture of the estate. He has been sent because of 'a great number of leases having expired'.

[12] William Carleton, *The Black Prophet* (1847), ed. by John Kelly, (Poole: Woodstock Books, repr. 1996), pp. 193-4. Further references to this edition are given after quotations in the text and the title shortened to *Prophet*.

Carleton approves of him because he is 'inaccessible to bribery' and does not allow 'his religious or political principles to degenerate into prejudice' (*Prophet*, pp. 280-1). He encounters the perennial problem of Ireland – namely, sub-letting:

> [H]e found the soil in many places covered with hordes of pauper occupants, one holding under another in a series that diminished from bad to worse in everything but numbers, until he arrived at a state of destitution that was absolutely disgraceful to humanity (*Prophet*, p. 291)

Sub-division results in holdings too small to produce enough, while continuous cultivation, with nothing left fallow, reduces fertility – in short, a downwards spiral.

Echoing Edgeworth, Carleton considers the middleman system 'one of the worst and most cruel systems that ever cursed either the country or the people' (*Prophet*, p. 101). On occasion, he appears to sympathise with middlemen faced with 'temptations to iniquity in the management of land' and the need for high levels of 'personal virtue and self-denial' (*Prophet*, p. 101) but this is probably ironic. The middleman's lack of long term interest in the estate encourages institutional violence:

> The middleman [...] very naturally endeavours to sweep from off the property he holds, whilst he holds it, by every means possible, as much as it can yield, knowing that his tenure of it is but temporary and precarious. (*Prophet*, p. 165)

Ireland's problems arise from 'the legislative wisdom' of 'those who possess position and ability' (*Prophet*, p. 215) and whose policies provoke the tenants

> [W]ithout the least disposition [...] to defend or justify any violation of the laws, we may be permitted to observe, that the very witnessing of such facts as these [Irish food exports], by destitute and starving multitudes, was in itself such a temptation to break in upon the provisions thus transmitted, as it was scarcely within the strength of men, furious with famine, to resist. (*Prophet*, p. 215)

Carts laden with food for export force their way through funeral cortèges and groups of starving tenants and the appalling spectacle inevitably results in agrarian violence. Carleton does not condone this violence but he understands what provokes it. He urges those in authority to treat those who have committed crimes because they are starving 'with the most lenient consideration and forbearance' (*Prophet*, p. 247) and condemns the Government's inaction:

> [O]ne would imagine that, after the many terrible visitations which we have had from destitution and pestilence, a legislature sincerely anxious for the health and comfort of the people, would have devoted itself, in some reasonable measure, to the humane consideration of such proper sumptuary and sanatory enactments as would have provided, not only against the recurrence of these evils, but for a more enlightened system of public health and cleanliness. (*Prophet*, p. 249)

If the Government had learned from earlier famines and then the Great Hunger could have been avoided.

As the Famine worsens 'the insane spirit of violence' spreads and creates 'a human mob' (*Prophet*, p. 251), but perhaps to soften the image of the violent Irishman – for 'our English neighbours' – Carleton shows how tenants put others before themselves with 'noble instances of self-denial and sublime humanity' (*Prophet*, p. 256). If only they were given 'peaceable employment [...] they would rest not only perfectly contented, but deeply grateful' (*Prophet*, p. 366). While Westminster politicians are partly responsible for Ireland's problems, Carleton believes that local '"politicians" – idle vagabonds' who incite violence – are as much to blame: 'wherever ribbonism and other secret societies do *not* exist, *there* they are certain to set them a-going.' (*Prophet*, p. 367).

The Famine plays a more central role in *The Squanders of Castle Squander* (1852) than in *The Black Prophet*. Carleton uses The Great Hunger as a backdrop and makes it clear that he is talking about the recent past. The first volume is essentially a re-working of *Castle Rackrent* while the second gives Carleton's views on the Land Question. *The Squanders* may not be Carleton's finest novel but it is still surprising that critics say so little about it. The most obvious reason for this neglect is that Carleton's analysis is controversial and particularly difficult to square with O'Donoghue's interpretation of the writer.

The Famine was the greatest human catastrophe to hit Ireland and is still seen as the most powerful symbol of Ireland's sufferings under British rule. A nationalist interpretation requires a reputable, substantial writer to depict the Famine. Carleton, the only contemporary Anglo-Irish writer of the Famine years and the 'Peasant novelist' too, appears to be the obvious choice. *The Black Prophet*, with its portrayal of an absentee landowner, a corrupt middleman and persecuted tenants, seems initially to be the key Famine novel. In *The Squanders*, however, we again encounter a depiction of profligate landowners, a corrupt agent and institutional violence. There are, however, important differences between the two novels. In *The Squanders*, Carleton not only portrays a famine but also attacks O'Connell, Young Ireland, Irish MPs, J S Mill, the Catholic Church, the Pope, aspects of Irish history and secret societies. Yet in a nationalist reading certainly O'Connell, Young Ireland and secret societies would surely be presented positively. In many ways, *The Squanders* is actually a more substantial Famine novel than *The Black Prophet* but it is difficult to use it to portray Carleton as a nationalist – hence its neglect. The same silence continues in more recent works in 'Famine Studies' – by writers like Melissa Fegan and Gordon Bigelow.

The superiority of *The Squanders* over *The Black Prophet* is evident in its unflinching exploration of the human implications of the Famine:

> [I]n this awful cemetery, were numbers of gaunt and starving dogs, whose skeleton bodies and fearful howlings indicated the ravenous fury with which they awaited an opportunity to drag the unfortunate dead from their shallow graves, and glut themselves upon their bodies. Here and there an arm; in another place a head (half-eaten by some famished mongrel, who had been frightened from his prey) or a leg, dragged partially from the earth, and half-mangled, might be seen. (*Squanders*, II, pp. 138-9).

This image of dogs feasting on festering body-parts is hard to forget. Carleton wants his readers – especially the English – to grasp the true effects of famine. He recounts a true story of an evicted family where the father resorts to cannibalism a particularly strong taboo for English readers in the wake of the loss of the Franklin Expedition (1845-48).

The title and some of the story echo *Castle Rackrent*. The first person narrator is again a loyal family retainer. We encounter a profligate, hedonistic, land-owning family – like the Rackrents – who become absentees in order to indulge themselves in London while demanding ever more rents. When the money runs out, they return to Ireland but get into debt through lavish entertaining. Finally, they hire an agent who, like Jason Quirk, craftily lends them money before taking their estate.

Carleton claims to be writing for 'my *country at large*' [sic] (*Squanders*, V. I, p. iii), but his tone towards the peasants is surprisingly harsh; he does 'not wish to see them give way to crime, nor become the ignorant slaves of either priest or landlord' (*Squanders*, II, p. iv). The Catholic Church and landowners pose a twin threat to tenants. Squire Squander is 'negligent and ignorant of his duties as a landlord-proprietor' and, again echoing the Edgeworths, 'unconscious that "property had its duties as well as its rights"' (*Squanders*, I, p. 46). Carleton has no objection to a landowner, however, so long as he behaves appropriately and 'look[s] into the state and circumstances of his property [...] observe modes of cultivation [and becomes] acquainted with the habits and character of [his] tenantry' (*Squanders*, I, p. 47).

The novel raises further problems for a nationalist reading. Nationalists like Daniel O'Connell and Richard Lalor Sheil regarded the 1832 Reform Act with mixed feelings. They generally approved of the Act because it promised to go some way to curb the landowners. Carleton agreed, praising the Act because it addressed the 'deep and atrocious corruption [of] the landlords'. He also approved of the Act, however, for another reason, one less likely to commend it to nationalists. It actually deprived 'forty-shilling freeholders' in Ireland of the right to vote. By the 1830s, rising land prices meant that a holding worth forty shillings a year scarcely amounted to a viable holding and hence, many freeholders were also tenants. Since to nationalists, tenants could almost be equated with Ireland, their disenfranchisement must have appeared a highly retrograde step, but Carleton disagrees; his first-person narrator despises 'forty-shilling freeholders' who 'lied [...] like devils' and believes 'the passing of the Act [...] very properly disenfranchised them' (*Squanders*, I, p. 209).

In *The Squanders*, Carleton attacks bad landowners who 'deliberately stooped to corrupt those who dwelt upon their own property – and all to gratify a low and selfish ambition' (*Squanders*, I, p. 210). Equally, he indicts Government corruption and the institutional violence that accompanies it – such as the sub-letting of land in order to accumulate votes. He also suggests that 'the peace of 1814' (*Squanders*, I, p. 214) was part of the problem. After the end of the Napoleonic Wars, export prices of Irish produce fell sharply. Carleton believes that the Government should have acted to help tenants and 'feelingly, and *honestly* adapted the rent to the produce of the soil, and prudently curtailed their own profligate expenditure' (*Squanders*, I, p. 216). Carleton's solution is to put the tenants' welfare above landowners' profits. His argument is reasonable but by placing the word '*honestly*' in italics, he stresses the corruption endemic in the Government and also implies that the seeds of The Famine were sown earlier in the century.

A conversation between Master Harry Squander and his Uncle Harry, reveals Master Harry's intention to evict tenants and benefit from the improvements they have made to the land. Uncle Harry, an enlightened and, significantly, northern landowner, considers this strategy 'oppression and legal robbery' and 'the practical motto of Irish landlordism' (*Squanders*, I, p. 252) that 'has fostered [...] dishonesty, envy, revenge, and murder' (*Squanders*, I, p. 254). Carleton admires landowner/tenant relations in his native north and, though believing its success is linked to Protestantism, still believes, echoing Adam Smith, that all will prosper if treated fairly.

The Squanders employment of 'Greasy Pockets', as their agent, marks the beginning of their fall. Greasy Pockets embodies the effects of the Famine – as Christopher Morash notes:

[P]roclaiming himself to be 'an embodied famine', Greasy Pockets is a response of horror to the demographic change brought about by the Famine.[13]

Outwardly, Greasy Pockets is full of *bonhomie* but he has a voracious appetite for land and destroys families. His prodigious appetite for food reflects an insatiable desire for estates and power. He swallows up estates just as the Ascendancy swallowed up Ireland. He uses the law to pursue his goals but admits that it is an obstacle to progress while '[e]ducation is in vain, so long as the Legislature neglects its duty' (*Squanders*, I, p. 285). Although these words are spoken by the most reprehensible character in the novel, the irony of the situation indicates that, like Edgeworth, Carleton supports just laws and education, believing 'the law between landlord and tenant has been the principal obstruction to the prosperity of Ireland' (*Squanders*, II, p. 151). The corruption in 'the administration of [...] public money' (*Squanders*, V. II, p. 113) and the misleading of 'English legislators [...] by the landlord class of Ireland' (*Squanders*, II, p. 151) are

---

[13] Christopher Morash, *Writing the Irish Famine* (Oxford: Clarendon Press, 1995), p. 163.

also to blame. Carleton has little time for 'Mr. Mill and Professor Hancock', accusing J S Mill of '*unacquaintance* with the cottier system' that has 'nothing whatsoever to do with the competition of land on Ireland' (*Squanders*, II, p. 153).

In *The Squanders*, Carleton consistently attacks O'Connell, holding him – together with the Catholic Church – responsible for the rising violence of the 1820s and 1830s.[14] O'Connell supported the introduction of the New Poor Law in Ireland[15] and hence some tenants viewed him as 'a political traitor to his country' (*Squanders*, II, p. 29). While O'Donoghue seeks to play down Carleton's opposition to O'Connell, *The Squanders* reveals the depth of his antipathy:

[I] feel confident in asserting, that the long course of agitation conducted by the late Mr. O'Connell [...] has inflicted upon the Irish people injuries of so serious a nature, that it will take years to raise and purify them from the consequences. Before that agitation commenced, the more respectable class of the peasantry were simple, honest, and sincere lovers of truth. (*Squanders*, II, p. 62)

O'Connell is blamed for destroying what was best in the Irish character; his agitation has turned them into dishonest, violent liars. O'Connell compares badly with Grattan who 'never for a moment substituted himself for his country' (*Squanders*, II, p. 64). Carleton's very personal attack culminates in the claim that '[t]he remote origin of that rebellion [1848] [...] was owing to the late Mr. O'Connell' (*Squanders*, II, p. 278). Conversely, Carleton insists that O'Connell's opponents, Young Ireland, were led by 'men of great talent' and 'of the highest personal character' who rejected 'the stale tricks and dishonest political dodges of O'Connell' (*Squanders*, II, p. 280). As we have seen, however, Carleton had insisted that he did not agree with the politics of Young Ireland or with what its supporters wrote in the *Nation*. While the leading men at the paper may have been Carleton's friends, contrary to O'Donoghue's assertions, they were not his political allies.

Carleton claims that 'Dan set the priests to work' (*Squanders*, II, p. 57) implying an unholy alliance between Irish politicians and the Catholic Church – 'fire-brand' priests threaten tenants with damnation 'unless he

---

[14] See *Squanders*, II, pp.57-73.
[15] Carleton, though aware of the limitations of the Poor Law, supported its introduction – see *Squanders*, II, p. 254.

shall vote as he [the priest] dictates to him' (*Squanders*, II, pp. 57-8). Carleton questions the integrity of priests and accuses them of hypocrisy when they allow a tenant to 'rob his landlord openly without a single reproof' but threaten 'God look to him, if he vote against his reverence's will!' (*Squanders*, II, pp. 68-9). Carleton admonishes priests:

> [I]t ought to be remembered that he did not enter into, or undertake his sacred mission, for the purpose of becoming a public politician; nor is such a purpose compatible with the pious and conscientious discharge of that mission. (*Squanders*, II, p. 58)

Priests should stay out of politics and obey their Bishops:

> [T]heir own bishops deemed it necessary to publish a general address to them, soon after the passing of the Emancipation Act, in which they embodied the same opinions we have written, and told them that their altars were built for other purposes than those of discussing public politics, or fomenting human enmity and ambition. (*Squanders*, II, p. 59)

Carleton asserts he is only repeating what the Church had already said. But approval of the leaders of the Church is qualified. The Pope himself, 'Pio Nono' [Pope Pius IX], is 'narrow-minded and unscrupulous' (*Squanders*, II, p. 303). Carleton fears that Ireland will be taken over by the Church and hence supports the Union. If the Catholic Church seeks to extend its power, that is bound to produce a violent reaction from the Protestants, especially the Orangemen. Education offers the best way to cure Ireland's problems, not least because it can curb creeping Catholic influence. Carleton supports the Maynooth Grant purely because it should produce a new class of educated but non-political priests who will not surrender their independence to the 'Popish Plot'.

The Squanders ends with Carleton ambiguously attempting to be positive about change:

> [T]he praise of modernization at the end of *Castle Squander* contradicts the logic of his narrative. The first volume of the novel begins by tracing the decline of the eponymous Castle Squander in a manner which, as the title suggests, is indebted to Maria Edgeworth's *Castle Rackrent*. While Carleton shares with other

Rackrentian Famine novels [...] the premiss that unsystematic estate management must be changed, he does so in a much more troubled way.[16]

Like Edgeworth, Carleton tries to balance his sympathy with tenants and his insistence that landowners must be encouraged to change within the existing political system. He struggled bravely to achieve this balance, though ultimately in vain.

Secret Societies

At first sight, *Rody the Rover* (1845) appears to support O'Donoghue's interpretation of Carleton. It portrays institutional violence orchestrated by the Castle and the shady spy-master Mr. Sharpe (a member of the Black Committee and who is so extreme that he has been expelled from the Orange Order). Ribbonism may be the undoing of the tenants but it is insinuated into their community by Rody, a Protestant spy.

In his Preface, Carleton claims he has written the novel with an 'anxious wish to benefit my countrymen'.[17] He refers to 'the curse of Ribbonism' and its 'blighting principles' (*Rody*, p. iii). However, his anti-Ribbon stance does not appear to be specifically anti-Catholic – as it had been in 'Wildgoose Lodge' (1833). Carleton's reputation as the 'Peasant novelist' is enhanced by his desire to tell the tale plainly rather than rely on readers understanding the sub-text – it is 'the moral lesson' (*Rody*, p. iv) in the tale that matters.

For Carleton, poverty is the main cause of Irish discontent and he believes – optimistically – that 'as poverty disappears, and industry with all its comforts returns, so does love, attended by his sweet and delightful retinue of the domestic virtues and affections' (*Rody*, pp. 16-17). Ballybracken is 'a specimen of filth, neglect, and ignorance' (*Rody*, p. 1) and only improves when the landowner is '*forced* to do from *shame* what he ought long ago to have done from *duty*' (*Rody*, p. 9). Northern Protestants appear as sober and industrious – in contrast to their southern countrymen – but Carleton believes that, given 'an adequate standard or model' (*Rody*, p. 11), all tenants can be taught to be equally industrious.

---

[16] Morash, p. 163.

[17] William Carleton, *Rody the Rover* (Dublin: James Duffy, 1845), p. iii. Further references to this edition are given after quotations in the text and the title shortened to *Rody*.

Rody defends his mission to destroy by asking, without irony, 'is it nothing to be able to say, that the Irish are a disaffected, riotous, unscrupulous, and blood-thirsty people, whom common laws cannot restrain?' (*Rody*, pp. 42-3). Tenants are deliberately provoked in order to allow the Government to persecute them and spy-master Sharpe reveals his true aim:

> [S]o long as we can attach a character of insubordination, violation of law, disregard of life and property, and habits of bloodshed and murder to the Roman Catholic inhabitants and Roman Catholic districts of the country, England and her legislators will look upon them as unfit to be trusted with civil privileges, or political power. (*Rody*, p. 132).

This is institutional violence at its most institutionalised; it is about the subjugation of Catholics. Sharpe implies that Catholics, with their first allegiance to the Pope and the Church, are interlopers rather than the indigenous inhabitants of Ireland.

Carleton sympathises with the tenants and seeks to help them. Tom M'Mahon, who takes the Ribbon oath, is a man who belongs 'to a degraded church and to a party deprived of [...] civil rights' (*Rody*, p. 74). Only later is M'Mahon told that he must swear in another fifty men – this is the insidious nature of secret societies so abhorred by Carleton. He blames Ribbonism rather than Catholicism for destroying the potential of Irishmen and of Ireland:

> I am not a friend to any of these secret societies, because they were nothing but curses to the country, and will be so long as it exists [...] The truth [...] is, if there can be an apology for Ribbonism, that it was nothing more or less than a reactive principle against Orangeism, of whose outrages it was the result. (*Rody*, p. 80)

Carleton advises tenants to adhere to 'the principles of their own Faith, the advice of their Leaders, and the earnest exhortations of their Clergy' (*Rody*, p. 211). Henderson is a fair agent but he is the one who evicts Molly Malone. Her neighbours, most of them Ribbonmen, help re-build her house but '[s]ympathy in the Irish heart is very often the cause of many an outrage' (*Rody*, p. 169) – indeed, they rename themselves 'The Molly Malones'. Carleton's position is contradictory however. He acknowledges that Ribbonmen sometimes act from the best motives but, recounting how Henderson's murder is blamed on a man framed by his fellow Ribbonmen, presents them as being cowardly killers. Still, Carleton's warning, at the end of the novel, reveals his sympathy for the tenants and his opposition to dubious Castle politics:

> [Tenants] are [...] surrounded by an invisible body of spies and detectives, trained and disciplined into the deepest reaches of treachery and iniquity, under the very sanction of government, which is not ashamed to degrade itself by double guilt of employing a class of men whose services are calculated to destroy the confidential intercourse of society at large, and are clearly at variance [...] with the spirit of a free constitution. (*Rody*, p. 248)

In *Valentine M'Clutchy* (1845), Carleton attacks the Orange Order. The novel is set in 1804 at the time of an earlier famine. Valentine M'Clutchy is foremost an Orangeman and it is the Orange Order that is the principle vehicle of oppression of Catholic tenants:

> I speak now of the North of Ireland. It was then, indeed, the seat of Orange ascendancy and irresponsible power. To find a justice of the peace *not* an Orangeman would have been an impossibility. The grand jury room was little less than an Orange lodge. There was then no law *against* an Orangeman, and no law *for* a Papist.[18]

Carleton deplores the inequality inherent in a system that institutionally discriminates against Catholics but, diplomatically, dissociates contemporary Tories from Orangeism:

> I deny [...] that modern Conservatism, is capable of adopting or cherishing the outrages which disgraced the Orangemen of forty years ago, or even of a later period. (*M'Clutchy*, p. xii)

In the novel, Lord Cumber, an absentee, consistently demands more rents. He replaces a good agent, Hickman, with 'Val the Vulture' M'Clutchy and encourages him to 'be generally angry, speak loud, swear roundly, and make [the tenants] know their place' (*M'Clutchy*, p. 73).

---

[18] William Carleton, *Autobiography* (1896), ed. Benedict Kiely (Belfast: The White Row Press, 1996), p. 48.

M'Clutchy follows Cumber's instructions but presents himself as the victim. He is besieged in his own house and threatened with death. Carleton, however, passes quickly over this episode of agrarian violence implying that the agent's crimes are so bad that he deserves his fate.

The cause of the mass eviction of Drum Dhu (later used by the Land League to exemplify institutional violence) is the tenants' decision to vote for Hartley (who gives them employment) rather than for Cumber's absentee brother. The focus is on the O'Regans, decent and industrious Catholic tenants, one of whose sons, Torley, is critically ill. We are told that '[w]inter had now arrived in all its severity' and the day chosen is 'Christmas eve' (*M'Clutchy*, p. 91). The ground is frozen hard, snow falling and a storm raging – into this maelstrom will be pitched a terminally ill boy. Carleton stresses that M'Clutchy's actions are entirely legal:

> Every step he took was strictly and perfectly legal, and the consequence was, that he had that strong argument, '*I am supported by the laws of the land*', to enable him to trample upon all the principles of humanity and justice – to gratify political rancour, personal hatred, to oppress, persecute and ruin. (*M'Clutchy*, p. 91)

M'Clutchy's actions are opposed – though only verbally – by the snobbish yet hypocritical local gentry who highlight the difference between themselves and M'Clutchy, who is both illegitimate and an Orangeman. However, both they and M'Clutchy use the law to benefit themselves and to persecute tenants.

M'Clutchy knows that '[r]emoval [...] in Torley O'Regan's case, would have been instant death' (*M'Clutchy*, p. 92), nevertheless the eviction goes ahead with M'Clutchy using Orangemen physically to remove the famine-struck tenants – emphasising the religious animosity behind the action. He is starting something that will end in his own violent death as '[f]rom many of the men [...] came stifled curses, and smothered determinations of deep and fearful vengeance (*M'Clutchy*, p. 96). The sentimental intensity of the scene reaches its height when, after evicting his own mother, M'Clutchy has Torley thrown out:

> His parents were immediately beside him, and took him now into their own care; but it was too late – he smiled as he looked into their faces, and then looked at his little brother, and giving one

long-drawn sigh, he passed without pain or suffering, saving a slight shudder, into happiness. (*M'Clutchy*, p.100)

The pathos of the scene is pronounced in order to engage the reader's sympathy. The tenants, having been shown who wields the power, are allowed back into their hovels rendering Torley's death completely unnecessary.

Institutional violence swiftly and inevitably leads to agrarian violence. Grimes, the key member of 'Deaker's Dashers' (Orangemen), is 'found murdered [...] with the slip of paper pinned to his coat, on which were written in a disguised hand, the words – "'Remember O'Regan's son, and let tyrants tremble"'(*M'Clutchy*, p. 103). Carleton, who does not describe this particular act of agrarian violence, appears to understand if not condone it:

Let it not be supposed that we are capable of justifying murder, or the shedding of human blood; but we are palliating, and ever shall palliate, that crime in the humble man, which originates in the oppression of the great man. (*M'Clutchy*, p. 337)

In Carleton's later novel, *The Tithe Proctor* (1849), written long after the Tithe War (1830-33),[19] he sees himself as being a champion for a 'country [...] disgraced by great crimes' and one 'disorganized by men whose hardened vices bring shame upon civilization itself'. Carleton determined to present Ireland '*as she is*' [sic] (*Proctor*, p. vi) and, although ostensibly set in 1830, the country is portrayed as quite as violent after the Famine as it has been before.

Despite the defeat of O'Connell's Repeal movement in 1843, Carleton still holds 'the leading advocates of Repeal' (*Proctor*, p. vii) responsible for ruining Ireland. Whiteboys and Repealers are equally responsible for the country's plight while landowners attract little criticism. Carleton attacks O'Connell and defends his own sympathy – though not total identification – with Young Ireland, claiming that its supporters are exempt 'from having any participation in bringing about results so disastrous to the best moral interests of the country' but 'that, as politicians, they were insane' (*Proctor*, p. vii).

---

[19] William Carleton, *The Tithe Proctor* (London: Simms and M'Intyre, 1849), p. vi. Further references to this edition are given after quotations in the text and the title shortened to *Proctor*.

To the tenants, the Purcells (devout Catholics and tithe proctors) are traitors to their class, community and religion. Purcell's employer is the avaricious Rev. Jeremiah Turbot, an absentee clergyman 'addicted to hunting and shooting' and who feels 'a keen and indomitable relish for the good things of this world' (*Proctor*, p. 54). Carleton's ironic tone works well in his depiction of Turbot (aptly named after a plump fish) as a fat, self-indulgent fool. Turbot, clearly a metaphor for the Church of Ireland, cares more for secular than theological matters, over-indulges in food and drink and expects tenants to pay for his excesses. Carleton implies that the engorged Church of Ireland, greedily demanding more tithes, is ultimately responsible for the deaths of tithe proctors. Only a severe lesson leads Turbot and the Church of Ireland to reform:

> That gentleman's double chin had followed the carnal fortunes of the church that supported it. [...] He was now leading, by compulsion, a reasonable and natural life, and not one so much at variance with the simple principles of his Religion, whatever it might be with those of the then Establishment. (*Proctor*, p. 230)

Carleton, the convert, believes that parsons should concentrate on religious issues rather than on secular luxuries. Mr. Temple, Turbot's curate and a good, enlightened minister, significantly emphasises the need to purge the Church of 'grossness and worldly feeling' (*Proctor*, p. 60) while opposing the use of force to collect tithes.

Although critical of the Church of Ireland, Carleton also berates Catholic priests for failing to prevent agrarian violence:

> [I]f the Catholic priesthood of Ireland were as anxious for the repression of crime as they are for a Repeal of the Union [...] the country would not be steeped in crime as it is, nor disgraceful to the religion which its perpetrators profess. (*Proctor*, p. 130)

Carleton questions the sincerity of the Whiteboys' professed faith believing they use Catholicism merely to give credibility to their actions. 'The Threshers' (forerunners of the Whiteboys) threatened priests and 'were as active in their attempts to diminish the income of the priest by intimidation, as they were that of the parson' (*Proctor*, pp. 226-7). Carleton blames the Catholic priesthood – especially 'Dr. Doyle [...] Bishop of Kildare and Leighlen' (*Proctor*, p. 101) – for stirring up anti-tithe feeling.

Despite O'Donoghue's attempts to minimise Carleton's opposition to O'Connell, however, Carleton makes it clear that he is virulently opposed to the Irish hero. O'Connell is to blame for the rise in agrarian violence. His guilt lies in his arrogant claim that the tenants have nothing to fear because, regardless of any Government action, 'he would undertake to drive a coach and six through the very severest of its penalties' (*Proctor*, p. 101). Carleton goes on to attack O'Connell's policy of passive resistance:

> [A] piece of advice which involved an impossibility in the first place, but which was as false in itself, as replete with dishonesty and imposture, as it was deceitful and treacherous to the poor people who were foolish and credulous enough to be influenced by it. (*Proctor*, p. 183)

The implication is that O'Connell must have realised that encouraging tenants to break the law by passive resistance would end in violence. Life became so cheap that 'men were openly and publicly marked for destruction, and negociations [sic] for their murder entered into in fairs, markets, and houses of entertainment' (*Proctor*, p. 184).

The end of the novel is characteristically ambiguous. Purcell and his sons die because they make extensive use of institutional violence and Buck English, leader of the Whiteboys, dies because he uses his men to exact personal revenge. Yet the women are spared and helped by English's brothers while Francis M'Carthy, the man who converted to Protestantism to study at Trinity College Dublin, emerges as the hero. Carleton's message is clear: as long as unjust tithes exist, so will secret societies like the Whiteboys.

Religion

Despite O'Donoghue's attempts to explain away the many paradoxes in Carleton's fiction, his work is characterised by glaring omissions and outright misinterpretation. O'Donoghue's dubious scholarship is evident in his desire to suppress some of Carleton's works:

> Carleton's fame would be rendered all the brighter by the suppression of some worthless writings, and readers ought to be

informed that those inferior productions still in circulation are not only dull, but positively offensive.[20]

When a biographer admits wanting to suppress works that he considers 'worthless', we are bound to ask whether he suppresses other things too. What is positively 'offensive' to O'Donoghue may not be so to other readers. When he talks of 'offensive' works, he has Carleton's early anti-Catholic stories in mind. To an extent, he does suppress them by playing down their significance – yet they are essential to a full understanding of Carleton.

O'Donoghue's reliance on the opinions of Dr Murray of Maynooth raises the question of Murray's own credibility. Murray's explanation of Carleton's religious position – taken up enthusiastically by O'Donoghue – is weak and his advocacy of 'the rigorous excision of all Carleton's preaching "asides"' is incompatible with the high standards of scholarship to be expected from a man in his position. It is striking that O'Donoghue does not mention Carleton's response to the letter from his cousin. It is possible that the reply may have disappeared but, if it defended the early anti-Catholic stories, O'Donoghue may have suppressed it because inclusion would have undermined his argument.

Carleton's letters and early works exhibit strongly anti-Catholic sentiments and consistently present the Catholic Church as the enemy of the tenants. Carleton may have been a tenant and raised as a Catholic but his conversion to Protestantism, as a young man, seems to have been entirely genuine. He often presents the Catholic Church as the enemy of the tenants, indeed his anti-Catholicism is the most strident of the writers so far examined. It is hard not to feel sympathy for revisionist commentators. On virtually every count, Carleton conforms to their ideal of a nationalist literary hero – but they cannot circumvent contradictory aspects of the man and the writer. Although born an Irish-speaking tenant, Carleton had become a middle class writer of literature in English. Yet he still lived in Ireland and wrote about Irish issues. While his novels may be national in sentiment they are certainly not nationalist in sentiment. Nationalist critics, like Daniel Corkery, cannot disown Carleton because that would leave them without any major novelist to plead their case and advance their cause. The only solution is to make light of Carleton's conversion and insist that somewhere there was a real Carleton

---

[20] O'Donoghue, I, pp.xi-xii.

who remained a Catholic throughout. As with Patrick Joseph Murray and the Banims, biography provided an opportunity to create a revised Carleton, a curious character but one who has now survived for over a century.

Given his background, it may seem appropriate to adopt the common description of Carleton as the 'Peasant novelist'. Carleton came from Ulster and was the son of a Catholic tenant who experienced serious Orange violence.[21] The family was so devout that the young Carleton was encouraged to become a priest. On a pilgrimage to Lough Derg, however, Carleton had a dream that led him not only to abandon any idea of the priesthood but also to reject Catholicism itself. Some writers make light of Carleton's apostasy, claiming that his conversion to Protestantism was prompted by a desire to rise in the world, to achieve middle class status, rather than by genuine rejection of Catholicism. It is true that Carleton did eventually become a respected writer, but not before he had spent some time as an apprentice stone-cutter and as a teacher.

Perhaps this is an apposite point at which to mention some basic though key differences between tenants and writers. Social advancement inevitably leads to change. While Carleton was undoubtedly born a tenant did he, as a successful author, die a tenant? After all, tenants live in the open air, the wind and rain, and their features become weather-beaten and their hands hardened and calloused. They are countrymen and are suspicious of towns. They are commonly illiterate and, even if they are not, they have little time for books and find writing slow and difficult. Their time sense is one of seasons rather than of days and hours. Writers are different in almost every respect. They spend their lives indoors, writing feverishly at their desks, surrounded by books. Their complexions are white and their hands, though perhaps ink-stained, soft and uncalloused. Although they may write of the countryside, they tend to live in towns – unless they have private means like Maria Edgeworth or are so successful that they can afford to buy an estate like Sir Walter Scott. If they can, they buy smart clothes to attend literary functions or visit their publishers. Their lives revolve around deadlines. If they have any sense, they take legal advice on contracts and royalties. Whatever they may write in their books, in their lives they are members of the professional class – no doubt sometimes in financial difficulty – but still a world away from the poverty of the tenant.

---

[21] Carleton, *Autobiography*, pp. 37-40.

Carleton's literary career began with a short story – 'The Lough Derg Pilgrim' (1828) – written for the *Christian Examiner* and hence, for O'Donoghue, precisely the kind of anti-Catholic literature that should be suppressed. Carleton describes the trials that pilgrims endured at the Holy site. Neither the pilgrims nor their devotions are ridiculed, but Carleton vilifies superstition and the Church that encourages it:

> Lough Derg [...] reposing there as the monstrous birth of a dreary and degraded superstition, the enemy of mental cultivation.[22]

Of course, O'Donoghue plays down Carleton's belief that the Catholic Church encouraged superstition in its adherents and implies that 'degraded superstition' is really a reference to surviving remnants of folk religions. It is clear, however, that Carleton means Catholicism itself. Consciously or unconsciously, he uses the language of the Protestant reformers of the sixteenth century. They had much to say about the superstition of the Catholic Church and Carleton must have known that his own use of the word would be interpreted in the same way. The fact that he was so deeply steeped in the language of the Reformation suggests more than a superficial conversion to Protestantism.

Carleton believed the Church exploited tenants through superstition just as landowners exploited them economically. He is against all exploitation including the Church's emphasis on personal guilt:

> [T]hat jealous spirit of mistaken devotion, which keeps the soul in perpetual sickness, and invests the *innocent* enjoyments of life with a character of sin and severity. (*T&S*, I, p. 243)

The Church's support for pilgrimages limits and undermines God's will; God's safeguards are weakened by the encouragement of superstition. Carleton rails against those in power, whether spiritual or secular, who keep tenants in ignorance. Initially, his antipathy to the abuse of power may appear initially to justify a nationalist interpretation, but his undeniable Protestantism and refusal to condemn all landowners fits uneasily with nationalist assumptions.

---

[22] William Carleton, *Traits and Stories of the Irish Peasantry* (1830, 2nd edn. 1833, final edn. 1843-44) (Gerrards Cross: Colin Smythe Limited, 1990), I, p. 234. Further references to this edition are given after quotations in the text, and the title shortened to *T&S*.

It is true that Carleton removed 'some offensive passages' (*T&S*, I, p. 237) from the definitive edition of his works, yet he did not go very far and anti-Catholicism was still a powerful element in the mature Carleton of the 1840s. The contradictions evident in Carleton's early stories may be related to the way that he wrote, as Barbara Hayley suggests:

> [H]e went back and reworked his old stories in edition after edition, rewriting, expanding, contracting, revising every story in some way.

In other words, a process of constant revision was bound to result in differences between what had been changed and what had not. As Carleton aged and changed, so did his attitude to Ireland's problems:

> Some of Carleton's most startling alterations concern the passages he removed or rewrote to avoid giving 'offence' to Catholics or others, according to his current religious views or his market [...] he actually added anti-Catholic passages to some of his *Christian Examiner* pieces for book publication.[23]

This rather casts doubt on any notion that Carleton was mellowing in his attitude towards the Catholic Church. He wrote for money. He needed to sell his books to provide for his family; consequently, his political and religious stance was extremely flexible.

'Wildgoose Lodge' provides one of the most disturbing descriptions of agrarian violence. The atrocities depicted in the tale are so horrific that Carleton feels obliged to insist on their authenticity stating '[t]his tale of terror is, unfortunately, true [...] the facts are pretty closely such as were developed during the trial of the murderers' (*T&S*, II, p. 362). 'Wildgoose Lodge' reveals Carleton's bitterness at being tricked into becoming a Ribbonman. Later versions of the story stress that both Ribbonmen and their victims are Catholics. As Hayley explains, however, the original described a Catholic attack on a Protestant by quoting Judge Fletcher who concluded that 'religious bigotry had no part in producing these monstrous crimes [...] it was Catholic against Catholic'. Yet more significant is that, in the original version of the tale:

---

[23] Barbara Hayley, *Carleton's Traits and Stories* (Gerrards Cross: Colin Smythe, 1983), pp. x-xi.

the Catholic Ribbon gang [set] off to attack 'the house in which this man (the only Protestant in the parish) resided'. In the first edition, he alters this phrase to 'the house in which this devoted man resided'.[24]

The original version is perhaps more crudely anti-Catholic than the later one; by reverting to the facts and making Ribbonmen and their victims Catholics, Carleton gives the tale an entirely different slant. His most disconcerting words concerning tenants come in his explanatory note about Devann – the murderer of eleven innocent people, including a baby. Despite this, '[t]he peasantry, too, frequently exclaimed, on seeing him, "Poor Paddy!" A gloomy fact that speaks volumes!' (*T&S*, II, p. 362).

The fact that the 'Captain' in 'Wildgoose Lodge' is the local schoolmaster and the meeting takes place in 'the parish chapel' (*T&S*, II, p. 350), indicts both Catholic education and the Church itself. The Captain tells lies at the altar, encourages drinking in a way that mimics the Mass, allows armed thugs to cavort in church and thumps the altar while tricking the men into agreeing to his demands. Superstition and the supernatural play key roles in this tale; only truly evil men could commit such atrocities. The combination of oratory and drink, in a familiar Catholic setting, succeed in transforming those involved into demons that would 'sicken any heart not absolutely diabolical' (*T&S*, V. II, p. 355). At Wildgoose Lodge, the Captain revels in murder:

[A] human head, having the hair a blaze, was descried, apparently a woman's [...] [she] rather shrieked, aloud, for help and mercy. The only reply to this was the whoop from the Captain and his gang, of 'No mercy – no mercy!' and that instant the former, and one of the latter, rushed to the spot [...] the head was transfixed with a bayonet and a pike, both having entered it together. (*T&S*, II, p. 359)

These are killers who enjoy their work. This has nothing to do with land-ownership or religious enmity, it is vindictive violence used to terrify and control tenants. Ribbonism is presented as being more concerned with the settlement of personal scores than with the real interests of the tenants:

[24] Hayley, p. 124.

[A] man appeared upon the side-wall of the house, nearly naked; his figure, as he stood against the sky in horrible relief [...] Every muscle, now in motion by the powerful agitation of his sufferings, stood out upon his limbs and neck, giving him the appearance of desperate strength ... the perspiration poured from his frame, and the veins and arteries of his neck were inflated to a surprising thickness. (*T&S*, II, p. 360)

This man is the informer and the Captain wants him dead. Carleton conveys the victim's desperation by closely observed description. Ribbonmen are portrayed as being wicked, savage beasts involved in the worst agrarian atrocities. Carleton knew this depiction of Ribbonmen put them beyond redemption. The closing words of the tale are bland to the point of naivety – or perhaps deliberately understated for ironic effect as the narrator notes 'how seldom [...] justice fails to overtake the murderer' (*T&S*, II, p. 362).

The Real Carleton?

O'Donoghue's biography produces conflicting evidence about Carleton's religious beliefs. He claims 'Carleton had been for many years more or less indifferent to all forms of religion'.[25] This assertion appears to rest on Carleton's statement in 1868 that '[f]or half a century or more I have not belonged to the Roman Catholic religion'.[26] O'Donoghue's assertion would be invalid, however, unless the Catholic religion was the only religion. He tries to circumvent this problem by concluding that Carleton had no strong beliefs – arguing that lack of belief made Carleton a Catholic by default. In other words, all Irish peasants are in some sense Catholics simply because they are Irish peasants. Several twentieth-century writers, like W B Yeats, Benedict Kiely and Barry Sloan, appear to accept this unlikely analysis.

Carleton wrote for a variety of publications ranging from the avowedly Protestant *Christian Examiner* and *The Dublin University Magazine* to the avowedly nationalist *Nation* and *The Shamrock*. O'Donoghue explains this astonishing range by claiming that Carleton accepted any commission 'for his children's sake'. Nevertheless, he admits that Carleton became a literary hack and that '[a]ny "side" that would pay for the service of his

[25] O'Donoghue, II, p. 326.
[26] O'Donoghue, II, p. 334.

pen, might command it'[27] which must undermine O'Donoghue's own attempt to identify Carleton's real allegiances. It is, however, Carleton's links with the *Nation* that most interests revisionist writers. He had many friends among the leaders of Young Ireland and was especially close to Charles Gavan Duffy, one of the editors. For Carleton, Young Ireland put tenants first, unlike Daniel O'Connell who, he believed, used them for his own ends. This is undeniable and O'Donoghue builds on it to imply that Carleton was a secret supporter of Young Ireland. He states Carleton 'soon became associated in the public mind with the politics and conduct of the paper'. Although Duffy denied that Carleton ever wrote for his paper, O'Donoghue states that he did, but tried superficially to keep his distance from it:

> Carleton was never a Nationalist, and was quite incapable of adopting the principles of the Young Irelanders. He never attended the weekly *Nation* suppers, even after he wrote for the paper, but went on excursions with some of the party, and was a frequent caller at the office, where he did not spare his applause or criticism of the work done by the young men. But he could not understand their aspirations.[28]

Thus, according to O'Donoghue, we have a writer who was 'never a Nationalist' but supported nationalism – truly a middle way. Carleton frequented the offices of the paper, socialized with its editors and contributors, gave his sought-after opinion on all matters, admired those involved even though, apparently, he did not fully agree with what they said or wrote. Yet, despite stating Carleton was not a nationalist, O'Donoghue asserts '[it] was the pressure of the Young Irelanders which caused Carleton to write books of a really Nationalistic character.' Also, he quotes John McKibben who states the writer 'deemed the young fiery fanatics of *The Nation* as the most brilliant men that ever broke lance with the English in Ireland'.[29] O'Donoghue's argument is, at best, confused.

A leader in *The Dublin Evening Mail* (3 July 1848) appears to support O'Donoghue's claim that, if not a nationalist, Carleton at least supported the nationalist cause, but while O'Donoghue approves of what he believes to be Carleton's position, the newspaper expressed outrage that a man so

---

[27] O'Donoghue, II, p. 45.
[28] O'Donoghue, II, pp. 56-7.
[29] O'Donoghue, II, p. 304.

closely associated with nationalist journals should have been awarded a pension by Lord John Russell's government:

> He became an early and zealous contributor to the *Nation*, and other journals of that stamp, wrote tracts and novels for Mr. Duffy's National Library, and was, from its first commencement, and is still, enrolled by name on the regular staff. An evening contemporary describes him as 'one of the proprietors of the *Irish Tribune* – a professed successor of the *United Irishmen* – and a devoted disciple of the Mitchel school. He is [...] the avowed author of 'Rody the Rover', 'Valentine M'Clutchy', and other popular stories, in which the right owners of property, and the Government of the country are held up to the hatred and contempt of the classes in which such publications are meant to circulate.[30]

Significantly, the newspaper fails to mention that Carleton was even-handed in his disapproval; while Orangeism is indeed condemned in *Valentine M'Clutchy*, Ribbonism is condemned in *Rody the Rover*. Carleton wrote an unpublished response to this bigoted attack:

> To these assertions I simply reply that I am, and ever was, opposed to the general politics of the *Nation* and other such journals; that I never wrote a political line in it or any other journal.

Carleton's reference to 'general politics' is ambiguous as it implies he is against everything the paper stands for. His claim never to have written a 'political line' seems to depend on a questionable distinction between political journalism, writing about politics in a novel and writing about religion and politics in journals and novels. Carleton believed his instructional and improving novels would never have been read by Catholic tenants – implicitly his intended audience – had they been published by 'Conservative booksellers' and seeks to explain his association with *The Tribune*:

> An engagement was proposed to me in the literary department of that journal [...] I was not in a condition, with a large family to

---

[30] O'Donoghue, II, p. 129.

support, to decline. When [...] I saw the lengths to which writers in that paper went I withdrew from it.

Carleton was a devoted family man and insisted that even his adult children remained at home. A lack of business skills added to his financial problems and he was often reduced to selling his copyrights for a fraction of their true value.

Carleton's defence of his political position is, characteristically, ambiguous:

I am not now nor have I ever been a Repealer, no Jacobin, no Communist, but a plain, retiring literary man who wishes to avoid politics, and to devote his future life to such works as he hopes may improve his country and elevate her people.[31]

The first part of this statement indicates he is not a nationalist but the second part reveals his aspirations to be a true Irish hero. The fact that Carleton did not support O'Connell presented O'Donoghue with a problem but he seeks to explain matters by claiming '[p]olitically, Carleton was opposed to O'Connell and his son, but he had a considerable regard for the latter'[32] – but liking O'Connell's son hardly compensates for disagreeing with O'Connell.

The battle over Carleton's literary soul began soon after his death: '*The Nation* [...] regarded him as the first and greatest of our Irish storytellers'. But *The Daily Telegraph*:

[N]ot only compared Carleton disadvantageously with Banim and Griffin and Miss Edgeworth and Lady Morgan, but attacked the Irish character itself. Because Carleton confined himself to Irish life, his critic accused him of holding 'the superstition that a true national literature must be written by Irishmen, on Irish topics alone, and must be printed and published in Ireland, upon Irish paper, and bound in Irish cloth of the real Irish colour'.

This was unfair and it is hard to dissent from O'Donoghue's comment:

---

[31] O'Donoghue, II, pp. 131-133.
[32] O'Dongohue, II, p. 274.

The article in the *Daily Telegraph* [...] is written in the most detestable style of insular prejudice, and is teeming with indications of ignorance and spite.[33]

Perhaps Carleton himself, 'the acquaintance of various literary men',[34] offers the best, if somewhat immodest, analysis:

The only three names which Ireland can point to with pride are Griffin's, Banim's and [...] my own. Banim and Griffin are gone, and I will soon follow them – *ultimus Romanorum*, and after that will come a lull, an obscurity of perhaps half a century, when a new condition of civil society and a new phase of manners and habits among the people – for this is a new *transition* state – may introduce new fields and new tastes for other writers.[35]

Carleton's words are prophetic for, after his death, no single writer dominated Anglo-Irish literature until the latter part of the century.

In the last resort, attempts to persuade readers that Carleton's background and his undoubted sympathy for the tenants must mean that he should be regarded as a political nationalist are not convincing. Julian Moynahan correctly defines Carleton as 'a political conservative and unionist' who 'had also come under the influence of Thomas Davis's tolerant and ecumenical form of cultural nationalism'.[36] Davis's attempts to link the past with national identity appealed to Carleton who wanted to define what it meant to be Irish. He believed a man could be Unionist, Protestant, patriotic, anti-violence and still be an Irishman. The fact that Davis was a Protestant and the son of an Englishman did not help endear him or his followers to nationalists; indeed, his ideas of Irish identity have been challenged by, among others, W B Yeats.

Carleton, like other agrarian novelists, feared mob violence but was also frightened of organised violence whether Orangeism or Ribbonism – as Terry Eagleton indicates:

Just as Carleton's style negotiates its unsteady path between British power and Irish experience, so his politics seek for a compromise

---

[33] O'Donoghue, II, pp. 340-341.
[34] O'Donoghue, II, p. 55.
[35] O'Donoghue, II, p. 293.
[36] Julian Moynahan, *Anglo-Irish* (Princeton: Princeton University Press, 1995), p. 47.

between what he sees as the most negative aspects of both. The typical Irish novelist – Banim, Griffin, Carleton – is petty-bourgeois in ideological outlook, as horrified by imperial arrogance as he is by the threat of popular insurrection.[37]

It is true that Carleton's path was indeed 'unsteady', but any definition of Irish identity as lying 'between British power and Irish experience' is perhaps too vague. As Moynahan indicates, Carleton considered himself to be an Irishman yet he was anti-Repeal, anti-Irish Parliament, a Protestant and a patriot:

> Carleton claimed that O'Connell's Catholic Association maintained hidden connections with seditious agrarian terrorist societies such as Ribbon Men, and that this conspiracy was abetted by the hedge schoolmasters [...]. Also privy to the plot were 'a great proportionate number of the Roman Catholic clergy who are educated in Maynooth College [...]'. A covering letter to the man charged with transmitting the memorandum to Peel contains an offer from Carleton to provide proof of his allegations.[38]

Carleton questions O'Connell's loyalty, attacks the Catholic Church and offers to become an informer. Yet this Memorandum was written by the author of *Valentine M'Clutchy* that left many Conservatives incandescent with rage:

> The journals of Irish Toryism were incoherent with fury and could only cry out that action should be taken against the writer as 'a fomenter of discontent and disloyalty'.[39]

But no true nationalist would offer to become an informer for the British Government. Moreover, in *Valentine M'Clutchy*, the targets of Carleton's attack are primarily corrupt agents and absentee landowners – similar targets to those found in Edgeworth's Irish novels.

Despite attempts by O'Donoghue and others, no evidence has been produced to prove that Carleton's conversion to Protestantism was

---

[37] Terry Eagleton, *Heathcliff and The Great Hunger* (London: Verso, 1995), p. 211.
[38] Moynahan, p. 48.
[39] Thomas Flanagan, *The Irish Novelists* (New York: Columbia University Press, 1959), p. 313.

insincere. Although Patrick Rafroidi states that Carleton's faith 'caused him much anguish, as did his political allegiance',[40] he was, by nature, a thinker and writer.

Carleton, ever contradictory, was a tenant who defended good landowners. He was associated with Young Ireland but rejected its politics. He liked O'Connell's son but despised the father. He championed the cause of Catholic tenants but attacked the Catholic Church. He attacked Catholic priests for their politics but, as spiritual ministers, held them to be 'an example worthy of imitation' (*Squanders*, II, p. 307). He believed the Government and Ascendancy were corrupt but supported the Union and opposed the return of a separate Irish Parliament.

There are striking similarities between Carleton and Edgeworth, and while Carleton knew more about cabin life and dealt more directly with the religious conflict, it is still Edgeworth's agenda that dominates his novels. Even though Edgeworth's name is conspicuously absent – possibly because of vanity – from Carleton's personal canon of Irish literature, her influence upon him was immense. Both were Protestants who supported the Union, opposed absenteeism and secret societies, sympathised with tenants' aspirations and believed in education. They certainly admired each other's works. Edgeworth readily agreed to help when asked to support a memorial for Carleton:

> I feel gratified, so much desiring to have our name and my testimony under my own hand, while yet I live, of my admiration of his talents and my esteem for his works, which gave with such masterly strokes and in such strong and vivid colours the pictures of our country's manners, her virtues, and her vices, without ministering to party prejudices or exciting dangerous passions, to produce authorship effect or to win temporary applause.[41]

Edgeworth's reference to Carleton's lack of 'party prejudices' is, however, puzzling in the light of 'Wildgoose Lodge,' *Rody the Rover* and *Valentine M'Clutchy* are considered. This, of course, returns us to the crux of the matter: was Carleton a true independent or was he nothing more than a literary hack – a pen for hire? The answer is probably that he was a bit of both. He certainly liked to think of himself as an independent, a literary

---

[40] Patrick Rafroidi, *Irish Literature in English* (Gerrards Cross: Colin Smythe, 1980), I, p. 129.
[41] O'Donoghue, II, p. 108.

explorer, but needed money to survive. Bearing in mind his satirizing of Edgeworth's agenda, his ambition to join the literary establishment may explain his effusive reaction to Edgeworth's letter, as recounted by O'Donoghue. This clearly reveals deep admiration:

> I never saw so strong an impression of gratified feeling in my life in anyone as he [...] evinced on my reading him [Edgeworth's] letter. He really could not find words to convey his emotions, and at last declared that he was sufficiently repaid for all the trials and troubles which had made him an author.[42]

Flanagan claims that *Valentine M'Clutchy* is a re-working of *Castle Rackrent*, but it is arguably more visibly a satirical re-working of *The Absentee*. Carleton seeks to show how Edgeworth's ideas would not have worked because of institutional corruption, religious antagonism and human nature. Unlike Edgeworth in *The Absentee*, Carleton does not fully believe in the credibility of happy endings. M'Clutchy's murder, Cumber's death in a duel and the enlightened Topertoe's inheritance all happen at speed and with little explanation.

Carleton felt Edgeworth's blueprint was untenable. He satirizes her novel but provides no realistic solution of his own. All he can suggest is the desperate idea of turning all tenants into Ulster Protestants. The only possible way that such a hopeless dream could be fulfilled would be through the Government – hence his support for the Union, his rejection of Repeal and his objection to an Irish Parliament. Essentially, he comes round to Edgeworth's way of thinking and embraces the landowners.

It is hard to make sense of Carleton, and O'Donoghue's portrayal of him has only served to make matters more complex. It is tempting to agree with men like Carter Hall who saw Carleton as a mere opportunist, but that would be unfair.

Perhaps Carleton was truly a man of principle and, in his own fashion, there may have been an underlying consistency about him. It was not illogical for a man to denounce oppression in all its forms – Orangeism, Ribbonism, the spiritual tyranny of the Catholic Church or the material oppression of landowners and middlemen. But if Carleton was against all these things, then what was he for?

---

[42] O'Donoghue, II, p. 111.

In his early works, Carleton's anti-Catholicism is evident in his extreme attacks on the Church. However, he also supports the tenantry from which he sprang. His works of the 1840s sometime appear to confirm the nationalists' claim that he was one of them: he attacks Ribbonism, Orangeism, landownership, the Ascendancy and the Government. Yet he is still a Protestant. The tenants' champion ultimately emerges as a moderate without a solution. If he supported the nationalists unconditionally, he would be supporting an independent Ireland in which the power of the Catholic Church, the embodiment of the slavery of superstition, would be hugely increased. If he gave unconditional support to Protestantism, he would be advancing the cause of the landowners, the peasants' other major oppressors. For Carleton, there was really no way out and his Ireland died with him, as Pádraig G Lane notes:

> The teeming world of the mud-cabins of William Carleton's pre-Famine Ireland, full of want and misery described by such writers as Lady Morgan, the Banim brothers and the Halls, withered away under the pressure of a market-driven economy.[43]

Lane's conclusion is echoed by Joep Leerssen who states, 'the feeling in post-Famine Ireland was that Carleton's peasantry, with its lore and pastimes, had been swept out of existence'.[44]

Carleton's own estimate of his literary worth may be conceited but it is not inaccurate; he was one of the best of the agrarian novelists, probably the most significant after Edgeworth. Yet he failed to exploit his advantage of a deep and abiding knowledge of and empathy with Catholic tenants to the full. His own desire for personal advancement coupled with the enduring problem – faced by all agrarian novelists – of trying to include too much in their novels, prevented him from writing the great Irish agrarian novel.

More specifically, he was unable to reconcile his religious and nationalist allegiances – hence his ultimate confusion about the Land Question. As we have seen, the Banims and Griffin believed that the only way forward was to placate the tenants – mainly because they feared the tenants. Carleton's situation was even worse for he both loved and feared

---

[43] Pádraig G Lane, 'Agricultural Labourers and the Land Question', in *Famine, Land and Culture in Ireland*, ed. by Carla King (Dublin: University College Dublin Press, 2000), p. 101.
[44] Joep Leerssen, *Remembrance and Imagination* (Cork: Cork University Press, 1996), p. 106.

the tenants but also hated the Catholic Church, the ultimate embodiment of Irish identity. It is hardly surprising that he could find no way forward.

Edgeworth, Griffin, the Banims and Carleton all abandoned the Irish agrarian novel well before they died. Edgeworth turned to writing social novels set in England, Griffin burnt his manuscripts and joined the Christian Brothers, the Banims wrote about Eastbourne, while Carleton switched to money-spinning romantic melodramas, often with 'Black' in the title, perhaps to remind people of his earlier works. So, why did they all give up?

Edgeworth, the most perceptive of the agrarian novelists in the first half of the nineteenth century, came to realise that her solutions no longer made sense in a changing and increasingly violent Ireland. It is striking, however, that although she knew about agrarian violence, Edgeworth says virtually nothing about it. She probably realised that any realistic portrayal of Ireland would have to include agrarian violence – yet such an inclusion would only damage her case that bad landowners, rather than bad tenants, bore the prime responsibility for Ireland's problems. It is ironic that the main contribution of Edgeworth's successors – Griffin, the Banims and Carleton – should have been the introduction of increasingly graphic accounts of the very agrarian violence that Edgeworth herself, supposedly the representative of Ascendancy values, hesitated to portray. It is ironic because the inclusion of agrarian violence weakened the tenants' case, so dear to later nationalist commentators, in the minds of readers. To take the irony further, Edgeworth really offers more comfort to the nationalist cause because she chooses not to portray the tenants' violence. If tenants are portrayed as violent, they become unattractive to readers, especially to English readers. There is always the underlying suspicion that, even if institutional violence is removed, the tenants will still be as bad as ever. The only way to explain the tenants' violence is to exaggerate institutional violence and that is exactly what Griffin, the Banims and Carleton do. Inevitably, the result is that Ascendancy landowners and the tenants seem to deserve each other. In short, while Griffin, the Banims and Carleton are searching for solutions, what they actually describe is an endless circle of violence – Ixion's 'wheel of torture'.

One of the key problems with the agrarian novelists is that they doubt whether their own class can solve Ireland's problems; they all lack confidence. A confident conservative writer would believe that aristocrats and landowners could save society – the message of Benjamin Disraeli's *Coningsby* (1844) and *Sybil* (1845). Edgeworth may have been a member of the aristocratic/landowning class but she knew too much about their faults to be really confident about their potential. A confident liberal would have confidence in the people – although with appropriate middle class leadership. There are hints of this in Dickens and in the early *Punch* fraternity. Griffin and the Banims belonged to the middle class but lacked real confidence in either the middle classes or the people. A confident Marxist would have confidence in the industrial proletariat. There were, however, hardly any industrial proletarians in Ireland to have confidence in and, anyway, most of this small minority were Ulster Protestants. Only one other possibility remains. The confident anarchist – and some Fascists of the *Blud und Boden* sort – would have confidence in the peasants/tenants. Perhaps the problem would resolve itself when a true peasant writer, like Carleton, appeared. Finally, we might encounter someone who had confidence in his own class. However, if a peasant writer did not have confidence in his own class – surely the 'soul of Ireland' – then the long search for a solution would have failed and Edgeworth's agenda would be totally exhausted.

In the progression – or perhaps regression – from Edgeworth to Griffin and the Banims, we observe a number of common features. The links between all four authors are surely strong enough to dispose of any suggestion that they belong in different camps. All are concerned with the same issues and all attempt to identify a solution based on their own class. All fail, and, indeed, the failure becomes more complete as the progression unfolds. Edgeworth probably comes closest to success. Her solution is more clearly articulated than anything proposed by her successors. She has some confidence in the capacity of her own class to mend its ways and some confidence that the tenants could do the same. Nevertheless, her confidence is qualified – hence the increasing pessimism of her later Irish novels. Griffin and the Banims are less confident still about landowners, tenants or indeed their own middle class. The basic difficulty with Edgeworth, and even more with Griffin and the Banims, is that all are honest enough to admit that their own class, at least in its present form, is as much part of the problem as the potential solution to it. Griffin's and the Banims' solutions are vaguer and more elusive than Edgeworth's and this may be because they are even less confident than she is.

Although Edgeworth, Griffin and the Banims all admit that their own class may be part of the problem, they are too bound up with that class to take the next step and acknowledge that it is *the* problem, not just part of it. The tenants themselves present an even bigger difficulty. Edgeworth, Griffin and the Banims are not tenants and, crucially, they know enough of agrarian violence, however excusable, to fear them. They can never fully endorse a solution based solely on the tenantry. We are bound to conclude, therefore, that for all their Catholicism, Griffin and the Banims can offer little more than a bourgeois imitation of Edgeworth's gentrified solution – with all its problems and only some of its merits. If the agrarian novel were to escape this impasse, a radically different approach would be needed.

So, was Carleton the saviour of the agrarian novel as some critics suggest? Carleton wrote:

> I found them [Irish tenants] a class unknown in literature, unknown by their own landlords, and unknown by those in whose hands much of their destiny was placed. If I became the historian of their habits and manners, their feelings, their prejudices, their superstitions, and their crimes; [...] it was because I saw no other person willing to undertake a task.[1]

The aim may be laudable but it should be noted that Carleton never suggests that he intends to write from the tenants' own point of view, or that he is one of them. The passage reveals a curious sense of detachment. A man who felt he belonged to the peasantry himself would hardly need to have 'found' them. Nor is there any reason why an 'historian' should necessarily identify with his subjects; indeed the references to 'prejudices', 'superstitions' and even more to 'crimes' suggests a definite element of hostility. So, Carleton is quite as detached from the peasants as any of his predecessors. He does not escape from the hole they have dug; rather he

---

[1] David J O'Donoghue, *The Life of William Carleton &c* (London: Downey & Co, 1896), II, p. 361.

deepens it further. Thus, Carleton remains in the same category as Edgeworth, Griffin and the Banims.

To describe Carleton as the 'Peasant Novelist' would be a contradiction in terms. The former tenant was a tenant no more and hence could fear them as much as any landowner or trader; however sympathetic. His attitude was bound to be ambiguous; with part of his mind, he might well despise tenants – after all, he had risen in the world and they had not. If Carleton was such a man – as he probably was – he would be even worse placed to find a tenant solution than Edgeworth had been to find a landowners' solution or Griffin and the Banims to find a middle class one. The difference is that Edgeworth might have found a landowners' solution and Griffin and the Banims might have found a middle class solution but Carleton could never have found a tenant solution. The prospects of progression do not improve with Carleton; they become bleaker than ever. Carleton could not find a tenant solution because he was not a tenant but if he had remained one, he could not have written at all. Since he was a writer, Carleton remained firmly locked in the fatal embrace of Edgeworth.

It is clear that the nationalist idea of progression within the Irish agrarian novel – from Edgeworth through Griffin and the Banims to Carleton – depends on a belief in a clear trend towards their own position. But they can only substantiate this belief by interpreting literary texts in a way that strains the reader's credibility. In short, nationalist readings tend to ignore what the agrarian novelists actually say in favour of what the commentator expects someone of a particular background to say. This approach has obvious flaws and may have even led the critics to concentrate on the wrong writers. They focus on Griffin, the Banims and Carleton, but say relatively little about Edgeworth.

Of course, it is hardly surprising that nationalist commentators probably supposed that Edgeworth – pro-Union, a Protestant and a member of the Ascendancy – would offer little to assist their cause. Yet it is interesting to speculate about what a nationalist interpretation of Edgeworth would look like. It might not be entirely convincing but it would probably be more convincing than the nationalist interpretations of Griffin, the Banims and Carleton. After all, Edgeworth accepts that Ireland can never be entirely like England and concludes that there is such a thing as a distinctly Irish identity. She is quite sympathetic to Catholicism – certainly more so than Carleton. She places the blame for Ireland's troubles squarely on the landowners and their supporters. She describes institutional violence but, unlike her successors, makes little mention of potentially damaging agrarian violence. In fact, Edgeworth actually presents quite an attractive possibility for a nationalist re-interpretation – but the opportunity was never grasped.

The notion of a distinct Irish identity – hinted at by Edgeworth and her successors – obviously involves an essentialism likely to be regarded with suspicion by modern cultural critics of all persuasions. Yet the Catholic tenant must surely be at the heart of any delineation or statement of an Irish *volksgeist*. One way of approaching the story of the agrarian novel is to see it as a journey to this goal. Edgeworth cannot really articulate the essence of 'Irishness' because she is neither a Catholic nor a tenant. Things improve with Griffin and the Banims who, at least, are Catholics but still not tenants. The next step in the supposed evolutionary chain is a writer who is both a Catholic and a tenant. He simply has to be both. Voltaire once said that if God did not exist, it would be necessary to invent him. Perhaps the same is true of the nationalist analysis of the agrarian novel. Without such a figure, the case would fall apart; and there is really only one candidate – Carleton. There was the slight difficulty in that Carleton was actually a middle class Protestant, but the nationalists had no choice – they had to present Carleton as a Catholic tenant, come what may. We may admire some critics' ingenuity while deploring their disregard for the truth. If we are right, there is no progression – it is more like regression or mere circularity. With Carleton, we are really back to Edgeworth again – an agrarian writer with some sympathy for the tenants but who is neither a tenant nor a Catholic.

What we must now consider is whether a political journalist, Charles Kickham, could offer the change that the imaginative novelists had so far failed to provide.

Part Two:
Beyond Ireland

When considering the chronological development of the agrarian novel, there is a substantial hiatus between the end of the Famine and the appearance of the next significant agrarian novels in the late 1860s. This requires some explanation.

Ireland experienced several famines prior to the Great Famine of 1845. Although it is possible to say when the Famine began, it is harder to determine when it and its effects ceased – if indeed they ever ceased. During the key Famine years of 1845-1849, the combination of starvation, disease (Typhus, relapsing fever, scurvy, marasmus, kwashiorkor and xerophtlamia), resulted in the loss of two million people, over one fifth of the population. Since the Irish economy was overwhelmingly a rural economy, dependent on tenants to work the land and on the survival of associated village communities, this was immensely destructive. Yet, as Christine Kinealy comments: 'Although 1851 marked the disappearance of blight, the effects of Famine continued to be felt'.[1]

The hiatus in literature may be due to the fact that Ireland had been so traumatised by the events of the Famine that any contemporary fictional representation of it would have seemed distasteful. Although, as we have seen, William Carleton tried to portray the devastation of the Famine first in *The Black Prophet* in 1847, and in *The Squanders of Castle Squander* of 1852, he failed, perhaps understandably, either to foresee or depict its possible long-term effects. After Carleton, no writer was to use the Famine as a setting or backdrop to a work of fiction until 1860, when Anthony Trollope published *Castle Richmond*. Thomas Flanagan argues:

[T]he development of the Irish novel had been cut short by the despair and silence which fell upon Ireland in the wake of the

---

[1] Christine Kinealy, *A Death-Dealing Famine* (London: Pluto Press, 1997), p. 151.

Famine. The decades which followed, years which are among the dreariest in Irish history, afforded barren soil for any kind of intellectual or political life.[2]

In other words, Irish writers, like politicians, were emotionally numb. The energy so evident in the fight for Catholic Emancipation and in the Tithe War had evaporated. Politics – and especially fiction – had to take second place to survival and re-building. In fact, economic revival did occur, especially in the 1850s, leading contemporary writers, like John M'Aleer, to assert: 'The growth and development of the prosperity of Ireland in the last eight or nine years have attracted much attention'.[3] Thus a combination of emotional paralysis and gradual economic growth may explain the lack of agrarian novels between Carleton's *The Squanders* and Charles Kickham's *Sally Cavanagh* (1869). In short, the people were too pre-occupied with re-building their lives to be sufficiently interested or motivated to pursue political change or agrarian violence.

As we shall see, Kickham's novels and those of honorary Irishman, Anthony Trollope, are very different to those of the pre-Famine years. Early agrarian novelists had struggled with the Irish Land Question and all had sought, however unsuccessfully, to find an Irish or at least Anglo-Irish solution. The key change in the novels of Kickham and Trollope is the central roles now taken by America and England. The focus shifts radically: urban-centred, American-inspired, Fenianism dominates Kickham's novels, ideas and solutions. However, where Kickham still regards the English and their Anglo-Irish landowner instruments as the problem – more extreme but not really so different from Griffin, the Banims and Carleton – Trollope introduces a dramatic change of direction. In Trollope, everything is the reverse of what it had been – Ireland has gone mad. Now it is the Protestant minority who are persecuted and murdered by their Catholic tenants. Politics are in the hands of Charles Stewart Parnell and the Land League. No-one listens to the voices of liberal-minded moderates; worse still, hunting has been disrupted.

---

[2] Thomas Flanagan, *The Irish Novelists* (New York: Columbia University Press, 1959), p. ix.

[3] John M'Aleer, *The Social Condition of the Population of Ireland &c.* (Dublin: Alex. Thom & Sons, 1860), p. iii.

Both Kickham and Trollope glimpse solutions to the Irish Land Question. Unlike their predecessors, their solutions are essentially foreign; but would salvation come from the West or from the East?

Chapter 5:
Charles Kickham – The Problems of Purity

As we approach the shores of the republic – when I think that in a few hours I shall stand, for the first time in my life, upon free soil – my pulse begins to beat quick [...]. This young giant, with hot blood in his veins, is an object more worthy of reverence, more provocative of high and holy aspirations, than all the crumbling relics of nations that have withered, put together [...] Magnificent Democracy! I kiss the hem of your garment. Bunker Hill! I worship you.[1]

From Moderation to Extremism

A basic tenet of nationalism holds that, while a people may receive just assistance from outside, in the last resort, they must find salvation and freedom from their own resources. Ultimately, Irish nationalists came to this conclusion too – hence 'Sinn Fein', 'ourselves alone'. At first sight, it is tempting to suppose that Charles Kickham's republic with its 'Magnificent Democracy', alludes to a future Ireland. In fact, it is an existing republic, the United States of America; any misunderstanding is removed by the reference to Bunker Hill. The passage suggests that Kickham saw America, rather than Ireland itself, as the solution to Ireland's problems. If America is Kickham's 'young giant', Ireland is no more than one of 'the crumbling relics of nations'. Later commentators have stressed that the purpose of *Knocknagow* (1879), Kickham's most significant and popular novel, seeks to identify 'some effectual measures of alleviation of the evils of which he wrote'.[2] Yet these 'measures of alleviation' depended heavily, if not solely, on America.

---

[1] Quoted in R V Comerford, *Charles J. Kickham* (Portmarnock: Wolfhound Press, 1979), pp. 62-3 (original source not identified).
[2] James J Healy, *Life and Times of Charles J. Kickham* (Dublin: James Duffy and Co. Ltd., 1915), p. 118.

At first glance, Charles J Kickham appears to fulfil all the requirements for an ideal nationalist writer. The nephew of John O'Mahony, one of the founders of Fenianism in America, Kickham has been seen as a patriot, a Fenian thinker and a political martyr, imprisoned by the British. His conviction for 'treason felony', affected his health (he had to be released after serving only four years of a fourteen year sentence) and coloured his attitude towards the English and their Parliament. Nationalist readings stress the alleged injustice of his trial: '[t]he trial proceeded – as all such trials did – on the jury-packing system'.[3] Others note that 'Kickham withdrew his counsel, and refused to make any further defence, convinced [...] that his conviction had already been decided upon'.[4] Thus Kickham emerges as a man of suffering whose personal experience is reflected in his art, his poetry and his three novels: *Sally Cavanagh* (1869), *Knocknagow* and *For the Old Land* (1886).[5]

Estimates of Kickham's literary achievements, however, are more varied. While describing Carleton as 'the great novelist of Ireland',[6] W B Yeats claims that only 'one man alone stands near him [...] – Charles Kickham, of Tipperary'.[7] J J Healy, an early biographer, insists that Kickham had a genius that 'was something akin to that of Dickens' and 'as a novelist he far outrivals Griffin and Banim, and was beyond doubt the greatest novelist Ireland has given birth to'. Healy dismisses 'Carleton's caricatures' and 'Lever's astute dog-boys'[8] as failing to depict Irishmen truly. He even compares Kickham to Shakespeare claiming that 'what Garrick said of Shakespeare might also be said of Kickham, namely that "he dipped his own pen in his own heart"'.[9] Healy's praise of Kickham is echoed by Sir Charles Gavan Duffy who ranked him 'next after Carleton, Griffin and Banim, and far before Lever and Lady Morgan as a painter of Irish manners'.[10] For another early biographer, Kickham provides 'the best pen pictures of Irish peasant life after the Famine ever written, and they serve to make the book [*Knocknagow*] [...] an immortal

[3] Healy, p. 25.
[4] William Murphy, *Charles J. Kickham* (Blackrock: Carraig Books, 1976), p. 4.
[5] Kickham died in 1882 with *For the Old Land* incomplete. It was left to the radical MP William O'Brien (1852-1928) to finish the novel.
[6] W B Yeats, *Stories from Carleton* (London: The Walter Scott Publishing Co. Ltd., n.d.), p. xvi.
[7] Yeats, p. xvii.
[8] Healy, pp. 61-68.
[9] Healy, p. 144, note for p. 89.
[10] R J Kelly, *Charles Joseph Kickham* (Dublin: James Duffy and Co. Ltd., 1914), p. 10.

work, which every Irish man and woman should read and treasure'.[11] Benedict Kiely compares Kickham to Henry James and insists that he represents the essence of Irishness:

> Any consideration of Kickham as a writer must inevitably be influenced by his nobility as a man and by the fact, too, that he is a national piety. But he who is still, I should hope and trust, so close to the heart of his people, observed and understood them with all the exactitude and intensity of the ideal Jamesian novelist, on whom nothing is lost.[12]

When the *Irish Fireside* conducted a survey to discover "the hundred best Irish books", it transpired that 'either *Sally Cavanagh* or *Knocknagow* was to be found near the top of almost every list submitted'.[13]

Yet even a nationalist interpretation reveals doubts. While the reservations seem mainly literary, there are hints of more profound concerns – although there is an obvious reluctance to articulate them clearly. Yeats concedes that Kickham's 'books are put together in a haphazard kind of way – without beginning, middle, or end'.[14] Daniel Corkery regards Kickham's writing as 'only good in parts, and not great anywhere'.[15] Kiely concludes: '[s]ophistication, particularly literary sophistication, was, to put it mildly, no part of his make up'[16] and admits '*Knocknagow* may not be the greatest novel of the Irish nineteenth-century nor the novel of that period that has most relevance to our own times'.[17] Even R V Comerford questions Kickham's literary merits:

> *Knocknagow* [...] is a poorly organised work, though not markedly worse in this respect than many other books composed originally as serials. It has several sub-plots but they are handled (or neglected) so badly that in the last few chapters a gigantic effort has to be made to tie up loose ends.

---

[11] Kelly, p. 55.

[12] Benedict Kiely, *A Raid Dark Corners* (Cork: Cork University Press, 1999), p. 111.

[13] Comerford, p. 297.

[14] Dr. W. B. Yeats, 'Charles Kickham: An Appreciation', in Charles Kickham, *The Valley Near Slievenamon*, ed. James Maher (no publication details, 1941), p. vii.

[15] Daniel Corkery, *Synge and Anglo-Irish Literature* (Cork: The Mercier Press, 1966), pp. 25.

[16] Kiely, p. 108.

[17] Kiely, p. 115.

For an alleged arch-nationalist, it is curious that Kickham seems to depend so heavily on English literary influences. Comerford does acknowledge that Kickham drew heavily on 'The Deserted Village' (1770) – by his fellow Irishman Oliver Goldsmith – not merely as a general theme but almost to the extent of plagiarism in his descriptions of the lost rural way of life. According to Comerford, both authors had the same purpose – to evoke a sense of loss. However, Comerford also identifies the influence of Dickens ('Kickham's favourite author'[18]) but hardly to Kickham's advantage, speaking of his 'disastrous imitation of Little Nell in *The Old Curiosity Shop*'. Comerford also suggests the influence of George Eliot's *Adam Bede* (1859) 'whose rural English midlands settings are much closer to Kickham's world than is Dickens's predominantly urban landscape'.[19] It seems that Comerford, at least, doubts Kickham's originality and even his competence as a writer.

In one important respect, Kickham reminds us more of Edgeworth than of the agrarian writers who came between them. Like Edgeworth, he appears to provide a solution. Whereas, seventy years earlier, Edgeworth's solution had been essentially Unionist, Kickham's solution was essentially nationalist. But does Kickham's nationalism represent the triumphant conclusion of a progression leading from Edgeworth's impressive but ultimately anti-Irish analysis of Edgeworth, through the well-intentioned but muddled searching of the Banims, Griffin and Carleton, to the clear realisation that Ireland must have a state of its own? This is the preferred interpretation of most critics. An alternative reading is to argue that it is not progression that we find but another example of the terrible circularity that dogged Irish agrarian fiction for so long.

Kickham was a Fenian, nationalist, writer and politician – yet ultimately, as this chapter will show, an isolated and contradictory anomaly. He looked around him in Ireland and saw little hope for the future. He looked across the Irish Sea and saw Ireland's nemesis but looked across the Atlantic and saw her salvation. He idolised the democratic giant, the republic of the United States, yet advocated a hierarchical Ireland. Though an Irish nationalist, Kickham had no faith in the Irish people. He believed that help had come from overseas – hence his involvement in Fenianism, more of an Irish-American movement than a purely Irish one. He implies that the only way to revivify Ireland was to give it a transfusion of the 'hot blood' from America. This image is

---

[18] Comerford, pp. 197-200..
[19] Comerford, p. 201.

curiously anticipatory of Bram Stoker's *Dracula* (1897), and to pursue the image further, it is Ireland that will receive the blood and America that will lose it. In other words, Ireland prefigures Count Dracula himself, not his victims.

For all her Unionism, Edgeworth had at least sought for a solution inside Ireland and the same is true of the Banims, Griffin, and Carleton. Kickham's focus upon an external solution suggests that he had a fairly low opinion of the Irish. An external solution is in itself a tacit admission of this – and, as we shall see – Kickham is not even sure that an external solution can be found. Irish agrarian fiction abounds in paradox; this, the most nationalist of the Irish agrarian writers, is actually the most anti-Irish, certainly more so than Edgeworth or any of her successors to date. Kickham's only rival in this respect is Anthony Trollope. Total opposites though they might seem, the two had much in common, not least in an extremism so different to the tradition of moderation and reconciliation, exhausted by the authors explored so far in this book.

With Kickham, the Irish agrarian agenda emigrates to the United States. Kickham's novels may be set in Ireland but America is a powerful, even dominant presence in his underlying analysis. Curiously, the agrarian novels echo major developments in Irish history. Edgeworth wrote about the Union and its aftermath from an Ascendancy perspective, the Banims and Griffin wrote about the effects of the Union, O'Connell and the struggle for Emancipation from a Catholic perspective and Carleton wrote about famines and their effects. Now, the metaphorical emigration of the agrarian novel correlates with the real mass emigration of the Irish to America.

In the past, there were four major elements in the story – landowners and tenants, England and Ireland. Now, there are five – landowners and tenants, England, Ireland and America. The extra dimension dramatically increases the number of possible permutations and plots. The agenda had been relatively simple and straightforward – though still complicated enough to give rise to serious misunderstandings about what the authors were really saying. Now things become more difficult and intellectually challenging. The crucial thing is that the introduction of America into the equation becomes the driving force behind the complete polarisation of positions. The Land Question becomes almost secondary and we face a clash of civilizations in which Ireland herself is a marginal player. For Kickham, the battle is really America versus England; but would this give Edgeworth's agenda a new lease of life?

163

1798-1848 – Unity and Disunity

For Kickham, 1798 represented the 'golden age' of Ireland's heroic history and its inspiration for the future. The Wolfe Tone rising, of course, failed, many hundreds of Irishmen died and the English then imposed an unequal Union. Nevertheless Kickham was attracted by the ideological purity of many of those involved. The United Irishmen had been genuinely and rarely united, indicating that a man could be Irish first and a Catholic or Protestant second. In short, 1798 provided Kickham with a vision of a common Irish identity, the last time that Irishmen united against the common enemy: England. The Act of Union, almost by definition, exacerbated division between Irish Catholics and Anglo-Irish Protestants. For Kickham, however, heroic failure was probably more important than a success sullied by compromise.

While he was growing up, Kickham's 'mother had emotive stories to tell of the sufferings of rebels and their families in 1798'.[20] He probably drew on these stories for his early poems such as 'Rory of the Hills', 'The Rebel Myles O'Hea; or, Eighty Years Ago', 'Carraig-Mocleara' and 'The Shan Van Vocht'. The last also refers to America, 'a land where all are free':

> And now, if ye be men,
> Says the Shan Van Vocht,
> We'll have them back again,
> Says the Shan Van Vocht,
> With pikes and guns galore;
> And when they touch her shore,
> Ireland's free for evermore,
> Says the Shan Van Vocht.[21]

In other words, it will be American 'pikes and guns' that will liberate Hibernia.

In his novels, especially *Knocknagow*, Kickham consistently links events back to the 'golden age' of 1798, as Comerford suggests:

---

[20] Comerford., p. 18.
[21] William Murphy, 'Poems of Charles Kickham', in *Charles J. Kickham*, (Blackrock: Carraig Books, 1976), pp.8-29.

Here a society pre-occupied with the ownership of land could presume to see an explanation of its own origins in a struggle against the vicissitudes of insecurity of tenure. Most important of all, here, painted in touching and memorable fashion, were all the virtues that this society prized, the emotions that it felt, and the values that it exalted.[22]

Kickham, however, also saw 1798 as the embodiment of English repression:

[P]oor Mrs. Donovan got that sad face of hers one bright summer day in the year '98, when her father's house was surrounded by soldiers and yeoman, and her only brother, a bright-eyed boy of seventeen, was torn from the arms of his mother, and shot dead outside the door. And then the gallant officer twisted his hand in the boy's golden hair, and invited them all to observe how, with one blow of his trusty sword, he would sever the rebel head from the rebel carcase [sic].[23]

Few agrarian novels depict a more gruesome scene, but Kickham emphasises that he is recounting an act that had occurred nearly a century earlier. Had things changed? Although the English may now appear more civilised, they remain capable of acts of incredible barbarity.

Knocknagow reveals a view of bygone Ireland that appealed to the romantic Fenian in Kickham. 1798 had been a noble, heroic struggle in which Catholic and Protestant Irishmen combined to 'drive the invader out of Ireland' (*Knocknagow*, p. 225). Morris, who 'received a 'shattered [...] knee in '98' (*Knocknagow*, p. 221), agrees with his fellow tenants' view that '[s]ecurity is the only thing to give a man courage' (*Knocknagow*, p. 220). Despite the local priest's condemnation of agrarian violence, Morris believes that, in a land where there is no justice for tenants, it is the only way to prevent eviction:

'I have my old pike yet – an' maybe I'd *want* id yet!' he exclaimed, with a look of defiance at the priest. 'An' the man that'd come to

---

[22] Comerford, p. 297.

[23] Charles J Kickham, *Knocknagow* (1879) (Dublin: M H Gill and Son Ltd., 1962), p. 368. Further references to this edition are given after quotations in the text.

turn *me* out on the road, as I see others turned out on the road, I'd give him the length uv id, as sure as God made Moses'. (*Knocknagow*, pp. 220-1)

This outburst is revealing. Kickham, no lover of the Catholic Church as an institution, clearly disapproves of the Church's stance on agrarian violence. He retained a romantic belief in the Irish people – faithful Christians, rather than subservient Catholics, willing to defend themselves and their neighbours against an unjust authority made up of the Catholic Church and the English State.

1798 was not however an isolated example of English brutality. If England murdered directly in 1798, they murdered indirectly, on a much larger scale, during the Great Famine. Thus Kickham emphasises England's terrible guilt in the 1840s:

And England – whose duty it was not to allow a single man, woman or child to die of hunger – when this glorious Republic offered to send food to the starving Irish if England would send her idle war-ships to carry it – England refused, and let the people starve, and now shouts in triumph that the Celts are gone with a vengeance. (*Knocknagow*, p. 584)

The Famine was nothing short of mass murder and Kickham 'burned for a conflict with the people's murderers'.[24] He perceived the Famine in personal terms and the experience confirmed his belief in an English conspiracy against the Irish. The belief that England, especially the Government, ignored the problems of the Irish remained with him throughout his life. Even when the British were fighting in other parts of the Empire, Healy attests that the poem, 'Patrick Sheehan' (1857), should warn the Irish of 'our enemy' England's ingratitude:

Kickham's idea was to give a vivid picture of England's gratitude for Irish valour when fighting her accursed battles against the manhood of Russia and India. Oh, how he would lash her if he was alive during the Boer War, when the brave Boers nobly fought the robber.[25]

---

[24] Healy, p. 16.
[25] Healy, p. 72.

In fact, Healy reveals more about himself than about his subject. A biographer who implicitly perceives the English as the 'enemy', can hardly be trusted to present a balanced interpretation of Kickham and his works. More significantly however, Kickham's interpretation is not accurate; during The Famine, some aid was sent both by the Government and by private charities. One such was the Quaker organisation in whose relief work W E Forster was involved in 1846, and the evidence points to considerable humantarian effort.

Kickham continued to blame the English for Ireland's ills – including the Famine. Even if the English had not created it, they took advantage of the situation by refusing proffered American aid. Kickham's hatred of the English never mellows – Healy's sympathies are also revealed:

> The political opinions he held when he was a suspected youth in the famine year, and the opinions he held when he stood in the dock in Green Street, Dublin (17 years later), he held until his dying day. His opinions never changed. He was ever a rebel to English rule in Ireland – and what *Irishman* is not? [26]

Whether or not the Irish were in despair, Kickham's despair at the lack of a current, pure, patriotic feeling must explain why he has to resort to America as Ireland's saviour. In other words, there was a crucial difference between 1798 and the Famine. In 1798, the Irish had been truly heroic but where was that heroism now? Although empathising with the tenants' plight and viewing himself as the 'People's Champion', Kickham deplored their apathy. Such apathy may have been understandable but it was hardly admirable. Kickham's argument – *pace* Healy – that '[d]espair and hunger' had destroyed rather than reinforced Irish patriotism would have dismayed a real nationalist who would have insisted that patriotism could be reawakened, without foreign intervention.

The Land Question

Kickham invariably refers to the English and the Celts rather than the British and the Irish, revealing a romanticised view of the conflict, one perceived in terms of a clash of ancient races rather than actual or potential nation states. But when he refers to the English, is he implying

---

[26] Healy, p. 18.

that they were exclusively to blame for The Famine? If he is talking about the English in Ireland – the landowners – then he undermines his argument for the inclusiveness of all Irish under one banner. His concentration on the English may be simply a means to further his own inclusive Irish agenda. This would appear to be yet another example of his confused and unrealistic argument, as Terry Eagleton notes:

> Charles Kickham [...] did not consider landlordism as an evil in itself, denounced the Land League as communistic, and like some of the Young Irelanders looked for support to a paternalist upper class. His anxieties about the Land League, a movement that betrayed the labourers and small tenants to the interests of the graziers and strong farmers, were farcically unfounded.[27]

Kickham was an Irish revolutionary who supported an independent Ireland but one tied to America. He wanted a republic but also wanted to retain a hierarchy that would return some land to the Irish yet keep landownership while cutting the 'graziers and strong farmers' down to size.

The flawed construction of Kickham's novels may result from the inclusion of too many themes – including the Land Question, which, itself, is more than a single problem with a single solution. In *Sally Cavanagh*, 'that shapeless novel', Kickham stresses that the law is the main tool of institutional violence. Without a lease or security, the Purcells are at the mercy of Oliver Grindem (the landowner). He is entitled to raise the rent as Purcell has improved the property. If the tenant cannot pay then the landowner will get a new tenant who, like the aptly named Grindem, will benefit from all Purcell's improvements but pay a substantially higher rent. Equally, in *Knocknagow*, Mick Brien, formerly a prosperous tenant, appears as 'blood gushed from' his mouth 'and flowed down the breast of his shirt' (*Knocknagow*, p. 255), when he is evicted, his home levelled and his world destroyed:

> Billy Heffernan looked around him, and felt the cold breeze as it whistled through the uncovered roof, and saw the once rosy farmer's wife crouching in a corner with a sick child pressed against her bosom. (*Knocknagow*, p. 256)

---

[27] Terry Eagleton, *Heathcliff and the Great Hunger* (London; Verso, 1995), p. 290.

Kickham's sentimentalized view of rural tenants is to the fore but lacks the immediacy of Carleton's descriptions. Although Kickham provides sufficient details, the scene is not contextualized. Unlike Carleton, Kickham does not provide much breadth of analysis; readers are encouraged to feel unconditional sympathy for the Briens, without explanation of the reasons behind the eviction. The emphasis is on the tenants' lack of security in their land-holdings. This point is underscored by the introduction of the narrator's voice (concerning another tenant), a technique considered manipulative and crude by exponents of subtler forms of social realism:

> [T]hough we cannot help sharing Phil Lahy's contempt for Tom Hogan's slavishness, we heartily wish he had a more secure hold of that little farm in which 'his heart was stuck' than the word of a gentleman who went on raising the rent as fast as Tom Hogan went on with his draining, and fencing, and liming, and manuring – to say nothing of the new slated barn and cow-house. (*Knocknagow*, p. 268)

Hogan is a good tenant who suffers dreadfully from institutional violence. He works hard to improve his farm but, since the law is on the landowner's side, every improvement he makes – at his own expense – only provides an excuse to raise his rent. Hogan's improvements do not secure his tenure; ironically, by making his farm more valuable, his own position becomes more precarious. Kickham explains:

> [I]t must be remembered, they [Irish tenants] were conceived and born under a notice-to-quit; it took the light out of their mother's smile, and ploughed furrows in their father's face while he was yet young; it nipped the budding pleasures of childhood as a frost will nip the spring flowers, and youth's and manhood's joys withered under its shadow; it taught them to cringe, and fawn, and lie. (*Knocknagow*, p. 294)

The full force of Kickham's argument against the unjust legal system is revealed when, in *Sally Cavanagh*, Father O'Gorman observes that he fears 'the people will continue to fly from a land where […] the laws are all for the landlord, and against the tenant. And if the peasantry and working farmers go, we are all down'.[28] This form of institutional violence reduces tenants to the level of animals:

> The greyhound was crunching the piece of hard oaten bread outside the door [...] seizing the hound by the throat, the boy pulled the fragment of the bread from between his teeth, and devoured it ravenously! (*Cavanagh*, p.184).

In *For the Old Land*, Kickham depicts the fear implicit in the tenants' position:

> If he goes with the landlord he'll be denounced and hooted, and degraded in his own eyes as well as in his neighbour's, so that life will be a burden to him. And if he goes with the other party – then comes the notice to quit [...].[29]

Perrington, the key landowner and magistrate, revels in the power and terror he commands and delights in working out who will be his next victim:

> [T]he occasional compression of the blanched lips and a catching of the breath betrayed the terror of him who feared the dreaded sentence of eviction would be pronounced that dismal day. (*Land*, p. 83)

Perrington is a twisted and cruel man who enjoys seeing his tenants suffer in the appalling weather while he deliberately keeps the 'drenched and shivering crowd' (*Land*, p. 84) waiting. As in other agrarian novels where the writer has nationalist sympathies, the stress is upon institutional violence rather than agrarian violence. Perrington's death is reported with pointed brevity simply as 'Mr. Perrington has been murdered' (*Land*, p. 126).

---

[28] Charles J Kickham, *Sally Cavanagh* (1869) (Dublin: James Duffy and Co. Limited, 1948), p. 166. Further references to this edition are given after quotations in the text and the title shortened to *Cavanagh*.
[29] Charles J Kickham, *For the Old Land* (1883) (Dublin: M. H. Gill and Son, 1892), p. 15. Further references to this edition are given after quotations in the text, and the title is shortened to *Land*.

As a political purist, Kickham is unable to include agrarian outrages in his vision of a noble struggle to free all Irishmen:

> [Kickham] had never condoned agrarian outrages, though he understood how an individual, maddened by injustice, could be moved to violence. The Land League [...] looked to him like organised outrage. '[...] [T]he thing is at best only Whiteboyism'.[30]

While Kickham goes as far as supporting direct action against 'rack-renting landlords' and seems to condone 'boycotting', he never really makes it clear who or what should decide when that agrarian violence is justified. Kickham's ambiguous attitude to violence is evident when he states that 'we are branded as a nation of murderers because a landlord happens to be shot once in half a dozen years'.[31] He conveniently interprets actions generally accepted as forms of agrarian violence as not agrarian violence at all. The best that can be said is that if a landowner is a 'rack-renter' he deserves to be subjected to agrarian violence and/or boycotting. These arguments come perilously close to hypocrisy:

> He did not disapprove of 'boycotting' as such. It had been utilised by tenant protection societies in the 1850s and the youthful Kickham had celebrated it in verse. Even in 1880 he advocated its use where there was justification.[32]

Romantic notions of 'boycotting' only add to the sense that Kickham is not fully aware of its dire consequences. Perhaps to prevent his anti-English argument being used as an excuse for agrarian violence, Kickham resorts to obfuscation:

> No word has ever escaped our pen intended to justify such a deed as that contemplated by this poor maddened victim of tyranny. [...] we find it hard to brand Mick Brien as a MURDERER. [...] [N]o one will for a moment class him with the human wild beasts with whom the writer of these pages was doomed to herd for years; and among whom at this hour Irishmen, whose only crime is

---

[30] Comerford, p. 153.
[31] Kickham, in Maher, p. 230.
[32] Kickham, in Maher, p. 153.

the crime of loving their country, are wearing away their lives in the Convict Prisons of England. (*Knocknagow*, p. 387)

Kickham's bitterness over his imprisonment and his unrelenting hatred of England are indicated by this narrative intervention in the tale. The attempt to mitigate Brien's actions is patent. It is emphasised that Brien is a good man, a good husband and father and a respectable farmer, who loses everything to lesser landowners who have used the law for their own gain. Kickham may claim overtly that he does not support agrarian violence but covertly he does. Tenants are driven to commit agrarian outrages by unrelenting institutional violence; their actions are reactive rather than pro-active – as Healy indicates:

> He claimed that concessions to Ireland had always been wrung from England by Fenianism in one shape or another.[33]

Kickham favours a 'Peasant Proprietary' (*Knocknagow*, p. 481) but never explains how this would work in practice. Although he sympathises with the tenants, he recognizes that the land is not just divided between landowner and tenant; between the two, there were invariably middlemen or lesser landowners. Sir Garrett Butler, the most senior landowner in *Knocknagow* and an absentee in England, is portrayed leniently:

> Notwithstanding all we heard of his kindness of heart and his simplicity, things go on just as in the old way since he came in for the property. He leaves all to the agent; and, so long as he sends him whatever money he requires, Sir Garrett seems not to care for his tenants or trouble his head about them. (*Knocknagow*, p. 479)

Butler is a decent, old fashioned landowner. Indeed, after having played a part in the tale disguised (not unusual in agrarian novels) as a musician, he appears as an enlightened landowner. He decides to remove the bad agent, Beresford Pender, and make up for his own former shortcomings as a landowner: 'I fear I have much to answer for, for all the wrong that has been done in my name' (*Knocknagow*, p. 561).

Kickham indicates that all is not well in his Ireland as the 'new landlords are such screws' (*Knocknagow*, p. 571). There are, once again,

---

[33] Healy, p. 26.

hints of positive feelings towards 'Old English' landowners. One character, Dr. Kiely, admits, 'some of them became more Irish than the Irish themselves' (*Knocknagow*, p. 595). Lesser landowners – like Lloyd, who is 'strongly condemned for the way he manages his property' (even though Benedict Kiely sees him as 'the amiable Protestant landlord'[34]) and Somerfield who 'thinks the more independent the tenantry become, the harder it will be to manage them' (*Knocknagow*, p. 423) – are the real enemy. Somerfield advises Butler not to give new leases to tenants but it is a different matter when he wants one himself:

> Mr. Sam Somerfield, J.P., applied for a new lease of Woodlands. [...] the arguments brought forward to show that long leases would prove advantageous both to the landlord and the tenant were so convincing, that the old baronet, with all his simplicity and want of experience, could not help wondering why his agents had always warned him against giving leases to his tenants [...] and pointed to the practice and example of this same Mr. Sam Somerfield in support of his assertion that leases would be ruinous to the landlord's interest. (*Knocknagow*, p.527)

Somerfield and his cohorts seek to prevent tenants having leases in order to grab land for themselves.

Kickham deplores the introduction of the Workhouse into Ireland and is incensed when families are torn apart:

> This poor woman was only admitted the week before with her husband and children, from whom, according to their infamous rules, she was at once separated. She now heard her husband's name read from the altar, and with a wild shriek of agony fell down, and was borne senseless out of the chapel. They did not even take the trouble to inform her that her husband was dead! Were human beings ever treated before as our poor people are treated? (*Knocknagow*, p. 541)

The question posed regarding 'our people' shows that Kickham is addressing his fellow Irishmen and encourages anti-English feeling.

---

[34] Kiely, p. 114.

Perhaps the strongest attack comes when he implicitly accuses the English Government of encouraging institutional violence:

> 'The Irish landlords were encouraged to exterminate the people', said Dr. O'Connor, 'and when the work was done, many of themselves were exterminated. England cares just as little for them as for the people'. (*Knocknagow*, p. 613)

This also appears to be an attempt to appeal to Irish landowners to side with their tenants against the Government. For Kickham, it should be Irishmen united against Englishmen rather than landowner against tenant. The only chance of finally settling the Land Question is with full Irish independence – Comerford claims:

> Kickham at all times assumed that a satisfactory and final solution to Ireland's agrarian problems would go hand in hand with the vindication of Irish nationhood. [...] To Kickham's way of thinking there was a mystical union between the two.[35]

Although much concerned with the Land Question, Kickham's approach is essentially political and, as we shall see, his views on economic issues are highly ambiguous. There may be special reasons for this. When Kickham was thirteen, an accident left him almost completely deaf and blind; thereafter he lived in his own world and developed his own political opinions in virtual isolation. He became intransigent believing that anyone 'who disagreed with him, churchman or politician, was in error. His certainty of the correctness of his own views was such that no allowance was made for the status of opponents'.[36] When John Mitchel, an extreme nationalist who had consistently denounced Home Rule, stood for election in Tipperary in 1874, Kickham saw an opportunity to reassert the anti-Parliamentarian stance that was a position he had adopted some years earlier:

> Kickham had lived through the awful times of the Famine and the still awful times that followed when eviction began its devils' work and the crowbar brigade stalked through the length and breadth of the land. [...] He saw the futility of constitutional agitation as then

---

[35] Comerford, p. 146.
[36] Comerford, p. 70.

placidly practised, how feeble the stand up was in 1852, how the Tenant Right Organisation's efforts were rendered futile by defection and treachery, how helpless people were.[37]

Kickham blames not only the English but also his fellow Irishmen (secular and clerical) who supported the renegades Sadleir and Keogh:

> [Kickham] interested himself in the Tenant Right movement, and became one of its most energetic workers. When that organisation failed, he was so disgusted with the perfidious conduct of Messrs. Sadlier and Keogh that he lost all faith in Parliamentary agitation from that time forward.[38]

Kickham regarded those who opposed him as traitors to the tenants' cause and 'never forgave what he saw as the perfidy of those who took the other side'.[39] So, when Mitchel ran for election promising that, if elected, he would never take his seat at Westminster, Kickham felt he could support him without compromising his hostility to Parliament.

Kickham adopted a patronising attitude towards Parnell and seriously underestimated his abilities:

> Don't know what Parnell means by saying that it is cheaper to buy the land than to fight for it. Something more precious than money or blood may be paid for it if *he* has his way. [...] If land-leaguers win, the old Faith goes with other old things.[40]

Hence Kickham found himself out of step with the new order in nationalist politics. He was a political purist and visionary, with a romantic, intellectual attachment to an ideal, rather than a pragmatist. In the last resort, he was convinced that the solution to the Land Question lay in an independent Ireland. If Ireland were free then Irish tenants could own the land they worked. This was a potent mix of politics and Romantic nationalism. Kickham claimed not to be anti-farmer though it is difficult to see how a true nationalist could be pro-farmer. Healy's biography of 1915 brings this out well:

---

[37] Kelly, pp. 49-50.
[38] Murphy, p. 2.
[39] Murphy, p. 38.
[40] Kickham, in Maher, p. 297.

Kickham was a genuine Nationalist [...] yet this is how he speaks of the class of people whom he calls 'graziers': – 'There is a class of Irishmen of whom we have never spoken, except incidentally, either in praise or blame. We mean the large farmers [...]. Yet we think it well to let these large farmers know that we are not ignorant of their existence. There are some good men among them; but, as a class, these men of bullocks are about the worst men in Ireland. They appear to have no more souls than the brutes which they fatten for the tables of our English masters'.[41]

Kickham's snobbery and selective anti-Irish stance is evident. However, while he sides with tenants against bad graziers, he allows that there are good graziers too. He also claims to sympathise with all Irish people without land, including manual workers in the towns and cities, yet still denounces the Land League for trying to introduce 'communism'[42] to Ireland (a curious posture that implies subscription to the British version of the law).

Perhaps Kickham's own position as a property owner – he inherited houses numbers 1 to 12A in Mullinahone from his father – and his implicit acceptance of the hereditary principle had something to do with his opposition to Communism and communal land-ownership. So uncompromising in all other respects, Kickham turns out to be surprisingly compromising about property.

The Religious Dimension

Previous agrarian novelists had stressed Protestant/Catholic divisions but Kickham does not adopt this stance; he was a Catholic, but not a religious zealot. He disliked politicized Catholic priests and an interfering Church but did not distinguish between Catholic or Protestant landowners:

[Kickham] was not opposed to landlordism [...]. Looking at nineteenth-century Irish rural society, Kickham did not see the pattern discerned by other nationalist propagandists – an alien landowning aristocracy exploiting native tenantry. Instead he saw Irishmen (of various social ranks) exploiting other Irishmen

---

[41] Cited in Healy, pp. 57-8.
[42] Comerford, p. 154.

because they were permitted, encouraged or even forced to do so by alien and unjust laws.[43]

It is true that Kickham disapproved of absentees but then so had all agrarian novelists since Edgeworth. Kickham's argument was with lesser landowners/agents who had only got their land because of the Irish propensity to sub-divide estates.

Kickham's presentation of priests and the Catholic Church is revealing. In *Sally Cavanagh*, the landowner's sister – 'proselytising among her brother's wretched tenantry' (*Cavanagh*, p. 55) – is portrayed as reprehensible. She disturbs dying Catholics and blackmails the poor into converting. When recounting the schoolmaster's story, Kickham's anti-Evangelical stance is evident:

> [T]he clergyman's wife met me, and inquired kindly for my mother. She also gave me a half a sovereign, which she desired me to give my mother to buy clothes for me. And when the clothes were bought we were both to call upon her. We did call upon her; and, to my poor mother's dismay, the lady offered to provide for me if she were allowed to bring me up as a member of the Established Church. [...] I am sorry to think the half sovereign which made me so happy was only a bribe. (*Cavanagh*, pp. 91-2)

Kickham implicitly reinforces his attitude to Evangelicals and to his own faith when Sally has to choose between conversion and survival:

> It was a grand picture: the noble mother, with hunger gnawing at her own vitals, prepared to see the children of her heart wither before her eyes, rather than expose them to the risk of losing the faith of their fathers, or imperil the priceless jewel, for which, in all her woe, and want, and misery, the daughters of Erin have been famed. (*Cavanagh*, p. 182)

Sally's choice results in the death of her children and her own descent into madness. Underlying this despair, however, there is a sense of hope. When Sally is in the Workhouse and finds out that all her children are dead, her only comforter is a Protestant woman. Kickham believed that

---

[43] Comerford, pp.148-149.

Protestants and Catholics should not allow those in power to drive a wedge between them, religious differences should take second place to common nationality.

In *Knocknagow*, Father Hannigan, while pro-tenant, consistently opposes agrarian violence. When Morris advocates violence, Hannigan says it is 'murder – wilful murder'. Morris's response that 'the prayers of the congregation would carry the man's sowl to heaven' (*Knocknagow*, p. 221) is a rejection of the priest's advocacy of non-violence. Nevertheless, Hannigan, a moderate, does recount one opinion with which he agrees:

> [An Irish judge] had sentenced several men to be hanged a short time before, and a gentleman present made some severe remarks, while discussing the subject of agrarian outrages, when Judge --- said: 'I never met an instance of a landlord being killed, who did not deserve – I won't say to be hanged, as I am a judge – but I do say, a case of the kind never came before me that the landlord did not deserve to be *damned*.' (*Knocknagow*, p. 223)

This implies that judges and priests share the same view that bad landowners need not be hanged as God's justice will be more severe. Kickham's belief that priests were against both agrarian violence and the tenants goes back to his Young Ireland days. Kickham, like Carleton, was a supporter of Thomas Davis, as Healy records:

> Irish he was to the heart's core, always full of Irish sympathies – Irish prejudices even – but under Davis, 'his prophet and his guide', his sound judgement and sterling patriotism 'grew with his growth and strengthened with his strength'.[44]

It was Davis and his romantic notions of Irish nationality that inspired Kickham. Like Davis, Kickham was 'against utilitarian industrial society' and, instead, believed in '[t]he glorification of an imaginary, pre-industrial past when all the social orders lived in mutually-beneficial harmony'.[45]

The Church often clashed with Young Ireland and Comerford cites an occasion when Kickham 'suffered the pain of hearing his parish priest refer to the deceased patriot [Davis] as a "dangerous man"'. Kickham also knew that, during the abortive rebellion of 1848, '[t]he priests in

---

[44] Healy p. 56.
[45] Comerford, p.149.

Mullinahone as elsewhere [...] used all their influence to oppose rebellion' – something Kickham found abhorrent. Kickham's attitude towards the Catholic Church and its representatives was ambiguous:

> [Kickham's] balanced intellectual position co-existed throughout his adult life with a most intense feeling of disillusionment (almost amounting to an obsession) with the majority of the clergy as he actually found them.[46]

According to Kelly, Kickham 'had a deep reverence for the sacred office of the priest and was a devout Catholic, but he found fault with the political action and utterances of certain high ecclesiastics of his day'.[47] His confused stance is evident in his account of Father Sheehy's death. Kickham sympathises with this eighteenth-century priest who was hanged by the English 'becase he wanted to save the people from bein' hunted, an' the whole counthry turned to pasture for sheep and cattle' (*Knocknagow*, p. 257). Kickham's real venom, however, is reserved for the Catholic Bishop, who was responsible for Sheehy's death and whose doorway was sprinkled with blood from his severed head:

> [H]e was all-in-all wud the great lords an' gentlemen; and for fear uv offendin' 'em, he wouldn't stir hand or fut to save the life uv the poor priest that had the rope about his neck. (*Knocknagow*, p. 257)

Not only did the Bishop let his priest die but also consorted with the enemy and put his own welfare above that of the tenants.

Kickham believed that corruption, especially materialism, was endemic in the Catholic Church and that priests enjoyed an unhealthily close relationship with the social elite:

> [Kickham] rebuked clerics for failing to live up to their own principles, and especially for the abuse of their religious office. The clergy in Ireland in the mid-nineteenth century enjoyed extensive prestige and social influence in their parishes. The temptation to subordinate the role of minister of religion and charity to that of

---

[46] Comerford, pp. 20-22.
[47] Kelly, p. 21.

petty local tyrant was strong, and for many irresistible. The classical expression of this abuse was the altar denunciation.[48]

For Catholics, particularly uneducated rural tenants, the threat of being damned by a priest was something truly to be feared. Kickham abhorred the way priests abused the tenants' trust. Kickham was a devout Catholic who told 'John O'Mahony of his gladness that Ireland was "as Catholic as ever", and adding that he himself would not "give up the old faith even for liberty"'. Yet these are the words of the man who wrote severely 'anti-clerical articles' in the *Irish People*. Kickham also deplored the unacceptable attempts by priests to retain control of their local communities:

> [A] parish priest who might react quite nonchalantly to an episcopal exposition of the theological and canonical objections to secret societies, would feel his personal position threatened by the sight of someone other than himself organising the pastimes of the local youth. This social dimension gave a particular seriousness and determination to the clerical onslaught on fenianism in the mid-1860s.[49]

Unlike the Catholic Church, Kickham saw no problem with being a Fenian and a Catholic – a view widely held:

> [T]he great majority of the fenian rank and file were instinctively loyal catholics who felt no conflict between their catholicism and their nationalism and had no appreciation of continental anti-clericalism.[50]

Kickham was not against Catholicism, he was against corruption and the abuse of power whether by priests or lesser landowners – as depicted in *Knocknagow*:

> Stubbleton [...] had his whole property cleared without as much as a paragraph in the newspapers about it. He divided it into large farms, then, and got heavy fines and a good rent that more than repaid him for what he had lost. The parish priest denounced him

---

[48] Comerford, p. 41.
[49] Comerford, p.69.
[50] Comerford, p. 73.

as an exterminator; but Stubbleton gave a farm to the priest's nephew, and put a stop to that. (*Knocknagow*, p. 290)

Yet Kickham admitted that not all priests were corrupt. Father M'Mahon is the kind of clergyman of whom Kickham approved:

> [M'Mahon] with the pure and noble soul and 'the proud walk', is a type of parish priest, if not altogether common, yet not rare. In him a highly cultivated intellect, a vivid and florid imagination, a fiery temperament, an utter self-forgetfulness, and the tenderest sensibility, with a hauteur of manner somewhat startling at first, are combined with a magnificent entity. Ireland may well feel proud and thank Heaven that she has still such Father M'Mahons.[51]

M'Mahon is Kickham's ideal priest who 'asked himself were the people he loved, and who loved him in their heart of hearts, doomed indeed to destruction?' (*Knocknagow*, p. 454) Kickham answers this question by cataloguing the unwarranted sufferings of his flock:

> Poor Father M'Mahon is heart-broken at the sufferings of the people. [...] Last Sunday, when requesting the prayers of the congregation in the usual way for the repose of the souls of those who died during the week, the list was so long that poor Father M'Mahon stopped in the middle of it, exclaiming with a heart-piercing cry, 'Oh my poor people! my poor people!' and then turned round and prostrated himself at the foot of the altar convulsed with grief [...] Then he got into a rage and denounced the government as a 'damnable government.' (*Knocknagow*, p. 540)

M'Mahon's is portrayed as a kind and popular priest. The level and constancy of institutional violence suffered by the tenants – often ending in death – is too much for the old man. The blame rests solely with the Government.

In *For the Old Land*, the key priest is Father Feehan who is central to persuading his flock to vote against the landowner's candidate. But local politics are dividing the Catholic Church:

---

[51] Healy, p. 115.

Father Feehan felt bitterly mortified when the parish priest of Ballinsoggarth, leading on a long array of voters, arrived at the polling place and announced, in the hearing of Lord Allavogga, that only five votes from his parish would be polled that day against Brummagem and O'Mulligan. Immediately after, Mr. Percy Perrington and Bill Kerrawan marched over a score of Father Feehan's parishioners, under their pastor's very nose, to vote for 'the hereditary enemies of their creed and country'. (*Land*, p. 116)

A tenant's failure to do as instructed by his priest would result in a public rebuke from the pulpit – as Martin Dwyer discovers when Feehan 'flayed the poor "black sheep" alive in his address from the altar' (*Land*, p. 118). Kickham abhorred the way that the Catholic Church instilled terror in the faithful, but his attack is directed at priests rather than at Catholicism. He questions their anti-Fenian stance and believes that they do not understand the aims of Fenianism and see it as a threat to their local power base. Kickham even portrays Feehan as a 'castle priest' (*Land*, p. 152) and hence a traitor to his faith, his people and his country. By the end of the novel, the writer (probably not Kickham) strongly implies that Fenianism was so successful that it resulted in the inclusion of '"Bright's clauses" in Mr. Gladstone's Land Act' (*Land*, p. 184).

Although Kickham was a devout believer in the Catholic faith, Father James Cantwell refused to allow Kickham's body to be honoured in Thurles Cathedral. This may have been due to a misunderstanding, but 'Cantwells' decision accorded with a strong political prejudice that he shared with a large number of priests in the archdiocese who remembered all the trouble they had had with Kickham's Fenian supporters down the years'.[52]

As with much else surrounding Kickham, his attitude to religion was ambiguous. His battle was primarily with the Catholic Church rather than with the Church of Ireland – largely ignored in his novels. Although his Catholic faith never diminished, his battle with the Church and its priests lasted throughout his adult life. While he believed in an independent, Catholic Ireland, he wanted a democratic Ireland, based on the American model, and not one run by the Catholic Church. He chose to ignore the fact that the American Constitution rejects the idea of a State religion and

---

[52] Comerford, p. 174.

that, in a truly Catholic Ireland, the Church hierarchy would inevitably be overwhelmingly influential.

The Land of Liberty

In *Sally Cavanagh*, Kickham stresses the sorrow at leaving Ireland rather than the excitement of a new start in America:

> Here Brian Purcell stood, watching the cars laden with the outcast children of Erin as they toiled wearily up the hill through the gap; and wail after wail of agony, as if hearts were rent asunder, was borne upon the breeze, as friend after friend turned back after bidding a *last* farewell. (*Cavanagh*, p.25).

Institutional violence is directly to blame for emigration. Kickham believed an independent Ireland would need all her children to rebuild the nation. Emigration was a necessary evil, though, hopefully, it would only be a temporary phenomenon. Those who left might escape death in Ireland, but having prospered abroad they should certainly return, with renewed vigour, to overthrow English rule.

In *Sally Cavanagh*, set in contemporary Ireland, Kickham explains how institutional violence forces Irishmen to emigrate. He believes that these emigrants, many now trained soldiers after fighting in the American Civil War, wish to return to Ireland to fight the English – very much the Fenian position:

> In September, 1865, [James] Stephens gave the order for action [...]. There was found a document from Stephens saying the military men from America should be paid at the rate of 750 dollars monthly for majors, and 115 dollars for second-lieutenants, and thirty officers were named as having arrived in Ireland to take part in the rising.[53]

Kickham's romantic notions of the returning Irish are represented by Conor Shea's son. The rest of the family has died in Ireland but he has

---

[53] Kelly, pp. 28-29.

survived because he emigrated with his father.[54] Now a man, he stands by his sibling's graves and, thinking of the arm he lost on an American battlefield, pledges 'an arm left – for Ireland' (*Cavanagh*, p. 251).

Kickham looked across the Atlantic to America and saw a romantic vision of Democracy. Moreover, unlike Ireland, America offered the prospect of vast amounts of land. In *For the Old Land*, the Dwyers dream of owning their piece of America:

> Old Martin thought himself quite a capitalist; and even Tom looked forward hopefully, and considered that they'd land in America with sufficient funds to purchase a good farm in one of the Western States'. (*Land*, p. 125)

America can do no wrong and carries the hopes of Ireland and the Fenians. Kickham, however, harboured a more romantic vision of the Irish in the American Civil War:

> My heart swelled with pride when I read of Tom's gallantry in re-capturing the green flag, and crying out, 'One more charge for the honour of old Ireland!' (*Land*, p. 153)

One day the 'young giant' would physically and militarily help free Ireland.

Kickham had a romantic and unrealistic vision of America; it stood for everything that Ireland, under English rule, did not. In *Sally Cavanagh*, Kickham's rhetoric is clear:

> Suppose he would fly with her to that great young nation, of which he was so enthusiastic an admirer. With his talents might he not rise to a height that would satisfy even her ambition? (*Cavanagh*, p. 87)

America is vibrant and fresh – unlike either Ireland or England. It is a land of opportunity where a man can rise and not be kept down by unjust laws, an Imperial power, politicized priests and the inability to own land. When tenants are evicted, they head for America – the beacon of hope for the likes of Norry Delany who can now 'go with her two brothers to

---

[54] See Murphy, p. 27, line 9 of 'The Shan Van Vocht: 'They are coming from the West [...]'. In Trollope, help comes from the East but, anticipating Stoker, death also comes from the East.

America (they had just been ejected from their little "spot of ground")'
(*Cavanagh*, p. 205). America not only offers dispossessed tenants hope but
is also 'the land of liberty'. Kickham believed that America would go to
war with England over Ireland. In a heavily contrived ending to *Sally
Cavanagh*, he portrays a united and inclusive scene. Nobody wants Shea,
the Irish nationalist hero, to leave again for America. It is left to the local
Parson, Mr. Stephens, to offer a warning to the Government:

> [I]f a war breaks out between the United States and these
> countries, our government will find they have committed a
> grievous mistake in driving the men who recruited our army, and
> contributed so much to the glory of England, into the ranks of our
> foes. For America does not love us. (*Cavanagh*, p. 243)

Kickham's interpretation of America's role in the Land Question is the
key difference between him and earlier agrarian novelists. Prior to
Kickham, all agrarian novelists agree that change is needed in the
relationship between landowner and tenant. Kickham's agrarian novels do
not, however, move the agenda forward or even represent a break with it.
The old, moderate agenda had run its course in Ireland and Kickham,
possibly subliminally, hoped to breathe new life into the sub-genre by
threatening to bring American extremism into the centre of the political
arena. In so doing, however, he took what should have been 'realist-
reactionary' novels into the realm of fantasy.

There are many exaggerations and distortions in Kickham. He even
claims to have found the solution to the Land Question. He recalls how
John Dillon wanted 'farmers and peasants to compel the landlords to
reduce the rents to a let-live level'. Kickham states that 'I am fully satisfied
that it would have settled the Irish Land question for ever'. Yet, as ever,
Kickham believed that the opportunity was lost because the early
advocates of this programme spurned his own prophetic and acute
insight, instead turning to politics and sending 'so-called representatives to
the British Parliament'.[55] Kiely endeavours to circumvent this problem
with Kickham's interpretation of events by claiming that 'you cannot have
him if you do not accept his myth and his mystique'[56] but this is
disingenuous as Kickham was, first and foremost, a nationalist and a
politician. He wrote about what he observed and his interpretation of it.

---

[55] Kickham, in Maher, p. 113.
[56] Kiely, p. 109.

His limitations as a novelist stem from his desire not just to act as an historian – like other agrarian novelists – but from his desire to be a political propagandist. He was prevented from being a true extremist by his love of and admiration for all things American.

As a Fenian, Kickham may be viewed as a radical but his opposition to violence and his gentleness are often stressed. Despite the best attempts of his biographers, there is no evidence showing him to be the revolutionary of nationalist myth. Instead, we are regaled with tales of his infirmity, kindness and love of children. Kickham, the property owner, advocated only a diluted form of Fenianism – as reflected in his trenchant opposition to Parnell, Davitt and the Land League. A certain level of paranoia and intellectual snobbery is also evident – as Healy reveals when citing Kickham's own words:

> [M]y tone would be somewhat different if my 'Notes' were
> appearing in the *Irish Monthly*. [...] I felt all the more constrained to
> speak out because I knew I had a host of foes on every side –
> Leaguers, Skirmishers, Nihilists, Repealers, Home Rulers, Whigs,
> Tories, and Radicals. [...] The worst of it is, I fear, that most of
> what I say is 'caviare to the general'; and do any cultured people
> read me at all? I would not quite despair of making an impression
> here and there if I had the right sort of audience.[57]

While Kickham clearly has a high opinion of his own abilities, he seems not to rate the Irish people very highly; yet it is they he claims to want to liberate.

Kickham, consistently opposed to Communism, supported America. Yet America, although rejecting the hereditary principle, was and is more committed to Capitalism and property-ownership than any other country. This leads to a fundamental tension in Kickham's argument. How, as a Fenian, can he attack the principle of property – especially inherited estates – and still support America? Of course, the other significant country to advocate Capitalism and a property-owning democracy – including the hereditary principle – was and is England. It is ironic that even America herself was ultimately forced into a war with England because of the desire to own land.

---

[57] Quoted in Healy, pp. 134-5.

Kickham attacks the English Parliament as corrupt and pointless. Yet America – whose politicians were also guilty of 'gerrymandering' – championed the principle of parliamentary democracy. Kickham also frequently attacks the law in Ireland but American law was written and administered in English and derived directly from English law. If Ireland became like America would her law be any less English? Kickham's problem was not that America and England were too far apart, rather they were too close together. In attacking aspects of English rule, Kickham actually weakened his own pro-American argument. For Kickham, America is the complete opposite of England and benefits from being so but, by focussing on America, Ireland almost disappears from the debate.

According to Kelly, Kickham once made a pronouncement which 'epitomised his beliefs of agrarian reform' – and also reflected his knowledge of the Bible:

> Leave to the labourer what belongs to the labourer, to the farmer what belongs to the farmer, and to the landlord what belongs to the landlord – do this and the greatest possible amount of good that any settlement of the Land Question can do for Ireland is done.[58]

Although it is not as clear cut as in *Knocknagow*, Kickham's position generally reflects this belief, one that leaves little room for Fenian agitation. Ultimate advocacy of the *status quo* is perhaps the most surprising thing about Kickham. By implication, this means that everybody should remain in their existing circumstances – a position not even advocated by Edgeworth, who recognized the need for change. Kickham, the radical Fenian activist and property owner, appears as a rather conservative revolutionary when it comes to the division of property. Indeed, he was none too keen to extend the franchise as that would threaten his vision of a hierarchical, property-owning Ireland. Equally, he opposed Parnell and the Land League because their actions risked the security of property in the Land War.

The 'realist-reactionary' agrarian novel was never written. Kickham wanted to be seen as a radical writer and visionary, but he was neither. He was not the true peasant nationalist as he and subsequent nationalist biographical interpretations have sought to claim:

---

[58] Kelly, p. 37.

Kickham was misunderstood [...]. This was inevitable. Most of the 19th century in Irish political life was a great misunderstanding, sometimes showy, sometimes squalid, but always more or less windy, unreasoning and intolerant.[59]

Kickham thought that, in American Fenianism – really an urban rather than a rural movement – he had found the solution to the Land Question. Yet when Fenians ceased to behave as he thought they should, he descended into despair and isolation. Despite the passage of time and the Famine, Edgeworth's agenda still remained dominant in the agrarian novel. The nationalist solution was simply too confused and too contradictory. It seems that, with Kickham, a final but doomed attempt had been made to extract some life from a moribund agenda. Kickham lacked the capacity to work through the Land Question; contrary to the claims of some critics, he was simply not in the league of contemporaries like Dickens and Eliot (neither Dickens nor Eliot attempted to tackle such an intractable subject).

If the introduction of America into the nationalist political solution had failed, was there any way in which the agrarian novel could still develop? Ireland itself was exhausted, the only possibility in the real world, was to find another external solution, to replace America with England, for the wheel to come full circle back to Edgeworth.

---

[59] William Bulfin, in Maher, p. 10.

Ireland for the Irish might be very well, but he did not at all want to have Ireland for the Americans.[1]

The Honorary Irishman

The prospect of 'Ireland for the Americans' that so alarmed Father Malachi in Anthony Trollope's *The Land-Leaguers* (1884) encapsulates the solution to the problems of Ireland advanced – though with some confusion – by Charles Kickham. As so often in Irish agrarian novels, Trollope's choice of names may be significant. Father Malachi, who speaks the words quoted above, may be named after an earlier Celtic saint. In the Middle Ages, St Malachi delivered a series of prophecies about the end of the Catholic Church. Perhaps, Father Malachi's comments may imply that an American Ireland means the end of a truly Catholic Ireland. St Malachi's prophecies were even more specific however. He believed that the last Pope, Peter II, would be an Englishman. Thus, in Father Malachi, there is an explicit reference to America and – perhaps – a subtle reference to England. Therefore in Malachi, actually not an attractive figure, therefore we see the three elements of the second, or external phase, of the Irish agrarian novel; America and England as the major players and Ireland as a relatively minor one.

Anthony Trollope is the only English novelist to be studied in detail in this book; his inclusion requires explanation. He lived in Ireland following his appointment as a Post Office surveyor in 1841 and later became Inspector of Postal Deliveries in South Western Ireland. Trollope claimed to have invented pillar-boxes while in Ireland; perhaps their robust construction reflects his concern for the security of the mail. Apart from

---

[1] Anthony Trollope, *The Land-Leaguers* (1884) (London: Penguin Group, 1993), p. 17. Further references to this edition are given after quotations in the text and the title shortened to *Land-Leaguers*.

his five explicitly Irish novels, Irish characters (notably Phineas Finn) figure prominently in Trollope's later 'Palliser' series, set in and around Westminster. Trollope's main interest outside of literature was politics and he was particularly fascinated by Parliament. Until the 1870s, Trollope was an admirer of Gladstone, but his enthusiasm faded after 1880 when Gladstone returned as Prime Minister and followed Irish policies Trollope considered wrong-headed. After long neglect, Trollope's Irish novels are now beginning to receive the attention they deserve:

> The matter of this chapter is Trollope's third series of fictions: 'Father Giles of Ballymoy' and 'The O'Conor's of Castle Conor, County Mayo', *The Macdermots of Ballycloran*, *The Kellys and O'Kellys*, *Castle Richmond*, *An Eye for an Eye* and *The Landleaguers*. I am not the first to recognise that Trollope tried to write Irish novels that would 'equal the appeal of his Barsetshire and other English books' – nor the only person to write that Trollope was 'arguably a great Irish novelist'.[2]

Melissa Fegan notes '[v]iolence is all-pervasive in Trollope's Irish fiction'.[3] Trollope wrote five specifically Irish novels: *The Macdermots of Ballycloran* (1847), *The Kellys and O'Kelly's* (1848), *Castle Richmond* (1860), *An Eye for an Eye* (1879) and *The Land-Leaguers*. Trollope was elderly and infirm by the time he wrote *The Land-Leaguers* and, as a Liberal opposed to Gladstone's Irish policy, now wrote from a conservative perspective. He laments the lost Ireland of the 1840s, when landowners, tenants and priests knew their places. Trollope is appalled by the agrarian outrages perpetrated by Land Leaguers and by the 'political terrorism' of Irish nationalist MPs at Westminster. Yet Trollope also portrays a world turned on its head. The ordered, rural society of *Castle Richmond* has disappeared, institutional violence has also disappeared, and agrarian violence rules almost unchallenged. Catholics – including politically motivated priests – now oppress Protestants. There are frequent and arbitrary acts of extreme and cruel agrarian violence, including the religious corruption of a young boy and followed by his callous assassination when he tells the truth.

We encounter, in Trollope, the opposite of Kickham – yet both were united in looking for a solution outside Ireland and then found that their

---

[2] Ellen Moody, *Trollope on the Net* (London: The Hambledon Press, 1999), p 34.
[3] Melissa Fegan, *Literature and the Irish Famine 1845-1919* (Oxford: Clarendon Press, 2002), p 111.

solution was no solution. While Kickham looked west to America, Trollope looked east to England. Everything is reversed; in Kickham, America is good and England bad whereas in Trollope, America is bad and England is good. In both cases, however, Ireland is the battleground for the struggle between the two giants.

The background to *The Land-Leaguers* is the Land War. Although officially over by 1882, the Land War continued intermittently until 1923 and saw tenants taking both violent and non-violent action against evictions. Parnell and the Land League were remarkably successful in mobilizing the tenants. But it was not simply a case of landowners versus tenants; the Catholic Church inevitably became embroiled. Many priests, previously loyal to their Church's guidelines, became politicized and were caught up, overtly or covertly, in agrarian violence.

Father Malachi, prompted largely by personal ambition, is unwilling to keep to his Church's line on issues affecting the lives of his flock. Tenants have become politicized with the introduction of Fenianism from America – and many priests have followed their lead. Malachi's problem is that, in order to advance his career, he needs a hierarchy; therefore, he has little time for republican ideas that reject all notions of hierarchy. Malachi's answer is a middle way: land to the tenants and primacy to a hierarchical Catholic Church within an independent Ireland. This would, of course, have been impossible; such an Ireland would be tied to and essentially governed by Rome. Secondly, America, with its historic rejection of State religion, would be less supportive, Britain would see danger to its western shores and the Ascendancy would see their land, homes, livelihood and security disappear. Even Kickham would have rejected this middle way because of the role of the Catholic Church. For Trollope, this was not a middle way at all but another extremist and hellish vision of Ireland's future.

In *The Land-Leaguers*, Trollope 'made up a story to fit his thesis'[4] and presents a ghastly picture of Ireland – very different to contemporary Irish novels like George Moore's *A Drama in Muslin* (1886), and Somerville and Ross's *Naboth's Vineyard* (1891). The Ireland that Trollope once knew has vanished. A simple pastime like hunting has become a weapon, friendly Catholic priests have become hostile and previously contented tenants turn to violence. In his final novel, Trollope seeks to show English readers the dangers inherent in the Irish situation; American Fenianism, Catholic

---

[4] R C Terry, *Anthony Trollope* (London: The Macmillan Press Ltd., 1977), p 192.

extremism and Land League MPs threaten the stability of Ireland and the Union itself. The only hope of saving Ireland is through resolute action – coercion – by the Government.

Although limited reference will be made to Trollope's other Irish novels, this chapter concentrates on *The Land-Leaguers,* principally because it is set in the early 1880s. It deals extensively with agrarian issues and provides the clearest counterpoint to Kickham. While *The Macdermots of Ballycloran* is indeed set in Ireland in the 1840s, secret societies remain in the background – with the exception of the violent hacking off of Hyacinth Keegan's foot that is used to incriminate Thady Macdermot. *The Kellys and the O'Kellys* consists of a series of intertwined love stories set against the backdrop of Ireland, while *An Eye for and Eye* is also essentially a love story. We will first consider Trollope's earlier experience of Ireland and its influence on his later attitude, go on to examine his reaction to the Famine and its political implications, and then engage in detailed study of the portrayal of agrarian violence in the novel. A consideration of Trollope's views on religion is followed by an examination of his attitude to America before a final analysis of his possible solution.

The Golden Age

In *The Land-Leaguers,* Trollope suggests that the 1840s had been a 'golden age' in Ireland. This seems a strange evaluation of the decade of the Famine, but Trollope's evident nostalgia for the 1840s was probably influenced by personal factors. When working for the Post Office in London in the 1830s, he had been unsuccessful and unhappy. The move to Ireland improved his fortunes – despite a reference from his former superior, Colonel Maberly, 'damning him as worthless'.[5] Trollope quickly became a part of local society and revelled in the experience. Ireland brought 'him out of his shell' and he developed a 'noisy, boisterous social manner' – a point made in Victoria Glendinning's informative biography:

> Some loved Anthony for this manner and some didn't. It was taken to be a particularly bluff, roast-beef kind of Englishness, and that is what in the end it became. But it was a mode he learned in Ireland.

---

[5] Victoria Glendinning, *Trollope* (London: Pimlico, 2002), p. 114.

Trollope enjoyed the freedom of his position, both socially and at work, and revelled in being the Englishman abroad.

In Ireland, Trollope developed a passion for hunting that lasted for the rest of his life; he included hunting in some twenty novels and stories. In particular, Trollope loved the supposed social inclusiveness of the chase:

> Hunting was also, in a place where he had no contacts, a great way of making friends. The whole point of hunting, in Anthony's opinion, was that anyone could join in who had the use of a horse. It made all kinds and classes of people equal 'for a time' [...]. This social intercourse, he wrote, was 'the best half of hunting' (*British Sports and Pastimes*). As a young English gentleman, humbly employed, who knew almost no one in Ireland, Anthony gained from this social promiscuity.

Trollope enjoyed dancing as 'it involved physical contact', watching horse racing and 'much deleterious drinking of whiskey punch'.[6] It was also in Ireland that he fell in love with Rose Heseltine who was to become his wife.

Trollope wrote his first novel, *The Macdermots of Ballycloran*, in Ireland in 1847 while the Famine still raged. As Glendinning points out, however, stories based in Ireland were not that popular:

> The word 'Ireland', to the average English reader, spelled religious and political problems, violence and, in literature, an unfamiliar and barbaric brand of regionalism.[7]

The English, bombarded with news about the Famine, may have felt they had heard quite enough about Irish suffering. The novel was not a success and nor was the next tale, *The Kellys and O'Kellys*; R C Terry notes, it had little 'connection with social affairs' and is his 'foray into the broad comedy of Lever and Maria Edgeworth'.[8] Yet the Trollopes appear to have been remarkably unaffected by the Famine 'carrying on their lives normally'. It is strange that a man so observant and sympathetic to Irish tenants could have initially been so unmoved:

---

[6] Glendinning, pp. 120-126.
[7] Glendinning, p. 161.
[8] Terry, p. 189.

Anthony, continuously on the road for his work between towns and villages, was in a better position than most to see what was going on during the Famine, but he was curiously anxious to play down the horror stories that appeared in the press. At home the Trollope's were half-insulated at first, like many middle-class urban people, from the disaster around them.[9]

Even in his *Autobiography* (1883), Trollope refers to the Famine only briefly, although admitting an anxiety 'to show that the steps taken for mitigating the terrible evil of the times were the best which the Minister of the day could have adopted'.[10] Only in *Castle Richmond* does Trollope deal with the reality of the Famine but, as Melissa Fegan comments, the novel's subtitle, 'A Tale of the Famine Year in Ireland', 'does not really fit the bill'.[11] The fact that Trollope had known what was going on is revealed in a letter to the *Examiner* quoted by Glendinning:

Anthony later wrote that 'those who were in the country during the period will never forget the winter of 1846 and the spring of 1847. The sufferings of the poor were awful. [...] He also remarked that while Irish landlords shrieked to the government for aid, they were at this stage unwilling to sacrifice their own comforts: 'no carriages were abandoned, no hounds destroyed, no retinues reduced'.[12]

These comments suggest that Trollope sought to excuse his apparent failure to react to the Famine by insisting that others, socially his superiors, also failed to react constructively.

On his last visit to Ireland, researching material for *The Land-Leaguers*, Trollope was in his late sixties and unwell. He stayed 'at country houses and in the better-class hotels'[13] and, consequently, spoke only to those in charge and received essentially biased information. He could not recognize the country he had once known so well; Ireland now seemed intent on descending into civil war. It is easy to understand why Trollope

---

[9] Glendinning, pp. 163-4.

[10] Anthony Trollope, *Autobiography* (1883), intro. by Michael Sadleir (London: Oxford University Press, 1961), p. 71.

[11] Fegan, p. 129.

[12] Glendinning, p. 165.

[13] James Pope-Hennessy, *Anthony Trollope* (London: Phoenix Press, 2001), p. 387.

felt so nostalgic for the 1840s – 'apt as we are to look back with fond regret to the happy, by-gone days of past periods'.[14] During Peel's second administration (1841-1846), the Anglo-Irish Ascendancy felt in control of the country and these years also coincided with the happiest period of Trollope's life. He hunted, drank, danced, flirted, got married and had immense fun and freedom. To an old man approaching death, the Ireland of his memories probably appeared ideal.

'The State of Ireland'

Despite his affection for the Irish, Trollope adopted a callous attitude towards the suffering of the Famine. His words still seem shockingly harsh:

> The famine and its results were terrible while they lasted; but they left behind them an amended state of things. When man has failed to rule the world rightly, God will step in, and will cause famines, and plagues, and pestilence – even poverty itself – with His own Right Arm. But the cure was effected, and the country was on its road to a fair amount of prosperity, when the tocsin was sounded in America, and Home Rule became the cry. (*Land-Leaguers*, p. 253)

While this view of the Famine as a natural, Malthusian solution to Ireland's over-crowding, seems hard-hearted, as Terry Eagleton suggests, many in England would have endorsed it:

> Even the Famine will yield a retrospective teleology of sorts, to those of a Malthusian frame of mind, and there were plenty in Victorian London who saw it as providential. [...] The moral crassness of this is as unoriginal as most of Trollope's pronouncements: the position is lifted wholesale from Malthus's *Essay on Population*, which sees famine as a last-ditch divine corrective to human vice. [...] Trollope [believed] the Famine is the consequence of God's mercy rather than his wrath, undoing

---

[14] Anthony Trollope, *The Kellys and the O'Kellys* (1848) (London; Penguin Books, 1993), p. 132.

the results of human folly and converting Ireland into a pleasant and prosperous land.[15]

It is strange that Trollope, not usually a callous man, should have thought thus. His position adopted in *The Land-Leaguers* may reflect a sense of frustration at old age. It is strikingly different to Trollope's line in earlier Irish novels, especially *Castle Richmond*. There, the tone is sympathetic to the tenants and the Famine is blamed on bad land management:

> [T]hus a state of things was engendered in Ireland which discouraged labour, which discouraged improvements in farming, which discouraged any produce from the land except the potato crop; which maintained one class of men in what they considered to be the gentility of idleness, and another class, the people of the country, in the abjectness of poverty.[16]

There appeared to be some truth in this analysis. Rapid population growth in the first part of the nineteenth century had not been accompanied by a similar growth in agricultural production. The main change had been a significant extension of sub-letting, leading to ever-smaller holdings. Mono-culture is inherently dangerous, and exclusive reliance on one crop – the potato – liable to result in famine if the harvests failed. There were several famines, of varying severity, between 1801 and 1845. In relation to its agricultural resources, Ireland was over-populated, especially in the 'congested' districts of the west. If agricultural improvement was impossible, lower numbers were the only way to restore a viable balance between population and resources – through famine or migration or a combination of both. Subscribers to this view believed that once the pressure of population had been reduced, Irish agriculture could be reorganized and the country escape from excessive dependence on the potato. Holdings would become larger and the whole system reorganized on more rational – that is more English – lines. Those who remained would enjoy better living standards and a more secure food supply.

---

[15] Terry Eagleton, *Heathcliff and the Great Hunger* (London: Verso, 1995), p. 15, and see p 15n.

[16] Anthony Trollope, *Castle Richmond* (1860) (London: Penguin Books Ltd., 1993), pp 120-140. Further references to this edition are given after quotations in the text and the title shortened to *Richmond*.

There are, however, objections. Perhaps, the Government should have done more to curb the evil of sub-letting and sub-division before the Great Hunger. Of course, such measures would have been unpopular with both landowners and middlemen – sub-division produced higher overall rental income – and with the land-hungry tenants themselves. From an enlightened Unionist position, one that Edgeworth might have endorsed, the true charge against the Westminster Government was really one of neglect – and there are hints of this in *Castle Richmond*.

Despite what some nationalist readings maintain, Trollope considered himself an honorary Irishman: 'I have known Ireland for more than forty years, - say from 1842 to 1882' (*Land-Leaguers*, p. 253). He returned to Ireland, during the Land War, and was appalled by what was happening. *The Land-Leaguers*, however, provides an incomplete picture of Trollope's view of the condition of Ireland. Only forty-nine of the planned sixty chapters were completed. His son's postscript reveals that little is known of what the remainder might have contained.

A key chapter is 'The State of Ireland' in which Trollope outlines his position on the Land War. Arthur Pollard notes that the chapter 'is pure fact and comment' and, as Trollope indicates, was probably 'intended as the preface':[17]

> It is necessary that this one chapter shall be written in which the accidents that occurred in the lives of our three heroines shall be made subordinate to the political circumstances of the day. This chapter should have been introductory and initiative; but the facts as stated will suit better to the telling of my story if they be told here. (*Land-Leaguers*, p. 251)

It is unclear why Trollope included this prefatory material so late in the novel; perhaps initial serialisation made it impossible to insert the chapter as a preface. However, Trollope was becoming increasingly incensed with the Land Leaguers and, after a second fact-finding trip, in July 1882, may have felt impelled to reinforce his fictional tale with new facts.

Trollope always regarded himself as a Liberal and, in 1868, had stood, unsuccessfully, as Liberal candidate for Beverley, Yorkshire. As late as 1880, Trollope would have been pleased when Gladstone appointed W E Forster Chief Secretary for Ireland on returning to the Premiership. Yet

---

[17] Arthur Pollard, *Anthony Trollope* (London: Routledge & Kegan Paul, 1978), p 23.

relations between Gladstone and Forster, once close friends, soon
deteriorated. Forster gave only reluctant support to the Land Act of 1881
and his outrage at the Kilmainham 'treaty' of 1882 made behind his back
and appearing to involve a deal with law-breakers, led to his resignation.
By 1882 it was clear that Gladstone's new Irish policy was quite unlike
that of his first administration (1868-74). Trollope agreed with his friend
and whist partner Forster and *The Land-Leaguers* may be seen as an *apologia*
for Forster.

Like Forster, Trollope believed that, during the Land War, 'property
has been jeopardised in a degree unknown for many years in the British
Islands' (*Land-Leaguers*, p. 251). He blames political agitators:

> [R]ents were readily paid up to 1878 and 1879; though abatements
> were asked for, – as was the case also in England; and there were
> men ready to tell the Irish from time to time, since the days of
> O'Connell downwards, that they were ill-treated in being kept out
> of their 'ould' properties by the rightful landowners. (*Land-Leaguers*,
> p. 252)

Trollope identifies with the landowners, the 'rightful landowners'. Yet
again he refers to English tenants; although in a similar position to the
Irish, they did not break the law. Trollope opposed 'Judge O'Hagan's
Land Court [...] with its various sub-commissioners' who would settle
'what rate land shall be let in Ireland' (*Land-Leaguers*, p. 255) because he
believed that the Court was destroying the long established links between
landowners and tenants. As an old-style Liberal, Trollope believed that the
market, not the Courts, should determine rents.

For Trollope, Gladstone's weakness was a prime cause of the Land
War; agrarian violence was inevitable if Government failed in its duty to
uphold the law:

> So it was in 1882. Tenants were harassed by needy landlords, and
> when they were served with forms of ejectment the landlords were
> simply murdered, either in their own persons or in that of their
> servants. Men finding their power, and beginning to learn how
> much might be exacted from a yielding Government, hardly knew
> how to moderate their aspirations. When they found that the
> expected results did not come at once, they resorted to revenge.
> (*Land-Leaguers*, p. 260)

After 1880, the Liberal Party became increasingly divided not just on Irish matters, but also over foreign and imperial policy and upon social and electoral reforms. These divisions reduced the effectiveness of Government and enabled Parnell and his followers to exploit its weakness both at Westminster and in the Irish countryside. Trollope sees a downward spiral into widespread violence:

> Did a neighbour occupy a field from which a Land-leaguing tenant had been evicted, let the tails of that neighbour's cattle be cut off, or the legs broken of his beasts of burden, or his sheep have their throats cut. Or if the injured one have some scruples of conscience, let the oppressor simply be boycotted, and put out of all intercourse with his brother men. Let no well-intentioned Land-leaguing neighbour buy from him a ton of hay, or sell to him a loaf of bread. But as a last resource, if all others fail, let the sinner be murdered. (*Land-Leaguers*, p. 260)

Violence is becoming arbitrary and is being used to settle personal vendettas. The pessimistic, even angry tone of *The Land-Leaguers* when it describes an Ireland mired in undeclared civil war, suggests a very different Trollope to the man of earlier years. The contrast with the more positive opinion of Trollope's *Autobiography* indicates the extent to which his had changed between 1876 and 1882:

> Home-rule no doubt is a nuisance, - and especially a nuisance because the professors of the doctrine do not at all believe it themselves. There are probably no other than twenty men in England or Ireland who would be so utterly dumfounded and prostrated were Home-rule to have its way as the twenty Irish members who profess to support it in the House of Commons. […] Home-rule is at any rate better and more easily managed than the rebellion at the close of the last century […] and very much less bloody than Fenianism.[18]

There is a distinct echo of earlier agrarian novelists, especially Edgeworth and Carleton, in Trollope's over-riding fear of mob rule and anarchy.

---

[18] Trollope, *Autobiography*, p 62.

Treacherous Tenants

Trollope depicts only agrarian violence in *The Land-Leaguers*. Philip Jones and his family, industrious farmers, become the target for local Land-Leaguers led by Pat Carroll. The initial outrage involves the smashing of sluice gates, destroying the work of thirty years; and, clearly, the sluice gates symbolise the law. Once the law is smashed, disorder, anarchy and violence, overwhelm good people like a flood. Carroll's prime objective is to destroy Jones and other landowners, although ultimately the trouble comes from America:

> There had been, so he [Jones] was told, a few demagogues in Galway town, American chiefly, who had come thither to do what harm they could; and he had heard that there was discontent in parts of Mayo. (*Land-Leaguers*, p. 11)

Mayo is significant because it was the birthplace of Michael Davitt. Davitt and the Land-Leaguers are 'the new aristocracy' (*Land-Leaguers*, p. 296) who oppose the old aristocracy with violence, intimidation and murder.

In *The Land-Leaguers*, Trollope portrays only good landowners – there is no sign of institutional violence. Jones, like other landowners, underestimates the power and abilities of the Land League. He is bemused by what occurs because he and his family have always been good landowners:

> [T]his man came to me and said that because the tenants away in county Mayo were not paying their rents, he could not pay his. And he can sell his interest on his holding now for £150. When I endeavoured to explain this to him, and that it was at my cost his interest in the farm had been created, he became my enemy. (*Land-Leaguers*, p. 7)

Things have changed so much that it is now the landowners who lose from their investment in improvements. As we have seen, in the novels of Carleton, it is the tenants who complain that landowners cheat them when they carry out improvements; everything is now the opposite to what it had been. County Mayo and County Galway, with backward rural economies, were prime targets for agrarian outrages. Jones, a rationalist, cannot understand why so many people turn against him. He concludes that any remaining tenants, not actively against him, dare not say anything in his defence; that would invite violent retribution from the Land Leaguers. Jones 'would have declared that no man in Ireland was on better terms with his tenantry than he' (*Land-Leaguers*, p.10). More is at stake than a tenant wanting better terms; the structure of the entire community is collapsing. Ellen Moody interprets Trollope's presentation of 'Irish rebels' as 'mad, evil people manipulated by outsiders (Americans), into demanding what is impractical and into committing barbarous acts'. She also highlights Trollope's commitment to the Rule of Law:

> Trollope dramatises and explains how a community of people normally tolerant enough of one another, who have worked together for years, can be transformed into individuals isolated by their fear of one another, and then into a violent mob. Trollope makes it clear to the reader why an unlawful authority, a 'new terrible aristocracy' is much worse than a lawful one. The former is based on 'aristocracy of hidden firearms', led by desperate, enraged and highly aggressive men. Unlike a legitimised authority whose laws control its instruments, the people who assume an unlawful authority need obey no law at all.[19]

The once paternalist relationship between landowner and tenant has changed irrevocably – but because of the tenants not the landowners.

In *The Land-Leaguers*, Carroll is supported not only by the local Catholic priest but also by the Land League:

> It was known that Pat Carroll had joined the Land-leaguers in the neighbouring county of Mayo with great violence, and that he had made a threat that he would pay no further rent to his landlord. The days of no-rent manifestation had not yet come, as the obnoxious Members of Parliament were not yet in prison; but no-rent was already fixed in the minds of many men, about to lead in the process of time to 'Arrears Bills,' and other abominations of justice. (*Land-Leaguers*, p. 86)

---

[19] Moody, p 44.

Trollope emphasises the link between the perpetrators of agrarian violence (like Carroll) and their masters in Westminster; those 'obnoxious Members of Parliament' should have been sent to prison.

Boycotting was one of the most effective forms of agrarian violence employed by the Land Leaguers. It is used to isolate and weaken the resolve of the Jones family at Castle Morony (the name echoing Castle Rackrent):

> Boycotting had commenced, and had already become very prevalent. To boycott a man, or a house, or a firm, or a class of men, or a trade, or a flock of sheep, or a drove of oxen, or unfortunately a county hunt, had become an exact science, and was exactly obeyed. [...] We can understand that boycotting should be studied in Yorkshire, and practised, - after an experience of many years. [...] But County Mayo and County Galway rose to the requirements of the art almost in a night! (*Land-Leaguers*, pp. 117-8)

Trollope despises boycotting. While recognizing that it is not unknown in England, he suggests that it appeals naturally to the Irish mind and that tenants, naïve and easily exploited by politicians, take readily to it. Boycotting is a callous and calculated act, incompatible with the English sense of fair play, and it affects every aspect of the Jones's life. Ada and Edith, Jones's two daughters, have to keep house, while Frank, the eldest son, has to run the whole estate with only occasional help from '"Emergency" men, who had been sent in from various parts of Ireland' (*Land-Leaguers*, p. 225). Trollope ensures that the stoic Jones family overcomes all the obstacles the Land Leaguers put in their way. The breakthrough in solving Florian's murder comes only when Teddy Mooney, an enthusiastic boycotter, realises that he is paying an even higher price than Jones. By joining a boycott, tenants inflict enormous damage on themselves and Trollope insists '[t]here is but the meditation of two minutes between Land-leaguing and Orangeism, between boycotting landlords and thorough devotion to the dear old landlord' (*Land-Leaguers*, p. 243).

Trollope regards hunting as a mark of civilization and attacks the practice of 'stopping the hunt'. In Ireland, the love and knowledge of horses was something common to all classes. Trollope, who favoured subscription hunts, supported the Liberal view on hunting – even the concept of ladies joining the hunt. Since he regarded hunting as socially unifying, hunt disruption was equal to social disruption, risking the stability of the whole community. In 'stopping the hunt', the tenants were able to inconvenience landowners with little risk to themselves:

> Fox hunting was an obvious target. The fact that so many MFHs [Master of Fox Hounds] and hunt servants were English didn't help. Nor were republican American agitators impressed by the sport of kings. 'Small wonder', wrote *Baily's*, 'if a sport which originated among the aristocracy of the land, and which, though broad and tolerant as the British Constitution itself, had always a most patrician savour about it, should be looked upon with suspicion, which all too soon turned to aversion'.[20]

'Stopping the hunt' was not only easy but satisfied national and class resentments with the disruptive influence of American republicanism again evident.

Black Tom Daly, MFH, is obsessed with hunting and cares only for horses and hounds. When the tenants decide to 'stop the hunt', he is drawn into the fray. Hitherto, Daly, although a Protestant, has had little time for either religion or politics and has treated everybody the same when out hunting. Trollope implies that, because of the violent actions of the Land Leaguers, people are forced to take sides – leading to increased bigotry and hatred. In addition, Daly is used to convey an unlikely idea to disconcert English readers:

> Now there had come a cloud over his [Daly's] spirit in reference to the state of his country. He could see that the quarrel was not entirely one between Protestant and Catholic as it used to be, but still he could not get it out of his mind, but that the old causes were producing in a different way their old effects. Whiteboys, Terryalts, Ribbonmen, Repeaters, Physical-Forcemen, Fenians, Home-Rulers, Professors of Dynamite, and American-Irish, were, to his thinking all the same. (*Land-Leaguers*, p. 58)

There are obvious similarities between Trollope and Daly: both are Protestants, love to hunt and see no difference between 'Home-Rulers', 'American-Irish' and members of violent secret societies. Trollope implies

---

[20] Jane Ridley, *Fox Hunting* (London: Collins, 1993), p 123.

that the violent activities of pre-Famine secret societies are being replicated at Westminster, where Parnell's filibustering is no less than 'political terrorism'. Trollope uses Daly to propose an extreme, though logical solution:

> The country can do nothing to put down this blackguardism. When they've passed this Coercion Bill they're going to have some sort of Land Bill, just a law to give away the land to somebody. What's to come of the poor country with such men as Mr. Gladstone and Mr. Bright to govern it? [...] Martial law with a regiment in each county, and strong colonel to carry it out, – that is the only way of governing left to us. (*Land-Leaguers*, p.137)

Trollope hated appeasement and believed that the result would be worse than if the Government stood its ground and Forster thought much the same. The former Chief Secretary's Quakerism differed from that of his fellow Liberal John Bright, an advocate of democracy who stirred up rural radicalism in England. Trollope certainly blamed Gladstone but felt that the real villain was Bright with his zeal for reform and his admiration for America.

When the hunt begins, there are no tenants at the covert on Bodkin's land. Although, as a Catholic landowner, he is acceptable to his Protestant counterparts, Bodkin's tenants still see him, first and foremost, as a Catholic Irishman. Things are different when the hunt moves to other coverts. No matter how far Daly rides, the tenants have always reached the coverts before him. This reveals the Land Leaguers' high level of organization and how a previously superficially stable society is being undermined:

> He was one Kit Mooney, a baker from Claregalway, who in these latter days had turned Land-leaguer. But he was one who simply thought that his bread might be better buttered for him on that side of the question. He was not an ardent politician; but few local Irishmen were so. Had no stirring spirits been wafted across the waters from America to teach Irishmen that one man is as good as another, or generally better, Kit Mooney would never have found it out. (*Land-Leaguers*, p. 64)

The Land War turns apolitical Irishmen into landowner-hating zealots. Like his mother, Trollope blames the American obsession with equality:

> Any man's son may become the equal of any other man's son, and the consciousness of this is certainly the spur to exertion; on the other hand, it is also a spur to that coarse familiarity, untempered by any shadow of respect, which is assumed by the grossest and lowest in their intercourse with the highest and most refined. This is a positive evil, and, I think, more than balances its advantages.[21]

Trollope's view of Americans was undoubtedly influenced by his mother's observations. Though he liked the Irish generally, Trollope did not really trust the tenantry. While some changes might be necessary, the social hierarchy in Ireland should be maintained.

At another hunt, Barney Smith (Daly's huntsman) is attacked and Daly, sorely provoked, responds violently:

> They said that the blackguard was hurt, but I saw him escape and get away over the fence. Then they all set on Tom, but by G— it was glorious to see the way in which he held his own. Out came that cross of his, four feet and a half long, with a thong as heavy as a flail. He soon had the road clear around him, and the big black horse you remember, stood as steady as a statue till he was bidden to move. (*Land-Leaguers*, p. 119)

Although Daly acts in self-defence and in defence of his injured employee, violence begets violence. The attack on Daly by a number of tenants is cowardly. This message is reinforced when Daly is falsely accused of riding down some tenants – an accusation that provides an excuse for yet another agrarian outrage: the destruction of his kennels by arson.

The threatening letters sent by Land Leaguers hark back to pre-Famine Ireland, reinforcing the links between secret societies both past and present. The pseudonym, 'Captain Moonlight' had a long history and echoes earlier events in England where names such as 'Captain Swing' and 'Captain Ned Ludd' had also been used in rural confrontations. McGrew, the Jones's butler, receives a threatening letter:

---

[21] Fanny Trollope, *Domestic Manners of the Americans* (1832) (Stroud: Alan Sutton, 1993), p 87.

Mr. PETER McGREW,

If you're not out of that before the end of the month, but stay there doing things for them infernal blackguards, your goose is cooked. So now you know all about it.

From yours,

MOONLIGHT (*Land-Leaguers*, p. 203)

McGrew is terrified, all the more so since he believes that Lax (the Land Leaguers' hired killer) can read his mind. The name Moonlight is an established part of Irish myth. It was easy – and cowardly – for anybody to write a letter using a name so well established in the tenants' psyche. It was a particularly effective way to operate.

The level of agrarian violence increases steadily throughout the novel and murder becomes the norm. Florian, newly converted to Catholicism, witnesses the destruction of the sluice gates. Carroll, a violent bully, threatens the boy with death if he reveals what he saw:

> 'Not a know; – an' if you main to keep yourself from being holed as they holed Muster Bingham the other day away at Hollymount'. The boy understood perfectly well what was meant by the process of 'holing'. The Mr. Bingham, a small landlord, who had been acting as his own agent some twenty miles off, in the County of Mayo, had been frightfully murdered three months since. (*Land-Leaguers*, p. 13)

The fact that Carroll forces a boy to lie to his father, the victim of the outrage, would not be lost on English readers and would make Land Leaguers seem even more loathsome.

Unlike Kickham, Trollope does not consider a tenant's security of tenure particularly important:

> [Trollope's] Anglo-Irish, Irish Catholic and Protestant landlords are all decent. The landlords are all virtuous and civic-minded men who need, or have the right to, an adequate return on what are presented as generous investments in Irish land [...]. The Irish rebels are presented as mad, evil people manipulated by outsiders (Americans), into demanding what is impractical and into

committing barbarous acts. [...] None of the landlords in this book rent-rack [sic] their tenants, and the need a tenant has to know that he has some security of tenure before he will invest in a property is never brought up.[22]

Trollope's stance is both patronizing and paternalistic while his reliance upon the decency of landowners echoes the early Edgeworth

Thomas Blake, another Protestant landowner, is Jones's closest friend:

> Mr. Blake was a man of good property, who, in former years, had always been regarded as popular in the country. He was a Protestant, but he had not made himself odious to the Roman Catholics around him as an Orangeman, nor had he ever been considered to be too hard as a landlord. He thought, perhaps, a little too much of popularity, and had prided himself a little perhaps, on managing 'his boys' – as he called the tenants – with peculiar skill. (*Land-Leaguers*, p. 23)

Blake's attitude is similar to that of Trollope and, so far, it had worked. Trollope thinks that religious moderation is the key. He does not approve of religious or political extremists, like Orangemen, who deliberately provoke Catholics. Blake has a Catholic counterpart in Sir Nicholas Bodkin:

> Sir Nicholas's neighbours, such of them at least that are Protestants, regard Sir Nicholas as equal to themselves. They do not care much for his religion, but they know that he is not a Home-Ruler, or [...] a Land-leaguer. He is, in fact, one of themselves as a country gentleman, and the question of religion has gone altogether into abeyance. Had you known the country thirty years ago [...] you would think that he was one of the old Protestants. [...] He liked to get his rents paid, as long as his tenants would pay them, he was at one with them. (*Land-Leaguers*, p. 53)

If Blake is an ideal, moderate, Protestant landowner, so Bodkin is his Catholic equivalent. Catholic landowners who hunt and carry their religion

---

[22] Moody, p 44.

lightly are acceptable to Protestants. Yet the reference to better days 'thirty years ago' is puzzling; in the early 1850s, Ireland was still in the aftermath of the Famine. Robert Morris, a further example of a Protestant landowner, is fair but eccentric. He has given his tenants so many abatements that he has halved his own income. His reward is to be callously murdered. He had been '"dropped" [...] from behind a wall built by the roadside. It had been done at about five in the afternoon, in full daylight' (*Land-Leaguers*, p. 227) – but nobody will admit to witnessing this outrage.

For the only time in his Irish novels, Trollope uses a boy, Florian, as the central character. He does this to enhance the despicable nature of his murder and hence to reveal the true nature of the Land League:

> Mr. Jones saw a mask, which he supposed to be mask worn by a man, through a hole in the wall just in front of him, but high above his head. And at the same moment he could see the muzzles of a double-barrelled rifle presented through the hole in the wall. [...] Then a trigger was pulled, and one bullet – the second – went through the collar of his own coat, while the first had had a more fatal and truer aim. The father jumped up and turning round saw that his boy had fallen to the ground. (*Land-Leaguers*, p. 187)

The attack comes from behind a wall and from a masked assassin – cowardice at its worst and contrary to all forms of civilized behaviour. A defenceless, ten-year-old boy, on his way to give evidence against men who have attacked his family, is shot for trying to tell the truth. Trollope's frustration and anger is evident in Jones's words:

> [Jones] had spent his time for many a long year in doing all in his power for those around him, and now they had brought him to this. [...] They had taught his boy to be one of them, and to be untrue to his own people. And now, because he had yielded to better teachings, they had murdered him. [...] The accursed Papist people were all cowards down to their backbones. [...] But they were terribly powerful in their wretched want of manliness. They could murder, and were protected in their bloodthirstiness one by another. [...] The honour and honesty of one man did not in these days, prompt another to abstain from vice. The only heroism left

in the country was the heroism of mystery, of secret bloodshed, and hidden attacks. (*Land-Leaguers*, p. 188)

Catholicism is directly linked to Land Leaguers and mindless agrarian violence. Jones's many good deeds count for nothing when mob violence is unleashed.

After Florian's murder, the level of agrarian outrages rises still further, Terry Carroll, the other prosecution witness and one of the perpetrators of the original crime, appears in the witness box only to be shot and killed in open Court. The crime is a direct insult to the Queen and shows that Land Leaguers can strike anywhere. The ease with which the murder is committed, along with the convenient lack of witnesses, demonstrates the effectiveness of the Land League's intimidation. The murder of Morris and many others shows how easy killing has become:

> He [the tenant] has not, of his own, much capacity for the use of firearms; but he had four pound ten, which should have gone to the payment of his rent, and of this four pound ten, fifteen shillings secured the services of some handy man out of the next parish. He had heard the question of murder freely discussed among his neighbours, and by listening to others had learned the general opinion that there was no danger in it. So he came to a decision, and Mr. Morris was murdered. (*Land-Leaguers*, p. 281)

Murder has become a profitable 'cottage industry', so commonplace that even 'the women would ask for fresh murders, and would feel disappointed when none were reported to them, craving, as it were, for blood' (*Land-Leaguers*, p. 282). Gentle, caring and religious Irish wives and mothers have become addicted to bloody murder. Trollope knew that English readers, especially women, would be horrified:

> Trollope makes the reader travel a slow curve of alarm, fear, dread and terror in a series of accidents, intimidations and single unexplained murders which culminate in a mass murder in a farmhouse.[23]

---

[23] Moody, p.44.

The murder of the Kellys (based on the real killing of the Joyce family) is described in terrifying detail:

> The six persons had been murdered, barring one child, who had been taken into Cong in a state which was supposed hardly to admit of his prolonged life. The others, who now lay dead at a shebeen house in the neighbourhood, consisted of an old woman and her son, and his wife and a grown up daughter, and a son. All these had been killed in various ways, - had been shot with rifles, and stoned with rocks, and made away with after a fashion that might come most readily to the hands of the brutes devoid of light, mercy, of conscience, and apparently of fear. (*Land-Leaguers*, p. 291)

These murders are especially abhorrent because unarmed women and children are killed in their own beds. Even worse, the atrocity is a family affair and primarily concerned with power among tenants themselves:

> [T]he Kellys were a tribe who had been strong in the land for many years. Though each of the ten [murderers] feared to be of the bloody party, each did not like not to be of it, for so the power would have come out of their hands. They wished to be among the leading aristocrats, though still they feared. And thus they came together, dreading each other, hating each other at last; each aware that he was about to put his very life within the other's power, and each trying to think, as far as thoughts would come to his dim mind, that to him might come some possibility of escape by betraying his comrades. (*Land-Leaguers*, p. 292)

Although *The Land-Leaguers* is unfinished, Trollope's message seems clear: if the Land League can turn families against each other, Ireland's future will be truly terrible. But, at the end of the novel, there is a faint glimmer of hope; this crime goes too far and finally witnesses come forward; religious divisions are no longer all important.

Religion

In *The Land-Leaguers*, Jones is consistently presented as moderate in religion:

The Jones's had been Protestants, the father and mother having come from England as Protestants. They were not, therefore, Ultra-Protestants, as those will know who best know Ireland. There had been no horror of a Catholic. According to Mrs. Jones the way to heaven had been open to both Catholic and Protestant, only it had suited her to say her prayers after the Protestant fashion. The girls had been filled with no pious fury; and as to Mr. Jones himself, some of the Protestant devotees in the neighbourhood of Tuam had declared that he was only half-hearted in the matter. (*Land-Leaguers*, p. 4)

Jones's attitude to Protestantism reminds us of Richard Lovell Edgeworth. Jones's religion could not fairly be used to justify his sufferings at the hands of Catholic Land Leaguers. Carroll may be a Catholic but what matters about him is that he is a violent, politically-motivated Land Leaguer. The problem is that Florian is dazzled by Catholicism and decides to convert. If he had not converted, he would not have been bound by his oath to the politicized Father Brosnan and could have revealed what he had seen earlier. His lies divide the family and allow Carroll, Lax and other Land Leaguers to continue with their murderous mayhem – while Castle Morony draws closer to financial ruin.

Although the storyline of Florian's conversion is far fetched, Trollope uses it to drive home the terrible intimidation practiced by extreme, American-influenced, politicized Catholics, men without morality who bully and frighten an innocent, naïve, young boy. Florian first has to deal with a masked man and his henchman, Carroll – perhaps an echo of Pip's first meeting with Magwitch in *Great Expectations* (1860-61):

You'd better mark him, that's all. If he cotches a hould o' ye he'd tear ye to tatthers, that's all. Not that he'd do ye the laist harum in life if ye'd just hould yer pace, and say nothin' to nobody. (*Land-Leaguers*, p. 12)

This physical threat would be enough to terrify anyone but, not content, Carroll grossly distorts the true message of Catholicism:

You're to remimber your oath, Muster Flory. You're become one of us, as Father Brosnan was telling you. You're not to be one of

211

us, and then go over among them schaming Prothestants. (*Land-Leaguers*, p. 14)

Florian now belongs to the tenants' side and a hooded woman accosts him at his own front door, warning '[y]ou're one of us now, Master Florian' (*Land-Leaguers*, p. 20).

Trollope notes '[t]here has come a change among the priests in Ireland during the last fifty years' (*Land-Leaguers*, p. 15). The new kind is not to his liking:

> There used to be two distinct sort of priests; of whom the elder, who had probably been abroad, was the better educated; whereas the younger, who was home-nurtured, had less to say for himself on general topics. [...] their feelings and aspirations were based then on their religious opinions. Now a set of men had risen up, with whom opposition to the rulers of the country is connected chiefly with political ideas. A dream of Home Rule has made them what they are, and thus they have been roused into waking life, by the American spirit, which has been imported into the country. (*Land-Leaguers*, p.16)

Trollope blames America for this sad change. He has no objection to Catholic priests as such, but as Glendinning notes, he sees those 'who stirred up the people as reprehensible'.[24] This point is elaborated by Jill Felicity Durey:

> For the law-abiding 70-year old Father Giles, Trollope has respect, but for the zealous young curate, Father Brosnan, Trollope has none. He had lost his sympathy for the Irish Catholic cause, and demonstrates more sympathy for the victimized Protestant Jones family. For him, the end did *not* justify the means. Trollope's early adoption of a balanced stance vis-à-vis Roman Catholicism swiftly turned into rejection once politics became the issue and murder became the means. Once again, he totally disapproved of a church becoming involved in politics.[25]

---

[24] Glendinning, p 495.
[25] Jill Felicity Durey, *Trollope and the Church of England* (Basingstoke: Palgrave Macmillan, 2002), p 160.

Trollope identifies three types of priest. Father Giles, 'a man seventy years of age', cared for his flock but also believed that they should 'do as they were bid by their betters' (*Land-Leaguers*, p. 16). The bane of his declining years is his curate, Father Brosnan, who puts politics before religion:

> He [Giles] had gone so far as to forbid Father Brosnan to do this, or to do that on various occasions, to make a political speech here, or to attend a demonstration there; - in doing which, or in not doing it, the curate sometimes obeyed, but sometimes disobeyed the priest. (*Land-Leaguers*, p.16)

Brosnan has no respect for anybody who disagrees with him or who gets in his way. He even regards Giles 'as half an infidel, and almost as bad as a Protestant' (*Land-Leaguers*, p. 18) and is totally opposed to landowners:

> Father Brosnan knew the application as to his rent which had been made by Pat Carroll to his landlord. He was of opinion that no rent ought to be paid by any Irish tenant to any landlord – no rent, at least, to a Protestant landlord. [...] He considered not at all the circumstances, whether, as had been the case on certain properties in Mayo, all money expended had been so expended by the tenant, or by the landlord, as had been the case with Pat Carroll's land. That was an injustice, according to Mr. Brosnan's theory; as is all property in accordance with the teaching of some political doctors who are not burdened with any. (*Land-Leaguers*, p.17)

Father Malachi takes the middle ground between the two extremes of Giles and Brosnan:

> [Malachi] had an inclination for Home Rule, and still entertained a jealousy against the quasi-Ascendancy of a Protestant bishop; but he had no sympathy with Father Brosnan. (*Land-Leaguers*, p. 17)

Trollope's implicit warning is that unless the Government acts, priests will become more extreme. Even selfish ones like Malachi, whose political beliefs are more moderate than Brosnan's, will be in a minority. Malachi's dislike of the prospect of an American Ireland probably stems from his ambition to become a bishop – he needs a native hierarchy to advance within the Catholic Church.

Jones is desperate to do something about '[t]he absurdity of the conversion' of his son. Malachi 'would no doubt have owned that the boy had been altogether unable to see, by his own light, the difference between the two religions. But he would have attributed the change to the direct interposition of God'. Trollope implies that, although Malachi was Florian's friend and knew the truth about his conversion, he was first and foremost a priest and 'the gaining of a proselyte under any circumstances would have been an advantage too great to jeopardise by any arguments in the matter' (*Land-Leaguers*, p. 75).

Brosnan takes advantage of Florian's youth and naïveté. He encourages the boy to convert for political rather than spiritual reasons. He tries to use Florian's gullibility and innocence to protect Carroll and destroy Jones. Like many other extremists, Brosnan cares little for the truth. Jones is a Protestant landowner and as such deserves to be punished:

> [I]n the quarrel which was now beginning all his sympathies were with the Carrolls at large, and not with the Jones's at large. At every victory won by the British Parliament his heart again boiled with indignation. At every triumphant note that came over the water from America […] he boiled, on the other hand, with joy. He had gleams in his mind of a Republic. He thought of a Saxon as an evil being. The Queen, he would say, was very well, but she was better at a distance. The Lord-Lieutenant was a British vanity, and English pomp, but the Chief Secretary was a minister of the Evil One himself. (*Land-Leaguers*, p. 18)

Brosnan is a rabid republican, strongly influenced by America, and against everything English:

> *The Landleaguers* […] is an indictment of this cause [Home Rule], the impetus for which, the novelist alleges, came originally not from the Irish but from the Americans, who used the younger generation of zealous priests like Father Brosnan to follow it through to completion, even if murder was used to achieve their goal. Trollope felt betrayed: fanaticism and violence were

anathema to him and *his* Church, and he could never condone such extremes. For him, this was worse than secularism.[26]

Brosnan does not represent the official position of the Catholic Church and even his fellow priests disagree with him. Trollope condemns him for his dangerous ignorance:

> He was a man thoroughly disloyal, and at the same time thoroughly ignorant, altogether in the dark as to the fitness for the duties of the priesthood, to which he had been educated, had no capability of perceiving political facts, and no honesty in teaching them. (*Land-Leaguers*, p. 18)

It is not entirely clear as to what or whom Brosnan is disloyal but, since he is loyal to his flock and to the Land Leaguers, he must be disloyal to the Catholic Church. Yet, when Florian is murdered, Brosnan condemns himself:

> [T]here seemed to be a feeling about the country that Florian Jones had deserved his fate. He had, it was said, been untrue to his religion. He had given a solemn promise to Father Brosnan, - of what nature was not generally known, - and had broken it. 'The bitherness of the Orange feud was in his blood', said Father Brosnan. But neither did he explain the meaning of what he said, as none of the Jones family had ever been Orangemen. (*Land-Leaguers*, pp. 189-190)

The general reaction to Florian's murder is hardly creditable to the tenants. They consider that it is acceptable to murder a child who has supposedly 'been untrue to his religion'. Brosnan refers to 'the Orange feud' but he is at least as extreme as any Orangeman. His failure to explain his statement suggests a limited grasp of politics. His bigotry contributes to the boy's murder, yet the tenants approve of the crime and think it right to regard Carroll as 'a martyr' (*Land-Leaguers*, p. 190). As Carleton despaired about Ireland's future when he saw the tenants' reaction to the death of the child-murderer Devann, so Trollope despairs when describing the tenants' attitude to Lax.

---

[26] Durey, p 165.

The American Threat

Trollope had mixed views on emigration to America. Unlike Kickham, he wanted emigrant Irishmen to stay in America and keep their revolutionary and republican ideas there too. In *Castle Richmond*, Trollope portrays emigration in a positive light because it gives Irish tenants far better opportunities:

> The poor cotter suffered sorely under the famine, and under the pestilence which followed the famine; but he, as a class, has risen from his bed of suffering a better man. He is thriving as a labourer either in his own country or in some newer – for him better – land to which he has emigrated. (*Richmond*, p.125).

Even in *The Land-Leaguers*, Trollope does not object to Irish emigration – quite the contrary. But America is no longer seen as the land of opportunity; it has become a convenient 'dumping ground' for disaffected and troublesome Irishmen. Jones, the landowner and chief victim of the Land Leaguers, is baffled by Carroll's unwillingness to emigrate to America:

> [Jones] had been willing to buy out from his [Carroll's] bit of land and let him go to America, so that they might all be in peace. (*Land-Leaguers*, p. 11)

Trollope shares his character's confusion. America has served as the beacon of hope for the Irish so long that Trollope cannot grasp that disaffected Irishmen now want to change Ireland rather than emigrate. The real problem, however, is that Irish emigrants are now exporting Fenianism back to Ireland.

Trollope sees America not as the solution to Ireland's problems but as the cause. He 'places the blame for recent troubles emphatically on American influence and money'[27] – or on what was becoming Irish-American influence:

> It is, I think, the general opinion that these evils have been occasioned by the influx into Ireland of a feeling which I will not

---

[27] Pollard, p 24.

call American, but which has been engendered in America by Irish jealousy, and warmed into hatred by distance from English rule. (*Land-Leaguers*, p. 252)

Many Irish emigrants saw parallels between the American Civil War and what was needed in Ireland. A good many joined the Union armies, thinking that the Southern plantation owners were the American equivalents of Ascendancy landlords and the black slaves the equivalent of Irish tenants.

Trollope believed that hatred of the English was driven by Smith O'Brien and American-based Fenianism:

Smith O'Brien achieved little beyond his own exile:- but his words, acting upon his followers, produced Fenianism. That died away, but the spirit remained in America; and when English tenants began to clamour for temporary abatements in their rent, the clamours were heard on the other side of the water, and assisted the views of those American-Irish who had revivified Ribandism and had given birth to the cry of Home Rule. (*Land-Leaguers*, p. 252)

There was thus a direct link between America, Ribandism/Ribbonism and Home Rule, and it is the latter that Trollope sees as the greatest threat to the *status quo*:

Home Rule coming across to us from America had taken the guise of rebellion. [...] [T]he latter-day Home-Rulers [...] brought their politics, their aspirations, and their money from New York, and boldly made use of the means which the British Constitution afforded them to upset the British Constitution as established in Ireland. That they should not succeed in doing this is the determination of all, at any rate on this side of the Channel. [...] England is still writhing in her attempt to invent some mode of controlling them. But long before any such mode had been adopted [...] the Government in 1881 brought out their plan for securing to the tenants fair rents, fixity of tenure, and freedom of sale. (*Land-Leaguers*, p. 258)

217

The seeds of Home Rule have come from America and brought violence with them. Trollope blames Gladstone for appeasing the Land Leaguers and rewarding their violence. His use of the neutral phrase 'securing for the tenants' disguises his belief that recent Land Acts amount to a surrender to the rebels and to the Land Leaguers' demand for the 'Three Fs' (fixity of tenure, fair rent and free sale).

Not content with attacking American influence, Trollope uses a sub-plot – the love story of Rachel O'Mahony and Frank Jones – to ridicule that influence along with Fenianism and Parnell. Rachel and her father, Gerald O'Mahony, share a surname with the co-founder of Fenianism in America, John O'Mahony. Gerald O'Mahony is as a lazy, American fool, willing to live off his daughter's potential while voicing ideas he lacks the intelligence to understand. This does not, however, stop him from stirring up discontent and, as Arthur Pollard suggests, he 'personifies the new American-Irishman who, in Trollope's view, was causing so much trouble'.[28] Victoria Glendinning agrees:

> Anthony blamed American Fenianism for the troubles. The villain of his piece is Gerald O'Mahony, an Irish-American rabble-rouser. 'No educated man was ever born and bred in more utter ignorance of all political truths than this amiable and philanthropic gentleman'.[29]

By a ridiculously contrived set of circumstances, O'Mahony becomes a Land League Member of Parliament. Trollope drives home his point by suggesting that the Irish MPs at Westminster believe that even the bumbling, ignorant and incompetent O'Mahony would make a better leader than Parnell.

Solution?

Ironically, Trollope, the Englishman, offers a more innovative inter-pretation of Ireland's problems than Kickham, the devout Irishman and Fenian. Trollope almost completely dismisses the old agenda and moves into fantasy when he identifies America as the epitome of all evil. In the last resort, he reiterates his mother's anti-Americanism:

---

[28] Pollard, pp. 24-25.
[29] Glendinning, pp. 495-6.

[N]o single feature in their [the American], national character, [...] that could justify their eternal boast of liberality and the love of freedom. They inveigh against the governments of Europe, because, they say, they favour the powerful and oppress the weak. You may hear this declaimed upon in Congress [...] listen to it, and then look at them at home; you will see them with one hand hoisting the cap of liberty, and with the other flogging their slaves. You will see them one hour lecturing their mob on the indefeasible rights of man, and the next driving from their homes the children of the soil, whom they have bound themselves to protect by the most solemn treaties.[30]

The fact that Trollope's novel is unfinished deprives us of what may have been his solution to the Irish crisis. Nevertheless, enough of the story has been written and sufficient is known about Trollope to reveal that he could offer no constructive blueprint to solve the Irish problem. He opposed Home Rule and longed for the past but suggested no solution that offered a viable future. His belief that Ireland should be kept in the Union, that priests should not be political, and that tenants should know their place is dated and unrealistic. Although Trollope wanted to be the voice of sanity and reason in discussions about the Land Question, as *The Land-Leaguers* shows, he ended up offering only a slightly crazed and nihilistic vision of Ireland.

---

[30] Quoted in Teresa Ransom, *Fanny Trollope* (Stroud: Alan Sutton Publishing Ltd., 1996), p 64.

By the time Kickham and Trollope wrote their agrarian novels, Ireland was again a central issue in British domestic politics. Agrarian violence, which had lessened after the Famine, spread at an alarming rate. Landowners and tenants who had co-existed fairly peacefully in the years after The Famine found themselves forced to take sides in an increasingly polarised country. While Fenian ideals were spread among the tenants and Gladstone gradually moved towards Home Rule, the Land War raged in Ireland. Ascendancy landowners found themselves without allies and surrounded by a newly confident and aggressive tenantry and a politicised Catholic priesthood.

Neither a politicised and violent Ireland, nor the introduction of America was able to inject new imaginative life into the agrarian novel. The momentum, such as it was, that had been built up by agrarian novelists, in the first five decades of the nineteenth century, had all but disappeared. Kickham's hope of an Irish nation re-vitalised by American republican vigour was doomed from the start. Irishmen who had emigrated did so to forge a new life away from Ireland and the Old World, and only a tiny minority had any intention of returning. Kickham liked to believe that the American Civil War offered an example to Ireland: the Ascendancy, like the Confederacy, would be soundly defeated. He saw the Irish who fought for the Union as heroes who could return to Ireland, trained and battle-hardened, ready to take on the English. In reality, most of those who had fought in the Irish regiments did so because they believed in and wanted to be a part of a new, unified America not because they wanted to be trained to fight for Ireland. Kickham, though principally a political writer, was, above all, a dreamer. As reality closed in on his dreams and his solution was revealed as absurd, he fell out with fellow Fenians, nationalists and the Catholic Church before retreating into a world of his own where he no longer had to suffer criticism.

For Trollope, the end of his literary career and his farewell to Ireland was equally sad. While Kickham, the political journalist, may be forgiven writing second-rate literature, it is harder to forgive Trollope. The liberal and encompassing attitude, evident in his earlier novels, gives way to an uncompromising diatribe against all change. Trollope professed to love Ireland and its people but there is little evidence of this in *The Land-Leaguers*; here, his main aim is to attribute blame. It is true that Trollope was old and infirm and died before completing the novel. His writing lacks direction rather than energy. Trollope's analysis of the Land Question is, uncharacteristically, simple and extreme. The enemy comes in many guises: America, Fenianism, tenants who do not know their place, politicised Catholic priests and a Prime Minister and a Liberal party that no longer holds firm. Trollope's stance is uncompromising: full support for Ascendancy landowners, suspension of *Habeas Corpus* and the use of the military to regain control and re-establish stability. As Gladstone was beginning to realise, it was too late for such tactics. At least superficially, Parnell's Home Rulers – and even the Land Leagues – were democratic movements supported by most of Ireland and watched with approval in much of Europe.

Charles Kickham and Anthony Trollope were of different nationalities, different religions and subscribed to different politics. One would expect their novels to reflect these differences and present the Land Question in radically different ways. The only similarity seems to be that they are both agrarian novelists – and not very good ones either. Yet Kickham and Trollope have more in common than first meets the eye. The best way of proving this point is by comparing extracts from their novels:

Kickham:

The dying foxhunter seemed to drop suddenly into a doze, from which a low fretful whine from one of the hounds caused him to awake with a start. 'Poor bluebell; poor Bluebell', he murmured. The hound named wagged her tail, and coming close to him, looked wistfully into his face. [...] He roused himself [...] and gazed once more upon the fine landscape before him, and again called upon the huntsman to sound the horn.[1]

---

[1] Charles J Kickham, *Knocknagow* (1879) (Dublin: M H Gill and Son, 1962), p 484.

Trollope:

He not only knew every hound in his pack, but he knew their ages, their sires and their dams; and the sires and the dams of most of their sires and dams. He knew the constitution of each and to what extent their noses were to be trusted. 'It's a very heavy scent to-day', he would say, ' because Gaylap carries it over the plough. It's only a catching scent because the drops don't hang on the bushes'.[2]

Kickham:

When he flung himself down among the fern on the mountain side, the greyhounds flung themselves down too [...] the sun was struggling through the mist that rested upon the opposite hill [...] Now the greyhounds were coiled up at his feet, breathing as regularly as if they were on the hearthstone before the kitchen fire; the sun was mounting high above the cloud-banks piled up around the horizon.[3]

Kickham:

'The fact is,' returned Mr. Armstrong, seriously, 'it is more costly to live now than it used to be. I find I must either sell my property or my pony. 'Tis a fine thing to be an "estated man"; it brings one troops of friends and invitations to dinner. [...] Don't imagine 'tis getting old I am', he continued, throwing back his shoulders, 'No such thing. That voyage across the Atlantic has added at least twenty years to my life'.[4]

Trollope:

'That is very true; - so true that I myself shall act upon the truth. But I will not make his last years wretched. He is a Protestant, and you are Catholics'. 'What is that? Are not ever so many of your

---

[2] Anthony Trollope, *The Land-Leaguers* (1884) (London: Penguin Group, 1993), p 56.
[3] Charles J Kickham, *Sally Cavanagh* (1869) (Dublin: James Duffy and Co. Ltd., 1948), pp 1-2.
[4] Charles J Kickham, *For the Old Land* (1886) (Dublin: M H Gill and Son, 1892), p 182.

lords Catholics? Were they not all Catholics before Protestants were ever thought of?'[5]

Trollope:

Nothing ever so strengthened the love of the Irish for, and the obedience of the Irish to O'Connell, as his imprisonment; nothing ever so weakened his power over them as his unexpected enfranchisement. The country shouted for joy when he was set free, and expended all its enthusiasm in the effort.[6]

Trollope:

With her, as with the world in general, religion was the point on which those prejudices were the strongest; and the peculiar bent they took was horror of hatred and popery. As she lived in a country in which the Roman Catholic was the religion of the poorer classes, and of very many persons who were not poor, there was ample scope in which her horror and hatred could work.[7]

Trollope:

[H]e acted as his father's agent over the property – by which I mean to signify that he occupied himself in harrowing the tenantry for money which they had no means of paying; he was occasionally head driver and ejector; and he considered, as Irish landlords are apt to do, that he had an absolute right over the tenants, as feudal vassals.[8]

Without attribution it would surely be hard to guess who had written what. There are passages in Trollope that seem remarkably like one's ideas

---

[5] Anthony Trollope, *An Eye for an Eye* (1879) (Gloucester: Dodo Press, n.d.), pp 57-8.
[6] Anthony Trollope, *The Kellys and The O'Kellys* (1848) (London: Penguin Group, 1993), p 2.
[7] Anthony Trollope, *Castle Richmond* (1860) (London: Penguin Books Ltd., 1993), pp 95-6.
[8] Anthony Trollope, *The Macdermots of Ballycloran* (1847) (London: Penguin Group, 1993), p 6.

of Kickham and some in Kickham that seem like Trollope. For all their political differences, they describe the same society in much the same way.

Together, so different and yet so similar, Kickham and Trollope take the Irish agenda out of Ireland and moved it to America and to England. For a while the move – in either direction – may have given a moribund and stale genre a new lease of life; yet had it really? The overseas solutions identified or at least hinted at by Kickham and Trollope were no more convincing than the domestic solutions sought by their predecessors. Was there anywhere else that the agenda could 'emigrate' to? There was only one possibility – it would have to abandon reality all together.

Part Three:
The Flight from Reality

Introduction:
Beyond Time and Space

At the beginning of this book, it was argued that Irish agrarian novels tend to follow the conventions of social realism first established in the eighteenth-century novel – and, up to this point, they have done precisely that. The chief reason why the novels examined so far remained firmly within the tradition of realism lies squarely with Maria Edgeworth. Edgeworth was a product of the Enlightenment, the Age of Reason. Since she dominated the sub-genre of the agrarian novel so completely, even those who disagreed with aspects of her analysis had to do so within the parameters of her rational and realist agenda. It could, however, have been very different.

If Edgeworth's influence had not been so pervasive, it is possible that Thomas Moore could have 'fathered' a 'family' as large and as important as Edgeworth's. Principally known as a poet, in *Memoirs of Captain Rock* (1824), Moore offers an entirely different interpretation and presentation of the Land Question. While Edgeworth's agenda is one of realism and rationality, Moore's is essentially fantastical – exemplified in Captain Rock, the nested narrator and chief character of *Memoirs*. Moore, an Irish Catholic, had unique advantages. He was a great friend of Robert Emmet, a leading United Irishman. His *Irish Melodies* (1808-34) were extremely popular and helped establish his reputation as 'the voice of Ireland'. Yet Moore lived much of his adult life in England, in particular, in London. As *The Memoirs, Journal, and Correspondence* (1853-6) show, Moore revelled in his role as the darling of London Society. It was against this background that he re-visited Ireland and for the first time became aware of the deprivations and suffering of Irish tenants.

The persona Moore adopts in *Memoirs* is that of the leader of the Whiteboys, the main secret society of the time. *Memoirs*, in some ways more of a history than a novel, is weak in characterisation – except for the extraordinary figure of Rock himself. Rock blames English misrule for Ireland's problems and, specifically, for the rise in agrarian violence. Moore, the 'pseudo-historian', attempts a chronological history of Ireland from its earliest days till the present (1824). Rock argues that the Land Question was created by the English and could equally be solved by the English. The seizure of Irish land, the introduction of the Penal Laws, the persecution of the Catholic Church and widespread institutional violence have forced the tenants to become Whiteboys; in short, institutional violence begets agrarian violence. Rock claims that he exists only because of institutional violence; if tenants were treated fairly, he would die. But is Moore's solution even as sound as Edgeworth's?

While Rock, as an individual, is not exactly immortal, his title, role and power are. But, if Moore's was the first of the agrarian novelists to apply fantasy to the Land Question, Bram Stoker was to take fantasy much further. The Protestant and socially-aspiring Stoker was the last agrarian novelist of the nineteenth century. In *Dracula* (1897), Count Dracula, unlike Captain Rock, is unambiguously immortal. Stoker takes the agrarian novel to Transylvania – with Dracula as the ultimate Ascendancy landowner, the Castle as the ultimate Big House, and the tenants the ultimate victims, literally drained both of money and of life. As we shall see, it is, in fact, too simplistic to see *Dracula* (1897) as merely a re-working of the standard Irish agrarian novel in a foreign setting. This complex novel wrestles with Ireland's past and with her new, emerging role at the dawn of the twentieth century. Stoker's interest in science, psychology, technology and the 'New Woman' issue provides *Dracula* with a host of themes new to the agrarian novel. But there is still one thing that unites Stoker with many of the agrarian novelists; like them, he is unsure whether he wants to destroy the Ascendancy or not.

[W]hile the progress of time produces a change in all nations, the destiny of Ireland remains still the same – that here we still find her, at the end of so many centuries, struggling, like Ixion, on her wheel of torture – never advancing, always suffering – her whole existence one monotonous round of agony.[1]

Tom Moore: Poet, Novelist or Historian

The inclusion of Thomas Moore's *Memoirs of Captain Rock* (1824) at this stage in the book requires some explanation. Moore's ability as a prose writer is not impressive and he is also very different to the authors previously discussed. At first sight, his inclusion may appear unnecessary or inappropriate, but further investigation will reveal that it is essential. Let us begin by identifying some of the differences that separate Moore from the authors discussed so far.

The novels we have considered, in earlier chapters, are set either in the present or – more commonly – in the near present. Some near present novels, including the Banims' *Crohoore of the Bill-Hook* (1825) and Carleton's *The Black Prophet* (1847) are really 'present novels' in disguise; contemporary issues are merely given a thin covering of the outward appearance of the previous generation. Thus, while several agrarian novelists acknowledge the influence of Scott, they do not follow him in one important way. Unlike Scott, and several English and French authors, they do not set their stories in the Middle Ages or in the seventeenth century – they are not historical novelists. In one sense, they are less like Scott than Moore is. While *Memoirs* ranges widely over time, there can be

---

[1] Thomas Moore, *Memoirs of Captain Rock &c.* (London: Longman, Hurst, Rees, Orme, Brown, and Green, 1824), p. ix. Further references to this edition are given after quotations in the text and the title shortened to *Memoirs*.

231

no doubt that its true centre is the seventeenth century, the period that also provides the setting for Scott's *Old Mortality* (1816).

A further difference is that, whatever their respective merits, the writers discussed to date are unquestionably novelists. Moore is first and foremost a poet and is often described as the National Poet of Ireland. *Memoirs* is certainly not a work of poetry, but is it really an historical novel? It is hard to put a label on *Memoirs*, which seems to straddle the frontier between fiction and history. Of course, the frontier is blurred and many historical novels introduce characters that actually lived and describe or allude to events that actually happened. However, in all cases, there is an element of what may be termed fictional licence. There is no claim, either explicit or implicit, to total historical accuracy. Historical novelists do not pretend to be historians. They do not organise their works like historians and rarely engage in anything approaching formal historical analysis – although, as we have seen, Trollope comes close to this in *The Land-Leaguers*. In *Memoirs*, however, we encounter something that looks more like a work of history than a novel. Chapters are introduced with a summary of their contents, there are references and footnotes and extended sections of analysis. As we shall see, however, *Memoirs* is not a real piece of historical writing. It might more accurately be described as 'pseudo-history' or, if that is too unkind, as 'fictional history'.

The qualities required in a poet differ from those needed in a novelist or in an historian so it is hardly surprising that *Memoirs* cannot be considered as a great success in literary or historical terms. All of the authors considered so far have at least some merit as novelists and have certainly not lacked defenders. It is true that Moore's biographer, James Burke, contends that the *Memoirs* contains '[h]umour and pathos [...] exquisitely combined, and all the varied powers of a mind which could range over every topic are lavishly displayed'.[2] Yet even Burke seems more impressed by Moore's passion and anger than by his literary skills:

> I have [...] drawn MOORE as an Irishman, and have delighted to present the reader those scathing passages in his writings in which he lashes with unsparing hand the misgovernment of his native land.[3]

---

[2] James Burke, *The Life of Thomas Moore* (Dublin: James Duffy and Sons, c.1879), p. 92.
[3] Burke, p. 6.

But it is hard to disagree with Rev. Mortimer O'Sullivan's view, in *Captain Rock Detected* (1824), that, at best, *Memoirs* is a second-rate work of prose literature. It is certainly tedious, repetitive, rambling, historically questionable and highly subjective. Try as he might, Moore is a bad novelist and a worse historian.

If *Memoirs* is to be included at all, it might seem more logical to have introduced it earlier in this book. After all, *Memoirs* appeared only seven years after Edgeworth's *Ormond* (1817), and a year before the Banims' *Tales of the O'Hara Family* (1825-26). So far, we have adopted a chronological approach. This has not, however, been chosen for its own sake, but because it has corresponded to a thematic analysis – that is the story of the creation, development and ultimate collapse of Edgeworth's agenda. Her agenda, formed between 1800 and 1820, and followed by the Banims, Griffin and Carleton, sought solutions to the agrarian problems of Ireland. Though more extreme and foreign-orientated, Kickham and Trollope still belong to the same tradition. Moore is only introduced now because he represents a radically different agenda, not envisaged by Edgeworth or by those who remained under her shadow. The new – or rather the alternative – agenda takes the agrarian novel away from realism and into the realms of fantasy. This is the true significance of Moore and provides the main justification for including *Memoirs* and, in particular, for introducing it at this stage in our analytical journey.

If, as suggested, Moore, essentially a poet, turned to pseudo-history or fictional history in *Memoirs*, we must consider his reasons. He may have felt so strongly about the situation in Ireland that he decided to speak out, concluding that, to achieve maximum effect and authority, he would have to write – more or less – as an historian rather than a poet. Moore must have known that he was not really an historian, or even an historical novelist, so how could he imagine *Memoirs* could actually pass for history? As we have seen, he went to some lengths to achieve this impression and even introduced the pretence that he was merely editing an historical manuscript that had actually been written by Captain Rock himself.

Moore certainly felt strongly about Ireland and its sufferings. Although the son of a Catholic grocer in Dublin, he attended Trinity College. According to Trench, Moore's ideas began to form when he was still a student. While at Trinity, '[h]e published, anonymously, a highly seditious *Letter to the Students of Trinity College*', with Lord Edward Fitzgerald as its hero.[4] Moore then entered Government service, taking a minor post in the Admiralty Prize Court in Bermuda. He later settled in England where literary – essentially poetical – success brought social advancement. Indeed, he remained in England for most of the rest of his life. Moore became a popular figure, perhaps because he seemed 'an Englishman's idea of what an Irishman ought to be'.[5] He mixed easily and his wide circle of friends included Mary Shelley, Scott, Byron (who asked Moore to be his biographer), Wordsworth, Coleridge, Thomas Babington Macaulay, Lord Lansdowne, Lady Holland, and Lord John Russell. He seems to have been particularly close to Russell. Curiously, Russell, later Prime Minister during the worst of the Famine and much blamed for his alleged neglect of Ireland, was to produce the first edition of Moore's *Memoirs, Journal and Correspondence* (1853-56). Whatever Moore may have said about England's treatment of Ireland, he clearly did not wish to cut himself off from English society.

The inspiration for writing *Memoirs* came to Moore on a tour of Ireland. He decided to keep a diary, which, though containing details of elaborate dinners and social visits, also includes many reflections on Ireland's past. His original intention was to turn the diary into a purely factual account of his tour. Moore, however, encountered something that evidently surprised him – the full extent of Irish poverty:

> Saw at Collan, for the first time in my life, some real specimens of Irish misery and filth; three or four cottages together exhibiting such a naked swarm of wretchedness as never met my eyes before.[6]

The experience so affected Moore that he abandoned his original plan in favour of "'History of Captain Rock and his Ancestors',[7] which may be more livelily [sic] and certainly more easily done'. The tone of the work

---

[4] W F Trench, *Tom Moore* (Dublin: At The Sign Of The Three Candles, 1934), pp. 16-17.
[5] Thomas Moore, *Tom Moore's Diary*, ed by J B Priestley (Cambridge: University Press, 1933), p. ix.
[6] Thomas Moore, *Memoirs, Journal and Correspondences of Thomas Moore*, ed. by Lord John Russell (London: Longman, Brown, Green, and Longmans, 1853), IV, 10 October 1823, p. 137.
[7] Russell, *Moore,* 1853, p. 103.

was in such sharp contrast to Moore's previous works that one reviewer at least insisted 'that Mr. Moore is not the author of Captain Rock'.[8]

We have noted that *Memoirs* bears some resemblance to historical novels produced in England, Scotland and France in that it is set – mainly – in the seventeenth century and hence differs from present or near present Irish agrarian novels. Yet the resemblance is merely superficial. More conventional historical novels portray the past as 'a foreign country',[9] a country whose values, moralities and self-identities differ profoundly from those of the present. Indeed, it is the great and widening gulf between past and present that constitutes much of the appeal of such novels. The past becomes so fascinating precisely because it is either disappearing or has already disappeared completely. In short, the beginnings of industrialisation in England and political convulsion in France made novelists and their readers eager to explore the lost worlds of earlier times. But how does Moore stand on this point? Unlike English and other historical novelists, he sees no contrast. Ireland has not changed: for him the past is the present and the present is the past.

Opposites

Since Moore, in *Memoirs*, aspired to be both a novelist and an historian, we must also compare him with an historian, with his friend Thomas Babington Macaulay. It is not enough to say that Macaulay and Moore are different; rather it must be stressed that, in almost every conceivable way, they are absolute opposites. The highlighting of these opposites serves several purposes; not only does it assist understanding of Moore, but, more fundamentally, it reveals much about underlying differences between England and Ireland. Of course, it is self evident that if Macaulay's version of history was accepted in England and Moore's in Ireland, then the differences between the mindsets and self-identities of the two countries would grow even further apart.

One way of viewing *Memoirs* is to see is as an attempt by a literary man to take over history. Yet Macaulay could represent an attempt by an historian to take over literature. Did not Macaulay say that he hoped that

---

[8] [Rev Mortimer O'Sullivan], *Captain Rock Detected &c.* (London: T. Cadell, 1824), p 360n. Further references to this edition are given after quotations in the text and the title shortened to *Detected*.

[9] L P Hartley, *The Go-Between* (1953), ed. by Douglas Brooks-Davies (London: Penguin Group, 2000), p. 5.

his *History of England* would supplant Scott as the favourite reading of young people, especially of young women? Indeed, despite many important historical novels, it could be argued that Macaulay was so successful that the English past came under the control of an historian. There was no Irish Macaulay and hence the Irish past was controlled by a poet and aspirant novelist, that is by Moore.

The most likely reason why Moore could have supposed that *Memoirs* could pass for authentic and accurate history was the lack of competition. In the nineteenth century, there was a remarkable dearth of serious historical writing about Ireland – at least until W E H Lecky. The same was also true of Scotland and Wales. In *The Isles* (1999), Norman Davies notes that, after 1707, Scottish historians largely abandoned the history of their own country in favour of the history of England. He attributes this to the effects of the Act of Union, and the later Union with Ireland may have had similar results. Of course, the British controlled the schools and encouraged them to teach British – really English – history. The study of history could lead to jobs in Government service. Significantly, British Civil Service examinations were to contain many questions on English history but virtually none on Celtic subjects. Schools and Colleges who wanted their pupils to do well in these examinations had little alternative but to arrange their syllabi accordingly. Here it may be noted that acceptance of History as an academic discipline long antedated acceptance of Literature.

There were special factors, however, at work in Ireland. The writing of a serious work of history probably requires more formal education than the writing of a novel. The most educated section of the Catholic community was the priesthood, but the Church viewed History with suspicion as the province of agnostics and doubters – *Philosophes* like Gibbon and Voltaire. More fundamentally, the Catholic mindset was anti-historical. The Church claimed to be the eternal Church whose doctrines, ceremonies and structure had remained unchanged since Apostolic times. To say anything else offered an opening to the Protestants' argument that they, not the Catholic Church of the nineteenth century, were closer to Apostolic Purity.

In the nineteenth century, to a greater extent than previously, History, in its 'von Rankean' mode, was essentially a matter of documents; sources such as oral history and folk traditions were regarded with suspicion by purists – good enough for novelists but not for historians. Traditional Irish culture was essentially non-literary; if documents existed, they represented the English dimension, the mindset of the landowners – the things nationalists deplored.

England and Ireland were inevitably influenced by their perceptions of their respective pasts. By any standards these pasts were different but the diametrically opposed interpretations produced by Macaulay and Moore may have made them appear even more divergent than they actually were. For Macaulay, the supreme representative of the Whig approach to History, the shadow of England's past was essentially benign. Virtually every century, from Roman times onwards, could be portrayed in positive terms. It was a wonderful story, leading logically and largely harmoniously to an even more wonderful present. For Moore, the shadow of the Ireland's past was almost entirely malign. Above all, the key message of *Memoirs* is that the history of Ireland had been extraordinarily violent. Perhaps it is here that Moore is revealed to be more of a novelist than an historian. The role of violence differs significantly in History and in novels. Violence is central to the artistic purpose of many novelists – it certainly was so to Moore – yet for historians, especially for historians like Macaulay, it was more of a distraction, impeding exposition of political and constitutional principles. Thus, Macaulay was temperamentally inclined to minimize the role of violence whereas Moore was temperamentally inclined to maximize it. Captain Rock positively revels in violence. While Macaulay refers to the English Civil War, he does not describe it in any detail, probably because he found its violence distasteful. He has much more to say about the 'Glorious Revolution' of 1688 and suggests that what made it glorious was that, in England at least, it was virtually bloodless. Macaulay also believed in progress and held that a reduction in violence was a crucial yardstick against which to measure such progress. So, when he discussed violent episodes, especially in the seventeenth century, Macaulay contrasted them with the peace and tranquillity of his own time – largely in order to substantiate his frequent assertion that the present was not only different from but also better than the past. For Moore, the present and the past are one and hence the present cannot be better or less violent than the past.

The Disputed Century

Both Macaulay and Moore both have much to say about the seventeenth century. It is true that Macaulay's *History of England* is mainly about that century, yet it is even more important to Moore. Macaulay never regarded the seventeenth century as the all-defining moment in English history. As his essay on *Hallam's Constitutional History* (1828) reveals, he could range widely over time and freely acknowledged the importance of the Medieval period and of the sixteenth century. He also recognised the crucial contributions of the eighteenth century and even more of his own times. For Moore, the seventeenth century is everything – there is very little before it and nothing afterwards. While the date on the Calendar may have changed, Ireland is still living in the seventeenth century.

Even if Macaulay regards the seventeenth century as perhaps the most important period in English history and acknowledges many of its short-comings, not least its violence, he still sees it in overwhelmingly positive terms. Charles I's attempt to set up Continental-style despotism is defeated and above all, the Glorious Revolution ensures the lasting victory of Whig principles of Parliamentary government. In short, the seventeenth century is so crucial because it sees the beginnings of political progress, a process that finally culminates in the Reform Bill of 1832. For Moore, however, the seventeenth century has no redeeming features and brings untold misery and oppression to Ireland. Indeed, some of the worst oppressors are the same people and institutions whose victory in England Macaulay so applauds.

One telling example of the growing divergence of English and Irish perceptions of the past concerns the reputation of Oliver Cromwell, surely one of the greatest monsters in the history of Ireland. Perceptions had not been so different at one time. In England, from 1660 to around the 1820s, it was considered bad form to mention Cromwell by name - 'the late usurper' was preferred. Yet Macaulay's essays in *The Edinburgh Review* in the late 1820s partially rehabilitated Cromwell. Some facets of the Lord Protector's character now appear attractive – as the champion of English greatness in the 1650s, as the creator of the first British State (including Ireland) and, above all, as a kind of proto-liberal. Cromwell was the champion of Parliament and, with the exception of Papists – notoriously intolerant themselves – an exponent of religious liberty, going to the extent of allowing the Jews to return to England in 1655. Cromwell was also seen as the forefather of non-conformist values and, after centuries of discrimination, non-conformists were now taking their rightful part in national life once more. It is true that Macaulay retained serious reservations about Cromwell, whose full apotheosis was to come with Thomas Carlyle's *Oliver Cromwell's Letters and Speeches* of 1845 – ironically the year when the Great Hunger began in Ireland.

Moore's treatment of what to him was clearly the defining moment in the tragedy of Ireland may anticipate more recent discussion on 'The General Crisis of the Seventeenth Century'. Some historians believe that calamitous events occurring across the world between 1620 and 1660 had an ultimate common cause. Thus, it has been suggested that climatic deterioration – perhaps caused by a cooling of the sun or by the effects of increased volcanic activity – may explain Civil War in England, the terrible events in Ireland and more besides. There was civil war too in France and Spain, the Thirty Years War in Germany, major disruption in the Ottoman and Mughal Empires, a change of dynasty in China, and Japan decided to isolate itself from the rest of the world. Everywhere, falling crop yields led to famines, plagues and mass migration – exactly as in Ireland in the 1840s. Governments sought to extend their authority to extract more tax from shrinking economies while the powerful used any means to acquire more land. Not surprisingly, large parts of Europe experienced peasant revolts on a massive scale, not least in Ireland and the Netherlands. The crisis deepened antagonisms already shaped by the Reformation, and extremism, even fanaticism, flourished in Catholic, Protestant, Orthodox, Jewish and Islamic societies. Many believed that the end of the world was at hand. It seems that, terrible as they were, Ireland's sufferings were not unique. Perhaps the real tragedy was that after 1660, while England and France experienced signs of recovery, there was no respite for Ireland. That is certainly the impression given in *Memoirs*. While Moore cannot be regarded as a serious historian, there is some truth in this analysis. Perhaps poets can achieve real historical insight after all.

Although *Memoirs* purports to be the autobiography of Rock, it is really an attack on England's mistreatment of Ireland – right up to 1824. Indeed, Terence de Vere White is surely right to say of *Memoirs* that 'as a statement of British misrule it is devastating'.[10] The most significant chapters in *Memoirs,* however, deal with the seventeenth century. They cover the great transfer – or rather theft – of land from Catholics to Protestants, the atrocities perpetrated by Cromwell, betrayal by Charles II, the defeat of the Catholic James II at the Boyne (1690) and Aughrim (1690), English failure to honour the Treaty of Limerick (1690) and the introduction of the Penal Laws. These, it is suggested, are the ultimate sources of the agrarian violence of the 1760s and later. Everything can be traced back to the disastrous seventeenth century.

---

[10] Terence de Vere White, *Tom Moore* (London: Hamish Hamilton, 1977), p. 184.

Few would deny that many of the problems faced by nineteenth-century Ireland, including the divisions between natives and settlers, Catholics, tenants and landowners, can be traced back to the seventeenth century. Memories of an earlier Ireland retreated into myth and fable. A new and troubled Ireland was born – an unfortunate timing. It is tempting to adopt a Freudian approach and to suggest that Ireland's metaphorically disturbed adulthood, in the nineteenth century, was the inevitable product of its traumatic birth and abused infancy, marked by such things as the 1641 rising and Cromwell's subsequent retribution.

Repetitions

As we have already seen, *Memoirs* purports to be an edited version of a manuscript autobiography of Captain Rock. Moore also employs the additional device of an anonymous editor – a man sent by 'a Society [based] on the model of the Home Missionary in London' (*Memoirs*, p iv) – seemingly to put an even bigger distance between himself and Rock. Of course, the device is transparent. There can be no doubt that there was no manuscript and that Moore himself wrote *Memoirs*. But we are bound to ask why Moore goes to such lengths: is it to buttress his slender claims to pass as an historian? Or, possibly, not to give too much offence to his English friends and patrons, or because he genuinely disagrees with Rock and finds some aspects of his character distasteful? All three considerations may be present. In his diary, Moore criticises O'Connell for agreeing to serve as counsel for 'Hickey […] a common gardener' who 'was a sort of Captain Rock'.[11] Nevertheless, while there may be reservations, surely the whole point of *Memoirs* is to give Rock a public platform.

Moore is careful to explain the origin of Rock's name, which is said to derive from the initials of 'Roger O'Connor King' (*Memoirs*, p 6). Yet 'Captain Rock' serves as both the name of an individual man and as the title of whoever is the current leader of the Rockites or Whiteboys. In short, Rock is a collective name. Indeed, Rock is clearly related to the many other 'Captains' – 'Moonlight', 'Ludd' and 'Swing' – the *noms de guerre* of the anonymous leaders of what almost amount to guerrilla armies who bring havoc to both Ireland and England. Whether one or many – and he is both – Rock is powerful and Moore records, that '[i]ntended

---

[11] Moore, in Russell, 11th August 1823, IV, p. 117.

riots at fairs [...] have been frequently put a stop to by orders from Captain Rock'.[12]

Moore, of course, is not a Freudian nor could he have been aware of later ideas about the 'General Crisis of the Seventeenth Century' – though, since, as we shall see, Rock is eternal, perhaps we should allow the possibility that he does know about these things. At least speaking through Moore, however, Rock must couch his story in terms more accessible to nineteenth-century readers. He must identify what makes Ireland so different to other countries and then explain that difference. The essence of Rock's case is contained in the quotation at the head of this chapter: all other nations change but 'the destiny of Ireland remains still the same' (*Memoirs*, p ix). The same message is repeated time after time and an impressive case is built up. There is no real change in the system of government:

> So like is one part of the history of Ireland to another that, in reading it, we are somewhat in the situation of that absent man, to whom D'Argeson lent the same volume of a work four successive times, and who, when asked how he liked the author, answered, 'il me semble qu'il se repete quelquefois'. The Government of Ireland 'se repete' with a vengeance! (*Memoirs*, p. 108n)

To say that the Ireland of the nineteenth century was essentially the same as what it had become in the seventeenth century did not mean that nothing of significance had happened: arguably far too much had happened. Unlike England, Ireland had not enjoyed the benefits of progress but neither had it experienced the quiet and calm of total stagnation. There had been change of a kind, but this had been cyclical rather than linear. It is here that the significance of the powerful image of Ixion's wheel, the 'wheel of torture' becomes apparent. Ireland never advances and always suffers, 'her whole existence one monotonous round of agony' (*Memoirs*, p. ix). But why does the wheel go round and round and never stop?

There were several ways in which it might have stopped. It would have stopped if Ireland had been totally destroyed – perhaps sunk like Atlantis under the waves of the Atlantic Ocean. This solution or something similar was proposed, perhaps in jest, by exasperated British

---

[12] Moore, in Russell, 11th August 1823, IV, p. 114.

statesmen from Sir Francis Walsingham to the Duke of Wellington. Wellington suggested that the populations of Ireland and the Netherlands be exchanged; the industrious Dutch would transform Ireland into a paradise while the Irish would neglect the Dutch dykes and all would be drowned. Moore had heard of Walsingham's idea and hints that Ireland's suffering had been so great that total extinction would have been preferable.

The wheel might have stopped if one or other of the contending parties became strong enough to achieve total victory. Perhaps this was the only answer, but the horrors of such victory would eclipse even those of the seventeenth century. Trench claims that Moore believed 'that Ireland must go through some violent and convulsive process' and 'if Separation [sic] was to be the price, it would be well worth paying, however dreadful would be the pain of it'. There is not much in *Memoirs* to suggest what such an Ireland would be, although Trench hints that Moore thought that Ireland could somehow return to happier times – though in reality they had probably not been much happier – before the arrival of the English:

> Moore put his heart into the learning of the airs [...] The music signified nothing less than the continuity of the Anglo-Irish Ireland of their [Moore's and Emmet's] immediate cognizance and to which their patriotic sentiment attached itself, with the Gaelic Ireland or an immemorial past.[13]

Yet was Irish victory over the English really likely? Rising after rising had failed and only added to the total of misery. The two sides were too finely balanced for either to be able to model Ireland entirely in its own image.

Another possibility would be for the parties to compromise, to show goodwill, mutual respect and tolerance. That was the solution proposed by Edgeworth and her successors and never completely abandoned even by Kickham and Trollope. The wheel might have stopped too if the Irish and Anglo-Irish had joined together against the English. Moore – though significantly not Rock – does toy with this possibility. He notes in his Diary:

---

[13] Trench, pp. 20-25.

[W]e cannot possibly judge how far the dawn of independence which rose upon Ireland in '82 might have brightened if it had been overcast by this general convulsion of the whole civilised world.[14]

Yet such dawns were rare and any opportunities soon evaporated. Rock certainly sees no chance of unity or compromise. A crucial difference between Moore and the novelists discussed previously is that he totally rejects any possibility of compromise. Moore, the diarist, certainly does not deny that the English (whom he knew and liked in their own country) had some good qualities, and the same is true of the Irish. However, as is explained in *Memoirs,* the problem is that for the past two hundred years and more, both have consistently revealed their worst sides in their dealings with each other:

[I]n this unhappy country it is only the *evil* of each system that is perpetuated – eternal struggles, without one glimpse of freedom, and an unrelaxing pressure of power, without one moment of consolidation or repose. (*Memoirs,* p. ix)

Rock describes the negative side of England at considerable length, associating it with the misdeeds of a number of major historical characters. He begins with James I, the Protestant son of the Catholic Mary Queen of Scots. Using the language of the nineteenth-century, Moore notes that James did not like 'reviewers'. James had declared that those who 'refuse the oath, are polypragmatic, and I leave them to the law'. In short, James is dismissed as a 'vain pedant' (*Memoirs,* p. 62). Yet, pedant or not, he behaved ruthlessly to Catholics and to Ireland. After the Gunpowder Plot of 1605, James took drastic measures aimed at crushing Catholicism in England and Ireland:

The exercise of their religion was strictly forbidden [...] All Catholics were obliged to assist at the protestant church service every Sunday and holiday; and thus they, who had been called 'imps of Anti-Christ', &c. for listening to a Latin mass which they did not understand, were now forced to listen to an English

---

[14] Moore, in Russell, 14th April 1823, IV, p. 57.

liturgy, which being Irish, understood quite as little. (*Memoirs*, pp 63-64)

Rock does not speculate if things would have been better if the Irish had been allowed to listen to a Protestant liturgy in their own language – a concession readily made to the Welsh. James, however, went much further. Above all, James's reign saw 'the first use made of English law [...] to rob thousands of the unfortunate natives of their property' (*Memoirs*, p 66):

> [A] system of spoliation was established throughout the whole country, and the possessions of every man placed at the mercy of any creature of the crown, who could detect a flaw or failure in his tenure. (*Memoirs*, p 67)

It was James who was largely responsible for the 'Plantation of Ulster' and the arrival of Protestant settlers into the North of Ireland: 'six entire counties of Ulster [...] were forfeited "at one fell swoop" to the crown'. Officially, the seizure was justified on the grounds of an Irish conspiracy, which Rock believes 'did not exist' (*Memoirs*, p 68).

Yet despite James's enormities, Rock stresses that his measures provoked surprisingly little resistance. Perhaps with some regret, Rock admits that, in James's reign 'the ROCKS did not flourish' (*Memoirs*, p 68). Indeed, it is stressed that neither in his own time nor subsequently was James regarded with the hatred that his actions probably deserved. James's successors may have far exceeded his atrocities but Rock is clearly puzzled by the relative indulgence shown to the first of the Stuart Kings of England. This indulgence was also noticed by other agrarian novelists, such as the Banims, who suggest that it was due to the fact that the Irish believed that James was descended from Milesius, the common ancestor of all Celts. Rock too seems to endorse this theory:

> [T]herefore, (like the Irishman lately, who was nearly murdered on Saint Patrick's day, but forgave his assailant 'in honour of the saint), we bore it all quietly in honour of Milesius. (*Memoirs*, p 69)

Rock implies that the Irish are too sentimental and too ready to be taken in by royal charm. They seem to regard 'a prince's promise' as a 'kind of convenient talisman, which may be broken over and over, without in the least degree, losing its charm' (*Memoirs*, p. 62). In this they are mistaken: no Irishman should trust an English monarch. Yet there are other, more prosaic, explanations.

Rock gives more credence to Sir John Davies who explained Irish inaction in the early seventeenth century as the logical result of military defeat and natural disasters – reinforced by firm English government and law. The Irish even seemed grateful:

> [T]he multitude being brayed, as it were, in a mortar with sword, famine, and pestilence together, submitted themselves to the English government, received its laws and magistrates, and most gladly embraced King James's pardon and peace in all parts of the realm, *with demonstrations of joy and comfort.* (*Memoirs*, p. 69)

Rock goes so far as to acknowledge that James himself may not have been responsible for the deceptive calm. It was more likely that corruption was the real cause:

> May it not have been the management of Parliaments [...] that a good deal diverted the attention of the people from more violent modes of asserting their rights? (*Memoirs*, p. 70)

If James gets off relatively lightly, subsequent rulers of Ireland are portrayed in darker colours. In the 1630s, England is represented by Thomas Wentworth, 1st Earl of Strafford, 'Black Tom Tyrant'. Strafford took appropriation of land to greater heights, abandoning any pretence of keeping even within the unjust laws introduced by James. He ensured that 'the whole province of Connaught became the booty of the crown and its minions' (*Memoirs*, p. 77), and appointed judges who were agents of the crown rather than impartial arbitrators. The continuing hatred of Strafford is evident when Rock mentions a house planned by the former Lord Lieutenant:

> [T]he haughty nobleman who built that mansion is, to this day, with a tenacity which does honour even to hate, recorded; and under the name of Black Tom, still haunts the imagination of the peasant, as one of those dark and evil beings who tormented the land in former days, and with whom, in the bitterness of his heart, he compares to its more modern tormentors. (*Memoirs*, pp. vii-viii)

Clearly, Wentworth's shadow is long and there can be few clearer statements of Rock's theory that the government of Ireland 'se répéte'. Yet even the shadow of Wentworth was not as malign as that of Cromwell. Indeed, while the Irish suffered under various monarchs, they were even worse off under 'the Parliamentary government':

> [W]ith the Lords Justice on one side, and Cromwell and Ireton on the other, assisted by a pestilence, which was the least cruel enemy of the whole, they were at last reduced to a state very nearly realizing that long-desired object of English policy – their extirpation. [...] [T]heir estates, which at that time, constituted at least nine-tenths of the landed property of the country, were divided among his [Cromwell's] officers and soldiers, and among those adventurers who had advanced money for the war. (*Memoirs*, pp 96-97)

The real significance of Cromwell, however, is that his example still determined the attitudes of British statesmen in the nineteenth century. Potentially, Wellington was another Cromwell:

> A certain military Duke, who complains that Ireland is but half conquered, would, no doubt, upon an emergency, try his hand in the same line of practice. (*Memoirs*, p. 98)

Similarly, the religious fanaticism of Cromwell's soldiers, who were told 'that the Irish were to be treated as the Canaanites were by Joshua' (*Memoirs*, p 99) was repeated – perhaps even exceeded – in the words and actions of modern day 'faithfully scriptural Orangemen' (*Memoirs*, p 101):

> A similar taste for the warlike passages of the Old Testament is observable in our modern Oliverians, Sir Abraham Bradley King, and his brother Orangemen; and, by a remarkable coincidence, it is from the same book, Joshua, that they, too, draw their charitable inspirations. How far these Orange heroes mean to carry their imitation of the soldiers of Joshua remains to be seen; but, I presume, the great victory which their leader Sir Abraham lately gained over the law by means of the House of Commons, was meant as a copy of the conquest of Jericho through the treachery

of the harlot, Rahab – the House of Commons enacting the part of Rahab on this occasion. (*Memoirs*, p. 100)

In short, Parliament had not changed; in the nineteenth century it was still the same 'harlot' it had been in the seventeenth. There was perhaps one thing to say in favour of Cromwell. If a land was to be ruined it was better that it should be ruined quickly – Cromwell's way – rather than suffer 'a slow lingering process of exclusion, disappointment, and degradation' (*Memoirs*, p. 97).

This had been Ireland's fate. Charles II had proved little better than Cromwell. Whoever was in charge – King or Parliament – the Irish were still punished. Cromwell had punished them for being Royalists; with the Restoration, their lands, power, freedom and independence would surely be restored. Charles II, however, upheld the Cromwellian land settlement, appreciating the political expediency of continuing to cast the Irish in the role of rebels. This meant, of course, that the English could keep their estates:

> [T]he path of iniquity lay clear and open; and upon such monstrous and insulting falsehoods was that Act of Settlement founded; 'by which,' says Lord Clare, 'seven millions eight hundred thousand acres of land were set out to a motley crew of English adventurers, civil and military, nearly to the total exclusion of the old inhabitants of the island.

The opportunity for change came with the Glorious Revolution, perhaps 'Glorious' for England but hardly so for Ireland. A few traitorous Irishman switched their allegiance from James II to the Protestant 'Prince and Princess of Orange' (*Memoirs*, p 112), but the real significance of William's victory was that the English embarked upon a new programme of land seizures:

> [T]hat rapacious spirit, which nothing less than the confiscation of the whole island could satisfy; and which having, in the reign of James I and at the Restoration, despoiled the natives of no less than ten millions six hundred and thirty-six thousand eight hundred and thirty-seven acres, now added to its plunder one million, sixty thousand, seven hundred and ninety-two acres more,

being the amount, altogether, [...] of the whole superficial contents of the island! (*Memoirs*, p113)

The defeated Catholics were then persecuted by the introduction of the Penal Laws. Moore blames James II for the defeat of Catholic Ireland and claims to respect William. He endeavours to drive a wedge between Orangemen and their seventeenth-century hero, William of Orange, by presenting, as historical fact, a letter of William's. It states that 'the Roman Catholics of that country [England] may enjoy liberty of conscience, and be put out of fear of being persecuted on account of their Religion' (*Memoirs*, p. 117). Shortly before the fall of Limerick, William had offered Catholics 'the free exercise of their religion, half the Church Establishment of Ireland, and the moiety of their ancient properties!' (*Memoirs*, pp. 118-119). William, however, did not keep his word anymore than earlier Kings had done – it was still the same story. The false promises of the Treaty of Limerick foreshadowed the equally false promises of Catholic Emancipation in the campaign for the Act of Union, with its 'marriage vows, false as dicers' oaths' (*Memoirs*, p. 111).

Orangemen still insultingly celebrate the ruin of Ireland on 12th July 1690. If the nineteenth century was like the seventeenth, the seventeenth century must have been like the nineteenth: 'the Bible society plan seems to have been tried upon the persecuted and confiscated Irish of those times' (*Memoirs*, p 62). Indeed, despite the repeal of the Penal Laws, little has changed. Power lies with those who hold the land and, in 1824, the English still hold the vast majority of the land with the native Irish little more than serfs. Rock approvingly quotes Henry Fielding:

The Irish had made a deuce of a clatter
And wrangled and fought about *meum* and *tuum*,
Till England stept in, and decided the matter,
By kindly converting it all into *suum*.
(*Memoirs*, p 65)

In the seventeenth century, as in the nineteenth, there might be the odd well-intentioned ruler but he is soon removed. The story of the Duke of Ormond[e], whose 'moderation' and 'wisdom' was 'hated and calumniated by the Protestant Ascendancy' (*Memoirs*, p. 109n) is repeated with Lord Wellesley, Wellington's more moderate brother. However, Ormonde and Wellesley are the exceptions. Overwhelmingly, it is story of almost uninterrupted oppression and theft. It had actually begun even earlier than the seventeenth century, in Norman times. It is an extraordinary story, so extraordinary that, if it was described in fiction, no-one would believe it. Yet, even more remarkably, even in the 1820s, there are many who, knowing 'that such proceedings once took place [...] still cling to the *principle* of those proceedings' (*Memoirs*, p 104)

The Wheel as Stage Machinery

English oppression forms the central part of Rock's analysis, though perhaps not the most interesting part. If it had been the whole story, we could well question the use of the symbol of Ixion's 'wheel of torture', powerful though that may be. In terms of simple mechanics, a force consistently exerted in one direction will not produce the circular motion associated with a wheel. From what we have seen so far, the image of a huge steam-powered hammer, steadily pounding the almost inert and prostrate body of Ireland, might seem better suited. For the wheel image to succeed, there must be opposite forces, or mechanical devices, in the shape of cranks which must be introduced to convert the dominant force – English oppression – into a circular motion. Moore, the poet, probably knew nothing of cranks, though he hints at their existence. He certainly has much to say about opposite forces. The opposite forces are represented by Rock himself. As we have seen, Rock is powerful enough to stop violence at fairs, but he sees himself in more grandiose terms, to the extent of comparing himself to the Czar of Russia:

> [L]et tyranny and turbulence, perfidy and plunder, be the order of the day among rulers and their subjects; and let Captain ROCK and the Czar of Russia divide the world between them. I shall not complain of my share in the arrangement and will answer for the magnanimous Alexander being equally satisfied with his. (*Memoirs*, p. 78)

While Rock generally adheres to the line, beloved of later nationalist readings, that Ireland's sufferings are unique, here he hints that they may not be. Strikingly, the reference is to Eastern Europe, an area identified earlier in this book as having something in common with Ireland. The closest approximation to Ireland is surely Poland, like Ireland a Catholic country, oppressed by a more powerful neighbour that also represents an alien faith. Poland is oppressed by Orthodox Russia and Ireland by Protestant England. Thus Russia and England may be one and the same, all the more so because, while England has always claimed to be enlightened, Russia finally has a Czar, Alexander, who claims to be equally so. In their dealings with Ireland and Poland, the hypocrisy of both is revealed. It is striking that, when O'Connell entered Parliament, he emerged as an ardent Russophobe, causing uproar by denouncing the present Czar's ancestor, Catherine the Great as 'that outrageous public prostitute', again the recurrent image of the harlot.

So it may be that Rock is claiming that he really shares the world with the King of England, or rather with the British Government. Rock represents Irish resistance to the English and *Memoirs* tells the story of the long succession of Irish risings, from the Rebellion of 1641, through 1798, to the Rockite campaign of 1821-24. As with the story of English oppression, little changes in the Irish response. The events of 1641 are described in detail and are supported by supposedly accurate footnotes. The self-conscious narrator/historian insists that he 'need not [...] apologize for the length of these extracts – they contain the concentrated essence of Irish history' (*Memoirs*, p. 90). While contemporary Protestants still regard the Rebellion of 1641 as 'an odious and unnatural rebellion', Catholics see this 'paroxysm of "wild justice"' (*Memoirs*, p. 92) as the result of Strafford's policies. Therefore, 1641 is seen as the source of Ireland's ills and the start of the pattern of agrarian violence that – with a brief respite in the first half of the eighteenth century – still continued in the 1820s. Rocks contention is that the long-term subjection of the Irish, the allegedly legitimate seizure of their lands and the persecution of their religion justifies reciprocal agrarian violence. It is English oppression that acts as Rock's recruiting sergeant; they give him 'a soul for right, and a soul for riot' (*Memoirs*, p. 106). The process is really quite simple:

> [I]n many places where the English had obtained settlements, the natives were first driven into insurrections by their cruelty, and then punished with double cruelty for their resistance [sic]. (*Memoirs*, p 80n)

Strangely, Rock does not seem to mind, although perhaps Moore does. English oppression has made Rock hard-bitten and cynical. He is an 'amateur' (that is a 'lover') of violence. He is also a man of some education, who knows something of the Italian Renaissance – perhaps a reference to Machiavelli. In his own way, he is actually grateful to the English. It is they who provide him with his pastime. In a memorable passage, he thanks them for creating a 'Fund of Discord' upon which he can still draw:

> I am not the less grateful to the 'wisdom of our ancestors' for that inexhaustible Fund of Discord which it has bequeathed to me and my family; nor a whit less alive to the merits of those personages of our own times [...] who contribute weekly, monthly, and annually their quotas to this venerable Fund, and promise to make it as large and lasting a blessing as the Debt of England itself. (*Memoirs*, pp 106-7)

Rock may be just being ironic, but with Rock we can never be entirely sure; that is partly why, for all its faults, *Memoirs* is so intriguing.

We have proactive English oppression and essentially reactive Irish resistance and agrarian outrages. This may go some way to explain the motion of the wheel, but we need to consider its operation more minutely. English oppression and Irish resistance are not completely separate forces, but are directly linked. Although they may greet examples of Irish resistance with horror and outrage, the English secretly welcome them. In fact, Irish resistance is actually part of their plan, so much so that, when they want more land, they deliberately set out to stir up a rebellion and are utterly unscrupulous in their methods. They follow the same tactics time after time, so it is almost as if they work to a script. They put on a play and the wheel turns on the stage of a theatre.

> The same drama, a little modernized, was acted over again in 1798; and the prompter's book and stage directions are still in hand in the archives of Dublin Castle, whenever an able Orange manager shall be found to preside over a renewal of the spectacle. (*Memoirs*, p 81)

It is striking that the Orangeman is only the manager. While he may produce the play, it is the proprietors – ultimately the English – who decide when it will be performed and how long it will run. So, the role of Orangemen on the wheel is merely that of government pawns. They are encouraged to provoke the Catholics – and, as ordinary people, they are inevitably exposed to Catholic counter-violence, while their masters can sit back in safety deciding how to derive maximum advantage for themselves. The pattern is clear: the Government supports landowners, as does the Church of Ireland. A Protestant hegemony uses the law and the military – institutional violence – to maintain order. Once this is achieved, the Government, perhaps with an eye to national or international politics, slightly loosens its grip. Emboldened, the Irish, covertly supported by the Catholic Church, seek to take advantage of this apparent leniency. The Government and the Ascendancy are neither willing nor able to understand the tenants' grievances. Once more they tighten their grip; naturally this elicits an equally violent response – and so the wheel turns again. Yet the role of the Orangemen is crucial, as Rock appreciates. To add to the sense of historical authenticity, Moore makes Rock refer to a family journal, which describes Sir John Clotworthy's provocation of Catholics. Clotworthy believed that the only way to convert Catholics is to have 'a Bible in one hand and a sword in the other'. With some relish the journal notes, '[t]his cannot fail […] to bring forth good fruit' (*Memoirs*, p. 82). Of course, 'good fruit' is Catholic rebellion.

Memoirs admits, tacitly, that Rock and his followers are serving the English purpose, just like the Orangemen. Both groups are tied to the wheel. Even the British Government, in some ways astonishingly naïve, is tied too. Indeed, virtually the full cast-list of stereotypical figures – who also appear in most of the other agrarian novels – are tied to it as well. They include: Protestant landowners, middlemen/agents, vulnerable ladies, Protestant and Catholic clergy, tenants and secret societies. The same is true of institutions: Monarchy, Government, the Churches, the Military, the Militia, the Judiciary, the Orange Order and the Nationalists. Names may change but the roles, the places on the wheel, never do. Many of the agrarian novels discussed earlier are open to the charge that their characters are not fully rounded and seem two-dimensional. Yet the charge is even more telling when applied to Moore. Because their roles remain unchanged, his characters, even Rock himself, are not real people. Inevitably, this reduces the literary effectiveness of *Memoirs*, though, interestingly, it also results in an unmistakable sense of the surreal.

Rock Modified

Memoirs provoked several responses (apart from the two key works discussed below) – as Tadgh O'Sullivan indicates:

Captain Rock in London was joined by Roger O'Connor's *Letters to his Majesty, George the Fourth* (1828), Charlotte Elizabeth Tonna's evangelical tract *The Rockite: An Irish Story* (1829) and anonymous travel book entitled *Captain Rock in Rome*.[15]

The most significant response came from Mortimer O'Sullivan, writing under the pseudonym of 'A Munster Farmer', in *Captain Rock Detected* (1824). O'Sullivan converted from Catholicism to Protestantism (Church of Ireland) and, though a Tory, opposed Ascendancy landowners.

O'Sullivan's interpretation of Irish history differs, unsurprisingly, from that of Moore. O'Sullivan believes the conquest of Ireland was carried out by English thugs and not by the various monarchs. Increased tithes are not the fault of Church of Ireland ministers but of landowners and middlemen. He condemns absenteeism and the sub-division of land that has created instability. The blame, however, does not lie entirely with the English: after the Reformation, the Irish had a choice between Pope and King – and foolishly they chose Rome.

In *Captain Rock Detected* (more a theological diatribe than a work of fiction), O'Sullivan – a Catholic looking through the glass of Protestantism – argues that it was the Penal Laws that drove Irish and English apart. Like Moore, O'Sullivan dislikes O'Connell claiming that he and Rock are in league. O'Sullivan not only opposes Catholic Emancipation – suggesting that even the Irish people themselves are not bothered about it – but also opposes Repeal.

As we have seen, O'Sullivan repeatedly claims 'that Mr. Moore is not the author of Captain Rock' (*Detected*, p. 360n), but this may be disingenuous. O'Sullivan, pre-empting Trollope – as in his reference to Malthus (*Detected*, p. 324) – is in favour of old Catholic priests who 'were educated gentlemen' he loathes the new priests who are 'arrogant and vulgar' and seek to 'conform to the habits of the lower orders' (*Detected*, pp. 258-9). Moreover, he repeatedly claims that Catholicism has no doctrine (*Detected*, pp. 382-3) and 'that the grand object of its ministers is its glory and stability not excluding certainly, the cultivation of Christian feeling' (*Detected*, p. 396).

O'Sullivan, as a 'humble and faithful historian' (*Detected*, p. 343), echoes Edgeworth:

---

[15] Tadgh O'Sullivan, 'Captain Rock in Print', unpublished MPhil thesis (University College Cork, 1998), p. 147.

[I] call upon the Irish gentry – I call upon the English people, to listen to my warning voice on the consequences of their misgovernment. (*Detected*, pp. 376-7)

Unlike later true agrarian novelists, he offers a simple solution:

I do not call for the return of the absentees; I do not call for English capital; *I demand only, that the landlords should join the government in giving some security that the tenant shall not be asked to pay more* THAN HIS FARM IS WORTH [sic]. (*Detected*, p. 419)

And also, echoing both Edgeworth and Adam Smith:

Give the Irish peasantry hope; let them be made to feel *that it is in their power to better their condition* [sic], and they will soon become desirous of improvement. (*Detected*, p. 420)

In 1825, *Captain Rock in London*, written by Michael James Whitty, appeared. In his dedication to George IV, Decimus Rock (the same forename as in Moore's *Memoirs*) outlines the closeness between the 'ROCKS of Ireland' and 'the Royal House of Brunswick'[16] but warns:

[I]t cannot fail to strike your Majesty that the wisdom of English legislation has entailed unheard-of grievances on my poor afflicted country, and that centuries of anarchy and seas of blood are allowing to that cursed policy which hopes to rule the people only by dividing them. (*London*, pt. 1, p. ii)

In the second dedication, in 1826, Rock announces the closure of *The Chieftain's Gazette* blaming it on his being too successful in enlightening the Irish people:

When I commenced my literary labours, the question of the forty-shilling freeholders came before the public; and I was the very first to oppose and expose Mr. O'Connell's advocacy of the two

---

[16] M J Whitty, *Captain Rock in London &c.* (London: James Robins & Dublin: Joseph Robins, 1825-26), pt. 1, p. i. Further references to this edition are given after quotations in the text and the title shortened to *London*.

pernicious measures then before legislature. […] I was the real and true friend of Ireland. (*London*, pt. 2, p. iv)

Despite the periodical's imminent demise, he still finds time to revel in the fact that he 'unveiled the character of that arch-hypocrite, William Cobbett' a man's whose ideas are 'tinged with quackery and delusion' (*London*, pt. 2, p. v).

Throughout the life of the *Gazette*, Rock frequently addresses landowners in his 'Letters to Irish Landlords' and reveals that, like Edgeworth and Moore, he cites excessive sub-division of the land as a major cause of Ireland's problems. Equally, Rock's admiration for Edgeworth and implicit acknowledgement of her influence is revealed in his review of the Banims' *Crohoore of the Bill-Hook*:

SINCE [sic] Miss Edgeworth, saturated with fame, retired from the literary field […] we have had scarcely any publications, purely Irish, worthy of attention, until within the last twelve months. (*London*, 14 May, 1825, pt. 1, p. 85)

A further implication is that, unlike Daniel Corkery, Rock is willing to view Edgeworth and the Banims as genuinely Irish. In stating that 'ROCKISM [sic] is immortal!!!' (*London*, pt. 1, p. 326) Rock is not an ordinary mortal; he is a 'time-lord' or one of the undead like Dracula. The point is made clearly when Captain Rock writes the obituary of his father, Captain Rock; individuals die but Captain Rock continues.

The 'Wheel of Torture': From Fantasy to the Surreal

Moore's *Memoirs*, like some other agrarian novels, reveals the pervasive influence of the seventeenth century upon subsequent events. For the Protestant Ascendancy, the source of Ireland's problems, particularly the violence, lies with the Catholic atrocities of 1641. For the Catholic Irish, the source lies with Cromwell's retribution at Drogheda and Wexford in 1649.

Ireland suffers from too much history and too few historians. Historians might conceivably have stopped or, at least, slowed the wheel because of historians' inherent need to be objective – no such constraint applies to writers of fiction. As a novelist, Moore is so despairing that all he can do is spin the wheel. He had little faith in political change if that

255

meant backing O'Connell whose leadership, according to Trench, Moore considered 'a sort of dictatorship'.[17] The cyclical history of Ireland is unique within Western Europe where the literatures of other countries reveal that, whether or not there was a 'General Crisis', they managed to pull away from their past histories. Ireland remained – perhaps still remains – tied to her 'wheel of torture'. There are few countries, in the twenty-first century where pictures of a seventeenth-century King, painted on the side of houses, are considered relevant to contemporary politics.

Among agrarian works, *Memoirs* offers a unique interpretation of the Land Question. The warning to Ascendancy landowners and the Government contained in Edgeworth's Irish novels has a positive undertone but Moore's warning is entirely negative and claims that continued violence is an inevitable result of English misrule. The practical blueprint offered by Edgeworth is replaced by an unreal agenda that offers no genuine hope and merely promises more violent agitation and the continued prosperity of secret societies like the Rockites. We have seen two failed solutions to the Land Question: the rational and fantastical. The route left unexplored is that of the surreal.

In conventional historical narrative – and indeed in socio-realist novels – things change. They change because the actors change; they are born, live out their lives whether long or short, and then they die. There is nothing so real as death. Yet in Moore, there is no change; although thousands may die, Rock does not. He is eternal, reincarnated time and again, as indeed are his enemies. The wheel cannot stop because those upon it do not die – indeed they cannot. Ireland has become the land of the undead – that is its essential tragedy. Of course, this is fantasy, a surrealist version of history. Such was Edgeworth's influence that few could see where Moore's logic was leading. Eventually, an author emerged who did understand; his name was Bram Stoker.

---

[17] Trench, pp. 16-17.

Chapter 8:
Bram Stoker – The Eternal Vampire

Ev'n already – long life to such Big-wigs, say I, For, as long as they flourish, we Rocks cannot Die.[1]

The vampire live on, and cannot die by mere passing of the time; he can flourish when that he can fatten on the blood of the living. Even more, as we have seen amongst us that he can even grow younger.[2]

From Satire to Surrealism

Although Stoker's *Dracula* (1897) was published more than seventy years after *Memoirs of Captain Rock* (1824), this chapter follows our discussion of Moore. Despite the substantial gap in time between them, Moore and Stoker follow the same alternative agenda, the non-Edgeworth agenda of fantasy and surrealism. Yet the time gap is still interesting. The fantasy agenda may have been crowded out, not just by the strength of the Edgeworth tradition, but also by the prevailing literary conventions of the Victorian period. *Memoirs* was published before the beginning of that period and *Dracula* almost at its end. Fantasy was never totally crowded out however; there are hints of the fantasy agenda in J Sheridan Le Fanu, even though, strictly speaking, he is not an agrarian novelist.

Captain Rock revels in that fact that he cannot die. The only thing that could kill him would be for the English to return Ireland to the Irish and Ascendancy landowners and to return the land to the tenants and so bring peace. Rock knows that this will never happen so he will continue to thrive. In *Dracula*, Bram Stoker seems to echo Moore's version of history by denying that matters inevitably improve 'by mere passing of the time'

---

[1] Thomas Moore, 'Captain Rock in London', in *The Poetical Works of Thomas Moore*, editor not named (London: Bliss Sands & Co., 1812), p. 412.
[2] Bram Stoker, *Dracula* (1897) (London: Penguin, 1979), p. 42. Further references to this edition are given after quotations in the text.

(*Dracula*, p. 286). In *Dracula*, Moore's hint that, if there is change, it will be for the worse, becomes more explicit. Dracula resembles Rock in that he does not die but, unlike Rock, he actually gets younger and stronger as he feeds on more and more blood. In other words, if, as seems possible, Dracula is really set in Ireland rather than in Transylvania, Moore's wheel of torture will spin faster than ever, no doubt, with added refinements of cruelty.

Dracula was published in 1897 in the dying days of the Ascendancy. The novel has a complex, fractured narrative structure that, like Shakespeare's *Macbeth*, accords with Tzvetan Todorov's model of equilibrium, disequilibrium, new equilibrium. Jonathan Harker, a respectable lawyer, visits an important client to arrange the purchase of a house. At this stage the world is ordered. Yet Harker's visit unleashes the vampire who travels to London to spread disorder. Only with Dracula's death is order restored and, with the vampire vanquished, a new order is established. The beginning and end of *Dracula* are fairly conventional. Though intellectually braver and more adventurous than other authors examined in this book, Stoker still subscribes to the orthodoxies and priorities of the 'well-made story' structure. It is only when Dracula is on the loose, when disorder reigns supreme, that the novel really comes alive.

There is now general agreement that *Dracula* is an important novel, but initial reaction was decidedly cool. As M J Trow notes:

> *The Athenaeum* found the book 'wanting in the constructive art as well as in the higher literary sense'. *Punch* wrote that it was 'the very weirdest of weird tales'. The *Bookman* damned with faint praise – 'we read nearly the whole with rapt attention'.[3]

While *Dracula* was an immediate success with the public, literary critics have spent a century trying to make sense of this complex and puzzling book. It has long been understood that *Dracula* is historically based, and Trow places it firmly in the historical context of Transylvania. Recently, however, *Dracula* has also become popular with Freudians, post-Freudians and post-Modernists. Trow notes that some commentators have given 'meanings to its passages that Bram Stoker probably never intended'. Much modern comment has focussed on sexual dimensions. Maurice Richardson describes *Dracula* as 'a kind of incestuous, necrophiliac, oral-

---

[3] M J Trow, *Vlad The Impaler* (Stroud: Sutton Publishing Limited, 2003) p. 33.

anal-sadistic all-in wrestling match', while Christopher Frayling notes that 'it has been read in terms of Freudian allegory, Marxist "cosmic racial conflict", feminist gender politics and so on'. This approach culminates in James Twitchell's claim that the success of *Dracula* lies in the fact that it represents 'sex without genitalia, sex without confusion, sex without responsibility, sex without guilt, sex without love – better yet, sex without mention'.[4] While these comments may be revealing about their authors, it is doubtful whether they really advance our understanding of *Dracula* or Stoker.

Some of the most perceptive comments on *Dracula* have come from Irish writers. Seamus Deane suggests that Dracula represents a dying Ascendancy clinging to life – or at least an after-life – while sliding towards inevitable oblivion:

> [L]andlord that he is, with all his enslaved victims, his Celtic twilight is endangered by the approach of a nationalist dawn, a Home Rule sun rising behind the old Irish Parliament. Dracula's dwindling soil and his vampiric appetites consort well with enough with the image of the Irish landlord current in the nineteenth century. Running out of soil, this peculiar version of the absentee landlord in London will flee the light of day and be consigned to the only territory left to him, that of legend.[5]

In Dracula's desperate attempt to escape the inevitable stake, we see the allegorical desperation of the Ascendancy; there is nowhere to run.

The suggestion of the link with Ireland is valuable and raises the question of whether *Dracula* should be placed within the tradition of agrarian fiction. At first sight, the proposition seems outlandish. *Dracula* appears to be an entirely new and unique novel, totally different from the conventional, predictable, over-lengthy and occasionally tedious works characteristic of the canon of agrarian fiction explored in this book. This is not the case, however, and *Dracula* does belong to the canon of Irish agrarian fiction – although not in the way that some critics suppose. Hence, while other literary traditions will be discussed, it is Stoker's interpretation of the Land Question that forms the focus of this chapter. It is the curiously sexless world of the novel's Anglo-Irish political subtext that especially concerns us.

---

[4] Trow, pp. 31-34.
[5] Seamus Deane, *Strange Country* (Oxford: Clarendon Press, 1997), p. 90.

This chapter considers the relationship between the Sensation novel and the agrarian novel before looking at the influence of Stoker's background on the genesis of *Dracula*. This will be followed by an analysis of the parallels between Stoker's Transylvania and Ireland and an exploration of the links between Captain Rock and Count Dracula. Finally, the importance of Norman Stone's theory of an 'inner' and 'outer' Europe and its relevance to *Dracula* is assessed.

Dracula Anticipated

Appreciation of the influence of the Sensation novels is important to a proper understanding of *Dracula*. As soon as Dracula appears, two key elements – vampirism and sexuality – dwarf all others. It is immediately obvious that *Dracula* is not merely a re-working of the Land Question. It is an extreme and irrational work, a curious blend of the agrarian novel, the Gothick novel, and the Sensation novel. While modern critics have often identified the novel's Irish parallels, they have missed its links to the agrarian novels. They have also failed to appreciate its debt to the circular interpretation of Irish history proposed by Moore and to the traditions of the Sensation novel exemplified by Le Fanu. It is noteworthy that the cool reception accorded to *Dracula* – and to other major innovative works of the 1890s, such as Oscar Wilde's *The Picture of Dorian Gray* (1891) and Kate Chopin's *The Awakening* (1899) – echoed the equally critical response to Wilkie Collins's *The Woman in White* (1859-60). Both Collins and Stoker reflect changes in society that produced unease in the conservative-minded; indeed, '[t]he 1890s has the reputation of being a "naughty" decade'.[6]

Although the Sensation novel was not specifically Irish, one of its greatest exponents, J S Le Fanu, was Anglo-Irish. Characteristics of the genre may be traced to the Gothick novel, exemplified in the works of Charles Maturin, an Anglo-Irish cleric. Stoker was influenced both by the Gothick novel and – to a greater extent – by the Sensation novel. According to David Punter, *Dracula* is 'a well-written and formally inventive sensation novel'[7] but the case argued here is that it is an amalgamation of the agrarian novel and the Sensation novel.

The Sensation novel was at its height in the 1860s but was prefigured in some of the Brontës' novels including *Jane Eyre* (1847) and *Wuthering*

---

[6] Trow, p. 31.
[7] David Punter, *The Literature of Terror* (Harlow: Pearson Education Limited, 1996), p. 16.

Heights (1847). Even Charles Dickens and George Eliot indulged in sensationalism – as evident in *Great Expectations* (1861) and *Adam Bede* (1859). The Sensation novel, however, became a media phenomenon with *The Woman in White* and Mary Elizabeth Braddon's *Lady Audley's Secret* (1862). Sensation novels, often based on newspaper reports of real events, set out to shock their predominantly middle class, female readers. They often involved unjust incarceration, sealed rooms, secret passages, abductions, murders, hints of the supernatural (real or imagined), and a host of evil characters. A key element was the inversion of the roles of conventional characters. Refined fathers, brothers and uncles emerge, not as the protectors of vulnerable women but as their persecutors; beautiful, cultured ladies turn into murderers of men; transgression of gender roles becomes the norm.

Le Fanu's *Uncle Silas* (1864) exhibits remarkable similarities with *Dracula*. In both, there are female protagonists whose roles differ radically from those delineated in more conventional novels. Le Fanu's Madame de la Rougierre is a study in transgressive sexuality and Maud Ruthyn fights for survival independent of male support; in *Dracula*, the 'New Woman', Mina, is independent and wilful. As some critics saw the Sensation novel as a literary disease that threatened disorder, so, in *Dracula*, the Count spreads disorder and disease. In the archetypal Gothick novel, horrors take place in the Appenines or Abruzzi but, in Sensation novels, they occur in the British home. In *Dracula*, the horrors occur both in remote mountains and in the home as the vampire travels from his Transylvanian lair to England. Terror is greater in a familiar, homely setting.

In Le Fanu's *The House by the Churchyard* (1863), Paul Dangerfield is a vampire, half-alive and half-dead. He glides through corridors rather than walks, as does Silas Ruthyn. Dangerfield is also described as a 'wher-wolf'.[8] Dracula is a vampire who, half-dead, must kill and drink blood to be even half-alive. He moves silently, appearing next to his victims without sound or warning. When he arrives at Whitby on the *Demeter*, he changes into a wolf-like dog to escape his pursuers and, later, in the same guise, attempts to enter Lucy's bedroom. Bartram Haugh, like Dracula's Castle, is a semi-derelict Big House. Madame de la Rougierre, like the Brides of Dracula, is herself implicitly vampiric in her apparent ability to lie with the dead before rising again:

---

[8] J Sheridan Le Fanu, *The House by the Churchyard* (1863) (London: Anthony Blond Ltd., 1968), p. 447.

Don't you love the dead, Cheaile? I will teach you to love them. You shall see me die here to-day, for half an hour, and be among them. That is what I love.[9]

While the Brides feed off the blood of the young, Madame de la Rougierre feeds off her hatred for Maud. Yet she too meets a suitably vampiric end when she is killed by Dudley Ruthyn, who uses 'a longish tapering spike' to dispatch her (*Silas*, p. 415).

In Silas Ruthyn we see a precursor of Dracula; both are associated with foul weather and wolves. While Dracula controls the wolves and becomes one himself, Maud perceives herself surrounded by wolves and is obsessed by a picture of a girl pursued by 'a pack of wolves' (*Silas*, p. 338). Dracula and Silas can enter and leave sealed rooms. Harker sees Dracula 'begin to crawl down the castle wall [...] *face down*, with his cloak spreading out around him like great wings' (*Dracula*, p. 47); Silas gets into and out of a sealed room to murder Charke. Lady Monica Knollys, the force for good in *Uncle Silas*, refers to Silas as 'an old enchanter in his castle' (*Silas*, p.144) and Maud's own description of her uncle could apply to Dracula:

> I saw him before me still, in necromantic black, ashy with a pallor on which I looked with fear and pain, a face so dazzlingly pale, and those hollow, fiery, awful eyes. (*Silas*, p. 194)

A further similarity between *Uncle Silas* and *Dracula* is that Harker, like Maud, is forced to write letters indicating all is well when, in reality, death is near; both hear their own graves being dug. While Maud attempts to persuade Tom Brice to take a note, begging for help, to Lady Knollys, Harker tries to send a similar note via the Szgany gypsies – but both are betrayed.

Although not a Sensation novel, the influence of Le Fanu's *Carmilla* (1871) upon *Dracula* is significant. The story concerns the lesbian vampire Carmilla's relentless pursuit of the innocent Laura. Baron Vordenberg, Laura's father, believes that '[a] suicide, under certain circumstances, becomes a vampire'.[10] In *Carmilla*, Le Fanu seeks to frighten his readers on two levels – also a feature of *Dracula*. First, Carmilla is frightening because

---

[9] J Sheridan Le Fanu, *Uncle Silas* (1864) (Oxford: Oxford University Press, 1968), p. 32.
[10] J Sheridan Le Fanu, *Carmilla* (1871) (New York: Scholastic Book Services, 1971), p. 111.

she is a woman who is out of control both sexually and physically. Secondly, like Dracula, she is a vampire, a revenant, who returns from the grave to create mayhem. Dracula's diseased blood infects all those who come into contact with him but Carmilla's blood is doubly diseased – it imparts both death and sexual deviance. Carmilla, in life Countess Mircalla, is pursued by a group of men through Styria, and is dispatched by 'a sharp stake [being] driven through the heart of the vampire' before her 'head was struck off' (*Carmilla*, pp. 106-7). In *Dracula*, Lucy is dispatched in a similar manner (*Dracula*, pp. 257-8). Christopher Frayling stresses Le Fanu's influence upon Stoker:

> Stoker seems to have been much taken by the strange and beautiful relationship between vampire and victim in *Carmilla*. Lucy and the brides of Dracula court their prey in ways which owe much to Le Fanu's listless *femme fatale* [...] *Carmilla*'s dream-like fantasy about sexually aware, and sexually dominant, women [...] would seem to have bitten deep into the psyche of two apparently prosaic, not-so-eminent Victorian males: Bram Stoker and his fictional counterpart, Jonathan Harker.[11]

In some ways, therefore Stoker looks to Ireland's literary past rather than to its future.

Le Fanu was not the only Anglo-Irish writer who influenced Stoker. Stoker married Oscar Wilde's former fiancée and it is possible that *Dracula* was written to compete with *The Picture of Dorian Gray* (1891). As with Moore's Rock and Le Fanu's Carmilla, Dorian Gray cannot die. Like other vampires, he is a serial murderer feeding off the misery, sorrow and deaths of others. Although, like Dracula, Dorian wants society to regard him as a cultured gentleman, as the critic of *The Scots Observer* notes, he is really 'a devil'.[12] Just as Dracula and the other vampires infect society so, as the critic of *The Daily Chronicle* observes, Dorian 'might go on for ever using his senses with impunity "to cure his soul", defiling English society with the moral pestilence which is incarnate in him' (*Gray*, p. 218). According to the critic of *The St. James's Gazette*, like the Sensation novelists, Wilde chose an established framework on which to base his story:

---

[11] Christopher Frayling, *Vampyres* (London: Faber and Faber, 1992), pp. 358-9.
[12] Oscar Wilde, *The Picture of Dorian Gray* (1891), ed. by Robert Mighall (London: Penguin Books, 2003), p. 218.

Why, bless our souls! haven't [sic] we read something of this kind somewhere in the classics? [...] Ah – yes – no yes, it *was* Horace![13]

When Dorian dies, we encounter a creature, ugly in death, stabbed through the heart:

> Lying on the floor was a dead man, in evening dress, with a knife in his heart. He was withered, wrinkled, and loathsome of visage. (*Gray*, p. 213)

All three Anglo-Irishmen, Le Fanu in the 1860s and 70s, Wilde and Stoker in the 1890s, feared revenants. Perhaps their fear came from their own personal and social insecurities. Le Fanu experienced agrarian violence at first-hand while Wilde and Stoker only found success as Irish outsiders in London.

The links between *Dracula* and earlier Anglo-Irish works are important for the agrarian novel and for Irish literature in general. Paul Murray refers to Roy Foster's identification of 'a line of supernatural fiction encompassing Maturin, Le Fanu, Stoker, W. B. Yeats and Elizabeth Bowen: "[t]heir preoccupation with the occult reflects a sense of displacement, a loss of social and psychological integration and an escapism motivated by the threat of a take-over by the Catholic middle classes" '. This may be partly true but Stoker, a Protestant with Catholic forebears, who lived mainly in England and supported Home Rule, did not fear Catholics in the way Foster suggests. Indeed, Stoker's all embracing Irishness is stressed by 'the English critic, David Glover' who believes that '*Dracula* [...] goes furthest in establishing Stoker's pedigree as a distinctly Irish writer'[14] while Terry Eagleton identifies the Irish literary genesis of *Dracula*:

> Jonathan Swift's *Gulliver's Travels*, Maria Edgeworth's *Castle Rackrent*, Maturin's *Melmoth*, Le Fanu's *Uncle Silas* and Joyce's *Ulysses* [are part of] 'a literary tradition [...] [of] largely unrealistic works', with Stoker and Maturin transcending realism altogether. This Irish Protestant Gothic might be dubbed the political

---

[13] Quoted in *Dorian Gray*, 2003, 'From The St. James's Gazette, June 1890', p. 215.
[14] Paul Murray, *From The Shadow of Dracula* (London: Jonathan Cape, 2004), p. 192.

unconscious of Anglo-Irish society, the place where its fears and fantasies most definitely emerge.[15]

The London Irish

Stoker is an enigma. Although educated at Trinity College Dublin, where he was a member of the College Historical Society, Stoker was a nationalist.[16] He came from a lower middle class, professional background and, along with his siblings, aspired to membership of the Ascendancy. He 'expressly approved' of 'British imperialism'[17] – except in Ireland where he wanted the land returned to the Irish. As Barbara Belford observes, Stoker is difficult to research:

> Stoker was not an obliging person to think about for five years. [...] He did not keep a personal dairy but a 'jotting diary,' focusing almost exclusively on Henry Irving's achievements. [...] In response to the question 'Who are you?' I imagine him saying, 'I am who you want me to be'.[18]

The same could be said of *Dracula*:

> As with all great art, the fairytale's deepest meaning will be different for each person, and different for the same person at various moments of his life.[19]

The lack of useful personal papers adds to the mystery surrounding Stoker and his novels. It is curious that a man who could write such a successful, multi-faceted novel was unable to replicate its success.

Stoker spent most of his working life as Henry Irving's manager and as theatre manager of the Lyceum Theatre in London, positions that brought him into contact with many important people. Stoker's *Personal Reminiscences of Henry Irving* (1906), written after Irving's death, has more about Stoker than Irving. Stoker emerges as extraordinarily vain, a man

---

[15] Quoted in Murray, p. 192.
[16] See Glover, p. 23.
[17] Joseph Valente, *Dracula's Crypt* (Urbana: University of Illinois Press, 2002), p. 68.
[18] Barbara Belford, *Bram Stoker* (London: Weidenfeld and Nicolson, 1996), p. xi.
[19] Keith Hopper, 'Hairy on the Inside: Re-visiting Neil Jordan's The Company of Wolves', in *Canadian Journal of Irish Studies*, 29, No. 2, Autumn, p. 17.

who takes every opportunity to ingratiate himself with the key figures of the day. Highly susceptible to flattery, he revelled in his grand acquaintances and had delusions about his own brilliance and importance. He even sent the Prime Minister unasked for copies of his novels. Stoker wanted the fame and adulation accorded to Irving and always notes that those he met were much impressed by his own opinions.

Murray traces Stoker's maternal ancestry: 'he was descended from the Blakes of Galway, one of the fourteen "tribes" of that city'.[20] Despite their Catholic ancestry, members of Stoker's family had a history of changing 'their religious allegiance'. By the time Stoker was born in Clontarf on 8 November 1847, the Stokers were loyal members of the Church of Ireland. Breaking free from his father's extreme conservatism, Stoker developed a 'lifelong emphatic support for parliamentary, as opposed to physical-force nationalism' and always took 'liberal attitudes on the intertwined issues of religion and politics in Ireland'.[21] Stoker Senior died before the publication of *Dracula*, although Belford is probably right to suggest that he would not have liked it:

> Beyond a veritable lexicon of Victorian taboos (seduction, rape, gang rape, group sex, necrophilia, incest, adultery, oral sex, menstruation, venereal disease, and voyeurism), there are obvious political, religious, and occult leitmotifs, ranging from the emergence of the New Woman to the polarization of East and West to an allegory on the tarot.[22]

Seán Lennon notes that Stoker's mother, Charlotte, witnessed horrors that later she described to her son:

> As a Sligo woman Charlotte had witnessed the consequences of the cholera epidemic of 1832, one dire example being the premature burial of distraught victims in order to avoid the further spread of disease.[23]

---

[20] Murray, pp. 7-10.
[21] Murray, pp. 8-19.
[22] Belford, p. 9.
[23] Seán Lennon, *Irish Gothic Writers* (Dublin: Dublin Corporation Public Libraries, n.d.), p. 15.

The nightmares that must have resulted from such tales and the fear of premature burial surfaced later in Stoker's attempt metaphorically to raise his characters from the dead. Murray also claims that Charlotte's belief in 'assisted emigration' became 'her son's panacea for Irish poverty'.[24] It was Charlotte's friendship with Dr. William Wilde and Jane Francesca Wilde (Oscar's parents) that enabled Stoker to move in a higher social circle. Later Stoker himself 'became friendly with [...] Lady Wilde, who, writing under the pen name of Speranza, had carved out a distinctive niche in the nationalist literature associated with the Young Ireland movement'.[25]

Stoker remained steadfast in his support for nationalism and, later, Home Rule. He did not, however, advocate a fully independent Ireland free from the English Crown; he clearly yearned for a hierarchy, so detested by Americans, to enable him to progress up the social ladder. Yet there was always ambiguity. Stoker was deeply influenced by John Bright, the pro-American enthusiast for democracy. In particular Stoker subscribed to Bright's ideas for reforms in Ireland – especially 'a plan of land purchase for tenants':

> Bright's aim, which Stoker shared, was to reform the landed interest in Ireland, to create 'contentment and tranquility' and thereby to underpin the union of Ireland and Britain. [...] In his politics, evident in his fiction, Stoker shared Bright's advocacy of ameliorative reform, combined with detestation of Fenianism.[26]

In fact, Stoker's views were quite close to those of his literary predecessors. Edgeworth wrote about the amelioration of Ireland, while the Banims, Griffin, Carleton and Kickham all loathed violence and secret societies. Stoker, like Carleton and Kickham, agreed with the nationalist ideas of Thomas Davis – who was himself influenced by Robert Kane's *The Industrial Resources of Ireland* (1844). With the exception Kickham (who rejected British parliamentary democracy in favour of the American version), the agrarian novelists supported change through political means – and never wavered in their allegiance to the English Crown.

When Home Rule became a real possibility, Stoker, as a Liberal, supported it enthusiastically. His support was influenced and encouraged

---

[24] Murray, p. 15.

[25] Murray, p. 14.

[26] David Glover, *Vampires, Mummies and Liberals* (London: Duke University Press, 1996), p. 51.

by his friends. Apart from the Wildes, who also supported Home Rule, Stoker had 'a close literary and political friendship with Justin McCarthy, the Irish nationalist writer [journalist] and politician' who was involved with Parnell. Stoker subscribed wholeheartedly to McCarthy's brand of Home Rule with its belief that 'economic development [...] would follow its implementation'.[27] His advocacy of Home Rule re-appears, in a Transylvanian context, in *Dracula*.

Dracula International

Agrarian novels are concerned with a series of flawed and polarised socio-political relationships: English and Irish, English and Anglo-Irish, Anglo-Irish and Irish, landowner and tenant, landowner and agent and tenant, Protestant and Catholic, Big House and cabin and institutional violence and agrarian violence. All these binaries find parallels in Stoker's *Dracula*.

In Stoker's Transylvania, Catholic Hungarians (the Protestant English) oppress the Orthodox native Romanians (the Catholic Irish). As in Ireland, the peasantry are overtly religious. The Romanians are 'just like the peasants at home' (*Dracula*, p. 11) and, being poor, have to travel on 'a leiterwagon' – the ordinary peasant's cart [...] calculated to suit the inequalities of the road' (*Dracula*, p. 17). Joseph Valente notes the similarities between Irish 'Big Houses' and Castle Dracula:

> Harker's description of Castle Dracula, grand but grim, dominant but desolate, recalls the Big House of latter day Anglo-Irish literature, a monument to misrule [...] obsolescence.[28]

Agrarian novels are littered with decaying Big Houses. Their deterioration reflects the failure of the Ascendancy as a class and lack of investment in the estates. In *Dracula*, Harker encounters a semi-derelict castle, learns that many rooms are shut up and that there are no servants. This corresponds closely to the actual condition of many of the Big Houses in Ireland. There are also parallels with The Castle in Dublin (where both Stoker and his father worked), and Castle Rackrent. Valente sees further links between Transylvania and Ireland:

---

[27] Murray, pp. 144-145.
[28] Valente, p. 53.

[T]he metaphorical logic of *Dracula* mirrors the political calculus of contemporaneous British foreign policy deliberations, in which the Irish Question and the Eastern Question bore upon and stood in for one another in a number of ways.[29]

Irish nationalists found it easy to identify with oppressed nations in other empires and their MPs often spoke on the iniquity of Russian oppression in Poland – Dracula, the oppressor, significantly escapes his pursuers on the *Czarina Catherine*. Valente outlines a real contingent relationship between Transylvania and Ireland:

Transylvania was in 1867 placed under the rule of Hungary, which at that time had achieved the sort of local autonomy shortly to be sought by moral force Irish nationalists: a semidetached status linking it to the empire solely through the Crown. When Isaac Butt [...] founded the Home Rule movement he floated the Hungarian arrangement as a blueprint for his own devolutionary scheme. [...] Parnell recirculated the Hungarian paradigm in October 1885 as a prospective settlement of the Irish Question [...] and his speech earned the approval of both the Tory leader Lord Salisbury, who judged the plan 'reasonable,' and [...] Gladstone, who thought the plan provided a workable basis for future bargaining. [...] sometime thereafter, Parnell played with the more hostile strategy of outright parliamentary withdrawal, which represented the very means whereby Hungary ultimately secured autonomy.[30]

Irish nationalists supported the aspirations of Hungarians who, before 1867, had been oppressed by the Austrians. Yet once the Hungarians had thrown off the Austrian yoke, they tightened their grip on the Romanians. Indeed, while in the 1860s and 70s, the Austro-Hungarian 'Augsleich' solution may have appeared as a possible blueprint for Ireland, the whole concept was doomed once Parnell adopted a more radical and potentially violent course.

As Terry Eagleton suggests, Dracula is the ultimate, surreal Ascendancy landowner:

---

[29] Punter, p. 54.
[30] Valente, pp. 54-5.

Dracula is an absentee landlord, deserting his Transylvanian castle to buy up property in London. Like many an Ascendancy aristocrat he is a devout Anglophile, given to poring over maps of the metropolis.[31]

Dracula, like many of the Ascendancy, comes from an old landowning family. Echoing Rock, Dracula 'speaking of things and people, and especially of battles [...] spoke as if he had been present at them all' (*Dracula*, p. 40). Dracula literally bleeds the tenants dry, just as Ascendancy landowners have done metaphorically in Ireland. As the Ascendancy is ultimately accountable to the English monarch, Dracula is accountable to Satan. There is nothing left to take, the land around the castle is dead and the locals are merely awaiting Dracula's final, fatal visit.

With these parallels in mind, we can see how Stoker envisages the fictional end of the Ascendancy. Dracula is supported only by the gullible (Harker), the insane (Renfield) and the dispossessed (the Sgzany gypsies). His world is empty of meaning and with no future, only a past. His bloodlust – analogous to institutional violence – drives him to commit endless murders that bring him no peace; he is, like the Famine, a plague upon the people. Despite the eroticism of the novel, the Count is sexless (even though he keeps three Brides, like pets, in his castle), impotent and unable to reproduce naturally, so his conventional line ends with him. Deane concludes:

> [T]he battle in this novel is a battle for reproduction – of the Undead against the living. The Undead are reproduced by a form of illicit and orgasmic sex; the living are reproduced by marriage. It is [...] the family against the mob; traditional piety against a revolutionary threat that produces, by perversion of the 'normal' – even to the contamination of blood – the ghastly, miasmic crowd.[32]

Dracula's only means of reproduction is to create a family of vampires that will, if successful, wipe out humanity and eventually themselves – the ultimate nihilistic mission. By the 1890s, the Irish Ascendancy was also doomed. The Liberals were committed to Home Rule and even the

---

[31] Terry Eagleton, *Heathcliff and the Great Hunger* (London: Verso, 1995), p. 215.
[32] Deane, p. 92.

Tories, hoping to 'kill Home Rule by kindness', prepared Land Acts to return land to Irish tenants. As Eagleton points out:

> Dracula, like the Ascendancy, is running out of land [...] His material base is rapidly dwindling, and without this soil [in his coffin] he will die. The Ascendancy, too, will evaporate once their earth is removed from them.[33]

The Ascendancy, like Dracula, is being marginalized: it belongs neither to England nor Ireland and is seen as an embarrassment by the English and as the embodiment of colonial oppression by the Irish. As the Ascendancy's lands are taken away so is its *raison d'être*. Its members will have nothing to pass on to their children who will have to choose to be either English or Irish. Either way, the Ascendancy is doomed. Just as Van Helsing uses science, rationality, psychology and the 'New Woman' to destroy Dracula, so the Government uses a new public mood at the dawn of a new century to destroy the Ascendancy.

Murray suggests that some of Dracula's characteristics may have been derived from Stoker's impressions of Irving or perhaps of Sir Richard Burton. Stoker was mesmerised by explorers like Burton and Henry Stanley. Burton's *Vikram and the Vampire or Tales of Hindu Devilry* (1870) contains 'blood-sucking demons' and a villain who can 'control the wolves'.[34] In *Personal Reminiscences*, Stoker notes that 'Burton's face seemed to lengthen when he laughed; the upper lip rising instinctively and showing the right canine tooth' and 'his canine tooth showed its full length like the gleam of a dagger'.[35] In *Dracula*, Lucy's 'teeth, in the dim, uncertain light, seemed longer and sharper than they had been in the morning' (*Dracula*, p. 192). Stoker also describes Stanley's face, 'through which the eyes seemed by contrast to shine like jewels [and] emphasised his slow speech and measured accents'. Stanley had the look of 'one who had traversed Heaven and Hell', had 'whitening of his hair' and 'looked more like a dead man than a living one'[36] – all characteristics that reappear in Dracula. More significant, however, is Burton's attitude to Home Rule:

---

[33] Eagleton, p. 215.
[34] Murray, p. 179.
[35] Stoker, *Reminiscences*, I, pp. 355-359.
[36] Stoker, *Reminiscences*, I, pp. 363-370.

Burton had definite ideas on the issue of Home Rule and advocated the adoption of the Austro-Hungarian constitution as a model for Ireland. He wrote on the parallels between the Irish and the Magyars and was familiar with the life and work of Arminius Vambery, the Hungarian writer and traveller who some believe first interested Stoker in Vlad the Impaler.[37]

Stoker reveals his gratitude to Vambery by having his alter-ego, Van Helsing, refer approvingly to 'the researches of my friend Arminius of Buda-Pesth' (*Dracula*, p. 359).

Stoker, like other agrarian novelists, was fascinated by history. Murray merely provides a brief overview of the influence of past writers on Stoker, but Joep Leerssen argues that the past is always evident in Ireland's present:

> The recurrence of the dead past, bursting into the living present; the awareness of buried, unfinished business yet awaiting definitive settlement – all this has important antecedents and begins perhaps with the cult of remembrancing initiated by Moore and the anti-Unionists. It fuels the 'Irish habit of historical thought'.[38]

Thomas Moore, like most Catholic writers, looks back to a romanticised past. His world is full of minstrels, a watchful Hibernia, a happy Catholic land, administered by Brehon Law and home to a contented people. Into this idyllic world come first the Normans and then the Protestant English who try to destroy the language, the culture and Catholicism. Despite all other influences, it is Moore's Rock, the fictional personification of Irish defiance, who has the biggest influence upon Stoker's Dracula. Indeed, as Leerssen suggests, *Dracula* is the inevitable by-product of nineteenth-century Anglo-Irish literature:

> It is no surprise that the figure of the aristocratic vampire, undead remnant of a feudal past battening on the vitality of the living, is an appealing one for Irish authors [...] The theme reverberates with worried reservations as to the straightforwardness of time, with an uncanny sense that Irish history, the sheer weight and bloodiness

---

[37] Murray, p. 178 and pp. 186-187.
[38] Joep Leerssen, *Remembrance and Imagination* (Cork: Cork University Press, 1996), pp. 222-223.

and persistence of it, will trouble the present's course towards the future.[39]

Moore would have agreed with Leerssen – the 'wheel of torture' is the past forever tainting the present and destroying hope for the future. The weight of the past is evident in *Dracula* with the Count's past being conveyed through historical details. Dracula is a vampire because of his forefathers' deeds as well as his own – exactly the story of the Ascendancy's history and subsequent decline. As Eagleton suggests '[t]here is an unspeakable foulness at the very heart of civility'.[40] Yet Stoker is not only attacking the Ascendancy, his target is also contemporary Irish culture:

> This cultivation of an undead past, which provides the blueprint and the ideals for future resuscitation, gives a morbid hue to the pretended vitalism of the Gaelic Revival and the Irish Renaissance.[41]

Stoker shows that a civilized, cultured exterior hides something much darker. '[T]he Gaelic Revival and the Irish Renaissance' adopted a myopic view of Ireland's cultural past. The past, especially the immediate past, was not confronted but avoided or ignored. As we have seen, Yeats' theory of 'Two Accents' in Irish literature reveals the selectivity of the Irish Revival. For Stoker, the Irish Revival has little substance because it fails to confront the realities of Irish history. While it seeks to create a new Ireland and culture, the only way it can succeed is by sanitizing the past. Instead of, metaphorically, stopping the 'wheel of torture', it seeks just to lock it away. Yet, as Dracula proves when he climbs out of the window of his locked room, the solution is not so easy.

Stoker was mesmerised by the East and especially by Burton's insistence that '[t]he desert has its own laws, and there – supremely of all the East – to kill is a small offence'.[42] While recalling the ease with which life is taken in the East, Stoker chooses to 'expand' the East to include

---

[39] Leerssen, p. 223.
[40] Eagleton, p. 216.
[41] Leerssen, p. 223.
[42] Stoker, *Reminiscences*, I, p. 359.

Eastern Europe. In *Dracula*, the East comes to the West.[43] However, Deane associates Dracula's need to take his home-soil with him to Irish history. The soil, in his coffin, is taken aboard the ship to England and 'is a literal version of the coffin-ship – that resonant image from the Famine times – that is wrecked on the Yorkshire coast, at Whitby'. He further suggests that 'it is a contaminated cargo; Dracula's soil is also his filth, his containment'.[44] According to Valente, 'Stoker's Transylvania has suffered a famine and a plague, and Dracula is symbolically associated with both: according to Stoker's working notes, the vampire brings on drought, and Dracula represents [...] a virulent force of contagion'.[45] This is a powerful image especially as Stoker believed that contagion came from the East.

In *Dracula*, Swales senses a contagion that 'tastes, and smells like death' approaching Whitby. The 'Russian' (*Dracula*, p. 94) ship 'with all sails set [...] was seemingly going westwards' (*Dracula*, p. 96). The ship, carrying death and contagion, will infect England; but just as England lies to the east of Ireland, so Ireland lies to the east of America. Deane's contaminated coffin ship is full of Irish going to America – implying that Ireland is defiling America. This raises the question of Stoker's attitude to the relationship between America and Ireland. If he had been a true nationalist, like Kickham, America would represent a beacon of hope and a temporary refuge for persecuted Irishmen – but, as Murray contends, this is not the case:

> [Stoker, in *The Lady of the Shroud* (1909),] proclaimed that society was rapidly becoming effete and that its regeneration depends on 'that personal purity which still exists with individuals'. This was especially true of America, where the Anglo-Saxon race was supposed to be dwindling and could never be restored to its former vigour by the new immigration from the East; the Irish were 'to serve to counterbalance effeteness in the American, and [...] may become in time the leading element of Western civilization.[46]

---

[43] In the opening paragraph, Harker states how he was 'leaving the West and entering the East', (*Dracula*, p. 9).

[44] Deane, pp. 89-90.

[45] Valente, p. 55.

[46] Murray, p. 37.

The East, only if defined relativistically, provides 'contagion' and 'regeneration'.

The perception that American society is becoming effete clashes with Stoker's portrayal of the Texan, Quincey Morris, in *Dracula*. Morris not only dies in his heroic attempts to defeat Dracula but is so highly regarded that the Harkers name their first child after him; indeed, Mina has 'the secret belief that some of our brave friend's spirit has passed into him' (*Dracula*, p. 449). Earlier, Dr. Seward claims that '[i]f America can go on breeding men like that, she will be a power in the world indeed' (*Dracula*, p. 209). While Seward's words appear complimentary, they also imply that America has not yet quite made the grade. Renfield pays an even more ambiguous compliment to America:

> Mr. Morris, you should be proud of your great state. Its reception into the Union was a precedent which may have far-reaching effects hereafter, when the Pole and the Tropics may hold allegiance to the Stars and Stripes. The power of Treaty may yet prove a vast engine of enlargement, when the Monroe doctrine takes its true place as a political fable. (*Dracula*, p. 291)

Although Renfield's words appear complimentary to America, we recall that he is in Dracula's power and is insane. The reference to the Monroe doctrine as 'a political fable' is strange and reveals a curious ignorance of what the Monroe doctrine actually entailed. Its essence was that the United States would not interfere in the affairs of the rest of the world provided that the rest of the world did not interfere in the Americas. Thus the expansion of the United States to include territory from the Pole to the Tropics in the Western Hemisphere would not have represented the abandonment of the doctrine. Of course, any such expansion could have been seen as a step towards eventual abandonment and presumably this is what Renfield has in mind. If the Monroe doctrine were to be abandoned, that would mean that the United States would be free to interfere in Ireland. While nationalists might welcome such interference, the fact that Stoker raises the possibility through the creature of Dracula – and hence, by definition, the agent of evil – suggests that he does not welcome the prospect.

It is clear that Stoker, unlike Kickham and the Fenians, does not regard the United States as the ideal instrument for the re-invigoration of Ireland. Stoker's attitude to America resembles Carleton's and even

Trollope's. Stoker was certainly no Unionist and Murray's assertion that – along with Sir William and Lady Wilde and Smith O'Brien MP – he believed that Ireland might regenerate the United States may well be true. Yet, contrary to what some nationalist readings claim, an Irish regeneration of America is not the same thing as an American regeneration of Ireland. It is clearly necessary to resort to such sleights of hand to keep Stoker within the nationalist fold. We have seen such things before.

There are other strange anomalies in Stoker's supposed nationalism. Murray even suggests that this supporter of Home Rule saw similarities between Dracula and Gladstone:

> [Stoker's notes] list Dracula's attributes, including connections with immortality and, obscurely, with Gladstone (Stoker may have been linking Gladstone with the Count in the sense that both had achieved a form of immortality, Gladstone in the political sense.)[47]

Not even Trollope would have dared make such a comparison. Murray's supposition, contained in parentheses, is plausible but lacks supporting evidence. Yet did not Gladstone rise from the political dead by returning to lead the Liberals in 1878 (after retiring in 1874) and the country in 1892, only finally retiring in 1894? It is unlikely, however, that Stoker really saw Gladstone as a vampire. Richard Shannon notes that 'Bram Stoker, Irving's manager, sent his *Dracula*, on the theme of "immortaliability" [to Gladstone], trusting that Gladstone would find nothing irreverent or base in it'.[48] He does not record Gladstone's reaction but, according to another biographer, Roy Jenkins, by 1897 Gladstone was 'half-blind and half-deaf'[49] so he may have been unaware even of the book's existence.

There was a more significant exchange between Gladstone and Stoker that nationalist readings have ignored. Stoker recalls how, during one of Gladstone's visits to the theatre, conversation centred on the implications of 'the Parnell Manifesto':

> [T]hough I was a philosophical Home Ruler, I was much surprised

---

[47] Murray, p. 172.
[48] Richard Shannon, *Gladstone* (Penguin: London, 1999), p. 586.
[49] Roy Jenkins, *Gladstone* (Macmillan: London, 1995), p. 619.

and both angry at and sorry for Parnell's attitude, and I told Mr. Gladstone my opinion. He said with great earnestness and considerable feeling: 'I am very angry, but I assure you I am even more sorry'.[50]

Stoker does not explain what he means by 'a philosophical Home Ruler' but he probably meant that he supported the intellectual concept of Home Rule rather than the practical reality. Nationalist readings, especially biographical ones, have always claimed Stoker as a full supporter of Home Rule but do not prove their case.

Vampirism is primarily concerned with blood and it is blood that defines a race – as Van Helsing states '[f]or the blood is the life' (*Dracula*, p. 280). It is easy for some nationalist interpretations to claim that *Dracula* is the transmogrification of the nationalist novel. It contains an unpopular, alien landowner, with tainted blood, who is trying fatally to infect his tenants. He bleeds the peasants dry and operates with no regard to the law while trying to make them converts to his heretical, alien 'religion' of the Undead. His insatiable lust for blood may be seen as the ultimate form of institutional violence.

On the surface, the religious situation in Transylvania is similar to that of Ireland. Yet the attempt, in nationalist readings, to stress the religious parallel is flawed because Dracula, as one of the Undead, has no recognized religion and is unconcerned with the religious beliefs of his tenants or victims. Yet Christian beliefs are central to events. Van Helsing reassures Mina about the scar (caused by the Holy Wafer burning into her forehead) and Harker, when given a crucifix by an elderly peasant woman, pointedly refers to his religious dilemma: 'as an English Churchman, I have been taught to regard such things as in some measure idolatrous' (*Dracula*, p. 13). 'Little England' – *pace* Valente – comprises of fervent Protestants. Abraham Van Helsing (who shares his creator's first name implying that Stoker identified with this intelligent, religious outsider) comes from Protestant Holland (as did William of Orange), Morris comes from Protestant America and the others from Protestant England. The faith of the Russian Orthodox peasants has singularly failed either to protect them or to destroy Dracula. If this were truly a nationalist novel, it would surely be unlikely that the victors would be, in essence, members of the Church of Ireland.

---

[50] Stoker, *Reminiscences*, II, p. 31.

This has not, however, prevented nationalist interpretations from minimising the Protestant element. Murray cites the necessity of 'Roman Catholic ritual and folkloric wisdom'[51] to destroy the vampire; by implication only Catholics have the knowledge and power to destroy Dracula. Murray points to 'Harker's struggle between a belief in the practical efficacy of these elements of Catholicism and his Protestant values'[52] but this is misleading. The history of the Christian Church and most of its central tenets are common to all Christians. Certainly characters hesitate at various points but few people could be prepared, by their particular denomination, for dealing with vampires especially if, as in Godalming's case, he has to participate in the staking and decapitation of his dead fiancée.

A key strand in *Dracula* is the Count's gradual destruction of Lucy – but she is no common victim since the name Westenra is linked to Lord Rossmore. His crime appears to be that he was an Orangeman. The Government overreacted and '[d]ismissed him from his position of magistrate' resulting in him becoming 'a Unionist martyr' and Murray perceives Stoker's use of the name as 'a hearty political joke'. In his confusing argument, Murray appears to present Lucy Westenra, 'Light of the West',[53] as the personification of Orangeism but, if that is the case, then Dracula – with all his negative and evil associations – becomes Catholic Ireland. Murray passes quickly over the fact that the maid, 'the worthless wretch' (*Dracula*, p. 200), who was left to guard Lucy, condemns her mistress by stealing the crucifix that protects her. However, Murray misinterprets the key role of Lucy: in fact, Lucy, who, this time, represents Hibernia, is the innocent victim of Dracula who represents Fenianism or the Land League. She is protected by Little England and initially survives only through blood transfusions from the Protestant Englishmen, Dutchman and American. Even after her fight for life ends, she is doomed to live on as one of the Undead, with her tainted blood, until selflessly saved by the actions of Little England.

When *Dracula* was written, 'the invasion novel' was popular and pandered to the paranoia of some sections of society. Murray postulates a nationalist-oriented idea that *Dracula* represents England justifiably under attack from the periphery of her Empire – even though Britain never had a European empire. He re-states his understanding that Stoker believed

---

[51] Murray, p. 166.
[52] Murray, p. 194.
[53] Valente, p. 65.

that 'the supposedly less developed Irish could reinvigorate these [British and American] cultures'. Yet, as we have seen, at best this idea is only hinted at in the novel – Murray's certainty is misplaced:

> *Dracula* presents a nightmare vision of a reverse reinvigoration, with an energetic, undead Count from the periphery spreading contagion in [...] the heart of the metropolis [...]. Count Dracula also undermines England's sense of its own centrality.

Regardless of whether *Dracula* is a nationalist or an Ascendancy novel, England must remain central – otherwise the novel's interpretation of the Land Question loses its context. Murray's attempt to portray the novel as depicting England under attack from its Empire's oppressed people backfires as he implies that the '"primitive" forces',[54] in this case, must be the Irish. His identification of them as 'primitive', blood-thirsty savages, hardly endorses the nationalist interpretation of the tenants. If the Fenians and/or Land Leaguers are indeed represented by Dracula then *Dracula* must be an Ascendancy novel. After all, it would be strange for a nationalist novel to portray its heroes as a contagion that preys on the vulnerable and is destroyed by devout Protestants.

Blood and Soil

Deane links the Irish obsession with their native soil to Dracula's need for his home soil:

> Dracula's dwindling soil and his vampiric appetites consort well enough with the image of the Irish landlord current in the nineteenth century. Running out of soil, this peculiar version of the absentee landlord in London will flee the light of day and be consigned to the only territory left to him, that of legend.[55]

Eagleton describes how 'the Dublin civil servant Bram Stoker was to pen another allegory of the collapse of the gentry'[56] while Leerssen claims 'that the figure of the aristocratic vampire [...] is an appealing one for Irish

---

[54] Murray, pp. 199-200.
[55] Deane, p. 90.
[56] Eagleton, p. 215.

authors from Boucicault [...] to Le Fanu to Stoker'.[57] Yet it is Valente who offers the most valid analysis:

> Ireland and the Irish Question may be said to constitute the 'other scene' of *Dracula*, a never fully present correlative to the official narrative concerning the Balkans and the Eastern Question, at once a supplementary shadow term and the novel's ultimate object of reference.[58]

There is a tradition of Irish writing dealing with vampires and myth. Stoker immersed himself in the history of Transylvania seeing in it parallels to Ireland's history. While he owes a literary debt to *Carmilla*, and even had to edit a section out of the original *Dracula* because it was too close to Le Fanu's work, his Transylvania is distinctly his own:

> [T]he literal meaning of the name *Transylvania*, 'beyond the forest', irresistibly suggests 'beyond the Pale', which historically refers to the broad expanse of Ireland that remained outside and resistant to British military and political control for most of the colonial epoch.

A further link to Irish myth is 'the penchant of Dracula and his harem for stealing and eating children'.[59] Stoker, having described the three voluptuous but carnivorous female vampires, reveals that their meal would consist 'of a half-smothered child' (*Dracula*, p.53). The mother's desperate plea for her child results in her being torn apart by wolves. Stoker underscores the heartlessness of his vampires including the English lady, Lucy. Echoing earlier Sensation novels – particularly *Lady Audley's Secret* with its blonde murderess Lucy Graham – Stoker has Lucy Westenra behaving in a most unladylike manner. He knew that it would be especially disturbing for his respectable female readers to see Lucy, 'callous as a devil' throw the child down 'growling over it as a dog growls over a bone' (*Dracula*, p. 253). While Valente correctly identifies influences such as Swift's *A Modest Proposal* (1729), Speranza's *Ancient Legends, Mystic Charms and Superstitions of Ireland* (1887) and Yeats's poem 'The Stolen Child' (1886), he fails to mention stories by Le Fanu like 'The Child That

---

[57] Leerssen, p. 223.
[58] Valente, p. 51.
[59] Valente, pp. 51-52.

Went With The Fairies' (1870). Nevertheless, he does identify other links between contemporary history and literature:

> [T]he figure of Dracula recalls Percy Bysshe Shelley's comment [...] that 'the Aristocracy of Ireland sucks the veins of inhabitants' or Fanny Parnell's reprobation of the same class as 'coroneted ghouls.' And surely Dracula is intended to bring to mind Michael Davitt's castigation of the Irish landowners as 'cormorant vampires' – after all, Dracula's initial assault on Lucy Westenra leaves her with 'an appetite like a cormorant' [...]. Lastly, Van Helsing's many impassioned admonitions to his fellows chime with William Smith O'Brien's exhortations of the Irish tenantry to 'fight like men' against the landowning 'bloodsuckers'.[60]

These semantic links to Ireland's political and literary history are reinforced by the name Stoker chose for the Count though its true meaning is characteristically ambiguous. Belford believes the name 'Dracula' has Irish origins since the 'Celtic phrase *dhroch fhola*, pronounced "druck ulla", [means] of bad blood'.[61] However, Murray claims a different provenance:

> The note on Dracula which Stoker took from William Wilkinson's *An Account of the Principalities of Wallachia and Moldavia with the Various Political Observations relating to them* was not strictly accurate but captured the essence of what the Wallachians meant by the term: 'Dracula in Wallachian language means DEVIL'.[62]

Dracula is not the first revenant in the agrarian novel as that dubious honour goes to Rock. Rock is Dracula's other face and represents the tenants' defiance. Both Rock and Dracula, these fictional, 'nationalist' heroes or anti-heroes, have rank. Rock has the military rank of Captain and Dracula the social rank of Count. At first sight, Rock and Dracula may appear total opposites. Rock is the metaphorical personification of all right-thinking Catholic, Irish peasants. Rock refers to 'the ROCK Dominion of Ireland, to which my son, now invested with the title

---

[60] Valente, p. 56.
[61] Belford, p. 264.
[62] Murray, p. 185.

Captain, succeeds'[63] thus emphasising that Rock will continue feeding, eternally, on Ireland's misery. Dracula feeds on blood but, as Punter indicates, 'Dracula is not merely an individual; he is […] a dynasty, a "house" '[64] – just like Rock. Dracula, when speaking about his history, invariably refers to himself as 'we' (*Dracula*, p. 42) implying that he is more than one individual. Rock too is more than one individual, 'the ROCK Dynasty' will continue 'through many a long year of distraction and tumult'.[65]

In a nationalist interpretation, Dracula is a representative of Ascendancy landowners finally getting what they deserve. Dracula, like Rock, cannot die. Just as Rock is doomed to continue to fight until Ireland is free, so too Dracula is doomed to live on in a world where increasingly he does not belong. However, where Moore sees the cycle of violence having no end, Stoker does see the end hence making his vision, bizarrely, more optimistic. While Rock feeds on the Irish hatred of the English, Dracula feeds on blood – anybody's blood. This reflects how much more complex the question of national identity, of Irishness, had become by the end of the century.

When Moore wrote *Memoirs* in 1824, the situation in Ireland was simpler than in 1897. Only twenty-four years had elapsed since the Union and only twenty-six years since the bloody events of 1798. Ireland was divided into two camps: Irish Catholic peasants and Anglo-Irish Protestant landowners. By the time Stoker was writing *Dracula*, the Ireland of Moore had long gone. Since Moore's time there had been Emancipation, the Tithe War, the Famine, Fenianism, dis-establishment of the Church of Ireland, the Land War, the possibility of Home Rule, Land Acts and the Aesthetic Movement. As Ireland moved inexorably towards independence, its socio-political situation became more complicated. This complexity is reflected in Dracula. It is too simplistic to claim that he merely represents Ascendancy landowners in decline.

Dracula is a novel about blood or, more specifically, about race. It is implied that Dracula, a landowner from the East, comes to England to taint the blood of those in the Metropolis. This may be seen as a metaphor for English landowners coming to Ireland, inter-marrying and tainting Irish blood. Yet Dracula's arrival in London implies that the English are the victims rather than the oppressors. Lucy may represent the

---

[63] Moore, *Memoirs*, p. 155.
[64] Punter, p. 17.
[65] Moore, *Memoirs*, p. 156.

archetypal English rose found in numerous Victorian novels, yet she is bitten and becomes one of the undead before being killed: Britannia is now the victim.

The strongest character, morally and spiritually, is Mina; for Stoker, she represents the future. She is representative of the 'New Woman' but is also a devout Christian Protestant and, as her use of new technology reveals, comfortable in both the old and new worlds. She is a loyal wife but insists on sharing the dangers encountered by the men and is strong enough to confront Renfield. The key relationship is that of Mina and Dracula. In a scene much analysed for its sexual connotations, he sucks her blood and she sucks Dracula's. After this exchange of bodily fluids, she is stronger spiritually, morally, psychologically and, initially, physically. It is her knowledge of Dracula's movements that enables Little England to destroy him. She is of mixed blood and is stronger because of it. Stoker implies, with echoes of the United Irishmen, that the mixed blood of the Ascendancy makes them stronger and an asset to Ireland. It is true that, having been bitten, Mina is dying and is only saved by Dracula's death but she is much stronger while he lives and, implicitly, after he is dead. After all, it is Mina who gives birth to the next generation and her son has the mixed blood of England, Holland, America and Transylvania – the living and the dead – running through his veins.

Stoker appears to be aware that his argument is incomplete. His main protagonist in the novel is a vampire, an anti-hero like Rock, and the symbol of an unresolved dilemma. The image of the vampire had been used, however, some years before the publication of *Dracula*. Murray notes how 'in February 1881 *Punch* featured a drawing of Gladstone strangling the three-headed monster of Irish terrorism, anarchy and sedition; the middle head, of terrorism, has long canines, just like Dracula'.[66] Murray reproduces two illustrations that appeared in rival periodicals in 1885. He cites "'The Irish Vampire' by John Tenniel featured in *Punch* on 24 October 1885'". This shows a prostrated, swooning Hibernia, shield at her side, with a giant bat hovering over her. On the bat's wings are written the words 'National League' and the bat's face is that of Parnell. Murray also shows "'The English Vampire" by an unknown artist, [that] appeared in the *Irish Pilot* of 7 November 1885'. This time Hibernia stands, sword in hand and shield raised defending her island against an obese bat. On Hibernia's shield are the words 'National League' and on the bat's copious

---

[66] Murray, p. 197.

stomach are the words 'British Rule'. The year 1885 marked the end of the Land War and emotions were running high. The ambiguous image of the vampire is potent in the public psyche. While it is seen in negative terms as sucking the life-blood of Ireland, one side's enemy is the other side's friend indicating that the relationship is more symbiotic than parasitic. For Unionists, Hibernia is a weak woman waiting to be dominated; for nationalists, she stands defiant against corpulent, British imperialism. Significantly, in neither case is the vampire either triumphant or defeated.

Perhaps the only way that Stoker – in this reading, the most ambiguous agrarian novelist – could attempt to work through the problems of Ireland was by escaping Edgeworth's agenda and moving it to Transylvania where its impasses and polarities could be explored in a surrealistic context. As we have seen, Stoker was a devout Protestant who had an equally devout Catholic family heritage. He disapproved of absentees but spent most of his adult life in England. He was a supporter of Home Rule but hinted at links between Dracula and Gladstone. He disliked the Ascendancy but was attracted by their eccentricities and longed to be a part of their world. *Dracula* took seven years to write and possibly Stoker originally intended to write an anti-Ascendancy novel but, like many of his subsequent readers, he became transfixed by Dracula and began to care more about him than those in colourless Little England.

Dracula on the Periphery

Norman Stone, in *Europe Transformed* (1981), claims that 'from 1870 to 1900, Europe changed at a faster rate than ever before or, arguably, since'. He investigates the European conflict between the forces of the *ancien regime* and those of Liberalism in the last decades of the nineteenth century. According to Stone, Liberals throughout Europe identified education as the prime instrument of change and improvement. The decline of the landowning class, exemplified by the fate of the Ascendancy, was observable from Ireland to Russia and from Scandinavia to Italy:

In the 1880s, aristocracies everywhere were in decline. By the early 1890s, they were often hysterical in their complaints. Agriculture had ceased to supply an income on which they could satisfactorily survive.

284

If we follow Stone's thesis, the Land War in Ireland becomes part of a wider phenomenon. Similar 'revolutions' were occurring in Russia, Germany and France – the Irish experience was not unique. Prior to 1870, landowners across Europe had done well as 'the advantage in economic life lay with agriculture'. 'The Great Depression', however, saw a shift away from agriculture to manufacturing and with it, a move from the country to towns. Landowners were unable to demand rents at the old levels because tenants suddenly had a choice. This freedom, though limited, led to increased violence:

> With the decline of agricultural prices, small peasant proprietors and wage-labourers sometimes also revolted – a factor that underlay the agrarian troubles of Ireland and Russia in the later 1870s and the early 1880s, and in central Italy in the middle of the decade.[67]

Nationalism in Ireland had been growing since the Famine. The old and relatively modest demand for the repeal of the Act of Union – which would have left Ireland still subject to the British Crown – was discarded in favour of a search for outright independence:

> In stagnating agrarian regions, such as Ireland or Croatia, there were often nationalists who could see their way out of stagnation only in an independent government that would take a similar view of economic problems.

Ireland fits a broader pattern in other respects. The response of the Irish tenants was echoed elsewhere:

> The floods of migrants from the countryside supplied endless quantities of building-labour in the great cities: Irish in Liverpool or Glasgow, where they made up a third of the population; Poles in Bochum, in the Ruhr; Slovak peasants in Budapest; Bohemian or Slovene peasants in Vienna; peasants from Pskov or Vologda in St. Petersburg; peasants from everywhere and anywhere in New York.[68]

---

[67] Norman Stone, *Europe Transformed 1878-1919* (London: Fontana), pp. 20-25.
[68] Stone, pp. 27-29.

Despite the drive towards education, many of these migrating tenants/peasants were illiterate and their experiences are reflected in a genre we may call European agrarian fiction – of which Irish agrarian fiction forms a significant, though not necessarily all-important, part.

Implicit in Stone is the idea that there was a fundamental division between 'inner' and 'outer' Europe. While Europe as a whole had its problems, by and large, gains outweighed losses in the prosperous 'inner' Europe; in the more deprived 'outer' Europe, losses may well have outweighed gains. Yet it is important to stress that the division between 'inner' and 'outer' Europe cut across national frontiers. Many states had regions in one or other of the two Europes. Thus, in France, the western parts of the country were in 'outer' Europe, while the eastern parts were in 'inner' Europe. Western Germany was in 'inner' Europe while areas such as East Prussia were definitely in 'outer' Europe. In Italy, the North – represented by Turin and Milan – was part of 'inner' Europe, while Naples and Sicily were in 'outer' Europe. Most of Britain was in 'inner' Europe but the Highlands of Scotland and virtually all of Ireland – with the possible exception of Ulster – were in 'outer' Europe. The division was really between areas where the dominant sector of the economy remained agriculture – especially peasant agriculture – and those where industry and commerce were now more important. So, there was much in common between such apparently diverse societies as Ireland, Spain, Poland, Hungary and Romania – and even places further afield such as Mexico.

These places all suffered from an economic backwardness associated with lack of industrialization. Their populations increasingly migrated to cities and those who remained felt the full force of agricultural depression as grain and other agricultural prices fell in relation to manufactured goods. Most strikingly of all, landowners in many of these areas were of a different race, language or religion to the peasant majority; above all, large numbers were absentees. In Hungary, aristocratic landowners often spent most of their time at the Court in Vienna, while in Russia, there was substantial internal absenteeism at the Court in St. Petersburg. At the North-western edge of Europe, Norway, formerly ruled by the Danes and now by the Swedes, was severely impoverished and even in England, the economic superpower of the day, conditions in Dorset were often described as resembling the poverty of Ireland.

Stoker's Transylvania belongs firmly to 'outer' Europe. It was part of the Austro-Hungarian Empire and was characterised by a rural economy with the classic features of absentee landowners and a virtually feudal tenantry. The fact that Stoker's account of Transylvania reminds us so powerfully of Ireland – as Irish nationalist interpretations admit – weakens any notion that Ireland was totally unique. *Dracula* exemplifies the tragedy of 'outer' Europe whether in Ireland or in Transylvania.

The dearth of historians of Ireland resulted in novelists unofficially taking their place. For the most part, agrarian novelists did manage to be historians and still write imaginative stories. Where Maria Edgeworth, Gerald Griffin, the Banims, William Carleton and Bram Stoker succeeded, however, Thomas Moore did not. His *Memoirs of Captain Rock* (1824) can hardly be regarded as a novel but neither is it a factually researched history. It is certainly unique and may best be described as a hybrid – fictional history. Yet, however classified, it offers a rather unsubtle analysis of the Land Question and, though it spawned a few ripostes in broadly the same style – including Rev. Mortimer O'Sullivan's *Captain Rock Detected* (1824) and *Captain Rock in London* (1825-26) by M J Whitty – Moore's interpretation of the Land Question was not taken up or even challenged by any subsequent agrarian novelist.

Stoker was certainly the most significant agrarian writer in the second half of the nineteenth century yet he offers no solution, only a mixture of confused analyses. He appears to approve of emigration – strongly influenced by his mother's ideas – but then shows that it will not work. However, in his creation of the vampiric Count, Stoker, from one angle, produced the ultimate Ascendancy landowner and an icon for the time and place. The days of the Ascendancy in Ireland were numbered as its vast estates were broken up by the Government and given to the tenants. The Ascendancy, like Count Dracula, was alone, wanted neither by the Irish nor by the English and an embarrassing reminder of past days of glorious hedonism. Yet Dracula also represents something positive. He may be the last full representation of a traditional Ascendancy landowner but he is unique, glamorous, strangely attractive and exciting; above all, he has stood the test of time.

Moore's solution is too simplistic. He believes that if all institutional violence is removed, and the tenants treated fairly, peace between landowners and tenants will surely follow. Ironically, his position is extremely close to Edgeworth. But Moore, unlike Edgeworth, fails to appreciate the extreme complexity of the relationship between classes and religions in Ireland. No change as simple as the one Moore proposes could have worked. Stoker is more subtle. He acts as a bridge between nineteenth-century Ireland, always looking backwards, and a new Ireland – represented by James Joyce – that looks forward to new forms of literature more appropriate to an urban Ireland, even an independent Ireland.

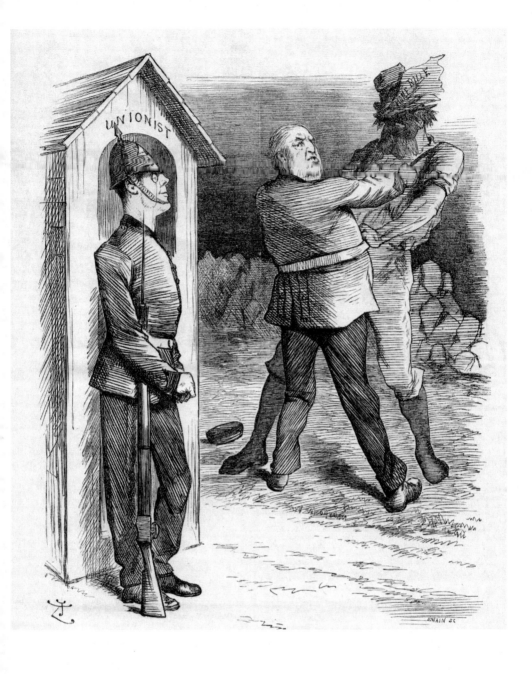

If you would know Ireland – body and soul – you must read its poems and stories. [...] They are Ireland talking to herself.[1]

The Anglo-Irish are gone but continue to haunt the imagination like a lost colony.[2]

Wider Horizons

As we have seen, unlike that of some later commentators, W B Yeats's approach at least has the merit of including the agrarian novel as part of Irish literature. Even if the agrarian novelists were actually read by the middle classes rather than by the rural poor, their works undoubtedly address key Irish issues. In the process, these authors also serve as chroniclers and historians, recording the culture and heritage of nineteenth-century Anglo-Ireland. Indeed, it is partly because of their novels that the Anglo-Irish 'continue to haunt the imagination' – even of twenty-first-century Ireland.

Yet despite its importance, the Irish agrarian novel has its limitations. Perhaps the most fundamental was the continued domination of Edgeworth's literary model. After a hundred years, every possible permutation of the scenarios derived from Edgeworth had been exhausted; in other words, by the end of the nineteenth century, the Irish agrarian novel was virtually dead. Of course, there were solutions; the most dramatic, adopted by Bram Stoker, was to move it into the realms of the 'undead', that is to adopt the 'Dracula Solution'. But we are still with a sense of 'might have beens'; were there other, less drastic opportunities for 'revitalisation'? If so, what were they and why were they not taken up?

---

[1] *Representative Irish Tales* (1891), ed. by W B Yeats (Gerrards Cross: Colin Smythe Ltd., 1979), p. 25.
[2] Julian Moynahan, *Anglo-Irish* (Princeton: Princeton University Press), 1995, p. xi.

For all writers, whether of fiction or of non-fiction, one crucial question must always be 'what is happening in other countries and can I use that in my own work? As we have seen, Norman Stone argues that the economic, social, religious and political problems of late nineteenth-century Ireland were part of a much broader phenomenon. Today, it certainly may be useful to compare the Irish agrarian novels with novels written in countries facing similar problems. For the most part, Irish literary critics, have not attempted such comparison and – to be fair to them – it is hard to detect much in the way of foreign influence in the works of the agrarian novelists themselves. Among the critics, there is one very significant exception: W B Yeats himself. Given Yeats's exacting standards, it is hardly surprising that the result is not flattering:

> No modern Irish writer has ever had anything of the high culture that makes it possible for an author to do as he will with life, to place the head of a beast upon a man, or the head of a man upon a beast, to give the most grotesque creation the reality of a spiritual existence.[3]

Yeats may have been excessively severe, but it is surely true that foreign comparisons could provide a way to assist our own understanding of Irish literature.

The absence of any significant 'foreign' dimension in the works of later Irish literary critics itself needs explanation. Since most of these critics rated the agrarian novelists even less highly than Yeats had done, their reluctance to engage in 'foreign comparisons' can hardly be attributed to any particular desire to protect the reputations of these writers. Almost by definition, nationalists are prone to a kind of tunnel vision. They regard their own nation as so unique and special that they give little thought to other ones – or to their literatures and cultures.

If the critics did not look elsewhere because they were too nationalist, perhaps the agrarian novelists' 'insularity' stems from the fact that they were not nationalist enough. If the novelists had been true nationalists, it might have been easier for them to identify with other oppressed or submerged nations. In reality, their nationalism was qualified; most found it difficult to decide conclusively that the problems of Ireland could be solved only by the severance of all ties with England. In this, and in so

---

[3] Yeats, *Representative*, p. 32.

many other ways, they were constrained by the continuing influence of the Edgeworth agenda. Irish history and Irish literature abound in paradox, but nothing is so paradoxical as the fact that writers and critics alike, whatever their nationalist inclinations, remained the prisoners of what was essentially an anti-nationalist agenda. They tried so hard to escape from an impossible dilemma that it is not surprising that they lacked the energy to do much else. Ultimately, it was not preoccupation with Ireland that made the novelists blind to what was going on in other countries; rather it was preoccupation with England.

We must still, however, investigate other models whose influence might have served to give new life to the Irish agrarian novel. A brief consideration of Thomas Hardy, Ivan Turgenev and Dmitri Grigorovich suggests many lost opportunities. Hardy, whose works depict rural life and poverty in Dorset, is surely England's greatest agrarian novelist. As in Ireland, English agriculture experienced serious depression after the end of the Napoleonic Wars. Yet, unlike his Irish counterparts, Hardy sees much good in the relatively recent past. Above all, he sees a continuing and generally benign interaction between characters and landscape that has been at work since Saxon times or even earlier. Yet Hardy's Wessex – essentially 'Greater Dorset' – suffers many of the same problems that afflicted Ireland: economic depression, harsh Land Stewards and religious rivalry (between the Established Church and the Dissenters). Thus, Barbara Kerr notes that 'Irish migrants avoided Dorset and Wiltshire where they recognised a poverty equal to their own'.[4]

Like Edgeworth, Carleton and Stoker, Hardy is a social commentator of great insight and stature. He uses a combination of 'his own first-hand experience, second-hand experience relayed to him in stories and traditions by his family and Dorset neighbours, and the products of his reading' to create his fictional world. Like Carleton, Hardy changed his religious beliefs. He was '[b]rought up as an Anglican [but] soon started moving towards Agnosticism in the religious sense of the word'.[5] The mature Hardy seems to regard religion as an obstacle to progress and, in this respect, his attitude, like some of the Irish agrarian novelists, appears almost post-Modernist. There are, however, major differences. While present in Hardy's novels, the religious dimension never swamps the story. Above all, Hardy does not seek to act as an historian.

---

[4] Barbara Kerr, *Bound to the Soil* (Wakefield: EP Publishing Limited, 1975), p. 107.
[5] Paul Turner, *The Life of Thomas Hardy* (Oxford: Blackwell Publishers Limited, 2001), p. 2.

In *Far From the Madding Crowd* (1874), Hardy portrays a way of life that is fast disappearing. The Industrial Revolution had drawn people away from the countryside and into towns and cities. Hardy writes about those who remain in the countryside, the people who are excluded or marginalized, and even denied a history. Kerr stresses the isolation and self-sufficiency of traditional rural life: '[a]ny village with a population over 500 was a self-contained community'.[6] However, industrialization was destroying the old ways, not just by drawing people to the new cities, but by actually invading the rural world. Change inevitably leads to instability, fear and discontent. The apparently safe world of Casterbridge is rocked by social change and violence: Bathsheba Everdene, a landowner, marries an NCO, Sergeant Troy, who is truly in love with Fanny Robin, a servant. Fanny's death and Troy's reappearance lead Farmer Boldwood, another landowner, to shoot Troy. Bathsheba's ultimate marriage to Gabriel Oak, a fallen landowner, reasserts the social hierarchy, but the safe, rural world has been forever tarnished.

Hardy, in *Tess of the D'Urbervilles* (1891), explores issues familiar to readers of Irish agrarian novels, but the characters are more rounded and the rural scene seems more accurately described. Tess Durbeyfield erroneously believes that she is related to a property-owning family, the D'Urbervilles. Parson Tringham reveals that the Durbeyfields may trace their descent 'from Sir Pagan d'Urberville [...] who came from Normandy with William the Conqueror' – just like the Old English settlers in Ireland – and once owned land 'in abundance'.[7] Nevertheless, just as Old English landowners were not considered to be truly Irish – Daniel Corkery's contention even in the twentieth century – so the d'Urbervilles, or Stoke d'Urbervilles, were neither truly aristocratic nor local. Mr. Stoke, a former moneylender in the North of England, moved south and 'd'Urberville [...] was annexed to his own name for himself and his heirs eternally'.[8] In *Tess* – as in *Wessex Tales* (1888), notably 'The Withered Arm' – Hardy portrays a rural world of thoughtless and wealthy property owners, poor tenants prone to drink, an unforgiving Church and extreme violence. These are the classic themes of the Irish agrarian novel, yet, despite a century of endeavour, no agrarian novelist treated them with anything approaching

---

[6] Kerr, *Bound*, p. 12.

[7] Thomas Hardy, *Tess of the D'Urbervilles* (1891), (London: Macmillan and Co Ltd, 1926), pp. 4-6.

[8] Hardy, *Tess*, p. 45.

Hardy's analytical eye or presented them with his depth of rural colour and humour.

Jude the Obscure (1895), Hardy's final novel, reflects social changes that also occurred in Ireland. *Jude,* published only two years before *Dracula,* points to the impending movement of the novel from countryside to town. When comparing the two novels, we glimpse what might have been. While Stoker produces a more urbanized Irish agrarian novel, Hardy's rural world is being replaced by a partly urban Wessex. At the beginning of the novel, Jude Fawley is aiming for Christminster/Oxford but his seduction by Arabella Doon – while still in this idyllic world – is ultimately responsible for the trials that follow. The Church and religion permeate the novel: Sue Bridehead works in a shop selling ecclesiastical items, Jude fails in his plans to enter the priesthood, they live together while unmarried and their arguments frequently contain Biblical references. Graphic violence enters when Jude and Sue's son, Old Father Time, hangs his two siblings and himself. In response to this horrendous act, Sue, penitent and claiming 'it is no use fighting against God!' returns to her husband and the Church while Jude – who 'did not often go to any service at the churches'[9] – returns to Arabella and excessive drinking before an early death. The uncertain ending of *Dracula* is paralleled in *Jude* with its overwhelming sense of nihilism in the face of unavoidable but barely intelligible progress.

In France, writers either sought to record a disappearing world – as in Balzac's *Scénes de la Vie de Campagne* (1833-44) – or confront the 'new' world as in Zola's *Germinal* (1885). The lack of agrarian and institutional violence in Balzac's rural stories is in sharp contrast to the violence and poverty found in Zola. In his depiction of a rural mining community in the 1860s, Zola compares bourgeois capitalism unfavourably with working class industrial solidarity. The mining company uses institutional violence to keep its miners working in horrific conditions and, when they strike, the soldiers are called in and fire on the miners – the ultimate in institutional violence.

George Watson emphasises the significance of the link between Irish and Russian agrarian novelists:

---

[9] Thomas Hardy, *Jude the Obscure* (1895) (London: Macmillan and Co, 1924), pp. 432-434.

[T]he Russian novelist was influenced by Scott's own source, the Irish novels of Maria Edgeworth. [...] the influence is said to date from Turgenev's first book, *A Sportsman's Sketches*.[10]

As we have seen, there were many similarities between the lives of peasants in Eastern Europe and Ireland but perhaps the closest link is between Irish peasants and their Russian counterparts. In 'Two Landowners', a short story in *Sketches From A Hunter's Album* (1852), Ivan Turgenev 'provides more evidence of the sickeningly callous treatment meted out by landowners to their serfs'.[11] He uses humour to bring out rather than hide unpalatable truths. The first landowner, 'the retired Major-General Vyacheslav Illarionovich Khvalynsky' (*Sketches*, p. 182), is unable to converse normally with social inferiors. Khvalynsky's stupidity is compounded by his choice of an agent, 'a retired sergeant-major who is a Little Russian and an extraordinarily stupid man' (*Sketches*, p. 183). Freed from his responsibilities but still demanding money, Khvalynsky chases young women and is atrociously sycophantic when lavishly entertaining dignitaries. Although it is tempting to laugh at these two ignorant men, their naïveté, prejudices and incompetence cruelly destroy the lives of the serfs. The second landowner, Mardary Apollonych Stegunov, seems strikingly similar to so many in Irish agrarian novels. This 'old style' (*Sketches*, p. 186) landowner's estate 'is managed by a bailiff drawn from among his peasants' while 'his house is run by an old woman' (*Sketches*, p. 187). Stegenov entertains freely, forcing vodka on normally abstemious priests, and generally following a lifestyle that contrasts vividly with that of his tenants who inhabit 'tiny huts [that] are horrible, cramped things' (*Sketches*, p. 189). However, Stegonov reveals a quasi-Medieval belief in the permanence of feudal hierarchies:

> In my way of thinking, if you're the master, you're the master, and if you're the peasant, you're the peasant. And that's that. (*Sketches*, p. 189)

---

[10] Maria Edgeworth, *Castle Rackrent* (1800), ed. by George Watson, (Oxford: Oxford University Press, 1991), p. 115.

[11] Ivan Turgenev, *Sketches From A Hunter's Album* (1852), trans by Richard Freeborn, (London: Penguin Books, 1990), p. 9. Further references to this edition are given after the quotations in the text, and the titled shortened to *Sketches*.

As far as Stegonov is concerned, the 'peasants are a bad sort' who 'won't give up breeding. They're so fertile, damn them!' Behind the humour, there is a dark side reminiscent of Carleton in novels like *Valentine M'Clutchy* (1845) and *The Squanders of Castle Squander* (1852). Landowners see the peasants as no different to animals, hence the demeaning reference to their 'breeding'. Stegunov also enjoys having his butler beaten keeping 'unconsciously in time with the blows: "'Chooky-chooky-chooky! Chooky-chooky! Chooky-chooky!"' (*Sketches*, p. 190). Yet, while Carleton does use humour to enhance his satire, he fails to combine it with the close observation and portrayal of peasant life so characteristic of Turgenev and, ironically, of his own short stories.

Nikolai Gogol also wrote about agrarian issues in 'Old-World Landowners', where corrupt middleman abuse their position:

> The steward, in conjunction with the village elder, robbed them in a merciless fashion. They had adopted the habit of treating their master's forest land as though it were their own; they made numbers of sleds and sold them at the nearest fair; moreover, all the thick oaks they sold to neighbouring Cossacks to be cut down for building mills.[12]

It is in the novels of Dmitri Vasil'evich Grigorovich, however, above all in *Anton* (1847), that we find the closest similarity to the Irish novels and arguably the most intriguing alternative model. *Anton* is based on a real event that could easily have happened in Ireland:

> Grigorovich's fellow-writer V. A. Sollogub, tells in his memoirs of a notorious local landlord, D. S. Krotkov, whose house was burned down by rebellious peasants and who was himself thrown into the flames by them.[13]

Anton is systematically persecuted by the Nikita Fedorych, the Land Steward – as Michael Pursglove notes:

---

[12] Nikolai Gogol, *The Complete Tales of Nikolai Gogol*, ed. and trans by Leonard J Kent (Chicago: The University of Chicago Press, 1985), II, p. 7.

[13] D V Grigorovich, *Anton/The Peasant* (1847), trans by Michael Pursglove and Nina Allen (Reading: Whiteknights Press, 1991), p. xvii. Further references to this edition are given after the quotations in the text and the title shortened to *Anton*.

The peasants themselves identify the steward as the source of their ills and view their absentee landlords with an indulgent eye. Indeed here, as in his later novels, Grigorovich does seem to imply that the age-old patriarchal system of master-serf relations would work well if only the masters would not allow themselves to be seduced away from the land by the charms of Petersburg. (*Anton*, Introduction, p. xviii)

In other words, all would be well if the absentees became residents, a solution as unrealistic in Russia as it was in Ireland. In *Anton*, Grigorovich conveys the harshness of Russian weather and the unremitting struggle waged by Russian peasants. As in Ireland, absenteeism goes 'hand-in-hand' with manors and Big Houses:

The shutters were firmly nailed up; some of them torn off by the wind, swung on one hinge or lay about the cracked and crumbling foundations; the paint on the roof, washed off here and there by the rain, revealed rot and woodworm; the panes in the crooked tower were almost all out; the decrepit exterior of the building, or more accurately of this ruin, was covered everywhere by irregular rows of swallows' nests. (*Anton*, p. 8)

We are reminded of the decay at Castle Rackrent where Thady stuffs rags into broken windowpanes to keep the rain out. However, the decay extends further; Anton's hut is in a 'ramshackle condition' and 'had almost rotted away' (*Anton*, p. 11). Although children are 'up to their knees in dirt' and young girls have 'babies in their arms' (*Anton*, p. 11), the peasants cling firmly to their religion, keeping an 'icon in the corner of the hut' (*Anton*, p. 14).

Anton's biggest problem is Fedorych:

He's got it in for me, the scoundrel. He's eating my whole life away. He's driving me off the face of the earth, but what can I do except put up with it? (*Anton*, p. 23)

Anton is forced by Fedorych – 'The Lord sent us a real beast in him' (*Anton*, p. 110) – to sell his horse, his last valuable possession, but it is stolen. Anton's struggle for survival and his attempts to recover his horse are used to highlight agrarian issues. Grigorovich, echoing Edgeworth, argues that not all landowners are bad and insists that the problem stems from absenteeism:

> Not all masters are so domineering, they go easy on their peasants. Those stewards who are like our friend [...] they're the worse [...] It's especially bad when their masters give them a free hand and don't live on the estate themselves. (*Anton*, p. 111)

In Edgeworth's *The Absentee*, the tenants become deliriously happy at the return of their masters, while the peasants in *Anton* view their social superiors as faultless and benevolent:

> Our masters, on the father's side, are too good and kind to wish harm to anyone. God grant them many years of health! My brother was in St Petersburg and says they're important people! But how can they do everything themselves? They've many estates themselves – they can't go round them all. [...] if they saw, for example, how the peasants are maltreated by the steward and suffer all sorts of privations, then, of course, they wouldn't allow it. (*Anton*, p. 113)

Everything is against Anton, the Russian 'Everyman'. He falls in with what, in an Irish agrarian novel, would have been called a secret society. Of course, his fate is inevitable but, before his trial and conviction, Anton is attacked by his fellow peasants:

> Anton's eyes were closed and only the convulsive twitching of his eyelids and forehead testified to the fact that he was alive. Blood was seeping through his clenched teeth on to his pale lips. The stout man [...] rained blows on him unceasingly. (*Anton*, p. 163)

Fedorych, who is 'just a peasant like us' (*Anton*, p. 113), stands aside and lets the violence continue. He has abused his position and used institutional violence to get his way – and all with the help of gullible peasants. Yet, whereas Grigorovich can attack the social and economic system in Russia, he is still able to create three-dimensional characters. In contrast, the Irish agrarian novelists – with the exception of Edgeworth in *Castle Rackrent* – fail to do this. They allow one issue, the Land Question, to dominate their novels to the detriment of their creative impulses.

Creativity Curtailed

Despite their considerable merits, the Irish agrarian novelists were too constrained by Edgeworth's agenda and hence produced little that is truly original. Their failure to propose coherent solutions exposes the limits of an agenda whose literary form is one of social realism; perhaps Stoker had no alternative but to take the agrarian novel into a surreal world. Whether agrarian novelists were pro- or anti-nationalist, Irish politics restricted their creativity. They were reduced to conducting political debates about Colonial occupation in novels premised on the comic conventions and structures of a publishing genre perfected at the Imperial centre. Agrarian writers were forced to be historians and that stopped them developing more original fiction. Their novels are certainly central to the debate over the Land Question but the need to be both useful and informed is their artistic undoing.

In the twentieth century, we encounter a new kind of Irish writer, often an exile, more urbanized, cosmopolitan and perceiving Ireland in a European context. In *John Bull's Other Island* (1904), George Bernard Shaw deals with Irish issues: violence, politics, nationalism and religion. Shaw avoids the stereotype of the ignorant Englishman: Thomas Broadbent is an Englishman with a conscience who claims 'now that South Africa has been enslaved and destroyed, there is no country left to me to take an interest in but Ireland'.[14] Shaw attacks the concept of the stage-Irishman: Pether Keegan, a former priest, diplomatically avoids getting embroiled in an England-versus-Ireland argument by stating that 'when you speak to me of English and Irish you forget that I am a Catholic'.[15] Loyalty to the Pope and the Catholic Church outweighs any national allegiance.

It is James Joyce, however, who best represents the move from the rural towards the metropolitan. Joyce came from a family who 'were [...] comfortably placed members of a class new to Irish life, Catholic bourgeois of strong nationalist outlook who expected Home Rule [...] to enter them on their true inheritance as an elite in the emerging Irish political and social structure'.[16] Joyce's exploratory use of epiphanies emphasises his creative literary abilities and his approach is certainly very

---

[14] George Bernard Shaw, 'John Bull's Other Island' (1904), in *The Complete Plays of Bernard Shaw* (London: Odhams Press Limited, 1937), p. 407.

[15] Shaw, 'John', p. 451.

[16] James Joyce, *The Dubliners* (1914), ed by Terence Brown (London: Penguin Books, 1992), p. x.

different to that found in the agrarian novels. Stories in *The Dubliners* (1914) examine a variety of dysfunctional individuals whose problems stem ultimately from their Catholicism. Joyce's semi-autobiographical novel, *A Portrait of an Artist as a Young Man* (1916), is a world away from *Memoirs of Richard L. Edgeworth* (1820). In *A Portrait of an Artist*, Stephen Dedalus's inner experiences chart, semi-ironically, his transition through the spiritual and sexual maelstrom of adolescence. Joyce abandons the chronological and linear structure of the agrarian novels in favour of an interwoven approach that produces its own dynamism. This innovative approach is taken further in *Ulysses* (1922) which focuses upon what 'happens' in a single day in Dublin. Unlike agrarian novels, *Ulysses* consciously looks out towards other European literatures both 'inner' and 'outer', ancient and modern.

With the possible exception of Elizabeth Bowen's *The Last September* (1929), Molly Keane, the last of the Anglo-Irish writers, represents the closest twentieth-century parallel with the agrarian novelists. Keane's novels, which concentrate on the relationships between the Anglo-Irish and Ireland, explore the final deterioration of Big Houses and their occupants. *Good Behaviour* (1981), *Time After Time* (1983) and *Loving and Giving* (1988), provide the final chapter in the history of the agrarian novel. Keane evokes the faded, emaciated social world of the Anglo-Irish Ascendancy, a world where only the remnants of people and places remain – the end is never far away:

> She tore at the handle and thrust against the door with her shoulder. It opened into the dark, shuttered room, quietly as though still dignified in service. [...] She ran, almost waltzing forwards across the boards, bared as for dancing, until – blind and unknowing – she plunged down through the gap where rotten boards were torn away and the empty drop was left unprotected.[17]

The Anglo-Irish realise they are doomed but do not know what to do. Many of Keane's characters suffer from creative exhaustion. Darwinism stresses the survival of the fittest through evolution, but the Anglo-Irish have not evolved and therefore, Keane believes, are doomed to extinction.

During the latter part of the twentieth century, it was fashionable to minimise the achievements of the agrarian novelists. Much of the criticism

---

[17] Molly Keane, *Loving and Giving* (1988) (London: Abacus, 1996), p. 232.

is justified, but this does not mean that their works should be ignored. To do so merely results in a skewed canon. The nationalists' motivation, certainly in the twentieth century, was entirely political – as Jonathan Clark suggests:

> Ireland was to terrorize and expel its Anglo-Irish elite, break in two confessional or ethnic lines in a way familiar in 1848, and achieve partial independence in the violent idiom of European racial nationalism.[18]

In terms of literature, nineteenth-century nationalist readings tried, rather clumsily, to re-interpret agrarian writers, most notably Carleton, as nationalists or as nationalist sympathisers. Twentieth-century nationalist interpretations were guilty of even greater distortion by trying to ignore the agrarian novelists. Even in the1990s, they were still trying to be selective in their choice of novelists before re-branding them as part of 'Irish Studies'. This approach is badly flawed, although it would be foolish to go so far as to claim greatness for a group of novels that too often re-work the same agenda. Only with later writers like Yeats – and especially Joyce – do we encounter post-Modern features such as symbolism, impressionism and the constructive note of what Arnold Bennett termed 'plotlessness'. When compared to these works, agrarian novels can appear plodding and old fashioned, devoted to orthodox social realism and picaresque structures.

Vindication

The agrarian novels still have a place, an important one, in any proper understanding of the development of Irish literature. In *A Room of One's Own* (1928), Virginia Woolf states that 'fiction [...] is not dropped like a pebble upon the ground, as science may be, fiction is like a spider's web, attached ever so lightly perhaps, but still attached to life at all four corners'.[19] Yeats, Joyce and subsequent Irish writers could not have achieved what they did without the agrarian novelists. But they did more than just prepare the way; writers like Edgeworth, the Banims, Griffin, Carleton and Stoker provide a vital link between Ireland's past and her future. Whether we think of them as good or bad writers is almost

[18] Jonathan C D Clark, *Our Shadowed Present* (London: Abacus, 2003), p. 105.
[19] Virginia Woolf, *A Room of One's Own* (1928) (London: Penguin Group, 2004), p. 48.

immaterial; it is surely absurd to form an Irish canon which omits the nineteenth century.

Agrarian novelists are often criticised for their lack of originality, but this can hardly be said of Edgeworth, the first 'regional novelist', who, as we have seen, influenced not only Scott but also Turgenev, Jefferies, Hardy, Mrs Gaskell, George Eliot, the Brontës, Charles Kingsley, R D Blackmore, R L Stevenson, J M Barrie, Arnold Bennett and D H Lawrence. It is, however, her influence upon Joyce that is most significant. Carleton was the first Irish 'Peasant novelist' and the first to portray peasant life in fiction from first-hand knowledge. Kickham's *Knocknagow* continued to be one of the best selling novels in Ireland well into the twentieth century. Stoker's *Dracula* is a sophisticated, allegorical re-working of the Land Question in a surreal, Transylvanian setting. The work is unquestionably original and survives in print, films and other media to this day.

Ireland has always been potentially politically explosive, and agrarian novelists had to be careful not to make things worse. Their novels needed both to entertain and to educate in true Victorian style. Yet they also appreciated the need to sell their books – often to a complacent English readership. Edward Said declared in his 'Culture and Imperialism' lecture:

> There was a kind of tremendous unanimity on the question of having an empire. There was very little domestic resistance to imperial expansion during the nineteenth century, although these empires were very frequently established and maintained under adverse and even disadvantageous conditions.[20]

This was the mindset against which the agrarian novelists had to write. They wrote when the British Empire was at its height and the city that mattered most was London not Dublin. The central themes of agrarian novels, however, such as colonialism, religious conflict, violent landowner/tenant relations, extreme poverty, emigration, famine and injustice have a universal relevance that goes beyond Ireland's own sufferings.

Agrarian novelists may not have produced great works but they did try to explore what it means to be Irish; after all, the real solution to Ireland's problems lies in producing a satisfactory definition of Irishness. Perhaps

---

[20] Edward W Said, *'Culture and Imperialism'* (Toronto: York University, 1993), URL:http//:www.zmag.org/zmag/articles/barsaid.htm, (para 11 of 34).

the best example of this may be found in the comparison of two visual symbols: the 'wheel of torture' and the Irish flag. The first image – a wholly negative one – of Thomas Moore's 'wheel of torture' represents an eternally divided nation. People will continue to misunderstand and mistreat each other and will be divided along religious lines, political lines and economic lines – and these divisions will be ruthlessly exploited by corrupt politicians, landowners and criminals. Poverty, famine and violence will continue to blight everyone's life and effectively prevent Ireland from ever becoming an independent nation. For Captain Rock and Count Dracula to continue to thrive, hopelessness, helplessness and despair must remain rampant.

The alternative symbol – a wholly positive one – of the Irish flag is inclusive, promoting the idea of peace and unity. On the Irish *tricolour*, the orange panel represents Protestants, the green panel represents Catholics, and the central white panel represents the peace between them. The aspiration to a peaceful and united Ireland – where Irishness is more important than religious affiliation – would have been applauded by many, including Wolfe Tone, Maria Edgeworth, William Carleton and W B Yeats. For all its shortcomings, the agrarian novel dominated Irish literary life for almost one hundred years. These were momentous years for Ireland because they witnessed the disintegration of the relative harmony of the eighteenth century and descent into a prolonged period of division and conflict. The value of agrarian novels is that, whatever perspective is adopted, they chronicle that descent. Perhaps we should not be too critical of their failure to produce workable solutions – for the simple reason that no such solutions were available at the time. In the twentieth century, part of Ireland did achieve independence but only at the high cost of partition. It remains to be seen whether the current Peace Process will finally provide something like the solution that the agrarian novelists strove so hard to identify. Of course, the essential first step towards solving any problem is to explain what it is – and the agrarian novelists certainly did that.

Primary texts:

Banim, John & Michael ('The O'Hara Family'), *Crohoore of the Bill-Hook and The Fetches* (1826), copyright edn, 2 vols (Belfast: Simms and M'Intyre, 1846)

Banim, John & Michael, *The Peep O'Day or, Life on the Mountains &c.* (1826), Arlington edn, (New York: Hurst & Company, n.d.)

Banim, John & Michael, *The Nowlans* (1826), (Belfast, Appletree Press, repr. 1992)

Banim, John & Michael ('The O'Hara Family'), *The Boyne Water* (1826), 2nd edn (New York: D. & J. Sadlier & Co., 1869)

Banim, John & Michael, *The Croppy; A Tale of 1798* (London: Henry Colburn, 1828)

Banim, John, *The Anglo-Irish of the Nineteenth Century* (1828), ed. by John Kelly (Poole: Woodstock Books, repr. 1997)

Bjornson, Bjornstjerne, *A Happy Boy* (1860) (Amsterdam: Fredonia Books, repr. 2002)

Bowen, Elizabeth, *The Last September* (1929), ed. by Victoria Glendinning (London: Vintage, repr. 1998)

[Brittaine, George], *Irishmen and Irishwomen*, 2nd edn. (Dublin: Richard Moore Tims, 1831)

Carleton, William, *Fardorougha the Miser: or, the Convicts of Lisnamona* (1839) (Belfast: The Appletree Press Ltd., repr. 1992)

Carleton, William, *Traits and Stories of the Irish Peasantry* (1842-44), 2 vols (Gerrards Cross: Colin Smythe, repr. 1990)

Carleton, William, *Rody the Rover or The Ribbonman* (Dublin: James Duffy, 1845)

Carleton, William, *Valentine M'Clutchy, The Irish Agent or, The Chronicles of Castle Cumber &c.* (1845) (Dublin: James Duffy, 1847)

Carleton, William, *The Tithe Proctor: A Novel: Being a Tale of the Tithe Rebellion in Ireland* (London: Simms and M'Intyre, 1849)

Carleton, William, *The Black Prophet: A Tale of Irish Famine* (1847), ed. by

307

John Kelly (Poole: Woodstock Books, repr. 1996)

Carleton, William, *The Squanders of Castle Squander*, 2 vols (London: Office of the Illustrated London Library, 1852)

Dickens, Charles, *The Old Curiosity Shop* (1841), vols VII & VIII (London: Chapman and Hall, 1858)

Dickens, Charles, *Christmas Books*, vol XXII (London: Chapman and Hall, 1858)

Edgeworth, Maria, *Castle Rackrent: An Hibernian Tale &c.* (1800), ed. by George Watson (Oxford: Oxford University Press, repr. 1991)

Edgeworth, Maria, *Castle Rackrent* and *Ennui* (1809), ed. by Marilyn Butler (London: Penguin Group, repr. 1992)

Edgeworth, Maria, *The Absentee* (1812), ed. by William J. Mc Cormack (Oxford: Oxford University Press, repr. 1988)

Edgeworth, Maria, *Ormond: A Tale* (1817), ed. by John Banville (Belfast: Appletree Press, repr. 1992)

Edgeworth, Maria, *Edgeworth's Tales and Novels*, 2nd edn, 18 vols (London: Baldwin & Cradock, 1832)

Eliot, George, *Adam Bede* (1859), ed. by Stephen Gill (Harmondsworth: Penguin Books Ltd., repr. 1985)

Friel, Brian, *Translations* (1981), 2nd edn (London: Faber and Faber Ltd., 2000)

Gogol, Nikolai, *The Complete Tales of Nikolai Gogol*, trans. by Constance Garnett, ed. by Leonard J. Kent, 2 vols (Chicago: The University of Chicago Press, repr. 1985)

Griffin, Daniel, *The Life of Gerald Griffin by His Brother*, American edn, vol X, (New York: D. & J. Sadlier & Co., n.d.)

Griffin, Gerald, *The Collegians: A Tale of Garryowen* (1829), American edn, vol I (New York: D. & J. Sadlier & Co., n.d.)

Griffin, Gerald, *The Rivals and Tracy's Ambition* (1829), American edn, vol. IV (New York: D. & J. Sadlier & Co., 1829)

Grigorovich, Dmitri Vasil'evich, *Anton/The Peasant* (1847), trans. by Michael Pursglove and Nina Allan (Reading: Whiteknights Press, repr. 1991)

Hall, Mrs. S. C., *The Whiteboy: A Story of Ireland in 1822* (1845) (London: Chapman and Hall, repr. 1855)

Hardy, Thomas, *Far From the Madding Crowd* (1874), ed. by Suzanne B. Falck-Yi (Oxford: Oxford University Press, repr. 2002)

Hardy, Thomas, *Tess of the D'Urbervilles* (1891) (London: Macmillan and Co. Ltd., repr. 1926)

Hardy, Thomas, *Jude the Obscure* (1895) (London: Macmillan and Co. Ltd., repr. 1924)

Heaney, Seamus, *Station Island* (London: Faber & Faber, 1984)

Joyce, James, *Dubliners* (1914), ed. by Terence Brown (London: Penguin Books, repr. 1992)

Joyce, James, *Portrait of an Artist as a Young Man* (1914 15), ed. by Seamus Deane (London: Penguin Group, repr. 2000)

Joyce, James, *Ulysses* (1922), ed. by Declan Kiberd, 4th edn (London: Penguin Group, 2000)

Joyce, James, *Finnegan's Wake* (1939), ed. by Seamus Deane (London: Faber and Faber, repr. 1975)

Keane, Molly, *Good Behaviour* (London: Abacus Books, 1981)

Keane, Molly, *Time after Time* (London: Abacus Books, 1983)

Keane, Molly, *Loving and Giving* (1988) (London: Abacus Books, repr. 1996)

Kickham, Charles J., *Knocknagow or The Homes of Tipperary* (1st published 1873, popular edn 1879) (Dublin: M. H. Gill and Son Ltd., repr. 1962)

Kickham Charles J., *Sally Cavanagh or, The Untenanted Graves: A Tale of Tipperary* (1869) (Dublin: James Duffy and Co. Limited, repr. 1948)

Kickham, Charles J., *For The Old Land: A Tale of Twenty Years Ago* (1886), 2nd edn (Dublin: M. H. Gill and Son, 1892)

Lawless, Emily, *Hurrish: A Study* (1886), ed. by Val Mulkerns (Belfast: Appletree Press, repr. 1992)

Le Fanu, Joseph Sheridan, *The House by the Churchyard* (1863) (London: The Cresset Press, repr. 1947)

Le Fanu, Joseph Sheridan, *Uncle Silas* (1864), ed. by William J. Mc Cormack (Oxford: Oxford University Press, repr. 1988)

Le Fanu, Joseph Sheridan, *Carmilla* (1871) (New York: Scholastic Book Services, repr. 1971)

Le Fanu, Joseph Sheridan, *Ghost Stories and Mysteries*, ed. E. F. Bleiler (New York: Dover Publications, repr. 1975)

Lever, Charles, *Lord Kilgobbin* (1872) (Belfast: The Appletree Press Ltd., repr. 1992)

Lover, Samuel, *Handy Andy: A Tale of Irish Life* (1842) (London: H. G. Bohn, 1851)

Morgan, Lady (Sydney Owenson), *Florence Macarthy: An Irish Tale* (1818), 4th edn, 4 vols (London: Henry Colburn, 1819)

Moore, Thomas, *The Poetical Works of Thomas Moore* (London: Bliss Sands & Co., 1812)

Moore, Thomas, *Memoirs of Captain Rock, The Celebrated Irish Chieftain, with some Account of his Ancestors*, 2nd edn (London: Longman, Hurst, Rees, Orme, Brown, and Green, 1824)

Moore, George, *A Drama in Muslin: A Realistic Novel* (1886), ed. by A. Norman Jeffares (Gerrards Cross: Colin Smythe, repr. 1993)

Moore, George, *Parnell and His Island* (London: Swan, Sonnenschein, Lowrey & Co., 1887)

O'Sullivan, Rev. Mortimer, *Captain Rock Detected &c.* (London: T. Cadell, 1824)

Scott, Sir Walter, *Waverley* (1814), ed. by Andrew Hook (London: Penguin Group, repr. 1985)

Shaw, George Bernard, *The Complete Plays of Bernard Shaw* (London: Odhams Press Limited, 1937)

Somerville, E. and Martin Ross, *Naboth's Vineyard* (Leipzig, Germany: Bernhard Tauchnitz, 1891)

Stoker, Bram, *Dracula* (1897) (London: Penguin Group, repr. 1979)

Swift, Jonathan, *Satires and Personal Writings*, ed. by W. A. Eddy (London: Oxford University Press, repr. 1967)

Swift, Jonathan, *A Modest Proposal and Other Satirical Works*, ed. by Candace Ward (New York: Dover Publications, 1996)

Trollope, Anthony, *The Macdermots of Ballycloran* (1847) (London: Penguin Group, repr. 1993)

Trollope, Anthony, *The Kellys and the O'Kellys* (1848) (London: Penguin Group, repr. 1993)

Trollope, Anthony, *Castle Richmond* (1860) (London: Penguin Group, repr. 1993)

Trollope, Anthony, *Lotta Schmidt and Other Stories* (London: Chapman and Hall, 1867)

Trollope, Anthony, *Tales of All Countries* (London: Chapman and Hall, 1867)

Trollope, Anthony, *An Eye for an Eye* (1879) (Gloucester: Dodo Press, n.d.)

Trollope, Anthony, *The Land-Leaguers* (1884) (London: Penguin Group, repr. 1993)

Turgenev, Ivan, *Sketches from a Hunter's Album* (1852), trans. by Richard Freeborn (London: Penguin Books Ltd., 1990)

Whitty, Michael James, *Captain Rock in London &c.* (London: Joseph Robins, 1825-26)

Wilde, Oscar, *The Picture of Dorian Gray* (1891), ed. by Robert Mighall

(London: Penguin Books Ltd., repr. 2003)

Woolf, Virginia, *A Room of One's Own* (1928) (London: Penguin Books Ltd., repr. 2004)

Yeats, William Butler, ed., *Representative Irish Tales* (1891) (Gerrards Cross: Colin Smythe Ltd., repr. 1991)

Yeats, William Butler, ed., *Stories from Carleton* (London: The Walter Scott Publishing Co., Ltd., n.d.)

Yeats, William Butler, *Four Years: 1887-1891* (1921) (London: Macmillan, 1977)

Yeats, W. B., *Essays and Introductions* (1961) (London: Macmillan Publishers Limited, 1989)

Young, Arthur, *A Tour of Ireland &c.*, 2 vols (Dublin: Messrs. Whitestone, Sleater, Sheppard, Williams, Burnet, Vallance, White, Beatty, Byrn, and Burton, 1780)

Secondary Texts:

To 1900

Anon., *Letters to a Friend in England, on the Actual State of Ireland* (London: James Ridgway, 1828)

Anon. ed., *The Poetical Works of Tom Moore* (London: Bliss Sands & Co., n.d.)

Burke, J., *The Life of Thomas Moore* (1852), 2nd edn (Dublin: James Duffy and Sons, 1879)

Carleton, William, *The Autobiography* (1896) (Belfast: The White Row Press, repr. 1996)

Croker, Thomas Crofton, *Researches in the South of Ireland* (1824) (Shannon: Irish University Press, repr. 1969)

Edgeworth, Richard Lovell, *Memoirs of Richard Lovell Edgeworth Esq., Begun by Himself and Concluded by his Daughter, Maria Edgeworth* (1820), 3rd edn (London: Richard Bentley, 1856)

Freeman, E. A., *History of the Norman Conquest: Its causes and its Results* (1867-1876), 6 vols (Oxford: Oxford University Press 1879)

Fitzpatrick, W. J., *Lady Morgan: Her Career, Literary and Personal* (London: Charles J. Skeet, 1860)

Froude, James Anthony, *The English in Ireland in the Eighteenth Century*, 3 vols (London: Longmans, Green & Co., 1895)

Froude, James Anthony, 'Ireland Since the Union: Being the last of a series of lectures delivered in the United States in October and November, 1872', *Short Studies on Great Subjects* (London: Longmans, Green, and Co., 1900), Vol II, 515-561

Geldart, Mrs. Thomas, *Stories of Ireland and Her Four Provinces* (London: Jarrold and Sons, 1851)

Hall, Samuel Carter, *A Book of Memories of Great Men and Women of the Age from their Personal Acquaintance* (1871), 3rd edn. (London: J. S. Virtue and Company Limited, n.d.)

Hare, Augustus J. C., ed., *The Life and Letters of Maria Edgeworth*, 2 vols (London, Edward Arnold, 1894)

Hare, Augustus J. C., ed., *The Life and Letters of Maria Edgeworth*, 2 vols (New York: Books for Libraries Press, 1971)

Hone, Joseph, ed., *John Butler Yeats: Letters to His Son W. B. Yeats and Others 1869-1922*, 3rd edn (London: Faber and Faber, 1999)

Hyde, Douglas, *A Literary History of Ireland* (1899) (London: T. Fisher Unwin, 1906)

Lecky, William E. H., *A History of Ireland in the Eighteenth Century* (1892), 2nd edn, 5 vols (London: Longman, Green & Co., 1902)

Le Fanu, William R., *Seventy Years of Irish Life: Being Anecdotes and Reminiscences* (London: Edward Arnold, 1893)

Lewis, George Cornewall, *On Local Disturbances in Ireland and On The Irish Land Question* (London: B. Fellowes, 1836)

Macaulay, Thomas Babington, *Collection of British Authors: Critical and Historical Essays by Macaulay*, Tauchnitz edn, 5 vols (Leipzig: Bernhard Tauchnitz, 1850)

Maguire, John F., *The Irish in America* (London: Longmans, Green, and Co., 1868)

M'Aleer, John, *The Social Condition of the Population of Ireland From the Year 1850: Their Progressive Prosperity* (Dublin: Alex. Thom & Sons, 1860)

Malthus, Thomas, *An Essay on the Principle of Population* (1798), ed. by Geoffrey Gilbert, 2nd edn (Oxford: Oxford University Press, 1999)

Mill, John Stuart, *The Irish Land Question*, 2nd edn (London: Longmans, Green, Reader, and Dyer, 1870)

Morgan, Lady Sydney, *Passages from My Autobiography* (London: Richard Bentley, 1859)

Murray, Patrick Joseph, *The Life of John Banim: The Irish Novelist* (London: William Lay, 1857)

O'Donoghue, David J., *The Life of William Carleton: Being His Autobiography and Letters; And An Account of His Life and Writings, From The Point At*

Which The Autobiography Breaks Off, 2 vols (London: Downey & Co., 1896)

Prendergast, John P., *The Cromwellian Settlement of Ireland* (London: Longman, Green, Longman, Roberst, & Green, 1865)

Round, J.H., *Feudal England: Historical Studies on the XIth and XIIth Centuries* (1895), (London: Swan Sonnenschein & Co Ltd, 1909)

Russell, Lord John ed., *Memoirs, Journal, and Correspondence of Thomas Moore*, 7 vols (London: Longman, Brown, Green and Longmans, 1853)

Stubbs, William, *Constitutional History of England* (1874-1878), 3 vols (Oxford: Oxford University Press 1926)

Thackeray, William M., *The Paris Sketch Book: The Irish Sketch Book: Notes on a Journey from Cornhill to Grand Cairo* (London: Smith, Elder, 1894)

Trench, W. Steuart, *Realities of Irish Life* (1868) (London: MacGibbon & Kee Ltd., 1966)

Trollope, Fanny, *Domestic Manners of the Americans* (1832) (Stroud: Alan Sutton, repr. 1993)

Trollope, Anthony, *An Autobiography* (1883) (London: Oxford University Press, repr. 1961)

Wilde, Lady ['Speranza'], *Ancient Legends, Mystic Charms, and Superstitions of Ireland* (Boston, USA: Ticknor and Company, 1888)

Wright, William, *The Brontës in Ireland, or Facts Stranger than Fiction* (London: Hodder and Stoughton, 1894)

Zimmern, Helen, *Maria Edgeworth* (London: W. H. Allen & Co., 1883)

Post 1900

Albright, Daniel, ed., *W. B. Yeats: The Poems* (London: J. M. Dent, 2004)

Aldous, Richard, *The Lion and the Unicorn: Gladstone vs. Disraeli* (2006), 2nd edn., (London: Pimlico, 2007)

Allen, Michael, and Angela Wilcox, eds., *Critical Approaches to Anglo-Irish Literature* (Gerrards Cross: Colin Smythe, 1989)

Allen, Walter, *The English Novel: A Short Critical History* (1954) (London: Penguin, repr. 1991)

Allison, Jonathan, ed., *Yeats's Political Identities: Selected Essays* (Michigan: University of Michigan Press, 1999)

Altick, Richard D., *Victorian People and Ideas* (New York: Norton, 1971)

Armstrong, Nancy, and Leonard Tennenhouse, eds., *The Violence of Representation: Literature and the History of Violence* (London: Routledge, 1989)

Backus, Margot Gayle, *The Gothic Family Romance: Heterosexuality, Child Sacrifice, and the Anglo-Irish Colonial Order* (London: Duke University Press, 1999)

Barden, J., *A History of Ulster* (Belfast: Blackstaff Press, 1992)

Bareham, Tony, ed., *Anthony Trollope* (London: Vision Press Ltd., 1980)

Bareham, Tony, ed., *Charles Lever: New Evaluations* (Gerrards Cross: Colin Smythe, 1991)

Barthes, R., *The Pleasure of the Text* (1973), trans. by R. Miller (Oxford: Basil Blackwell, 1990)

Bartlett, T., C. Curtin, R. O'Dyer, and G. Tuathaigh, eds., *Irish Studies: A General Introduction* (Dublin: Gill & Macmillan, 1988)

Bartlett, T., *The Fall and Rise of the Irish Nation: the Catholic Question, 1690-1830* (Dublin: Gill & Macmillan, 1992)

Bateman, John, *The Landowners of Great Britain and Ireland* (1883), 4th edn (Leicester: Leicester University Press, 1971)

Beames, Michael, *Peasants and Power: The Whiteboy Movements and Their Control in Pre-Famine Ireland* (Brighton: Harvester Press, 1983)

Beckett. J. C., *The Making of Modern Ireland, 1603-1923*, (London: Faber and Faber, 1966)

Beckett, J. C., *Confrontations: Studies in Irish History* (London: Hutchinson & Co., 1971)

Beckett, J. C., *The Anglo-Irish Tradition* (London: Faber & Faber, 1976)

Begnal, Michael, *Joseph Sheridan LeFanu* [sic], (Lewisburg: Bucknell University Press, 1971)

Belanger, Jacqueline, ed., *The Irish Novels in the Nineteenth Century: Facts and Fictions* (Dublin: Four Courts Press, 2005)

Belford, Barbara, *Bram Stoker: A Biography of the Author of Dracula* (London: Weidenfeld and Nicolson, 1996)

Bell, Anne Olivier, and Andrew McNeillie, eds., *The Diary of Virginia Woolf*, American edn, 5 vols (New York, Harcourt Brace Jovanovich, 1982)

Bell, Quentin, *Virginia Woolf: A Biography*, 2 vols (London: The Hogarth Press, 1973)

Bevington, Merle M., *The Saturday Review: Representative Educated Opinion in Victorian England* [1941], 2nd edn (New York: AMC Press, 1966)

Bilboul, R. R., and F. L. Kent, eds., *Retrospective Index to Theses of Great Britain and Ireland, 1715-1950, Volume One: Social Sciences & Humanities* (Oxford: ABC-Clio Press, 1975)

Bigelow, George, *Fiction, Famine, and the Rise of Economics in Victorian Britain and Ireland* (Cambridge: Cambridge University Press, 2003)

Blake, Robert, *Disraeli*, 2nd edn (London: Methuen and Co. Ltd., 1969)

Bovill, E. W., *English Country Life 1780-1830* (London: Oxford University Press, 1962)

Boehmer, Elleke, *Colonial and Postcolonial Literature* (Oxford: Oxford University Press, 1995)

Booth, Bradford T., *Anthony Trollope: Aspects of His Life and Art* (London: Edward Hulton, 1958)

Botting, Fred, ed., *The Gothic* (Cambridge: D. S. Brewer, 2001)

Bourne Taylor, Jenny, *In the Secret Theatre of the Home: Wilkie Collins, Sensation Narrative, and Nineteenth-Century Psychology* (London: Routledge, 1988)

Boyce, D. George, ed., *The Revolution in Ireland 1879-1923* (Basingstoke: Macmillan Education, 1988)

Boyce, D. George, *Nineteenth-Century Ireland: The Search for Stability* (Dublin: Gill & Macmillan, 1990)

Boyce, D. George, *Ireland 1828-1923: From Ascendancy to Democracy* (Oxford: Blackwell Publishers, 1992)

Boyce, D. George, *Nationalism in Ireland*, 3rd edn (London: Routledge, 1995)

Boyce, D. George, and Alan O'Day, eds., *The Making of Modern Irish History: Revisionism and the Revisionist Controversy* (London: Routledge, 1996)

Boyd, E., *Ireland's Literary Renaissance* (Dublin: Figgis, 1968)

Boycott, Charles Arthur, *Boycott: The Life Behind the Word* (Ludlow: Carbonel Press, 1997)

Boylan, H., *A Dictionary of Irish Biography* (New York: St. Martin's, 1988)

Bradley, Ian, *The Call to Seriousness: The Evangelical Impact on the Victorians* (London: Jonathan Cape, 1976)

Brady, A. M., and B. Cleeve, *A Biographical Dictionary of Irish Writers* (New York: St. Martin's, 1985)

Bramsback, Birgit, and Martin Croghan, eds., *Anglo-Irish and Irish Literature – Aspects of Language and Culture – Proceedings of the Ninth International Congress of the International Association for the Study of Anglo-Irish Literature Held at Uppsala University, 4-7 August, 1986*, 2 vols (Stockholm: Almqvist & Wiksell International, 1988)

Brand, Gordon, ed., *William Carleton: The Authentic Voice*, Irish Literary Studies 53 (Gerrards Cross: Colin Smythe Limited, 2006)

Briggs, Asa, *Victorian People: A Reassessment of Persons and Themes 1851-67* (1954), 3rd edn (London: Penguin, 1990)

315

Briggs, Asa, *The Age of Improvement 1783-1867* (1959), 2nd edn (London: Longman, 1996)

Briggs, Julia, *Virginia Woolf: An Inner Life* (London: Allen Lane, 2005)

Broeker, G., *Rural Disorder and Police Reform in Ireland 1812-1836* (London: Routledge and Kegan Paul, 1970)

Brown, Malcolm, *The Politics of Irish Literature: From Thomas Davis to W. B. Yeats* (London: George Allen & Unwin Ltd., 1972)

Brown, Stephen J., ed., *Ireland in Fiction: A Guide to Irish Novels, Tales, Romances and Folklore* (London: Maunsel and Company, 1916)

Brown, Terrance, *The Life of W. B. Yeats: A Critical Biography*, (Oxford: Blackwell Publishers Limited, 2001)

Brown, Thomas N., *Irish-American Nationalism 1870-1890* (New York: J. B. Lippincott Company, 1966)

Buckley, Jerome H., *The Victorian Temper: A Study in Literary Culture* (London: Frank Cass & Co. Ltd., 1966)

Bull, Philip, *Land, Politics and Nationalism: A Study of the Irish Land Question* (Dublin: Gill & Macmillan Ltd., 1996)

Butler, Harriet Jessie, and Harold Edgeworth Butler, eds., *The Black Book of Edgeworthstown and Other Edgeworth Memories 1585-1817* (London: Faber & Gwyer, 1927)

Butler, Marilyn, *Maria Edgeworth: A Literary Biography* (Oxford: Clarendon Press, 1972)

Butler, Marilyn, *Romantics, Rebels and Reactionaries: English Literature and its Background, 1760-1830* (Oxford: Oxford University Press, 1981)

Butler, Marilyn, *Jane Austen and the War of Ideas*, 2nd edn (Oxford: Clarendon Press, 1997)

Butler, W. F. T., *Confiscation in Irish History* (1917), 2nd edn (New York: Kennikat Press, 1970)

Byron, Glennis, ed., *Dracula: Bram Stoker* (Basingstoke: Macmillan Press Ltd., 1999)

Cahalan, James W., *Great Hatred, Little Room: The Irish Historical Novel* (Syracuse: Syracuse University Press, 1983)

Cahalan, James, *The Irish Novel: A Critical History* (Dublin: Gill & Macmillan Ltd., 1988)

Cairns, D., and S. Richards, *Writing Ireland: Colonialism, Nationalism and Culture* (Manchester: Manchester University Press, 1988)

Calder, Angus, *Revolutionary Empire: The Rise of the English-Speaking Empires from the Fifteenth Century to the 1780s* (London: Jonathan Cape, 1980)

Campbell, R. H., and Andrew S. Skinner, eds., *An Inquiry into the Nature*

316

and Causes of the Wealth of Nations (1776), 2 vols (Oxford: Clarendon Press, 1976)

Campbell, Mary, *Lady Morgan: The Life and Times of Sydney Owenson* (London: Pandora Press, 1988)

Carpenter, A., ed., *Place, Personality and the Irish Writer* (Gerrards Cross: Colin Smythe, 1977)

Campion, J. T., 'A Critical Memoir of John Banim and His Works' (1883), unpublished (London: British Library), MS. 18,489

Cavaliero, Glen, *The Supernatural and English Fiction* (Oxford: Oxford University Press, 1995)

Chadwick, Owen, *The Victorian Church: Part 1, 1829-1859* (1966), 3rd edn (London: SCM Press Ltd., 1987)

Clark, Samuel, and James S., Donnelly Jr., *Irish Peasants: Violence and Political Unrest 1780-1914* (Wisconsin, USA: The University of Wisconsin Press, 1983)

Clark, Jonathan C. D., *Our Shadowed Present: Modernism, Postmodernism and History*, (London: Atlantic Books, 2003)

Clarke, Isabel C., *Maria Edgeworth: Her Family and Friends*, (London: Hutchinson, 1949)

Clyde, Tom, *Irish Literary Magazines: An Outline History and Descriptive Biography* (Dublin: Irish Academic Press, 2003)

Cobban, A., *Edmund Burke and the Revolt against the Eighteenth Century* (London: George Allen Ltd., 1929)

Colby, R. A., *Fiction With A Purpose: Major and Minor Nineteenth-Century Novels*, (Indiana: Indiana University Press, 1967)

Colvin, Christina, ed., *Maria Edgeworth: Letters from England 1813-1844* (Oxford: Clarendon Press, 1971)

Colvin, Christina, *Maria Edgeworth in France and Switzerland* (Oxford: Clarendon Press, 1979)

Comerford, R. V., *Charles J. Kickham: A Study in Irish Nationalism and Literature* (Dublin: Wolfhound Press, 1979)

Comerford, R. V., *The Fenians in Context: Irish Politics and Society 1848-82* (Dublin: Wolfhound Press, 1998)

Connolly, S. J., ed., *The Oxford Companion to Irish History*, 2nd edn (Oxford: OUP, 2002)

Connolly, James, *Labour in Ireland: I. Labour in Irish History, II. The Re-Conquest of Ireland* (1916) (Dublin: The Sign of the Three Candles, c.1922)

Connolly, Peter, ed., *Literature and the Changing Ireland* (Gerrards Cross:

Colin Smythe, 1982)

Constable, K., *A Stranger within the Gates*, (Maryland: University Press of America, 2000)

Corbett, Mary Jean, *Allegories of Union in Irish and English Writing, 1790-1870: Politics, History, and the Family from Edgeworth to Arnold* (Cambridge: Cambridge University Press, 2000)

Corish, P. J., ed., *Radicals, Rebels and Establishments* (Belfast: Appletree Press, 1985)

Corkery, Daniel, *Synge and Anglo-Irish Literature* (1931) (Cork: The Mercier Press, repr. 1966)

Cornish, W. R., *Crime and Law in Nineteenth-Century Britain: commentary on the criminal justice and punishment, legal administration, civil disorder and police volumes in the I.U.P. reprint series of British Parliamentary papers*, (Dublin: Irish Academic Press, 1978)

Cornwell, Neil, *The Literary Fantastic: From Gothic to Postmodernism*, (Hemel Hempstead: Harvester Wheatsheaf, 1990)

Courtney, C. P., *Montesquieu and Burke* (Westport: Greenwood Press, 1975)

Cronin, John, *Gerald Griffin (1803-1840): A Critical Biography*, (Cambridge: Cambridge University Press, 1978)

Cronin, John, *The Anglo-Irish Novel: The Nineteenth-Century, Volume 1*, (Belfast: Appletree Press, 1980)

Cronin, S., *Irish Nationalism: A History of its Roots and Ideology* (Dublin: Academy Press, 1980)

Crossman, Virginia, *Politics, Law & Order in Nineteenth-Century Ireland* (Dublin: Gill & Macmillan, 1996)

Cruse, A., *An Englishman and His Books in the Early Nineteenth-Century* (London: Harrap, 1930)

Curtis, L. P., *Coercion and Conciliation in Ireland, 1880-1892* (Princeton: Princeton University Press, 1963)

Curtis, L. P., *The Cause of Ireland: from the United Irishman to Partition* (Belfast: Beyond the Pale Publications, 1994)

Dangerfield, George, *The Damnable Question: A Study in Anglo-Irish Relations*, (London: Constable, 1977)

Daraul, Arkon, *A History of Secret Societies* (1961) (New Jersey: Citadel Press/Carol Publishing Group, 1997)

Davie, Donald, *The Heyday of Sir Walter Scott* (London: Routledge & Kegan Paul, 1961)

Davies, Norman, *The Isles: A History* (London: Macmillan, 1999)

Davis, Paul E. H., ' "Talk talk talk ...": Virginia Woolf, Ireland and Maria

318

Edgeworth', *Estudios Irlandeses*, ed. Rosa González, 1, 2006, 32-38 [www.estudiosirlandeses.org]

Davis, Robert, *Gerald Griffin* (Boston: Twayne Publishers, 1980)

Deane, Seamus, *A Short History of Irish Literature* (London: Hutchinson, 1987)

Deane, Seamus, ed., *The Field Day Anthology of Irish Writing*, 3 vols (Derry: Field Day, 1991)

Deane, Seamus, *Reading in the Dark* (London: Jonathan Cape, 1996)

Deane, Seamus, *Strange Country: Modernity and Nationhood in Irish Writing Since 1790* (Oxford: Clarendon Press, 1998)

De Blacam, Aôdh, *A First Book of Irish Literature* (Dublin: The Educational Company of Ireland Limited, n.d.)

De Vere White, T., *Tom Moore: The Irish Poet* (London: Hamish Hamilton, 1977)

Diamond, Michael, *Victorian Sensation Or, the Spectacular, the Shocking and the Scandalous in Nineteenth-Century Britain* (London: Anthem Press, 2003)

Dickson, David, *New Foundations: Ireland 1660-1800* (1987), 2nd edn (Dublin: Irish Academic Press, 2000)

Dooley, Terence, *The Decline of the Big House in Ireland: A Study of Irish Landed Families 1860-1960* (Dublin: Wolfhound Press, 2001)

Dowden, Wilfred S., ed., *The Journal of Thomas Moore*, 6 vols (Newark: University of Delaware Press, 1984)

Dowling, P. J., *The Hedge Schools of Ireland*, 2nd edn (Cork: Mercier Press, 1968)

Drabble, Margaret, ed., *The Oxford Companion to English Literature* (1932), 5th edn (Oxford: Oxford University Press, 1985)

Drudy, P. J., ed., *Anglo-Irish Studies* (Chalfont St. Giles: Alpha Academic Press, 1976)

Duffy, Bishop John, *On Lough Derg* (Dublin: Veritas Publications, 1988)

Dunbabin, J. P. D., *Rural Discontent in Nineteenth-Century Britain* (London: Faber, 1974)

Dunne, Tom, ed., *The Writer as Witness: Literature as Historical Evidence* (Cork: Cork University Press, 1987)

Durey, Jill Felicity, *Trollope and the Church of England* (Basingstoke: Palgrave Macmillan, 2002)

Duytschaever, Joris, and Geert Lernout, eds., *History and Violence in Anglo-Irish Literature* (Amsterdam: Rodopi B. V., 1988)

Eager, A. R., *A Guide to Irish Bibliographical Material: A Bibliography of Irish Bibliographies and Sources of Information* (Westport, USA: Greenwood,

1980)

Eagleton, Terry, *Literary Theory: An Introduction* (Oxford: Basil Blackwell Ltd., 1990)

Eagleton, Terry, *Heathcliff and the Great Hunger: Studies in Irish Culture* (London: Verso, 1995)

Eagleton, Terry, *Crazy John and the Bishop and other Essays on Irish Culture* (Cork: Cork University Press, 1998)

Eagleton, Terry, *Scholars and Rebels in Nineteenth-Century Ireland* (Oxford: Blackwell Publishers Ltd., 1999)

Edwards, P. D., *Anthony Trollope: His Art and Scope* (New York: St. Martin's Press, 1977)

Edwards, R. Dudley, and T. Desmond Williams, eds., *The Great Famine: Studies in Irish History 1845-52* (Dublin: Browne and Nolan Limited, 1956)

Eglinton, John, *Irish Literary Portraits* (London: Macmillan & Co. Ltd., 1935)

Elliott, Marianne, *Wolfe Tone, Prophet of Irish Independence* (New Haven: Yale University Press, 1989)

Ellman, Richard, ed., *Selected Letters of James Joyce* (London: Faber and Faber, 1975)

Ellmann, Maud, *Elizabeth Bowen: The Shadow Across the Page* (Edinburgh: Edinburgh University Press, 2003)

Elton, O., *A Survey of English Literature 1830-1880* (London: Edward Arnold, 1961)

Escott, T. H. S., Anthony Trollope: His Public Services, Private Friends and Literary Originals (1913) (Port Washington, New York: Kennikat Press, Inc., 1967)

Everitt, A. M., *The Pattern of Rural Dissent* (Leicester: Leicester University Press, 1972)

Fallis, R., *The Irish Renaissance: an Introduction to Anglo-Irish Literature* (Dublin: Gill, 1978)

Fay, Brian, Philip Pomper, and Richard T. Vann, eds., *History and Theory: Contemporary Readings* (Oxford: Basil Blackwell Ltd., 1998)

Fegan, Melissa, *Literature and the Irish Famine 1845-1919* (Oxford: Clarendon Press, 2002)

Finneran, Richard, ed., *Anglo-Irish Literature: A Review of Research* (New York: The Modern Language Association of America, 1976)

Finneran, Richard J., ed., *Recent Research on Anglo-Irish Writers: A Supplement to Anglo-Irish Literature: A Review of Research* (New York: Modern

Language Association of America, 1983)

Fitzpatrick, B., *Seventeenth-Century Ireland: The War of Religions* (Dublin: Gill & Macmillan, 1988)

Flanagan, Thomas, *The Irish Novelists 1800-1850* (New York: Columbia University Press, 1959)

Foley, Tadhg, and Sean Ryder, eds., *Ideology and Ireland in the Nineteenth Century* (Dublin: Four Courts Press, 1998)

Foster, J. W., *Fictions of the Irish Literary Revival: a Changeling Art* (Syracuse: Syracuse University Press, 1987)

Foster, J. W., *Colonial Consequences: Essays in Irish Literature and Culture* (Dublin: Lilliput, 1991)

Foster, John Wilson, ed., *The Cambridge Companion to the Irish Novel* (Cambridge: Cambridge University Press, 2006)

Foster, John Wilson, *Irish Novels 1890-1940: New Bearings in Culture and Fiction* (Oxford: Oxford University Press, 2008)

Foster, Roy F., *Modern Ireland 1600-1972* (London: Penguin Books, 1989)

Foster, Roy F., *Paddy & Mr. Punch: Connections in Irish and English History* (London: Penguin Books, 1995)

Foster, Roy F., *W. B. Yeats: A Life: I The Apprentice Mage 1865-1914* (Oxford: Oxford University Press, 1997)

Foster, Roy F., *The Irish Story: Telling Tales and Making it Up in Ireland* (London: Penguin, 2002)

Foster, Roy F., *W. B. Yeats: A Life: II The Arch-Poet 1915-1939* (Oxford: Oxford University Press, 2003)

Fraser, Antonia, *Cromwell: Our Chief of Men* (1973) (London: Mandarin Paperbacks, 1993)

Fraser, D., ed., *The New Poor Law in the Nineteenth-Century* (Basingstoke: Macmillan, 1976)

Frawley, Oona (ed.), *Memory Ireland*, Vol I History and Modernity (Syracuse, NY: Syracuse University Press, 2011)

Frayling, Christopher, *Vampyres – Lord Byron to Count Dracula* (London: Faber and Faber, 1992)

Freeman, T. W., *Pre-Famine Ireland: a Study in Historical Geography* (Manchester: Manchester University Press, 1957)

Freeman, T. W., *Ireland: A General and Regional Geography*, 4th edn (London: Methuen, 1969)

Geary, Laurence, and Margaret Kelleher, eds., *Nineteenth-Century Ireland: A Guide to Recent Research* (Dublin: University College Dublin Press, 2005)

Genet, Jacqueline, ed., *The Big House in Ireland: Reality and Representation*,

(Dingle: Brandon Book Publishers Ltd., 1991)

Genet, Jacqueline, ed., *Rural Ireland, Real Ireland?* (Gerrards Cross: Colin Smythe, 1996)

Gibbons, Stephen Randolph, *Rockites and Whitefleet: Irish Peasant Secret Societies 1800-1845* (Southampton: University of Southampton, 1982)

Gibbons, Stephen Randolph, *Captain Rock, Night Errant: The Threatening Letters of Pre-Famine Ireland, 1801-1845* (Dublin: Four Courts Press, 2004)

Giddings, Robert, *The Author, The Book and The Reader* (London: Greenwich Exchange, 1991)

Gilbert, Alan D., *Religion and Society in Industrial England: Church, Chapel and Social Change, 1740-1914* (London: Longman, 1976)

Gill, W. S., *Gerald Griffin: Poet, Novelist, Christian Brother* (Dublin: M. H. Gill, n.d.)

Gillespie, Raymond, *Seventeenth-Century Ireland: Making Ireland Modern*, 2nd edn (Dublin: Gill & Macmillan, 2006)

Gilmour, Robin, *The Novel in the Victorian Age: A Modern Introduction* (London: Edward Arnold, 1986)

Glendinning, Victoria, *Trollope*, 2nd edn (London: Pimlico, 2002)

Glover, David, *Vampires, Mummies, and Liberals: Bram Stoker and the Politics of Popular Fiction* (London: Duke University Press, 1996)

Godechot, Jacques, *France and the Atlantic Revolution of the Eighteenth Century, 1770-1799* (London: Collier-Macmillan Publishers, 1965)

Goldring, Maurice, *Pleasant Scholar's Life: Irish Intellectuals and the Construction of the Nation State* (London: Serif, 1993)

Goodbody, Rob, ed., *Transactions of the Central Relief Committee of the Society of Friends During the Famine in Ireland, in 1846 and 1847* (Dublin: Edmund Burke Publisher, facsimile repr. 1996)

Graham, Kenneth, *English Criticism of the Novel 1865-1900* (Oxford: Clarendon Press, 1965)

Griffith, Arthur, *Thomas Davis: The Thinker & Teacher* (Dublin: M. H. Gill & Son Ltd., 1914)

Grubgeld, Elizabeth, *Anglo-Irish Autobiography* (New York: Syracuse University Press, 2004)

Hadfield, Andrew, and John McVeagh, eds., *Strangers to that Land: British Perceptions of Ireland form the Reformation to the Famine* (Gerrards Cross: Colin Smythe, 1994)

Haining, Peter, ed., *Vampires at Midnight: Seventeen chilling tales of the ghoulish Undead*, 2nd edn (London: Warner Books, 1993)

Hall, N. John, ed., *The Letters of Anthony Trollope* (Stanford: Stanford University Press, 1983)

Hall, N. J., *Trollope: A Biography* (Oxford: Clarendon Press, 1991)

Hall, Mrs. S. C, *Tales of Irish Life and Character* (1910) (London & Edinburgh: T. N. Foulis, 1913)

Hall, Wayne E., *Dialogues in the Margin. A Study of the Dublin University Magazine* (Gerrards Cross: Colin Smythe Ltd., 2000)

Halperin, John, ed., *Trollope Centenary Essays* (London: The Macmillan Press Ltd., 1982)

Hammond, J. L., *Gladstone and the Irish Nation* (London: Longmans, Green & Co., 1938)

Hand, Derek, *A History of the Irish Novel* (Cambridge: Cambridge University Press, 2011)

Harmon, M., ed., *Image and Illusion: Anglo-Irish literature and its context festschrift for Roger McHugh*, (Dublin: Wolfhound Press, 1979)

Harner, J. L., *Literary Research Guide: A Guide to Reference Sources for the Study of Literatures in English and Related Topics*, 2nd edn (New York: Modern Language Association of America, 1993)

Hartley, Leslie P., *The Go-Between* (1953), 2nd edn (London: Penguin Group, 2000)

Hawlin, Stefan, 'Seamus Heaney's "Station Island": The Shaping of a Modern Purgatory', *English Studies: A Journal of English Literature*, ed. by T. Birrell and J. Blom, 73:1, 1992, 35-50

Hawthorne, Mark D., *John and Michael Banim ("The O'Hara Brothers"): A Study in the Early Development of the Anglo-Irish Novel* (Salzburg: Institut Fur Englische Sprache Und Literatur, Universitat Salzburg, 1975)

Hayes, R. J., ed., *Manuscript Sources for the History of Irish Civilization*, 11 vols (Boston: G. K. Hall, 1965)

Hayes, R. J., ed., *Sources for the History of Irish Civilization: Articles in Irish Periodicals*, 9 vols (Boston: G. K. Hall, 1970)

Hayes, R. J., ed., *Supplement to Manuscript Sources for the History of Irish Civilization*, 3 vols (Boston: G. K. Hall, 1979)

Hayley, Barbara, *Carleton's Traits and Stories and the 19th Century Anglo-Irish Tradition* (Gerrards Cross: Colin Smythe, 1983)

Healy, James J., *Life and Times of Charles J. Kickham* (Dublin: James Duffy and Co. Limited, 1915)

Hennessy, James Pope, *Anthony Trollope* (London: Jonathan Cape, 1971)

Heilbroner, Robert L., ed., *The Essential Adam Smith* (Oxford: Oxford University Press, 1986)

Herlihy, Jim, *The Royal Irish Constabulary: A Short History and Genealogical Guide* (Dublin: Four Courts Press, 1997)

Hobsbawm, Eric, and G. Rudé, *Captain Swing* (1969) (London: Phoenix Press, 2001)

Hogan, Robert, ed., *The Macmillan Dictionary of Irish Literature*, 2 vols (Basingstoke: Macmillan Press, 1980)

Hogan, S., and G. Walker, *Political Violence: the Law of Ireland* (Manchester: Manchester University Press, 1989)

Holland, Merlin, and Rupert Hart-Davis, *The Complete Letters of Oscar Wilde* (New York: Henry Holt and Company, 2000)

Hollingworth, Brian, *Maria Edgeworth's Irish Writing: Language, History, Politics*, (Basingstoke: Macmillan Press Ltd., 1997)

Home Office, Great Britain, *Public Order, Discontent and Protest in Nineteenth-Century England, 1820-1850*, 49 reels (Brighton: Harvester Press, 1981), reel 48, 1840: Correspondence M-Q (HO 52 46)

Home Office, Great Britain, *Civil Disturbance, Chartism and Riots in Nineteenth-Century England*, 16 Reels (Brighton: Harvester Press, 1982), reel 1, boxes 41-53

Hooper, Glenn and Leon Litvack, eds., *Ireland in the Nineteenth Century: Regional Identity* (Dublin: Four Courts Press Ltd., 2000)

Hooper, Glenn and Colin Graham, eds., *Irish and Postcolonial Writing: History, Theory, Practice* (Basingstoke: Palgrave Macmillan, 2002)

Hoppen, K. Theodore, *Elections, Politics & Society in Ireland 1832-1885* (Oxford: Clarendon Press, 1984)

Hoppen, K. Theodore, *Ireland since 1800: Conflict and Conformity* (1989), 2nd edn (London: Longman, 1999)

Hopper, Keith, 'Hairy on the Inside: Re-visiting Neil Jordan's *The Company of Wolves*', *Canadian Journal of Irish Studies*, 2003, 29:2, 17-26

Horn, Pamela, *The Rural World 1780-1850: Social Change in the English Countryside* (London: Hutchinson, 1980)

Horsman, E. A., *On the Side of Angels? Disraeli and the Nineteenth-Century Novel* (Otago, New Zealand: University of Otago Press, 1976)

Houghton, Walter E., *The Victorian Frame of Mind 1830-1870* (New Haven: Yale University Press, 1957)

Howatson, M. C., ed., *The Oxford Companion to Classical Literature*, 2nd edn (Oxford: Oxford University Press, 1993)

Howes, Marjorie, *Yeats's Nations: Gender, Class, and Irishness*, 2nd edn (Cambridge: Cambridge University Press, 1998)

Hull, Eleanor, *A Text Book of Irish Literature*, 2 vols (Dublin: M. H. Gill &

Son, Ltd., 1908)

Hufton, Olwen, *Europe: Privilege and protest, 1730-1789* (London: Fontana, 1980)

Hurst, Michael, *Maria Edgeworth and the Public Scene* (London: Macmillan and Co., Ltd., 1969)

Hutchings, Peter, *Dracula* (London: I. B. Tauris & Co. Ltd., 2003)

Hyde, Douglas, *A Literary History of Ireland: From Earliest Times to the Present Day* (London: T. Fisher Unwin, 1906)

Hyland, Paul, and Neil Sammells, eds., *Irish Writing: Exile and Subversion* (Basingstoke: Macmillan, 1991)

Inglis, Brian, *The Freedom of the Press in Ireland 1784-1841* (London: Faber, 1956)

Inglis, Brian, *The Story of Ireland* (London: Faber & Faber, 1956)

Inglis-Jones, Elisabeth, *The Great Maria: A Portrait of Maria Edgeworth*, (London: Faber and Faber, 1959)

Innes, C. L., *Woman and Nation in Irish Literature and Society* (New York: Harvester Wheatsheaf, 1993)

Jackson, T. A., and C. D. Greaves, eds., *Ireland Her Own: An Outline History of Irish Struggle for National Freedom and Independence* (London: Lawrence & Wishart, 1971)

Jaeger, Muriel, *Before Victoria* (London: Chatto and Windus Ltd., 1956)

James, Louis, *Print and the People 1819-1851* (London: Penguin, 1976)

James, Louis, ed., *English Popular Literature 1819-1851* (New York: Columbia University Press, 1976)

Jeffares, A. Norman, *The Anglo-Irish Literature: Volume One: The Nineteenth Century* (New York: Schocken Books, 1982)

Jenkins, Roy, *Gladstone* (London: Macmillan, 1995)

Johnston, E. M., *Great Britain and Ireland 1760-1800: a Study of Political Administration* (Edinburgh: Oliver and Boyd, 1963)

Johnston, Edith Mary, *Ireland in the Eighteenth Century* (Dublin: Gill and Macmillan, 1974)

Jones, D. J. V., *Crime, Protest, Community and Police in Nineteenth-Century Britain* (London: Routledge, 1982)

Jones, Howard M., *The Harp that Once: A Chronicle of the Life of Thomas Moore*, (New York: Holt, 1937)

Jordan Jr., Donald E., *Land and Popular Politics in Ireland: County Mayo from the Plantation to the Land War* (Cambridge: Cambridge University Press, 1994)

Keane, Maureen, *Mrs. S. C. Hall: A Literary Biography* (Gerrards Cross:

Colin Smythe, 1997)

Keating, Peter, *The Haunted Study: A Social History of the English Novel 1875-1914* (London: Fontana Press, 1991)

Kee, Robert, *The Green Flag: Volume One: The Most Distressful Country*, 2nd edn (London: Penguin, 1989)

Kee, Robert, *The Green Flag: Volume II: The Bold Fenian Men*, 2nd edn (London: Penguin, 1989)

Kee, Robert, *The Laurel and the Ivy: The Story of Charles Stewart Parnell and Irish Nationalism* (London: Penguin, 1994)

Kee, Robert, *Ireland: A History* (London: Abacus, 1995)

Kelley, Leo. P., ed., *The Supernatural in Fiction* (Mission Hills: Glencoe, 1973)

Kelly, R. J., *Charles Joseph Kickham, Patriot and Poet: A Memoir* (Dublin: James Duffy and Co. Ltd., 1914)

Kelly, Ronan, *Bard of Erin: The Life of Thomas Moore* (Dublin: Penguin Ireland, 2008)

Keneally, Thomas, *The Great Shame: A Story of the Irish in the Old World and the New* (London: Chatto & Windus, 1998)

Kenny, Kevin, ed., *Ireland and the British Empire* (Oxford: Oxford University Press, 2004)

Kerr, Barbara, *Bound to the Soil: A Social History of Dorset 1750-1918* (Wakefield: EP Publishing Limited, 1975)

Kerr, D. A., *Peel, Priests and Politics: Sir Robert Peel's Administration and the Roman Catholic Church in Ireland, 1841-46* (Oxford: Clarendon, 1982)

Kettle, Arnold, ed., *The Nineteenth-Century Novel: Critical Essays and Documents*. 2nd edn (London: Heinemann, 1977)

Kiberd, Declan, *Inventing Ireland: The Literature of the Modern Nation* (London: Vintage, 1996)

Kiberd, Declan, *Irish Classics* (London: Granta Books, 2000)

Kiely, Benedict, *Poor Scholar: A Study of the Works and Days of William Carleton (1794-1869)*, (London: Sheed & Ward, 1947)

Kiely, Benedict, *A Raid into Dark Corners and Other Essays* (Cork: Cork University Press, 1999)

Killeen, Jarlath, *Gothic Ireland: Horror and the Irish Anglican Imagination in the Long Eighteenth Century* (Dublin: Four Courts Press, 2005)

Kinealy, Christine, *A Death-Dealing Famine: The Great Hunger in Ireland* (London: Pluto Press, 1997)

Kinealy, Christine, *The Great Irish Famine: Impact, Ideology and Rebellion* (Basingstoke: Palgrave, 2002)

King, Carla, ed., *Famine, Land and Culture in Ireland* (Dublin: University College Dublin Press, 2000)

Kinsella, Thomas, *Davis, Mangan, Ferguson? Tradition and The Irish Writer* (Dublin: The Dolmen Press, 1970)

Kinsella, Thomas, *The New Oxford Book of Irish Verse* (Oxford: Oxford University Press, 1986)

Knight, Denis, ed., *Cobbett in Ireland: A Warning to England* (London: Lawrence & Wishart, 1984)

Krans, Horatio Sheafe, *Irish Life in Irish Fiction* (1903) (New York: AMS Press, repr. 1966)

Krause, David, *William Carleton the Novelist: His Carnival and Pastoral World of Tragicomedy* (Maryland, USA: University Press of America, n.d.)

Kreilkamp, Vera, *The Anglo-Irish Novel and the Big House* (Syracuse: Syracuse University Press, 1998)

Ladurie, E. Le Roy & Guy, J., *Tithe and Agrarian History from the Fourteenth to the Nineteenth Centuries: An Essay in Comparative History* (Cambridge: Cambridge University Press, 1982)

Laing, Kathryn, 'Virginia Woolf in Ireland: A Short Voyage Out', *South Carolina Review*, 34, 180-187

Lamont, William, ed., *Historical Controversies and Historians* (London: UCL Press, 1998)

Lampson, G. Locker, *A Consideration of the State of Ireland in the Nineteenth Century* (London: Archibald Constable & Co. Ltd., 1907)

Lane, Maggie, *Literary Daughters* (London: Robert Hale, 1989)

Lawless, Emily, *Maria Edgeworth* (London: Macmillan & Co. Limited, 1904)

Laxton, Edward, *The Famine Ships: The Irish Exodus to America 1846-51* (London: Bloomsbury, 1996)

Leavis, F. R., *The Great Tradition* (1948), 2nd edn (Harmondsworth: Peregrine Books, 1983)

Leavis, Q. D., *Fiction and the Reading Public* (1932) 2nd edn (London: Penguin, 1979)

Lee, Hermoine, *Virginia Woolf* (London: Vintage, 1997)

Leerssen, Joep, *Mere Irish and Fíor-Ghael: Studies in the Idea of Irish Nationality, its Development and Literary Expression prior to the Nineteenth Century*, 2nd edn (Cork: Cork University Press, 1996)

Leerssen, Joep, *Remembrance and Imagination: Patterns in the Historical and Literary Representation of Ireland in the Nineteenth Century* (Cork: Cork University Press, 1996)

Lennon, Seán, *Irish Gothic Writers: Bram Stoker and the Irish Supernatural Tradition* (Dublin: Dublin Corporation Public Libraries, n.d.)

Lernout, Geert, ed., *The Crows Behind The Plough: History and Violence in Anglo-Irish Poetry and Drama* (Amsterdam-Atlanta: Rodopi B. V., 1991)

Lester, D., ed., *Irish Research: A Guide to Collections in North America, Ireland, and Great Britain* (New York: Greenwood, 1987)

Litton, Helen, *Irish Rebellions, 1798-1916: An Illustrated History* (Dublin: Wolfhound Press Ltd., 1998)

Llewellyn-Jones, Margaret, *Contemporary Irish Drama and Cultural Identity* (Bristol: Intellect Books, 2002)

Lloyd, David, *Anomalous States: Irish Writing and the Post-Colonial Moment* (Dublin: The Lilliput Press, 1993)

Loeber, Ralf, and Magda Loeber, *A Guide to Irish Fiction 1650-1900* (Dublin: Four Courts Press, 2006)

Lukacs, Georg, *The Historical Novel* (1937), trans. by Hannah and Stanley Mitchell, 3rd edn (London: Merlin Press, 1989)

Lyan, A., *Land Law in Ireland* (Dublin: Oak Tree Press, 1994)

Lydon, James, *The Making of Ireland: From Ancient Times to the Present* (London: Routledge, 1998)

Lyons, F. S. L., *Ireland since the Famine*, 2nd edn (London: Weidenfeld and Nicolson, 1971)

Lyons, F. S. L., and R. A. J. Hawkins, eds., *Ireland under the Union: Varieties of Tension: Essays in Honour of T. W. Moody* (Oxford: Clarendon Press, 1980)

MacDonagh, M., *Daniel O'Connell and the Story of Catholic Emancipation* (Dublin: Talbot Press, 1916)

MacDonagh, Oliver, *The Life of Daniel O'Connel, 1775-1847* (London: Weidenfeld and Nicolson, 1991)

MacDonagh, Oliver, *States of Mind: Two Centuries of Anglo-Irish Conflict 1780-1980* (London: Pimlico, 1992)

MacFie, A. L., and D. D. Raphael, eds., *The Theory of Moral Sentiments* (1759) (Oxford: Clarendon Press, 1976)

MacLysaght, Edward, *Irish Life in the Seventeenth Century* (Cork: Cork University Press, 1950)

McCaffrey, Lawrence J., *The Irish Diaspora in America* (Bloomington: Indiana University Press, 1976)

McCaffrey, Lawrence J., *Textures of Irish America* (New York: Syracuse University Press, 1992)

McCaw, Neil, ed., *Writing Irishness in Nineteenth-Century British Culture*

(Aldershot: Ashgate Publishing Limited, 2004)

Mc Cormack, William J., *Sheridan Le Fanu and Victorian Ireland* (1980), 2nd edn (Dublin: The Lilliput Press, 1991)

Mc Cormack, William J., *From Burke to Beckett: Ascendancy, Tradition and Betrayal in Literary History*, 2nd edn (Cork: Cork University Press, 1994)

Mc Cormack, W. J., *Dissolute Characters: Irish literary history through Balzac, Sheridan Le Fanu, Yeats and Bowen* (Manchester: Manchester University Press, 1994)

McDowell, R. B., *Public Opinion and Government Policy in Ireland 1801-1846* (London: Faber, 1952)

McDowell, R. B., *The Irish Administration 1801-1914* (London: Routledge & Kegan Paul, 1964)

McDowell, R. B., *Ireland in the Age of Imperialism and Revolution 1760-1801* (Oxford: Clarendon Press, 1979)

McGaw, N., ed., *Writing Irishness in Nineteenth-Century British Culture* (Aldershot: Ashgate, 2004)

McHenry, Dr. James, *Hearts of Steel* (Dublin: Thomas Tegg & Co., 1838)

McHugh, Roger, and Maurice Harmon, *A Short History of Anglo-Irish Literature: From its Origins to the Present Day* (Dublin: Wolfhound Press, 1982)

McKenna, B., *Irish Literature 1800-1875: A Guide to Information Sources* (Detroit: Gale, 1978)

McNally, Raymond T., and Radu Florescu, *In Search of Dracula: The History of Dracula and Vampires* (London: Robson Books, 1995)

McNeillie, Andrew, ed., *Essays of Virginia Woolf*, 2 vols (London: The Hogarth Press, 1986)

McNicholas, Anthony, *Politics, Religion and the Press: Irish Journalism in Mid-Victorian England* (Bern, Switzerland: Peter Lang, 2007)

Macintyre, Angus, *The Liberator: Daniel O'Connell and the Irish Party 1830-1847* (London: Hamish Hamilton, 1965)

MacLysaght, Edward, *Irish Life in the Seventeenth Century*, 2nd edn (Cork: Cork University Press, 1950)

Mackey, J. P., ed., *The Cultures of Europe: The Irish Contribution* (Belfast: The Institute of Irish Studies, Queen's University of Belfast, 1994)

Mackenzie, David, *Violent Solutions, Revolutions, Nationalism and Secret Societies in Europe to 1918* (Lanham Md.: University Press of America, 1996)

Maddox, Brenda, *George's Ghosts: A New Life of W. B. Yeats* (London: Picador, 2000)

Maher, James, ed., *The Valley Near Slievenamon: A Kickham Anthology &c.* (no publication details, 1941)

Mannin, Ethel, *Two Studies in Integrity: Gerald Griffin and the Rev. Francis Mahony ('Father Prout')* (London: Jarrolds, 1954)

Mansergh, Nicholas, *Ireland in the Age of Reform and Revolution* (London: Allen and Unwin, 1940)

Mansergh, Nicholas, *The Irish Question, 1840-1921* (London: George Allen and Unwin, 1975)

Manzoni, Alesandro, *On the Historical Novel* (Nebraska: University of Nebraska Press, 1984)

Martin, David, *John Stuart Mill and the Land Question* (Hull: University of Hull Publications, 1981)

Marx, Karl, and Friedrich Engels, *The Communist Manifesto* (1872), ed. David McLellan (Oxford: Oxford University Press, repr. 1998)

Matthews, Mike, *Captain Swing in Sussex and Kent: Rural Rebellion in 1830* (Hastings: The Hastings Press, 2006)

Maume, Patrick, *'Life that is Exile': Daniel Corkery and the Search for the Irish Ireland* (Belfast: The Institute of Irish Studies, 1993)

Maxwell, Constantia, *The Stranger in Ireland: From the Reign of Elizabeth to the Great Famine* (London: Jonathan Cape, 1954)

Meckier, Jerome, *Hidden Rivalries In Victorian Fiction: Dickens, Realism, and Revaluation* (Lexington: The University Press of Kentucky, 1987)

Meek, R. L., D. D. Raphael, and P. G. Stein, eds., *Lectures on Jurisprudence* (1762-3) (Oxford: Oxford University Press, 1978)

Mercier, V., and E. Dillon, eds., *Modern Irish Literature: Sources and Founders* (Oxford: Clarendon Press, 1994)

Mighall, Robert, *A Geography of Victorian Gothic Fiction: Mapping History's Nightmares* (Oxford: Oxford University Press, 2003)

Mill, John Stuart, *Chapters and Speeches on the Irish Land Question*, 2nd edn (London: Longmans, Green, Reader, and Dyer, 1870)

Miller, John, ed., *The Glorious Revolution*, 2nd edn (London: Longman, 1997)

Mills, D. R., *Lord and Peasant in Nineteenth-Century Britain* (London: Croom Helm, 1980)

Moley, R., *Daniel O'Connell: Nationalism without Violence – an essay* (New York: Fordham University Press, 1974)

Moody, Ellen, *Trollope on the Net* (London: The Hambledon Press, 1999)

Moody, T. W., and F. X. Martin, eds., *The Course of Irish History*, 3rd edn (Dublin: Mercier Press, 1994)

Morash, Christopher, *Writing the Irish Famine* (Oxford: The Clarendon

Press, 1995)

Morris, Jan, ed., *Travels with Virginia Woolf* (London: The Hogarth Press, 1993)

Mossner, Ernest Campbell, and Ian Simpson Ross, eds., *The Correspondence of Adam Smith* (Oxford: Clarendon Press, 1977)

Moynahan, Julian, *Anglo-Irish: The Literary Imagination of a Hyphenated Culture* (Princeton: Princeton University Press, 1995)

Mullen, Richard, *Anthony Trollope: A Victorian in his World* (London: Gerald Duckworth & Co., 1990)

Mullen, Richard, and James Munson, *The Penguin Companion to Trollope* (London: Penguin Books, 1996)

Murphy, Frank, *The Bog Irish (Who They Were and How They Lived)* (London: Penguin, 1987)

Murphy, James H., *Irish Novelists and the Victorian Age* (Oxford: Oxford University Press, 2011)

Murphy, Sharon, *Maria Edgeworth and Romance* (Dublin: Four Courts Press, 2004)

Murphy, William, *Charles J. Kickham: Patriot, Novelist, and Poet* (1903) (Blackrock: Carraig Books, facsimile repr. 1976)

Murray, Patrick, *Maria Edgeworth* (Cork: The Mercier Press, 1971)

Murray, Patrick Joseph, *The Life of John Banim: The Irish Novelist* (London: William Lay, 1857)

Murray, Paul, *From The Shadow of Dracula: A Life of Bram Stoker* (London: Jonathan Cape, 2004)

Newby, P. H., *Maria Edgeworth* (London: Arthur Baker Ltd., 1950)

Nowlan, Emer, *Catholic Emancipations: Irish Fiction from Thomas Moore to James Joyce* (Syracuse, New York: Syracuse University Press, 2007)

Norman, E. R., *The English Catholic Church in the Nineteenth Century* (Oxford: Clarendon Press, 1984)

Nowlan, Kevin B., and Maurice R. O'Connell, eds., *Daniel O'Connell: Portrait of a Radical* (New York: Fordham University Press, 1985)

O'Brien, G., ed., *Parliament, Politics and People: Essays in Eighteenth-Century Irish History* (Dublin: Irish Academic Press, 1989)

O'Connor, J., *History of Ireland 1798-1924*, 2 vols (London: Edward Arnold, 1926)

O'Day, Alan, and John Stevenson, eds., *Irish Historical Documents Since 1800* (Dublin: Gill & Macmillan, 1992)

O'Donoghue, David, *Sir Walter Scott's Tour of Ireland 1825* (Dublin: O'Donoghue & Gill, 1905)

331

O'Faolain, Sean, *The Irish*, 2nd edn (London: Penguin, 1980)

O'Farrell, P., *Ireland's English Question: Anglo-Irish Relations 1534-1970* (London: Batsford, 1971)

O'Farrell, Patrick, *England and Ireland since 1800* (Oxford: Oxford University Press, 1979)

Ó Gallchoir, Clíona, *Maria Edgeworth: Women, Enlightenment and Nation* (Dublin: University College Dublin Press, 2005)

Ó Gráda, Cormac, *Ireland: A New Economic History 1780-1939* (Oxford: Oxford University Press, 1995)

Ó Gráda, Cormac, *The Great Irish Famine* (Cambridge: The Press Syndicate of the University of Cambridge, 1997)

Ó Gráda, Cormac, *Black '47 and Beyond: The Great Irish Famine in History, Economy, and Memory* (Princeton: Princeton University Press, 1999)

O'Hart, J., *The Irish and the Anglo-Irish Landed Gentry* (Shannon: Irish University Press, repr. 1961)

O'Hegarty, P. S., 'Kickham's novels', *Irish Booklover*, xxvi (1938), 41

O'Malley, W. T., *Anglo-Irish Literature: A Bibliography of Dissertations 1873-1989* (New York: Greenwood Press, 1990)

O'Rourke, Rev. John, *The History of the Great Irish Famine of 1847, with Notices of Earlier Irish Famines*, 3rd edn (Dublin: James Duffy and Co., Ltd., 1902)

O'Tuathaigh, Gearoid O., *Ireland before the Famine 1798-1848* (1972) 2nd edn (Dublin: Gill & Macmillan, 1990)

Obelkevich, James, *Religion and Rural Society: South Lindsey 1825-1875* (Oxford: Clarendon Press, 1976)

Pakenham, Thomas, *The Year of Liberty: The History of the Great Irish Rebellion of 1798*, 2nd edn (London: Orion Books, 1992)

Palmer, R. R., *The Age of the Democratic Revolution: A Political History of Europe and America 1760-1800: The Challenge* (Princeton: Princeton University Press, 1959)

Palmer, R. R., *The Age of the Democratic Revolution: A Political History of Europe and America 1760-1800: The Struggle* (Princeton: Princeton University Press, 1964)

Parker, Geoffrey, and Lesley M. Smith, eds., *The General Crisis of the Seventeenth Century*, 2nd edn, (London: Routledge, 1985)

Partridge, A. C., *Language and Society in Anglo-Irish Literature* (Dublin: Gill & Macmillan Ltd., 1984)

Percival, John, *The Great Famine: Ireland's Potato Famine 1845-1851* (London: BBC Books, 1995)

Philpin, C. H. E., ed., *Nationalism and Popular Protest in Ireland* (Cambridge: Cambridge University Press, 1987)

Plumb, J. H., *England in the Eighteenth Century* (Harmondsworth: Penguin Books, 1950)

Pollard, Arthur, *Anthony Trollope* (London: Routledge & Kegan Paul, 1978)

Pollard, Arthur, *The Victorians*, 2nd edn (London. Sphere Books, 1988)

Pomfret, J. E., *The Struggle for Land in Ireland 1800-1923* (1930) (New York: Russell and Russell, repr. 1969)

Pope-Hennessy, James, *Anthony Trollope*, 2nd edn (London: Phoenix Press, 2001)

Porritt, E., and A. G. Porritt, *The Unreformed House of Commons Parliamentary Representation before 1832*, 2 vols (Cambridge: Cambridge University Press, 1909)

Porter, R. J., and J. D. Brophy, eds., *Modern Irish Literature: Essays in Honor of William York Tindall* (New York: Twayne Publishers, 1972)

Powell, K. T., *Irish Fiction: An Introduction* (New York: Continuum, 2004)

Prebble, John, *The Highland Clearances* (London: Secker & Warburg, 1963)

Prest, John, *Lord John Russell* (London: The Macmillan Press Ltd., 1972)

Priestley, J. B., ed., *Tom Moore's Diary* (Cambridge: University Press, 1933)

Pritchard, John, *The New Penguin Guide to the Law*, 3rd edn (London: Penguin, 1993)

Purcell, Deirdre, and Liam Blake, *On Lough Derg* (Dublin: Veritas Publications, 1988)

Punter, David, *The Literature of Terror: A History of Gothic Fictions from 1765 to the Present Day* (Harlow: Pearson Education Limited, 2003)

Quin, James and Eilis Ni Dhuibhne and Ciara McDonnell, *W. B. Yeats: Works & Days* (Dublin: The National Library of Ireland, 2007)

Radice, Betty, *Who's Who in the Ancient World: A Handbook to the Survivors of the Greek and Roman Classics* (London: Penguin, 1973)

Rafferty, Oliver P., *Catholicism in Ulster 1603-1983* (London: Hurst & Company, 1994)

Rafferty, Oliver P., 'Carleton's ecclesiastical context: the Ulster Catholic experience', *Bullan: an Irish Studies Review*, 2000, 4:2, 105-124

Rafroidi, Patrick, *Irish Literature in English: The Romantic Period*, 2 vols, (Gerrards Cross: Colin Smythe, 1980)

Rafroidi, Patrick, and M. Harmon, eds., *The Irish Novel in Our Time* (Lille: Publications de l'Universite de Lille III, 1976)

Rance, Nicholas, *The Historical Novel and Popular Politics in Nineteenth-Century England* (London: Vision Press, 1975)

Rance, Nicholas, *Wilkie Collins and Other Sensational Novelists: Walking the Moral Hospital* (Basingstoke: Macmillan, 1991)

Ranelagh, John O'Beirne, *A Short History of Ireland*, 2nd edn (Cambridge: Cambridge University Press, 1994)

Ransom, Teresa, *Fanny Trollope: A Remarkable Life*, (Stroud: Alan Sutton Publishing, 1996)

Rauchbauer, O., ed., *Ancestral Voices: the Big House in Anglo-Irish Literature: A Collection of Interpretations* (Hildesheim: Olms, 1992)

Read, C. A., *The Cabinet of Irish Literature: Selections from the Works of the Chief Poets, Orators, and Prose Writers of Ireland with Biographical Sketches and Literary Notices*, 4 vols (New York: P. Murphy & Son, 1903)

Reaney, Bernard, *The Class Struggle in 19th Century Oxfordshire: The Social and Communal Background to the Otmoor Disturbances of 1830 to 1835* (Oxford: History Workshop, 1970)

Ridley, Jane, *Fox Hunting* (London: Collins, 1993)

Roberts, Marie Mulvey, and Hugh Ormsby-Lennon, eds., *Secret Texts: The Literature of Secret Societies* (New York: AMS Press, 1995)

Sadleir, Michael, *Trollope: A Commentary* (London: Constable & Co., 1927)

Sadleir, Michael, *XIX Century Fiction: A Bibliographical Record Based On His Own Collection*, 2 vols (London: Constable, 1951)

Sage, Victor, *Le Fanu's Gothic: The Rhetoric of Darkness* (Basingstoke: Palgrave Macmillan, 2004)

Said, Edward, 'Culture and Imperialism', lecture delivered at York University, Toronto, February 10, 1993 [www.zmag.org/zmag/artic-les/barsaid.htm]

Sambrook, James, *William Cobbett* (London: Routledge & Kegan Paul, 1973)

Scally, Robert James, *The End of Hidden Ireland: Rebellion, Famine, and Emigration* (Oxford: Oxford University Press, 1995)

Scott, Sir Walter, *The Journal of Sir Walter Scott 1825-32* (1890), 2nd edn., (Edinburgh: David Douglas, 1910)

Seaman, L. C. B., *Victorian England: Aspects of English and Imperial History, 1837-1901* (London: Methuen & Co. Ltd., 1973)

Selden, Raman, *A Reader's Guide to Contemporary Literary Theory*, 2nd edn (Hemel Hempstead: Harvester Wheatsheaf, 1989)

Selden, Raman, *Practising Theory and Reading Literature: An Introduction* (Hemel Hempstead: Harvester Wheatsheaf, 1989)

Senior, Hereward, *Orangeism in Ireland and Britain, 1795-1836* (London: Routledge & Kegan Paul, 1966)

Shannon, Richard, *Gladstone: Heroic Minister 1865-1898* (London: Allen Lane/The Penguin Press, 1999)

Shannon, William V., *The American Irish* (New York: The Macmillan Company, 1966)

Shaw, Rose, *Carleton's Country* (Dublin: The Talbot Press Limited, 1930)

Shearman, H., *Anglo-Irish Relations* (London: Faber & Faber, 1948)

Sloan, Barry, *The Pioneers of Anglo-Irish Fiction 1800-1850* (Gerrards Cross: Colin Smythe, 1986)

Smalley, Donald, ed., *Trollope: The Critical Heritage* (London: Routledge & Kegan Paul, 1969)

Smith, M. L. R., *Fighting for Ireland? The Military Strategy of the Irish Republican Movement* (London: Routledge, 1997)

Snell, K. D. M., ed., *The Regional Novel in Britain and Ireland 1800-1990* (Cambridge: Cambridge University Press, 1998)

Snell, K. D. M., ed., *The Regional Novel in Britain and Ireland* (Cambridge: Cambridge University Press, 1998)

Somerset Fry, Peter and Fiona, *A History of Ireland* (London: Routledge, 1993)

Southall, R., *Literature, the Individual and Society: Critical Essays on the Eighteenth and Nineteenth Centuries* (London: Lawrence and Wishart, 1977)

Speck, W. A., *Stability and Strife – England 1714-1760* (London: Edward Arnold, 1988)

Speck, W. A., *Literature and Society in Eighteenth-Century England 1680-1820: Ideology, Politics and Culture* (Harlow: Addison Wesley Longman Limited, 1998)

Sperber, Jonathan, *Revolutionary Europe 1780-1850* (Harlow: Pearson Education Limited, 2000)

Strachey, Lytton, *Eminent Victorians: The Definitive Edition* (1918) (London: Continuum, repr. 2002)

Steele, E. D., *Irish Land and British Politics: Tenant-Right and Nationality 1865-1870* (Cambridge: Cambridge University Press, 1974)

Stoker, Bram, *Personal Reminiscences of Henry Irving*, 2 vols (London: Macmillan & Co. Ltd., 1906)

Stone, Norman, *Europe Transformed 1878-1919* (London: Fontana Paperbacks, 1983)

Suess, Barbara A., *Progress and Identity in the Plays of W. B. Yeats 1892-1907* (New York: Routledge, 2003)

Sutherland, John, *The Longman Companion to Victorian Fiction* (Harlow:

Longman Group UK Limited, 1988)

Swedenborg, Emanuel, *Heaven and Hell: From Things Heard and Seen* (1758) (London: The Swedenborg Society, repr. 1966)

Teeling, C. H., *History of the Irish Rebellion of 1798: Together with: Sequel to the History of the Irish Rebellion of 1798* (Shannon: Irish University Press, facsimile repr. 1972)

Teissedon, J., *Politics and Literature in the Nineteenth-Century* (Lille: Université de Lille III, 1974)

Terry, R. C., *Anthony Trollope: The Artist in Hiding*, (London: The Macmillan Press Ltd., 1977)

Terry, R. C., *Victorian Popular Fiction, 1860-80* (London: Macmillan, 1983)

Thorne, Tony, *Countess Dracula: The Life and Times of Elisabeth Bathory, The Blood Countess* (London: Bloomsbury Publishing plc, 1977)

Tobias, J. J., *Nineteenth-Century Crime: Preventions and Punishment* (Newton Abbott: David and Charles, 1972)

Todorov, Tzvetan, *Introduction to Poetics*, 2nd edn (Minneapolis: University of Minnesota Press, 1981)

Todorov, Tzvetan, *The Fantastic: A Structural Approach to a Literary Genre*, 2nd edn (Ithaca: Cornell University Press, 1975)

Tóibín, Colm, and Diarmaid Ferriter, *The Irish Famine: A Documentary* (London: Profile Books Ltd., 2001)

Tomalin, Claire, *Jane Austen: A Life* (London: Viking, 1997)

Tomalin, Claire, *Thomas Hardy: The Time-Torn Man* (London: Penguin Group, 2006)

Torchiana, Donald T., *W. B. Yeats & Georgian Ireland* (1966), Critical Studies in Irish Literature, Vol. 2. (Washington, DC: The Catholic University of America Press, 1992)

Townsend, Molly, *Not by Bullets and Bayonets: Cobbett's Writings on the Irish Question, 1795-1835* (London: Sheed and Ward, 1983)

Townshend, C., *Political Violence in Ireland: Government and Resistance since 1848* (Oxford: Clarendon, 1984)

Tracy, Robert, *Trollope's Later Novels* (Los Angeles: University of California Press, 1978)

Tracy, Robert, *The Unappeasable Host: Studies in Irish Identities* (Dublin: University College Dublin Press, 1998)

Trench, Charles Chenevix, *Grace's Card: Irish Catholic Landlords 1690-1800* (Dublin: Mercier Press, 1997)

Trench, W. F., *Tom Moore* (Dublin: At the Sign of the Three Candles, 1934)

Trevor, William, *Beyond the Pale and Other Stories* (London: The Bodley Head, 1981)

Trevor-Roper, Hugh, ed., *The History of England* (1848-61) (London: Penguin Classics, 1986)

Trow, M. J., *Vlad the Impaler: In Search of the Real Dracula* (Stroud: Sutton Publishing, 2003)

Turner, Paul, *The Life of Thomas Hardy: A Critical Biography* (Oxford: Blackwell Publishers Limited, 2001)

Valente, Joseph, *Dracula's Crypt: Bram Stoker, Irishness, and the Question of Blood* (Urbana: University of Illinois Press, 2002)

Vance, Norman, *Irish Literature: A Social History: Tradition, Identity and Difference* (Oxford: Basil Blackwell Ltd., 1990)

Vaughan, W. E., *Landlords and Tenants in Mid-Victorian Ireland* (Oxford: Clarendon Press, 1994)

Vaughan, W. E., ed., *A New History of Ireland*, 10 vols (Oxford: Clarendon Press, 2003)

Walshe, Eibhear, and Gwenda Young, eds., *Molly Keane: Essays in Contemporary Criticism* (Dublin: Four Courts Press, 2006)

Walton, James, *Vision and Vacancy: The Fictions of J. S. Le Fanu* (Dublin: University College Dublin Press, 2007)

Ward, Sir A. W., and A. R. Waller, eds., *The Cambridge History of English Literature: Volume XIV: The Nineteenth-Century, Part III* (Cambridge: CUP, 1967)

Warner, A., *A Guide to Anglo-Irish Literature* (Dublin: Gill & Macmillan, 1981)

Watson, C., *Snobbery with Violence: Crime Stories and Their Audience* (London: Eyre and Spottiswoode, 1971)

Watson, G., and I. R. Willison, eds., *New Cambridge Bibliography of English Literature* (Cambridge: Cambridge University Press, 1969-77)

Wedgewood, C. V., *Thomas Wentworth, First Earl of Strafford*, 2nd edn (London: Phoenix Press, 2000)

Weekes, A. O., *Irish Women Writers: An Uncharted Tradition* (Lexington: University Press of Kentucky, 1990)

Welch, Robert, ed., *The Oxford Companion to Irish Literature* (Oxford: Clarendon Press, 1996)

Wheeler, Michael, *English Fiction of the Victorian Period 1830-90* (New York: Longman, 1985)

Wheeler, James Scott, *Cromwell in Ireland* (Dublin: Gill & Macmillan, 1999)

Whelan, Kevin, *The Tree of Liberty: Radicalism, Catholicism and the Construction of Irish Identity 1760-1830* (Cork: Cork University Press, 1996)

White, Hayden, *Metahistory: The Historical Imagination in Nineteenth-Century Europe*, 2nd edn (London: The John Hopkins Press Ltd., 1973)

Williams, T. D., ed., *Secret Societies in Ireland* (Dublin: Gill & Macmillan, 1973)

Wilson, David A., *United Irishmen, United States: Immigrant Radicals in the Early Republic* (Dublin: Four Courts Press, 1998)

Winstanley, Michael J., *Ireland and the Land Question 1800-1922* (London: Methuen, 1984)

Wolf, Eric R., *Europe and the People without History*,(Berkeley: University of California Press, 1997)

Wolff, Robert Lee, Introduction to *The Chronicles of Castle Cloyne* (1886) (New York: Garland Publishing Inc., 1979)

Wolff, Robert Lee, *William Carleton: Irish Peasant Novelist: A Preface to His Fiction* (New York: Garland Publishing, 1980)

Wolff, Robert Lee, *Nineteenth Century Fiction: A Bibliographical Catalogue: Based on the collection formed by Robert Lee Wolff*, 5 vols (New York: Garland Publishing Inc., 1988)

Woodham-Smith, Cecil, *The Great Hunger: Ireland 1845-1849*, 2nd edn (London: Penguin, 1991)

Woodgate, M. V., *The Abbé Edgeworth (1745-1807)* (Dublin: Browne and Nolan Limited, c.1944-45)

Woodward, E. L., *The Age of Reform 1815-1870*, 2nd edn (Oxford: Clarendon Press, 1962)

Woolf, Virginia, *The Common Reader* (1925) (London: The Hogarth Press, repr. 1948)

Wu, Duncan, ed., *A Companion to Romanticism* (Oxford: Blackwell Publishers Ltd., 1998)

Young, G. M., *Portrait of an Age: Victorian England* (Oxford: Oxford University Press, 1936)

Young, G. M., *Early Victorian England 1830-1865*, 2 vols (London: Oxford University Press, 1934)

Theses (unpublished):

Buckley, Sean Patrick, 'Writing the Nation: the Prose Fiction of the Banim Brothers and Gerald Griffin, 1825-1830,' unpublished PhD thesis, University of London, 2002

Gilligan, David W., 'The Banim Brothers: 1796-1874 – A Study of the

Emergence of the Native Anglo-Irish Novel in its Political, Social and Artistic Contexts,' unpublished DPhil thesis, University of Ulster, Coleraine, 1990

O'Flaherty, Gearoid Noel Patrick, 'Wilde and Shaw: Nationalism, Socialism and Sexuality, A selective comparative study of Oscar Wilde and George Bernard Shaw's Identities, Ideologies and Contribution to Anglo-Irish Literature,' unpublished PhD thesis, University of Kent, 2002

O'Sullivan, Tadgh, 'Captain Rock in print: Literary Representation and Irish agrarian Unrest, 1824-1833', unpublished MPhil thesis, University College, Cork, 1998

Index